CRITICAL READINGS: MEDIA AND GENDER

in CULTURAL and MEDIA STUDIES

Series editor: Stuart Allan

Published titles

News Culture
Stuart Allan

Modernity and Postmodern Culture
Jim McGuigan

Sport, Culture and the Media, 2nd edition
David Rowe

Television, Globalization and Cultural Identities
Chris Barker

Ethnic Minorities and the Media
Edited by Simon Cottle

Cinema and Cultural Modernity
Gill Branston

Compassion, Morality and the Media
Keith Tester

Masculinities and Culture
John Beynon

Cultures of Popular Music
Andy Bennett

Media, Risk and Science
Stuart Allan

Violence and the Media
Cynthia Carter and C. Kay Weaver

Moral Panics and the Media
Chas Critcher

Cities and Urban Cultures
Deborah Stevenson

Cultural Citizenship
Nick Stevenson

Culture on Display
Bella Dicks

Critical Readings: Media and Gender
Edited by Cynthia Carter and Linda Steiner

Critical Readings: Media and Audiences
Edited by Virginia Nightingale and Karen Ross

Media and Audiences
Karen Ross and Virginia Nightingale

Critical Readings: Sport, Culture and the Media
Edited by David Rowe

Rethinking Cultural Policy
Jim McGuigan

Media, Politics and the Network Society
Robert Hassan

CRITICAL READINGS: MEDIA AND GENDER

Edited by
Cynthia Carter and Linda Steiner

OPEN UNIVERSITY PRESS
Maidenhead

Open University Press
McGraw-Hill Education
McGraw-Hill House
Shoppenhangers Road
Maidenhead, Berkshire
England SL6 2QL

email: enquiries@openup.co.uk
world wide web: www.openup.co.uk

2962843

302·23082 CAR

First published 2004
Reprinted 2007, 2008
Copyright © Cynthia Carter and Linda Steiner 2004

A catalogue record for this book is available from the British Library.

ISBN-10: 0 335 21097 X   (pb)   0 335 21098 8 (hb)
ISBN-13: 978 0 335 21097 8   (pb)   978 0 335 21098 5 (hb)
Library of Congress Cataloging-in-Publication Data has been applied for

Typeset by YHT Ltd, London
Printed in Great Britain by Bell & Bain Ltd., Glasgow

CONTENTS

SERIES EDITOR'S FOREWORD

Critical Readings: Media and Gender offers an exciting introduction to a wide range of research approaches, each of which continues to shape the ongoing development of feminist and gender-sensitive scholarship. Care has been taken by Cynthia Carter and Linda Steiner, the editors, to select contributions which demonstrate the conceptual and methodological richness of these diverse approaches. While no one volume can claim to be comprehensive in its scope, this one succeeds in highlighting important interventions while, at the same time, providing a sound basis for future enquiries.

This Reader begins with an introductory essay by the two editors, both of whom are leading figures in the field. This essay maps the contours of feminist media theory from the 'images of women in the media' approaches prevalent in the 1970s through to contemporary discussions of masculinity, globalization and cyberculture. Next, the Reader divides into three sections, each engaging with issues central to critical investigations into gender and media forms, practices, institutions and audiences. The contributions to Part I, *Texts in Context*, provide a historical analysis of configurations of femininity in advertising, an examination of the feminization and sexualization of the popular press, news reporting of sexual violence, portrayals of lesbian characters on television, and 'tough' images of femininity in women's magazines. Part II, *(Re)Producing Gender*, focuses on the various ways in which gender is continuously reconstructed across different media sites. Chapters address the impact of media monitoring on media imagery of women, the representation of women in the rock music press, how women reflect on their own media practice, the commercialization of contemporary masculinities, and women's involvement in the development of the Internet. Part III, *Audiences and Identities*, explores men's use of pornography, Aframerican and Latina women's depiction in Hollywood cinema, women's negotiation of soap opera narratives in everyday life, daytime talk shows, and girl gamers in the brave new world of cyberspace. Looking across the range of the Reader's chapters, spanning as they do some thirty years, it is readily apparent how strategically significant this kind of work is for ongoing efforts to improve the quality of women's and men's lives today.

The *Issues in Cultural and Media Studies* series aims to facilitate a diverse range of critical investigations into pressing questions considered to be central to current thinking and research. In light of the remarkable speed at which the conceptual agendas of cultural and media studies are changing, the series is committed to contributing to what is an ongoing process of re-evaluation and critique. Each of the books is intended to provide a lively, innovative and comprehensive introduction to a specific topical issue from a fresh perspective. The reader is offered a thorough grounding in the most salient debates indicative of the book's subject, as well as important insights into how new modes of enquiry may be established for future explorations. Taken as a whole, then, the series is designed to cover the core components of cultural and media studies courses in an imaginatively distinctive and engaging manner.

Stuart Allan

ACKNOWLEDGEMENTS

Cynthia Carter would like to thank Linda Steiner for agreeing to co-edit this Reader without hesitation and with great excitement. Her passionate commitment to feminist politics and the importance of her scholarship has been central in the development of feminist media research. I especially appreciate her friendship, her tireless efforts to see this Reader through and her unquestionable expertise in juggling! I am extremely grateful, as always, to Stuart and Geoffrey for their love and support throughout. I would like to dedicate this Reader to my grandmother, Meta Stairs, who is one of the strongest women I know.

Linda Steiner wishes to thank Cynthia Carter for her patient good humour in explaining UK vernacular and popular culture references, and especially for her intellectual seriousness; collaborating with her on this project has been challenging in the very best sense of the word. I wish to express appreciation to Edward Salomon, Sarah Salomon and Paul Salomon, for, among many other things, their combined and individual success in subverting a range of role expectations. I dedicate this to the memory of Frank Steiner and to Helen Steiner.

We would both like to express our sincere thanks to Lisa McLaughlin for her significant contribution to the development of the Reader in its early stages. Her political commitment to feminist media studies and her intellectual integrity is unquestionably evident here. We are also grateful to Justin Vaughan, who was with Open University Press when the Reader was contracted, for his early commitment to this project, and to Cathy Thompson, Shona Mullen and finally to Christopher Cudmore for his help in seeing it through to completion. Thanks also go to Miriam Selwyn who was editorial assistant at Open University Press when we started this book. Miriam was of invaluable help, particularly in the early stages, answering the sometimes staggering number of questions we had about the process of putting together a Reader. Thanks also go to Eleanor Hayes who guided us through the treacherous waters of editing, proofreading and indexing. Last, but certainly not least, our warmest thanks go to our series editor Stuart Allan, for his intellectual guidance, encouragement and unfailing enthusiasm for the project.

ACKNOWLEDGEMENTS FOR READINGS

The authors and publishers wish to thank the following for permission to use copyright material:

Myra Macdonald for 'From Mrs Happyman to Kissing Chaps Goodbye: Advertising Reconstructs Femininity', in *Representing Women: Myths of Femininity in the Popular Media*, Arnold (1995). Reproduced by permission of Hodder Arnold and the author.

Patricia Holland for 'The Politics of the Smile: "Soft News" and the Sexulization of the Popular Press', in *News, Gender and Power*, Carter, C., Branston, G. and Allan, S. (eds), Routledge (1998). Reproduced by permission of Routledge and the author.

Saraswati Sunindyo for 'Murder, Gender and the Media: Sexualizing Politics and Violence', in *Fantasizing the Feminine in Indonesia*, Sears, L. J. (ed.), © 1996, Duke University Press. All rights reserved. Reproduced with permission.

Marguerite J. Moritz for 'Old Strategies for New Texts: How American Television is Creating and Treating Lesbian Characters', in *The Columbia Reader on Lesbians and Gay Men in Media, Society and Politics*, Gross, L. and Woods, J. D. (eds), © 1999, Columbia University Press. Reproduced with the permission of the publisher.

Sherrie A. Inness for 'Pretty Tough: The Cult of Femininity in Women's Magazines', in *Tough Girls, Women Warriors and Wonder Women in Popular Culture*, © 1999 University of Pennsylvania Press. Reprinted by permission of the University of Pennsylvania Press.

Margaret Gallagher for 'The Final Analysis', in *Gender Setting: New Agendas for Media Monitoring and Advocacy*, Zed Books in Association with WACC (2001), reproduced by permission of Zed Books and the author.

Helen Davies for 'All Rock and Roll is Homosocial: The Representation of Women in the British Rock Music Press', in *Popular Music*, Vol. 20, No. 3, pp. 301–19, © 2001, Cambridge University Press. Reproduced by permission of the author.

Carmen Ruíz for 'Losing Fear: Video and Radio Productions of Native Aymara Women in Bolivia', in *Women in Grassroots Communication: Furthering Social Change*, Riaño, P. (ed) © 1994, Sage Publications, Inc. Reproduced by permission of Sage Publications, Inc.

John Beynon for 'The Commercialization of Masculinities: From the "New Man" to the "New Lad"', in *Masculinities and Culture*, Open University Press (2002). Reprinted by permission of Open University Press and the author.

Anne Scott, Lesley Semmons and Lynette Willoughby for 'Women and the Internet: the Natural History of a Research Project', in *Information, Communiation and Society*, Vol. 2, No. 4 (1999), pp. 541–65. Reprinted with permission of Taylor & Francis, Ltd. and the authors.

Robert Jensen for 'Knowing Pornography', in *Violence Against Women*, Vol. 2, No. 1 (1996), pp. 82–102, 1996, Sage Publications, Inc. Reprinted by permission of Sage Publications, Inc and the authors.

Elizabeth Hadley Freydberg for 'Sapphires, Spitfires, Sluts and Super-bitches: Aframericans and Latinas in Contemporary Hollywood Film', in *Black Women in America*, Kim Marie Vaz (ed.), © 1995, Sage Publications, Inc. Reprinted by permission of Sage Publications, Inc.

Mary Ellen Brown for 'Resistive Readings', in *Soap Opera and Women's Talk*, 1994, Sage Publications Inc. Reprinted by permission of Sage Publications Inc. and the authors.

Jane Shattuc for 'Freud vs. Women: The Popularization of Therapy on Daytime Talk Shows', in *The Talking Cure: TV Talk Shows and Women*, 1997, Routledge, Inc. Reproduced by permission of Routledge, Inc., part of the Taylor & Francis Group.

Heather Gilmour for 'What Girls Want: The Intersections of Leisure and Power in Female Computer Game Play', in *Kid's Media Culture*, Kinder, M. (ed) 1999, Duke University Press, reproduced by permission of Duke University Press.

Every effort has been made to trace the copyright holders but if any have been inadvertently overlooked the publishers will be pleased to make the necessary arrangement at the first opportunity.

1 | INTRODUCTION TO *CRITICAL READINGS: MEDIA AND GENDER*

Cynthia Carter and Linda Steiner

Why Study Media and Gender?

The media are important for many reasons, including their long acknowledged power to represent 'socially acceptable' ways of being or relating to others, as well as to allocate, or more usually withhold, public recognition, honour and status to groups of people. Already in the 1860s, for example, feminists in the UK and USA who were arguing for more progressive and egalitarian definitions of womanhood complained bitterly that the newspapers and magazines of the day either ridiculed or ignored the so-called 'New Woman' – women who sought greater social, educational, political and economic rights. The suffragists (or 'first wave' feminists) of the late nineteenth and early twentieth centuries were nearly unanimous in calling for the establishment of their own periodicals – which many regarded as being crucial to the political campaigns around increased rights for women, one of the most important being the vote (see Holland, Chapter 4 in this volume, for a discussion of women's historical relationship to the news). A century later, US feminist Betty Friedan's *The Feminine Mystique* (1963) emphasized the impact of popular women's magazines, whose articles, fiction and advertising celebrated a very particular form of domestic, suburban femininity, one that operated in a sphere almost completely separate from that of men. In so doing, magazine content naturalized the idea that women's 'normal' sphere of operation and influence is not only completely separate from that of men, but also less socially valued (see Macdonald, Chapter 3 in this volume).

It was not until the 'second wave' of the women's movement in the 1960s that systematic research into media images of women flourished. Almost immediately, feminist scholars and activists began to examine how women were being portrayed in a wide array of media forms – including films, prime-time television dramas, newspapers, pornography, news magazines, Saturday morning cartoons, women's and girl's magazines, popular music, comic books, advertising and soap operas. The concern was that the sexist messages of these media forms socialized people, especially children, into thinking that dichotomized and hierarchical sex-role stereotypes were 'natural' and 'normal'. Feminists quickly realized that effective challenges to certain standard ways of representing women in the media and popular culture depended on being able to provide empirical evidence of sexism. Scholars following this line of inquiry intended to use their research to help explain why more women were not successful in the public work world, especially in professions that were dominated by men. They also hoped that their studies might elucidate why so many women apparently felt unable to transcend their second-class citizenship in society, a status based on a prevailing assumption that unpaid domestic labour was less socially and economically valuable than paid labour in the public sphere.

Critical forms of feminist inquiry emerging in the 1970s went even further by examining the ways in which media representations supported the interests of two interlocking systems: patriarchy and capitalism. A highly productive concept informing some of this research was that of hegemony. For Italian political theorist Antonio Gramsci (1971), the notion of hegemony provides an explanation of how and why 'dominant' classes in society have to constantly renegotiate their powerful positions in relations to the 'subjugated' classes. To maintain power, these élites must rule by winning public consent for an economic system that privileges those already in dominant positions, rather than maintaining their control through coercion or repression. When the hegemonic definitions and ways of being of the powerful are naturalized and made to seem 'normal', they are presented to everyone as if no other definitions are possible – in other words, as 'common sense'.

The media are instrumental in the processes of gaining public consent. Media texts never simply mirror or reflect 'reality', but instead construct hegemonic definitions of what should be accepted as 'reality'. These definitions appear to be inevitable, 'real' and commonsensical. Thus, media images dissemble the extent to which they are aligned with the interests of powerful groups in society. Feminists have redeployed the notion of hegemony in order to argue that most of us cannot see how patriarchal ideology is being actively made to appear as 'non-ideological', 'objective', 'neutral' and 'non-gendered'.

That said, hegemonic realities must be continuously renegotiated, contested, reconstructed and renaturalized. Along with the media, other social institutions are central to these processes, including the education system, religion, and the family. Even with considerable propping up, however, there are ideological seams through which leak out evidence of flaws in the system and of the politically constructed nature of hegemonic ideology. Counter-hegemonic impulses of resistance and struggle are always possible. For instance, oppositional forces such as the women's movement may attempt to recast media definitions of femininity in order to advance the political objective of gender equality. One way that they have achieved this is through the establishment of alternative media forms where the aim is to offer more progressive and positive representations of women and girls. Nevertheless, as critical feminist media research has shown, the mainstream media have increasingly incorporated or co-opted this counter-hegemonic view, particularly when it has proven to be in their economic interest. In so doing, the media have at times unwittingly contributed to the support and advancement of oppositional gender realities (see Gilmour, Chapter 17 in this volume, for a consideration of girls' use of computer games in the formation of non-traditional feminine identities).

In any case, media texts, institutions and audiences have changed, in part, because of feminists' persistent advocacy over many years. Feminists have deployed their research on behalf of an enormous range of interventions, from boycotts and letter-writing campaigns, to lobbying for legal and regulatory changes. Some campaigns have been dramatic but episodic, such as the feminist take-over of the male publisher's office at the *Ladies Home Journal* in 1970 (most of the other major US women's magazines also had male publishers at the time). Longer-term and more consistent changes have resulted from women's vehement insistence that media organizations hire and promote on the basis of gender-fair procedures (often backed up by formal 'affirmative action' or 'equal opportunities' policies).

Another important development that shaped feminist activism and scholarship in the 1970s was that a distinction was made between *sex* (based on biological differences – male/female) and *gender* (masculinity/femininity). Gender, it was argued, is a social construction rather than a 'natural' fact. Thus, gender cannot be reductively 'read off' from sexual difference (male/female), nor can it be assumed that there are universal and homogenous definitions of gender that apply to all cultures across time. This insight led to an explosion of feminist research across academic disciplines and has been a central feature of media studies research for over thirty years now. For a long time, however, investigations into the media construction of masculinity did not undergo the same kind of scholarly scrutiny in media and cultural studies that had been given to femininity. Research was rarely undertaken, in part, because one principle of the women's liberation movement of the 1970s was to take women's issues seriously and to redress a historical lack of interest and research into them. However, the situation is changing. There is now a fast-growing scholarly interest in understanding how masculine identities are produced, represented and made sense of by audiences (see Beynon, Chapter 11 in this volume; Craig 1992; Jackson et al. 2001; Kama 2002; Tincknell et al. 2003). What is particularly interesting (and heartening) is that an increasing number of male media scholars appear to be taking gender much more seriously now, rather than simply continuing to leave critiques of masculinity to their female colleagues.

In part, the growth of research on gender issues has been linked to the entry of substantial numbers of women into media and communication departments in the USA and UK over the course of the past 30 years. Upon entering the academy, many women from this post-war 'baby boomer' generation insisted upon the importance of research that would explore all aspects of women's relationships to the media – an area that had largely been ignored by their male colleagues up to that time. Not surprisingly, there is also an economic dimension to the proliferation of this scholarship. The gender/media nexus is one of those important issues that can be studied without huge, expensive research laboratories, a consideration that has been crucial for many women scholars, since most have had limited or no access to such research facilities or financial support (van Zoonen 1994).

What we understand as the 'media' has also undergone dramatic rethinking over the past 30 years. In that time, major new technologies have emerged, including desktop computers, the Internet, satellite television, video recorders and games, cable television and mobile phones, to name only a few. Moreover, the academic study of the media has become an extremely popular field of study in schools and universities, and the growth of scholarly research over this period has been enormous. There has also been an increasing convergence of various media technologies. For example, television services now often include Internet and e-mail access; mobile telephones are now able to transmit images across satellite links around the world. Of course, with the development and circulation of each of these new technologies, issues around gender access and participation have been at the forefront.

Let us be clear about one thing – sexism is not merely an issue of media representations. It cannot be remedied simply by the inclusion of more 'realistic' and 'positive' images of women and girls in the media. Official statistics gathered by governments, unions, non-governmental organizations, businesses and pressure groups document the continuing material effectivity of sexism in employment. In both the UK and the USA, for example, women continue to earn less, per capita, than men. In 2002, the *New Earnings Survey* published by the British National Statistics Office (NSO) reported that the gap in pay between men and women had widened from the previous year. Specifically, women who are working full time earn 81.2 per cent of the average full-time male wage (compared to 81.5 per cent in 2001). Moreover, 180,000 of the part-time jobs done by women pay less than the minimum wage, compared to 50,000 of those by men. In the USA, we find a similar story. According to US Census Bureau (2000) data, in 1999 women were paid 72.2 per cent of men's annual wages ($26,324 for women, $36,476 for men). The US Department of Labor's (2002) statistics for 2001 are only slightly better, with women working full-time earning $511 a week or 76 per cent of a male full-time worker's weekly salary of $672. With respect to US media, the Annenberg Public Policy Center at the University of Pennsylvania reported in 2002 that men continue to dominate key decision-making positions. For example, in the top entertainment conglomerates, women make up only 13 per cent of executives and 14 per cent of the directors, while they are 14 per cent of US newspaper publishers and 32 per cent of the news executives in the seven national commercial television broadcasting corporations.

Such inequalities are even more severely marked in some 'developing' countries, where women often lack certain basic human rights – rights to an education, economic security, political enfranchisement, freedom from domestic violence, access to high quality, affordable healthcare, and reproductive control. Feminist scholars in these countries have long argued for the need to engage with the ways in which the media help to shape the norms, values and beliefs that underpin these gender inequalities. Over the past decade or so, critiques of the media are becoming increasingly globalized in their orientation (see Sunindyo, Gallagher and Ruíz, Chapters 5, 8 and 10 respectively in this volume). For example, when the harsh and extreme sexism of the former Taliban government recently was brought to public attention in the Western media, many people around the world became involved in campaigns to raise public awareness further. Some lobbied through local, national and international governmental bodies to put pressure on the Taliban government; others created global support networks with Afghani women's groups, sometimes using the Internet to organize quickly and create effective opposition. So, while the media have unquestionably contributed to the (re)production of sexist norms, values and beliefs, they are also capable of playing a significant role in bringing to world-wide attention the material harms that women may suffer as a result (see Scott, Semmens and Willoughby, Chapter 12 in this volume, for a discussion of women's historical relationship to the Internet).

This Reader's Structure and Organization

Instead of trying to define the media/gender canon of the last thirty years, this Reader reflects a particular political agenda. That is, our allegiances are closely linked with research that attends to the ways in which gender inequalities are both structurally (re)produced as well as negotiated, contested and challenged by audiences. For us, to engage with questions around gender, power and social inequality necessarily means that one must attend to societal structures, social divisions and inequitable distributions of social and economic power. What we are trying to do with this Reader is to construct a different kind of narrative – one that is openly critical in its orientation. That said, we are not in any way attempting to offer an alternative canon. Aside from the fact that a book of this length could not hope to achieve this goal, our aim is a very different one – to offer our readers a critical resource that is broadly indicative of the current state of critical, gender-sensitive research and that directly addresses our own concerns around the role that the media play in (re)producing structural inequalities.

This book provides a sense of how rich and exciting this area of research is, given that its readings engage with diverse theories as well as a variety of media audiences and genres. We have also taken care to present a fairly wide array of research methods, from large-scale surveys to textual analysis and ethnography and studies of media forms that have long interested feminist researchers, as well as more recent media texts and sites. Current attention goes, on the one hand, to the institutional, financial and organizational structures and procedures affecting how and why specific texts are produced, and, on the other, to the specific technological, interpersonal and even physical contexts in which audiences are situated.

No single Reader can encompass the entire trajectory of research on gender and media. Research findings from the 1970s and 1980s may no longer be relevant to what is happening today, including those from important studies which have been enormously influential in shaping the research agenda of media and cultural studies research. Many early studies that provided essential quantitative evidence about gender differences in media employment are now largely outdated too. A rapidly changing media environment (technological developments, media convergence, media globalization, changing media employment and ownership patterns, media education and so on) may also undermine the relevance of much more recent research from the 1990s. Even the methodological tools of researchers have changed since the 1970s and 1980s, when many studies involved fairly simplistic and literal 'counting' of individual women and men appearing in a body of media text. In such studies, scholars tended to assume that these texts were 'transmitted' to 'receivers' essentially intact, and that researchers' understandings of texts corresponded, more or less exactly, with how receivers understood them. Nor can one simply assume that the 'meaning' of a media text is embedded within it and merely needs to be uncovered by an astute semiologist. Such analyses have been largely supplanted by a range of more nuanced methods, often used in conjunction with each other, including ethnography, historical/archival research, participant observation, focus group interviews and discourse analysis, to name only a few.

Even with respect to the current generation of scholarship, no single book can tackle all of the theories or methods that are being used in gender-sensitive research, across all media forms and genres. Regrettably, we could not include all of the essays that we had envisaged when we first proposed this Reader and have had to redact some of the readings republished here so that we would not go over our 'word limit'. In part, it is the economic logics of academic publishing in the West that have been central in constraining what we have been able to include in this Reader. A longer book would not have been affordable. We hope that you will agree, however, that within these structural constraints, we have been able to put together a volume that will provide our readers with a useful starting point for the study of media and gender research.

Turning then to the Reader's contents, essays in Part I explore the very narrow ways in which femininity typically has been represented in mainstream media texts. The first reading (Chapter 3), by Myra Macdonald, provides a lively and expansive historical examination of the advertising industry's construction of domesticized, consumerist forms of femininity over the past century. Patricia Holland's essay (Chapter 4) refutes the claim made by publishers of the *Sun*, an UK tabloid newspaper, that its increasing emphasis on sexualization has been a force for gender democratization. Sexualization is also the central theme for Saraswati Sunindyo (Chapter 5), who demonstrates how the Indonesian press construct sexually active women as 'bad women' who are to blame for any violence that men use against them. Despite significant changes in social attitudes to homosexuality over the past few decades, Marguerite Moritz (Chapter 6) shows how US television portrays lesbian characters as 'asexual' and therefore non-threatening to heterosexuals, thus undermining the political significance of such social change. Part I of the Reader ends with an essay by Sherrie Inness (Chapter 7) in which she argues that although women's magazines are increasingly apt to represent strong, independent women, such images actually undermine women's potential toughness by clearly linking it to restrictive, socially acceptable feminine identities.

From investigations into media texts, we turn in Part II to an examination of some of the ways in which media institutions and production processes contribute to unequal gender relations. Margaret Gallagher's research into women's employment and representation in the news around the world makes the case for media monitoring as a way of accumulating cross-cultural evidence of women's stereotyping and marginalization (Chapter 8). In a classic case of the double bind, Helen Davies argues in Chapter 9 that the heavily male-dominated UK rock music press sexualizes female musicians and female rock journalists. This then fuels a belief that these women are less serious than their male counterparts, and thus less worthy of press attention in the case of female musicians, or space to write their reviews in the case of female rock journalists. To counter such barriers, some women have argued that women's alternative media appear to be the only place where the voices of women can be heard. Supporting this claim, Carmen Ruíz (Chapter 10) reports on a women's grassroots communication project in Bolivia that enabled a group of rural women to produce their own media forms, a project that left the women involved feeling empowered and active participants in the public sphere. The production of masculine identities is the focus of John Beynon's review of contemporary young men's magazines in the UK (Chapter 11). Beynon concludes that while these publications incorporate a wider, more open range of masculine identities, the least progressive masculine identity, 'laddism', appears to dominate, an identity in which 'real men' are defined by their consumerism. Our attention turns in the final paper in Part II from the formation of masculine identities in magazines to femininities and cyberspace. Anne Scott, Lesley Semmens and Lynette Willoughby conclude in Chapter 12 that one of the most pressing issues that feminists now need to address is how the new social geographies of Internet access are being gendered in ways that may severely constrain women's computer use and, perhaps, ultimately, their participation in the public sphere.

Part III of the Reader documents how gender matters when audiences try to make sense of media texts. Robert Jensen's article (Chapter 13) offers a critical, reflexive analysis of his own experiences of using pornography, concluding that it constructs an ideology of male dominance and female subordination that naturalizes men's control over women in society.

Elizabeth Hadley Freydberg (Chapter 14) makes a similar claim, arguing that in Hollywood cinema Aframericans and Latinas have been typically portrayed in stereotypical ways – as lustful, sexual objects of white men's desire, as 'bad' women whom white men need to exploit sexually as well as control. Turning to soap opera audiences, Mary Ellen Brown demonstrates in Chapter 15 that women's knowledge of this television genre can form the basis of female support networks through which such knowledge is legitimated and where women are empowered to resist its often constrictive messages about femininity. Similarly, Jane Shattuc (Chapter 16) argues that the discursive space provided by US television talk shows offers their predominantly female audiences a unique opportunity to form collective feminine identities from which they are able to articulate their shared experiences of gender subordination in society. In the final paper in Part III, Heather Gilmour insists in Chapter 17 that the gaming software currently being developed for girls contributes to the reproduction of hierarchical gender difference between boys and girls rather than to breaking it down. At the same time, however, she notes that girl gamers are resisting these restrictive definitions of femininity and finding pleasure in the formation of more heterogeneous, alternative identities.

In this brief introduction, we have attempted to show why the field of media and gender research is important, interesting and exciting. Some people might think that gender equality has been achieved and therefore that the issues we are addressing in this Reader are no longer relevant. We would agree that much progress has been made and that most women enjoy more personal, political and economic power and freedom. However, women as a group are still in a structurally subordinate position to most men. Around the world, women continue to make less money than do men; they often endure appalling experiences of a criminal justice system that fails to support them when attempting to press rape charges; they still have a much more difficult time getting promoted in their jobs than men; women's domestic labour and motherhood is undervalued in relation to paid labour in the public sphere; women continue to be sexualized, dehumanized and objectified in most mainstream media content.

There is still a great deal to learn about the ways in which the media contribute to women's secondary social and economic status. In any case, a now substantial and fast-growing array of new journals, edited volumes, monographs, conference presentations and special conventions is clearly evidence of an ongoing interest in the field of media and gender research. Feminist insights have clearly had a transformative effect on the fields of media and cultural studies. Losing sight of this fact is rather easy to do, given that most scholars now take for granted that their research must be sensitive to questions of gender, as well as those of class, 'race', ethnicity and sexuality, among other forms of identity. As recently as 15 to 20 years ago, many researchers still regarded these assumptions to be questionable, if not problematic. From the vantage point of today, however, such views seem almost anachronistic. This change has been an important one for feminist and critical media scholars. It has provided them with the institutional support needed to undertake systematic studies into a range of important issues and problems around gender – although such research does not itself solve them. Clearly, much more work remains to be done.

References

Annenberg Public Policy Center of the University of Pennsylvania (2002) *The Glass Ceiling in the Executive Suite: The 2nd Annual APPC Analysis of Women Leaders in Communication Companies.*

Craig, S. (ed.) (1992) *Men, Masculinity and the Media.* London and Thousand Oaks: Sage.

Friedan, B. (1963) *The Feminine Mystique.* New York: Norton.

Gramsci, A. (1971) *Selections from the Prison Notebooks of Antonio Gramsci*, ed. and trans. Q. Hoare and G. Nowell Smith. New York: International Publishers.

Jackson, P., Stevenson, N. and Brooks, K. (2001) *Making Sense of Men's Magazines.* Cambridge: Polity.

Kama, A. (2002) The quest for inclusion: Jewish–Israeli gay men's perceptions of gays in the media, *Feminist Media Studies*, 2(2): 195–212.

National Statistics Office (2002) *New Earnings Survey 2002*, www.statistics.gov.uk/pdfdir/nes1002/pdf (accessed 1 November 2002).

Tincknell, E., Chambers, D., van Loon, J., and Hudson, N. (2003) Begging for it: 'new femininities', social agency and moral discourse in contemporary teenage and men's magazines, *Feminist Media Studies*, 3(1): 47–63.

US Department of Labor, Bureau of Labour Statistics (2002) *Highlights of Women's Earnings 2001.*

van Zoonen, L. (1994) *Feminist Media Studies.* London: Sage.

MAPPING THE CONTESTED TERRAIN OF MEDIA AND GENDER RESEARCH

2

Cynthia Carter and Linda Steiner

The whole point of gender dimorphism, as it has been constructed for centuries, is that it means that someone – almost invariably someone who isn't female – gets to judge what is and isn't acceptable for women.... It is still much harder for women than for men to express themselves as individuals and the penalties for failing to conform remain high...

(Smith 1997: 166–7)

Most men are still culturally propelled to incorporate dominance, whether in terms of crude physical strength or displays of 'masculine' rationality and competence, into the presentation of self. Of course, by presenting gender as cultural and performative, the paradigm that holds that masculinity and femininity are straitjackets into which all biological males and females are automatically fitted, begins to be severely undermined.

(Beynon 2002: 11)

This introductory essay maps out what we believe to be the most important and relevant conceptual concerns around gender in the fields of media and cultural studies today. Since we understand media in terms of a highly inter-structured or 'articulated' relationship among texts, institutions and audi-ences, we offer brief accounts of current scholarly debates around representation found in Part I: Texts in Context; we examine media eco-nomics and workplace issues in Part II: (Re)producing Gender; and outline a range of insights generated by critical audience research in Part III: Audiences and Identities. Given the triangular relationships among texts, media organizations and industries, and audiences' practices, at some level, one cannot discuss one theme without raising the other two. That said, the sections below sketch key terms and issues, broadly outlining the historical, theoretical and methodological contexts for what is now a wealth of gender-sensitive research.

Texts in Context

Central to the stereotypes of masculinity and femininity in the Western media is the idea that they are opposites, and that boys and girls are 'naturally' and fundamentally different. Not surprisingly, children's media – like their toys – are among the first contexts that each of us encounters for demonstrating how masculinity and femininity 'ought' to be performed. Boy's action figure 'GI Joe' in the USA or 'Action Man' in the UK depicts a muscled, tough and aggressive character armed with the latest guns, missiles and explosives. Currently, popular films such as *Gladiator, Lord of the Rings, Men in Black* and *Spiderman* indicate what are deemed to be 'normal' or 'appropriate' forms of masculine behaviour. While a 'real man' may use his intelligence to outwit an opponent, in the end, the most valued attribute of a man in these films is his physical prowess. The threat of violence is often all that is needed to reconfirm one's masculine credentials, although a willingness and ability to use it must necessarily and credibly back up that threat. On children's television, cartoons such as *Digimon: Digital Monsters* and *Yu-gi-oh* combine images primarily of boys and men who use their smarts, strength and superhuman monsters to exert their will/superiority over others. Each week, the cast of characters must employ certain masculine skills and repertoires of expertise to defeat similarly inclined enemies and, finally, to confirm their superiority.

For girls, quite opposite points of identification were already apparent in early fairytales, many of which date to the seventeenth century. For example, female characters in *Cinderella, Rapunzel* and *Sleeping Beauty* are portrayed as being beautiful, emotional and timid, waiting for a man to come along to rescue them (preferably a prince or a knight in shining armour!). Nineteenth-century industrialization and the relocation of work from the family and farm to the factory and the town shop contributed to the development of unequal, gendered spheres of work (the 'public' sphere of men and political affairs versus the 'private' sphere of women and domesticity). Girls were raised to be the consumers of the future – domestic, caring, and objects of beauty – rather than producers. This idea was widely cultivated and promoted by newspapers and women's magazines. Continuing through the twentieth century, the modern media contrasted good girls (pretty, quiet, sensitive, selfless and nurturing) with 'evil' girls, who are assertive, sexual, stubborn and selfish. Since 1959, the 'Barbie' doll has provided several generations of girls with an image of 'ideal' (white, het-erosexual) femininity – a figure who is attractive, impossibly thin, long legged and big breasted – accessorized with the latest fashions, accom-modation, transport and boyfriend Ken.[1]

Although many clearly gendered stereotypes still inform media content today, the rigidity of such hierarchical feminine gendered identity has nevertheless begun to break down. An increasingly varied array of feminine images and role models is now available, some of which offer progressive and sometimes challenging alternatives. For example, in *Star Wars: Episode 1* (1999) one of the main female characters is the teenaged Queen Amidala who, through a combination of intelligence and exceptional military planning and fighting skills, is able to help defeat the evil that threatens her people. *Harry Potter and the Chamber of Secrets* (2002) features the pre-teen character Hermione Granger, who is portrayed as possessing knowledge of magic superior to her closest friends, Harry Potter and Ron Weasley. Nevertheless, socialization into not merely different but also unequal gender roles and behaviours has not disappeared altogether. Likewise, it is important to keep in mind that such socialization continues to have real, negative material (economic, social, political) effects on the life chances of girls (as well as boys) as they grow up (Mattelart 1986).

Turning to a consideration of the historical development of gender and media content research, it is important to note that as early as the 1960s media scholars influenced by concepts emerging from early 'second wave' feminism sought to understand and explain how the media depicts unequal gendered relations. The reason for this, of course, was to collect evidence of media sexism in order to intervene and substitute more positive and realistic images – ones that did not confine women to passivity and inferiority. A key concept generated by an early generation of media content researchers was that of 'symbolic annihilation'. This term was initially used by US mass communication scholars George Gerbner (1978) and Gaye Tuchman (1978) to describe the claim that powerful groups in society suppress the less powerful by marginalizing them to such an extent that they are ren-dered virtually invisible as a representable group. The media function – at least in the period they were describing – by either effectively erasing women's presence, by fundamentally denying their humanity, trivializing or mocking them, or by reducing them to a single 'feminine' characteristic, even if that characteristic could be regarded as 'positive' (like 'innocent', 'nurturing' or 'concerned for others').

Much of the generation of research inspired by these notions confirmed that media images through to the end of the 1980s tended to stay within a narrow set of sex role stereotypes, primarily limiting women to a domestic/

private sphere that experienced uncertain, if not low social status compared to that of men. Studies often concluded that men were usually depicted in a wider range of occupational roles, primarily in the public sphere, which enjoys higher social status. Feminist researchers generally assumed that the limited portrayals of women contributed to sexist and therefore harmful attitudes. For example, scholars argued that sexist stereotypes encourage people to believe that women are suited only (and always) to so-called 'traditional' female sex roles and discourage people from accepting women who are strong, assertive, independent and self-confident, thus inhibiting women's ability to realize their full personal and professional potential. Scholars and activists joined in a movement to challenge the media to depict women more fairly, in a wider array of occupational roles and with variation in intellectual and emotional traits. Meanwhile, pressure was also brought to bear on the media to portray men in ways that suggest that they can be sensitive, emotional and interested in and committed to their parenting and domestic responsibilities (see Craig 1992). Some changes did result from these efforts, although much work remains to be done.

In any case, role reversals are not the point. Altering mediated images of women and men to portray them in a wider range of roles is at best a start. Certainly the point of advocating change is not merely to argue that prime-time dramas should feature women as career-driven attorneys or that music videos should portray women as whip-wielding dominatrices. That a new US television series *The Bachelorette* will counter an existing one for men, *The Bachelor*, is not really a sign of gender progress. Analyses and critiques of media forms, institutions and production practices need to be very carefully constructed to show how media discourses contribute to, or conversely, challenge the structural (re)production of gender inequalities. That is, the political issue to be addressed is not merely either 'positive' or 'negative' images of a given fictional character's occupational role and surface-level indicia of their emotional stability (or lack thereof). Ideology researchers argue that the analysis of media texts can shed important light not only on the ideologically gendered assumptions underpinning their narratives but also on the gendered mode of address to their audiences. Which audiences are being served? Are women and men addressed differently, via texts with different varieties of intellectual and emotional content? To understand how gender difference is (re)produced ideologically in the media, attention needs to be paid to the ways in which media forms aimed at men are regarded as normatively the 'correct' ones, while those for women are marked as 'different', 'alternative', 'marginal' or, in other words, as non-normative. For example, the national television news and broadsheet press in both the USA and UK are widely considered to be 'objective' (non-ideological/non-gendered = masculine) while television talk shows like *Oprah* in the USA or *Richard and Judy* in the UK are regarded as 'subjective' (ideological/gendered = feminine) (see Allan 1999).

Recently, feminist researchers have been more insistent about the importance of analysing media texts produced primarily for female audiences (see Inness, Brown and Shattuc – Chapters 7, 15 and 16 in this volume). Day-time talk shows (Shattuc 1997), women's films (Lloyd and Johnson 2003; Stacey 1994; Vares 2002), women's magazines (Ballaster et al. 1991; Basu 2001; Beetham 1996; Currie 1999; Hermes 1995), soap operas (Brunsdon 2000; Brown 1994; Geraghty 1990) and other texts primarily intended for women have long been widely regarded as marginal and trivial, not only by many in the media audience, but also in 'mainstream' media scholarship. Why is this the case, these researchers enquire, and what is the significance of these perceptions? Media forms coded as 'gendered'/feminine have tended to be regarded by the academic administrators in positions of power over hiring and promotion as tangential to 'real' media scholarship – for a long time largely synonymous with studies of journalism and the news (see Brunsdon 2000). This effectively discouraged some from focusing on analysis of 'women's genres'. Much like the system of reward and punishment associated with boys' and girls' compliance to traditional gender roles, an academic system based on gender difference was used to construct and maintain a system of unequal scholarship relations (see Shirvani et al. 2002). Again, as essays in this volume show, this is now (slowly) changing. A lively and productive generation of scholarship taking these forms seriously is now beginning to thrive.

Representations in the media of people, events and relationships never simply appear from 'no place'. At some level, of course, this assertion that media messages do not simply appear like Venus emerging from the sea is obvious, but often discussions of content either begin and end with that content, or acquire explanations that turn immediately to highly macro-level societal conditions: patriarchy accounts for sexist content. Media organizations and the gendered issues attendant to those organizations are certainly responsive to social–political movements – and to the reactions against them – as well as to broad economic and social changes. However, between the very broad, general conditions and power relations in the world and the ideological messages which shape media texts that are delivered to audiences is an important system of production. Messages emerge from complex – indeed, extremely complex and often hierarchical – co-ordinated activities of increasingly globalized media organizations. The next section of this essay turns to examine the processes of producing media texts and the impact of gender difference within media institutions.

(Re)producing Gender

How gender is (re)produced in the media demands a consideration of the ways in which media forms are produced.[2] Just as gender itself cannot be understood in isolation from 'race', class and sexuality, so media production cannot be seen as solely a result of media workers, or owners. Nor, as catchy as McLuhan's idea was in *Understanding Media: The Extensions of Man* (1964), is the sole answer that 'the medium is the message'. What is critical is the complex interaction of institutional structures, organizational/ corporate constraints, the basis of financing and the possibility of advertiser pressure, the regulatory context, as well as the predispositions of individual workers and owners. For social movements trying to create alternative media, certain technical, technological and socio-economic factors also loom large. Can a newspaper or magazine physically get distributed to its potential readers? What kinds of skills and equipment are necessary to produce content? What is the cost of access to a medium – not so much the cost to consumers of purchasing or consuming a single 'issue' than the cost of buying (or starting) and operating a media organization such as a newspaper or radio station? Are potential audiences literate? Furthermore, like the analyses of texts, the analyses of media organizations (from hiring and promotion patterns to structures for decision making) need to be grounded in a dual systems approach that takes note of both 'gender biases' and the interests of commercial organizations in maximizing profit.

A brief historical detour to assess women's long presence in newsrooms raises many of the questions that are relevant to how work routes, divisions of labour, the need to find practical financing structures and a host of other features of textual production interact in the media construction of gender difference. To succeed economically, editors and especially publishers have long understood that newspapers need to obtain enough subscribers of a kind that would attract a sufficient number of advertisers. By this logic, it is perhaps not surprising that early newspapers in both the USA and UK (and in other industrialized countries) were largely masculine enterprises. Men were the most desired readers, so newspapers were written to attract them. The assumption was that women writers would be unable to cover issues of interest to men or to write in ways that men would find appealing. Initially, the few women who managed to enter newsrooms were nearly always the sisters, daughters or wives of newspaper and magazine publishers and editors (Sebba 1994). Later, a few women were hired specifically to write about things of interest to that somewhat marginalized audience, women (Mills 1990). It was assumed that female journalists were best suited to writing about fashion, domestic chores and social news. More to the point, the women's page has always been regarded as a 'low-rent ghetto' within journalism. 'Women's journalism' is not 'real' journalism (see Stott 1973; Mills 1997; van Zoonen 1998). Men did not want to write about things of interest to women nor, as their autobiographies attest, did women want to write for women's pages (Steiner 1998).

Women in the USA with access to money and the ability to make purchases for themselves and their families eventually became desirable markets. The *Delineator*, which lasted until the 1930s, was started in 1872 by Ebenezer Butterick to promote tissue patterns for sewing, as was *McCall's*. In 1837, Sarah Josepha Hale merged her *Ladies Magazine* with her competitor's *Godey's Lady's Book*, and ran it for 40 years. Other women's magazines have lasted for more than a century – the *Ladies' Home Journal* goes back to 1883, *Good Housekeeping* to 1885. The point is not that 'refined' middle-class women were in particular need of moral uplift, but that magazine publishers became convinced that they needed to ensure this. These magazines were not only cheap to produce and easy to read, but their staffs worked hard to convince women that they needed the magazines' models of 'proper' womanhood. Women became an ever more attractive market for advertisers as their spending power increased (see also Beetham 1996).

Women's magazines continue to raise a host of crucial issues for a consideration of gender. First, a logic within capitalism demands that femininity be defined and continually re-defined in ways that are financially profitable (see Macdonald, Chapter 3 in this volume). Particular definitions are tied to specific products that women are told that they need or that they can be made to desire and need through advertising. The emergence in the twenty-first century of multiple identities for women constitutes a boon to publishers and advertisers. There are now more niche markets. Marketing consultants have identified a growing number of feminine identities, each of which can be sold a range of products, although many of these identities are soon abandoned after they turn out not to be profitable (McCracken 1993). Each member of a niche market – whether defined by age, size, career, 'race', hobbies or even marital status – is handed her own set of problems and challenges which can be explained and solved by subscribing to the magazine and by using the products and services it advertises. In some cases, readers might not even know that they had such problems until discovering them in the magazine. Recently, many of the same issues have emerged in the new men's magazines, including the invention of successive styles of masculinity (see Beynon, Chapter 11 in this volume; see also Jackson et al. 2001). Nevertheless, the intense pressure from advertisers on women's magazines to offer complementary copy – essentially free advertising disguised as editorial copy run in conjunction with advertising – may signal both a particular lack of respect for women and the idea that women's anxieties about femininity can continue to be manipulated for financial gain.

Feminists who have tried over the last 150 years to establish their own media institutions have not necessarily avoided these financial pressures and constraints, even when they have been wholly uninterested in making a profit (Steiner 1992). Suffrage newspapers of the 1870s and 1880s, sex education journals of the 1920s and radical separatist magazines of the 1970s found it difficult or impossible to operate without some advertising revenue, but also found it difficult or impossible to attract this revenue when they wanted it. Even when the labour is donated, production, transmission and distribution of media forms can cost a lot of money. Questions revolving around funding and advertising have continued to be particularly troublesome for alternative media organizations, including those produced by feminists hoping to offer alternative definitions of femininity and portray non-hierarchical gender relations. Potential advertisers often assert that the readership of such media are not sufficiently interested in consumption, or at least in the specific products and services that advertisers have been accustomed to aiming at women. Alternatively, advertisers have pressured the feminist media to run certain kinds of stories, covers and illustrations, often in ways that were inconsistent with the politics of these organizations.

In the USA, certain feminist newspapers, magazines, radio shows and cable television programmers have succeeded, but usually only when they are the brainchild of an individual woman or because they are produced by relatively non-hierarchical collectives. Gloria Steinem (1990), one of the co-founding editors of *Ms.*, which is by far the largest feminist periodical published in the USA, famously described how the magazine's refusal to let itself be co-opted by advertisers meant the loss of many potential accounts. In 1980, for example, Revlon halted its plans to advertise in *Ms.* after four Soviet women exiled for publishing underground samizdat (self-published, usually photo-copied news written by political dissidents) appeared on a *Ms.* cover without make-up. In another incident, when *Ms.* not only refused to provide com-plementary copy but also reported that hair dyes might be carcinogenic, Clairol stopped advertising in the magazine. Relying on high subscription rates, from 1990 until 2002 *Ms.* ran no advertising at all. Its current owner, the US feminist organization Feminist Majority, however, has decided to accept some advertisements from progressive organizations and businesses.

Although the gatekeeping function of news media is well known, the gendered character of gatekeeping processes within news organizations is rarely systematically studied (van Zoonen 1998). That is to say, little attention has been paid to the extent to which organizational and bureaucratic procedures by which stories are selected and assigned are male dominated. While news decisions reflect certain institutional decisions about 'newsworthiness', exclusivity and the availability of credible sources, among other considerations, gendered power dynamics are also inflected when stories are changed to fit legal standards, editors' and owners' prejudices, community culture and advertiser demands (Christmas 1997; Mills 1997; Rhodes 2001).

Outside the news, there are even fewer systematic studies of the organizational impacts of gender, although anecdotal stories circulate about how, on one hand, individual politicians or feminist groups have complained about television or film plots, and on the other, how scripts have been changed when something seems too controversial. The structure of media institutions – in terms of the relative flexibility and adaptability of various technologies as well as the constraints imposed by certain economic and financing systems – has necessarily figured in debates about gender. The point of such work is to encourage a critical examination of how and when gender matters to media professionals and in media workplaces.

The production of messages also involves questions of genre, given media organizations' preference for and reliance on well-established ones like soap operas, daytime television talk shows and women's magazines, since these are seen to have enduring audience appeal. Even here, it is worth noting that the production of these and other gendered media genres has specific consequences for women. For example, in television soap operas, narrative time rarely follows clock time; plots continue for years, constituting the television soap as a serial form that resists narrative closure (Modleski 1982). In addition, soaps emphasize dialogue, problem solving, intimate conversation and domestic settings. On one hand, then, it can be argued that these devices are deployed to offer familiarity and thereby provide pleasure to women viewers in the home. However, one could also argue that these features are specifically employed as a commodity in order to hook a market for the commercials, to keep women watching, day after day, and month after month (see Brunsdon 2000).

John Fiske (1987: 308) has made a similar point about television news, referring to it as a 'masculine soap opera'. Like soaps, television news relies on a serial/continuous format for its stories about the world of men and resists narrative closure. So too does the news emphasize dialogue (through journalist/source interviews, for example) and problem solving (how to manage post-war Iraq as the focus of seemingly endless discussions, for instance). Where conversation is intimate in soap operas and related to women's experiences in the private sphere, the news instead emphasizes collective conversation in a public (masculine) setting. The discursive devices used in television news are ones that are well known to their (largely male) audiences, providing viewers with pleasures associated with their familiarity of the genre and its largely masculine mode of address. So too does the news discursively invite male viewers to return to the narrative, day in, day out, to follow stories as they unfold. In the UK, the evening news bulletins attract some of the largest audiences of the viewing day. These audiences are not only highly attractive to advertisers on the commercial television stations (because of their large numbers and relatively high disposable income), but also to the BBC, which needs to bring in large audiences in order to justify its continuing reliance on funding from the television licence fee.

In the context of commercial television in the USA, maintaining and expanding audiences for soap operas is driven by the commercial logics of advertisers who demand reliable and consistent access to this consumer market. Here the central interest of television producers is to sustain a market on behalf of advertisers, while serving the particular interests of an audience is of secondary importance (Modleski 1982). Similarly, popular romance novels – which major publishing houses like Harlequin and Mills & Boon produce several times a week, nearly by an assembly line, using simple and standardized narrative formats – are designed to keep their fans buying. The point is, as a particular popular culture genre, the romance novel is written to be consumed easily and quickly so that the reader shortly needs to buy yet another one (a similar logic to that of women's magazines). The actual story may be displaced within this scenario by the act of consuming the product itself. To put this point more bluntly, although it is tempting to think that media products are not produced in the same ways and for the same reasons as toothpaste and chairs, as commodities, the logic is pretty much the same. Indeed, whether the media product is a soap opera, romance novel, women's magazine or newspaper, it is not the product that is the central commodity, but the audience itself – an audience that can be sold to advertisers who want to sell to that audience other commodities.

The institutional processes and systems that give rise to media forms are largely indiscernible to their audiences. Such invisibility works to the economic and ideological advantage of media organizations, which face fewer challenges and enjoy greater resonance when audiences cannot step back to think who is responsible for the selection and production of texts but instead merely accept texts as 'mirrors of reality'. Nonetheless, students – in the broadest sense of the word – are becoming increasingly interested not only in the texts that media producers are currently providing for audiences but also who are producing them, what or who is missing, and who is not being addressed. Sometimes analysis of the sexist and capitalist interests of media institutions may be disruptive and may even spoil the fun of (unthinking) media consumption. That said, understanding the issues can also stimulate new ideas and political interventions in media institutions. We would argue that in most cases, as the next section on gendered audiences shows, understanding how the media operate, and why, and how they produce certain content can enormously enhance one's pleasure and appreciation of specific media genres.

Audiences and Identities

Media and cultural studies scholars understand audiences as comprising human actors who are necessarily active meaning-makers, although there is some debate over the extent to which viewers can be described as self-determining individuals. The messages of media texts never simply mirror or reflect 'reality', but instead construct hegemonic definitions of what should be accepted as 'reality'. To understand how audiences 'decode' media texts, it is important to understand how the hegemonic conditions of their encoding encourage audiences to make sense of them in certain 'preferred' ways – ones that help to (re)produce hegemonic definitions of 'reality'. Stuart Hall's (1980) 'encoding/decoding' model of communication underscored how audiences might accept hegemonic definitions of 'reality' although they might also partially resist them, or indeed read messages oppositionally. During the 1980s and 1990s, feminist and critical scholars variously investigated the conditions of production and reception of television soap operas, popular romance fiction, Hollywood cinema and women's magazines, often with the ambition of showing how female audiences negotiate the media's hegemonic constructions of the 'reality' of gender difference. Quite often this research argues against the common assumption that femininity is inferior to masculinity in popular culture, and advocates a revaluing of so-called feminine media forms and a reassessment of female audiences.

Audience scholars have been quite innovative in borrowing from other disciplines a range of methodological tools, including letters from readers and fans, ethnography, questionnaires, personal and focus group interviews and participant observation. The brief sketches of some key studies in this field that follow below also show how this still-emerging body of research takes seriously the genres and audiences that had been ignored or marginalized by previous generations of research. These studies are broadly grouped, first, into those that were undertaken within the context of the household, where researchers were seeking to understand how everyday interactions among family members shaped the gendered dynamics of media consumption. Second, we examine those studies that were conducted in other settings, such as in workplaces, university classrooms and cafés, where comprehending how gendered household dynamics shaped audience reception was not central to the study.

Two relatively early examples of British media research that address media use in domestic contexts include important studies by Dorothy Hobson and David Morley. In Hobson's (1980) pioneering research on housewives' use of the media in their everyday lives, she interviewed young, working-class women with small children.[3] Hobson discovered that these young mothers tended to prefer those media genres related to a 'woman's world'. For example, soap operas, popular radio programmes and women's magazines were all viewed favourably for their focus on women's problems in relationships, with the family and in dealing with the gendered dynamics of social relations outside the home. Conversely, the women showed little interest in media that they understood as more closely related to concerns in a 'man's world' (the news, current affairs and scientific and documentary television programmes). They considered such texts to be 'both alien and hostile to the values of women', although they also viewed them as important and serious (Hobson 1980: 109). Hobson emphasized the importance of women's own distinction between media related to a 'woman's world' and a 'man's world'. While women's use of the media provides them with a connection to the 'outside' world, it also reinforces 'the privatised isolation by reaffirming the consensual position – there are thousands of other women in the same situation, a sort of "collective isolation"' (1980: 94–5). By discursively positioning women within the private sphere, she concluded, the media actively (re)produced a hierarchical sexual division of labour.

David Morley's research on household media consumption patterns involved detailed interviews with 20 families in southeast England and observations of their media use in their homes. He reported his findings in the book *Family Television* (1986) where he argues that the micro-politics of the household fundamentally shape how individual members make sense of media messages. Understanding how men and women relate to each other within the household and how sexual politics influences media consumption (in terms of genre preference, style and length of viewing, who has control of the remote, and so on) helps explain how the relations of gender inequality in both the private and public spheres are reproduced in everyday life. While gender identities are never permanently fixed and are open to contestation, there are nevertheless certain patterned ways in which family members are interpolated which are largely tacit and therefore difficult to resist. For instance, like Hobson, Morley found that many women were not interested in the national news, largely because they did not see how it might link in any meaningful way to their daily lives. However, a number of women indicated that they liked to watch local television news. They were interested in what these programmes could tell them about local crimes, for instance, which 'they feel they need to know about [...] both for their own sake and their children's sakes' (1986: 169). It seems clear that women's interest in this type of story forms part of what Hobson referred to as a 'woman's world'. That is, women regard local news outlets as relevant to their family roles and duties (the care and protection of family members, particularly children, being fundamental). Said one of Morley's respondents: 'Sometimes I like to watch the [national] news if it's something that's gone on – like where that little boy's gone and what happened to him. Otherwise, I don't, not unless it's local only when there's something that's happened local' (1986: 169).

Ann Gray's (1992) *Video Playtime* followed up on this line of argumentation through an examination not only of the gendered patterns of media preferences (soap opera, family drama) but also of media technology use.[4] Gray discovered that women displayed a particular affinity for the video recorder and the telephone. Videos, she concluded, enable women to record programmes to be played back when daily household labour is complete or at times when they can be shared with female friends. The telephone is also important because it allows women to keep in touch with other women in the household and to maintain familial relationships.[5] In terms of the women's media preferences, women use soap opera, for example, as a way of facilitating their female friendships and validating the importance of the genre in women's lives (men tend to dismiss soaps as trivial). The programmes women enjoy provide them with periods of escape from the mundane routines of everyday life and, however temporarily, normative definitions of femininity.

Moving to audience research conducted outside the household, we note that some of the most important studies have combined analysis of texts and political economy of media industries with feedback from fans or audience questionnaires. Janice Radway's (1984) *Reading the Romance*, for example, conducted focus group and long interviews with romance fiction fans in a US Midwestern town she called 'Smithton'.[6] Radway also provided her own interpretation of the typical plots of romance novels, and she studied the institutional processes by which those novels were written, published and distributed. Instead of relating to romance plots in the 'preferred' way (accepting the patriarchal definitions of love, marriage and women's subordinate position in marriage), what she found was that these women regarded the female heroines as independent, assertive and powerful. Additionally, they all seemed able to incorporate these traits into their own (positive) self-image as women. In other words, these fans managed to read 'against the grain' of the narrow definitions of femininity on offer in romance texts, using the novels as a way of claiming a space for personal leisure. Romance reading constituted their declaration of independence from family and domestic responsibilities. Family members understood that when a wife or mother was reading a romance, she was to be left alone (even if they then violated this tacit understanding). Despite the discursive spaces that the romance genre provides for women to challenge normative assumptions about a woman's 'natural' roles in life (wife and mother), however, these texts do not offer a critique of patriarchal hegemony. As Radway (1984: 217) reasons:

> Because it refurbishes the institution of marriage by suggesting how it might be viewed continuously as a courtship, because it represents real female needs within the story and then depicts their satisfaction by traditional heterosexual relations, the romance avoids questioning the institutionalised basis of patriarchal control over women even as it serves as a locus of protest against some of its emotional consequences.

In the end, romance fiction does nothing to undermine the structural (re)production of the patriarchal control in the public sphere of work and political decision making.

Television talk shows provide another example of a feminized media genre that has undergone feminist analysis in recent years. Jane Shattuc's (1997) investigation of US daytime talk shows begins in an interesting way by offering a short cultural history of 'sob sister journalism' of nineteenth-century tabloids, which she regards as a possible forerunner of today's television talk shows. She also undertakes an extensive analysis of the industrial production requirements for these shows, including the logic of choosing themes, steering guests and experts, and manipulating audience members at home and in the studio.[7] The narratives of daytime talk shows, like soap operas, are woman-centred and celebrate women's agency and assertiveness. Still, the goal is to manufacture an expert consumer, not a feminist critic of capitalism. Although, as with Radway, little was made in the book of her survey data, Shattuc also distributed questionnaires to healthcare and hospital workers and visitors at two Boston hospitals. Two focus groups discussions gave Shattuc more thoughtful (and more critical) notions of how viewers use the talk shows than did her survey data, exposing an understanding of the shows' manipulative sensationalism and even some anger at how the shows construct people as 'trash'.

Yet another example of such triangulated, rigorous research is Amy Erdman Farrell's tough-minded critique of *Ms.* as a magazine offering a popular version of liberal feminism, indeed the first and perhaps only commercial magazine in the USA to espouse feminism. Farrell interviewed magazine staffers, went through its archives and examined all issues, including the 'No Comment' section that was contributed by readers. But a key feature of *Yours in Sisterhood* (1998) is her analysis of all the letters published in *Ms.* from 1972 to 1989, as well as a significant portion of the unpublished letters. Farrell shows how *Ms.* readers wrote, or rewrote, the magazine for themselves, specifically working to 'right' the magazine, to return it to the promise they had seen in it as a feminist resource. Not surprisingly for a magazine that was explicitly intended to be reader-centred, its readers developed a relationship of reciprocity and identification with the magazine that was reinforced by a second and highly adversarial relationship of resistance and contestation. Ultimately, Farrell was pessimistic about the likelihood of success for hybrids of feminism and commercial popularity, but they do provide crucial – and necessary – sites of intervention.

Other research has been much more specifically grounded on gathering audience data. Ien Ang based *Watching Dallas* (1985) on letters written by 42 Dutch fans of the US night-time dramatic (or melodramatic) serial *Dallas*. She placed an advertisement in a Dutch women's magazine asking women to write to her to tell her why they like to watch the programme. The main premise of her study was that programmes like *Dallas* had 'feminist potential'. They could be analysed by feminists to highlight some of the pleasures generated by such programmes as well as other forms of popular culture produced for largely female audiences that media scholars often derided as trivial or that were condemned, especially by international media critics, as symbolizing US cultural imperialism. In Ang's view, *Dallas* and similar 'weepies' could no longer be simply condemned, given the pleasure they inspired in fans, for their psychological realism, albeit one based on a deeply tragic structure of feeling and focus on domestic horrors, similar to the daytime soap operas. The visual stylization of *Dallas* and its extreme degree of external 'unrealism' are acknowledged, but she argues that the pleasure in the fantasy of *Dallas* need not necessarily lead to political passivity or anti-feminism.

To examine more closely some of the ways in which the media construct feminine identity and how women respond to these constructions, Andrea Press conducted extensive open-ended interviews with 20 working-class and 21 middle-class women of different generations.[8] Reporting the results of her study in the book *Women Watching Television* (1991), Press showed how class and generational differences influence how women make sense of television programming. She refuted the then academically fashionable claim that audiences always resist mediated cultural hegemony as well as the claim that the media determine how audiences make sense of their messages. Instead, she insisted that gender, social class and generation are fundamental factors, among others, influencing audiences' perceptions. For example, she found that the working-class women tended to relate to television most closely in terms of their class identity rather than their gender. For middle-class women, the reverse turned out to be true. Examining generational differences, both the youngest and oldest women, however, largely identified with gender aspects of television programming rather than those related to social class. As Press (1991: 177) notes: 'Younger women [are] more critically suspicious of television's images picturing women's changing social positions, and older women more hopeful and accepting of the stories these images tell.'

Phillip Schlesinger et al.'s UK study provides an examination of women's responses to violent film and television content.[9] The book coming out of this research, *Women Viewing Violence* (1992), was based on focus group interviews and surveys with female audiences of varying cultural backgrounds, personal experiences of male violence and social class; they were asked to respond to media representations of violence against women. For some of the women in the study, media violence made them remember terrible incidents of violence in their lives. For others, it contributed to a general fear of being attacked. Still others, with no personal experience of violence, regarded the mediated violence as abstract and distant from their everyday lives. How women viewed the violence very much depended on their social background and any direct experiences of violence. In other words, the study provided clear evidence for the argument that audiences should never be seen as a homogeneous group. That said, while ethnicity, social class and experience of violence tended to differentiate women from one another, a strong similarity among women was a fear of male violence in general, and rape in particular. As active critics of media violence, the group of women in the study insisted that the media must portray violence realistically and with the aim of educating the public about women's everyday experiences of violence. What must be taken into consideration in all media portrayals of violence against women is how they might affect women who have been victims of violence or who fear such violence. As the authors conclude, '*the issue is not whether depictions of violence increase the likelihood of similar violence among potential perpetrators, but the feelings and reactions that it creates among those who are the actual or potential victims of violence'* (1992: 170, emphasis in the original, see also Carter and Weaver, 2003).

For more than four decades, an enormously popular television genre, particularly with female audiences, has been the soap opera. Mary Ellen Brown's focus group discussions with US soap opera fans published in *Soap Opera and Women's Talk* (1994) concludes that, despite a widespread view that this is an exploitative genre that simply reproduces hegemonic notions of femininity, female fans often use soap narratives as a way of resisting restrictive forms of feminine identity.[10] Similar to Radway's (1984) argument about romance novels, soaps create opportunities for their predominantly female audiences to construct social networks where their talk about the programmes can be seen as an instance of resistive pleasure against patriarchy. Resistance to patriarchy, Brown insists, need not only be theorized at the macro level – that is of social changes in women's gender roles. Instead, it may also be achieved through micro-level changes in people's consciousness about gender – through a 'constant awareness of contradiction and the struggle to secure a space for the voice of the female spectator who speaks as well as sees' (1994: 182).

Female spectators are at the centre of Jackie Stacey's investigation into feminine identification, published as *Star Gazing: Hollywood Cinema and Female Spectatorship* (1994). Stacey's study is based on an analysis of letters and questionnaires sent to her by women who were avid cinema spectators in the 1940s and 1950s.[11] One of its aims was to challenge what she perceived to be universalistic arguments of psychoanalytic theorizing around female spectatorship prevalent at the time – much of which assumed that women view film through a 'male gaze' (Mulvey 1975). This claim, Stacey argued, largely ignored the historical realities of women's experiences as film audiences. Centred for analysis in her study was the historical and contextual place and importance of female movie stars in female spectators' memories of war-time and post-war Britain. To understand the relationship between sexual difference, spectatorship and visual pleasure, Stacey argued for the need to provide historical accounts of the relationship between female spectators and stars. This meant abandoning the assumption that female audiences passively accept what they see at the cinema. This claim was borne out in her audience research, where she found that women were aware of the impossibility of attaining the feminine ideal image as presented in Hollywood cinema. Nevertheless, they all took real delight in looking back to the youthful pleasures they experienced in the cinema – of identification (with the star), commodity consumption, glamour and escape from the monotony of everyday life. What these women highlighted was their contradictory experiences of the restrictiveness as well as the fluidity of feminine subjectivities – thus challenging claims around women's almost complete subordination in patriarchal war-time and post-war Britain.

While most critical audience research from the late 1980s and 1990s assumed that audiences are active and critical daily consumers of media, Joke Hermes's study of women's magazine use, published in her book *Reading Women's Magazines* (1995), makes a very different point.[12] Based on interviews with women of various ethnic, social class, educational backgrounds and ages, Hermes concluded that women's magazines might not be terribly important in their lives after all. While most of the women to whom she spoke find these publications to be accessible and pleasurable, they also regard them as having little cultural value or meaning. This finding, Hermes insists, challenges the view that media texts are always deeply significant to audiences. The place and importance of these magazines in women's lives is that they are easily incorporated into the demands of everyday life. She concludes, 'Women's magazines as a text [sic] are not highly significant, but as an everyday medium they are a means of filling a small break and of relaxing that does not interrupt one's schedule, because they are easy to put down' (1995: 144). These publications are perhaps the easiest to pick up when time permits and put down when the demands of childcare leave 'little time or energy, and accordingly narrows down your choice of media to relax with, to learn from or to be diverted by' (1995: 152). The speculation, then, is that perhaps their importance to women has been overestimated in previous research into this genre.

Each of the studies sketched out here is used to highlight the need to examine the taken-for-granted assumptions about communication processes in order to make apparent the often subtle and uneven ways in which unequal gender relations structures are (re)produced when audiences make sense of media texts. This is where audience research comes into its own – in the way that it can render problematic taken-for-granted ideas and beliefs circulating in society about gender. Such investigations show us how constructed these preferences are (in the name of audience differentiation, niche marketing and so on). Audience research contributes to a 'denaturalization' of gender difference and demonstrates in whose interest it tends to operate. In other words, it shows us that gender is a social construction and that while the media play a role in (re)producing gender norms, audiences do not automatically accept what they are seeing as the 'truth' of gender identity. The research outlined here shows that the ways in which audiences make sense of messages about gender in the media varies, sometimes considerably, from largely accepting traditional definitions of femininity to outright rejection (and somewhere in between). At its best, it contributes to efforts to challenge common-sense assumptions about gender by providing a wealth of empirical evidence that sometimes turns these assumptions on their head. As such, audience research is able to make apparent the fact that gender identities are culturally constructed, and therefore open to challenge, rather than 'natural', unchangeable and inevitable.

Conclusion

In explaining the extent to which the media contribute to the perpetuation of hierarchical forms of gender difference, many scholars are increasingly attentive to the interlocking interests of two ideological systems: capitalism and patriarchy. Interests in maximizing profit, it is argued, combine with male dominance, thereby shaping quite fundamentally the production of mainstream media texts' norms, values and beliefs. The power of these systems, however, can be challenged and contested. Indeed, in many industrialized societies the rigidity of masculine and feminine identity has diminished in recent years. The view currently prevailing may be that women 'have it all' and men are experiencing a 'crisis in masculinity'. Indeed, many media producers are now more alive to feminist thought and in developing the feminist sensibilities of their audiences. Media forms often 'play' with sexist imagery, for example, in a 'knowing' or reflexive manner, implicitly acknowledging the media's past complicity in portraying women in narrow, demeaning and sometimes offensive ways.

On the flip side, it is worth examining not only what has changed but also what remains problematic and as yet uncontested. Gender, always socially constituted, continues to be ruled by conventions, albeit in dynamic processes and expectations that have changed over the years. As Whitehead and Barrett (2001: 23) point out with regard to masculine identity: 'No matter how definitions of masculinity change, they are always in contrast to some definition of femininity and always elevated over this. In this way . . . anti-femininity lies at the heart of masculinity.' Pointing to examples of 'hard men' such as US boxer Mike Tyson and Vinnie Jones, the former British soccer player turned film actor, they (2001: 7) add:

> Countless numbers of men still act dominant and 'hard', deny their emotions, resort to violence as a means of self-expression, and seek to validate their masculinity in the public world of work rather than the private world of family and relationships. Moreover, such performances not only often go uncriticised, they are in fact lauded by many, both women and other men.

That is, the concept of masculinity is no more a biological given or stan-dardized certainty than is femininity, and no less a problem. Masculine identities are becoming increasingly complex and fractured, and perhaps no less unhealthy, as the percentage of young men with eating disorders and body distortion problems seems to suggest. Many researchers connect boys' muscle dysmorphia (also called bigorexia) to the proliferation of media images of men with 'perfect' and highly muscular bodies (Pope et al. 1999; Beynon 2002). Trying to buck conventions about femininity or masculinity continues to be scary and even risky for both girls and boys.

Sexism has not yet been eliminated from the media, as several essays in this volume show. In particular, the continuing proliferation of porno-graphic representations in print, film and more recently on the Internet points to a continuing objectification and dehumanization of women. Sin-cere people may disagree about whether particular representations are pornographic, whether particular forms of pornography can be said to have 'pro-social' uses and, more generally, whether pornography can be defined neatly enough to be legally regulated. But people do not sincerely disagree that most pornography promotes a highly narrow and even false sexual script, suggesting that women are always sexually available and that even when women say 'no' they mean 'yes'.

Furthermore, although both woman-centred texts and female audience members have a new found status in the academy, scholars are right to highlight the power of commercial and consumer values that constrain and limit audience agency. In a climate of complacency around issues of gender inequality, we would argue that now, perhaps more than ever, feminist and critical gender research investigation is needed of the ways in which the media perpetuate narrow gender identities and sexual hierarchies. The authors' work included in this Reader contributes to a political agenda that seeks to deconstruct and subvert these conventions and expectations, challenging taken-for-granted assumptions about their inevitability and paving the way for genuinely democratic gender relations. We hope that our readers will find this Reader to be an intellectually exciting and indis-pensable resource for the important task of making sense of the gendered structures of media texts, production and audience reception.

Notes

1. For a discussion of the globalization of Barbie, see Hegde (2001).
2. We use the term '(re)production' rather than 'reproduction' to signal that while the media may represent femininity in certain narrow and restrictive ways, none

the less gender identity is constantly being redefined, renegotiated and struggled over in the processes of production and reception of media texts. While we acknowledge that gender binarisms continue to disadvantage women and girls, we also think that gender identity has always been (to varying degrees) more open, fluid and challengeable than some feminists have suggested.

3. Hobson (1980) undertook tape-recorded interviews and participant observation in the women's homes, asking them about a wide range of experiences in their everyday lives, including their use of the media.

4. There were 30 women of various ages and social classes interviewed in their homes. Gray began her study in 1984 when video technology was still in its infancy and thus little research had yet been undertaken. Interviews were organized around a set of loosely structured questions, with each interview lasting approximately 1½ hours.

5. Lana Rakow's (1992) ethnography of telephone use in a Midwestern rural community which found that women relied on the telephone in distinctive ways – ways that were often very different to men's telephone use.

6. Radway's (1984) audience research consisted of two four-hour focus group interviews in a US Midwestern town she called 'Smithton' with 16 female romance fiction fans and long individual interviews with five of the most articulate women out of this group. She also used obtained information about female romance fans from 'Dorothy Evans' who also provided her with names of romance readers she might interview. Radway also described the institutional production of these novels and analysed the typical plots.

7. Shattuc's (1997) fieldwork involved distributing questionnaires to healthcare workers and visitors to cafeterias at two Boston hospitals in March 1995. Her sample of 118 responses includes 79 women, 32 men. Sixty-four per cent of the women in the same were aged 21–40 years old and college educated; around 60 per cent of the same identified as 'white', 27 per cent as 'black', 5 per cent 'Hispanic', 2 per cent Native Americans and 1 per cent Asian. Nursing, social work, hospital administration and medical technology were the most frequently cited occupations.

8. Press's (1991) research was based on open-ended, long interviews with 20 working-class and 21 middle-class women of different generations (from 17 to 78) in the San Francisco Bay area in 1985–86. Additional interviews were undertaken during 1986–88 in Southern Florida and Lexington, Kentucky to strengthen her findings.

9. Schlesinger et al. (1992) included interviews with 91 women, 52 of whom had directly experienced violence. The women were organized into 14 viewing groups, based on experience of violence and national background, ethnicity and class and were shown *Crimewatch UK, Update*, one episode of the soap opera *EastEnders*, and the television drama *Closing Ranks* or the feature film *The Accused*. Group discussions lasted for seven hours. They were also asked to fill out a questionnaire containing their personal data and another questionnaire asking them about each of the programmes that they were viewing that day.

10. Brown's (1994) fieldwork consisted of focus group interviews with 30 US daytime television soap opera fans, 26 of whom were female and 4 male. Out of these, 11 were adults, 9 were young adults in their early twenties and 10 were teenagers. She broke this larger group into seven smaller ones. In all of the groups she included people who were related to one another or who were living in the same household for other reasons (college students) in order to be able to say something about kinship and friendship networks.

11. Stacey's (1994) audience study consists of 350 letters and 280 long questionnaires sent to her by British women who were keen cinema goers from the 1940s and 1950s in response to her advertisement in two weekly UK women's magazines.

12. Hermes (1995) interviewed 80 people who read a fairly wide variety of Dutch women's magazines (from weeklies to glossies), both men and women, of different ages, economic backgrounds, ethnicities in both Amsterdam, where Hermes lives, and in rural areas. Interviews largely took place where she found people reading these magazines, in railway stations, coffee shops and other public places. Interviews were semi-structured and were audio-taped for later transcription and analysis. In addition to this interview material, she also undertook textual analysis of selected women's magazines.

References

Allan, S. (1999) *News Culture*. Buckingham and Philadelphia: Open University Press.

Ang, I. (1985) *Watching Dallas: Soap Opera and the Melodramatic Imagination*. London and New York: Methuen.

Ballaster, R., Beetham, M., Frazer, E. and Hebron, S. (1991) *Women's Worlds: Ideology, Femininity and the Woman's Magazine*. London: Macmillan.

Basu, S. (2001) The blunt cutting-edge: the construction of sexuality in the Bengali 'feminist' magazine *Sananda, Feminist Media Studies*, 1(2): 179–96.

Beetham, M. (1996) *A Magazine of Her Own? Domesticity and Desire in the Woman's Magazine, 1800–1914*. London and New York: Routledge.

Beynon, J. (2002) *Masculinities and Culture*. Buckingham and Philadelphia: Open University Press.

Brown, M.E. (1994) *Soap Opera and Women's Talk*. Thousand Oaks and London: Sage.

Brunsdon, C. (2000) *The Feminist, the Housewife and the Soap Opera*. Oxford: Clarendon.

Carter, C. and Weaver, C. K. (2003) *Violence and the Media*. Buckingham and Philadelphia: Open University Press.

Christmas, Linda (1997) *Chaps of Both Sexes? Women Decision-makers in Newspapers: Do They Make a Difference?* London: BT Forum/Women in Journalism.

Craig, S. (ed.) (1992) *Men, Masculinity and the Media*. London and Thousand Oaks: Sage.

Currie, D. (1999) *Girl Talk: Adolescent Magazines and Their Readers*. Toronto, Buffalo and London: University of Toronto Press.

Farrell, A.E. (1998) *Yours in Sisterhood*. Chapel Hill: University of North Carolina Press.

Fiske, J. (1987) *Television Culture*. London: Methuen.

Gerbner, G. (1978) The dynamics of cultural resistance, in G. Tuchman, A.K. Daniels and J. Benét (eds) *Hearth and Home: Images of Women in the Mass Media*. New York: Oxford University Press.

Geraghty, C. (1990) *Women and Soap Opera*. Cambridge: Polity.

Gray, A. (1992) *Video Playtime: The Gendering of a Leisure Technology*. London and New York: Routledge.

Hall, S. (1980) Encoding/decoding, in Centre for Contemporary Cultural Studies, (ed.) *Culture, Media, Language: Working Papers in Cultural Studies, 1972–79*. London: Hutchinson.

Hegde, R. (2001) Global makeovers and manoeuvres: Barbie's presence in India, *Feminist Media Studies*, 1(1): 129–33.

Hermes, J. (1995) *Reading Women's Magazines*. Cambridge: Polity.

Hobson, D. (1980) Housewives and the mass media, in S. Hall et al. (eds) *Culture, Media, Language*. London: Hutchinson.

Jackson, P., Stevenson, N. and Brooks, K. (2001) *Making Sense of Men's Magazines*. Cambridge: Polity.

Lloyd, J. and Johnson, L. (2003) The three faces of Eve: the post-war housewife, melodrama and home, *Feminist Media Studies*, 3(3): 7–25.

Mattelart, M. (1986) *Women, Media, Crisis*. London: Comedia.

McCracken, E. (1993) *Decoding Women's Magazines: From* Mademoiselle *to* Ms. London: Macmillan.

McLuhan, M. (1964) *Understanding Media: The Extensions of Man*. New York: McGraw-Hill.

Mills, K. (1990) *A Place in the News: From the Women's Pages to the Front Page*. New York: Columbia University Press.

Mills, K. (1997) What difference do women journalists make?, in P. Norris (ed.) *Women, Media, and Politics*. New York and Oxford: Oxford University Press, 41–55.

Modleski, T. (1982) *Loving with a Vengeance: Mass-Produced Fantasies for Women*. New York: Methuen.

Morley, D. (1986) *Family Television: Cultural Power and Domestic Leisure*. London: Comedia.

Mulvey, L. (1975) Visual pleasure and narrative cinema, *Screen*, 16(3): 6–18.

Pope, H.G., Olivardia, R., Gruber, A. and Borowiecki, J. (1999) Evolving ideas of male body image as seen through action toys, *International Journal of Eating Disorders*, 26: 65–72.

Press, A. (1991) *Women Watching Television: Gender, Class and Generation in the*

American Television Experience. Philadelphia: University of Philadelphia Press.

Radway, J. (1984) *Reading the Romance: Women, Patriarchy and Popular Literature*. Chapel Hill and London: University of North Carolina Press.

Rakow, L.F. (1992) Gender on the Line: Women, the Telephone, and Community Life. Urbana, Ill: University of Illinois Press.

Rhodes, J. (2001) Journalism in the new millennium: what's a feminist to do?, *Feminist Media Studies*, 1(1): 49–53.

Schlesinger, P., Dobash, R.E., Dobash, R. and Weaver, C.K. (1992) *Women Viewing Violence*. London: BFI.

Sebba, A. (1994) *Battling For News: The Rise of the Woman Reporter*. London: Sceptre.

Shattuc, J. (1997) *The Talking Cure: TV Talk Shows and Women*. London and New York: Routledge.

Shirvani, S., Carter, C., Ross, K. and Byerly, C. (2002) Media associations project, International Communication Association annual conference, *Reconciliation through Communication*, Feminist Scholarship Division Panel, Seoul, Korea, 15–19 July.

Smith, J. (1997) *Different for Girls: How Culture Creates Women*. London: Chatto & Windus.

Stacey, J. (1994) *Star Gazing: Hollywood Cinema and Female Spectatorship*. London and New York: Routledge.

Steinem, G. (1990) Sex, lies and advertising, *Ms.*, July/August.

Steiner, L. (1992) Conceptions of gender in reporting textbooks, 1890–1990, *Journalism Monographs*, 135.

Steiner, L. (1998) Newsroom accounts of power at work, in C. Carter, G. Branston and S. Allan, (eds) *News, Gender and Power*. London and New York: Routledge.

Stott, M. (1973) *Forgetting's No Excuse*. London: Faber & Faber.

Tuchman, G. (1978) Introduction: the symbolic annihilation of women by the mass media, in G. Tuchman, A.K. Daniels and J. Benét (eds) *Hearth and Home: Images of Women in the Mass Media*. New York: Oxford University Press.

van Zoonen, L. (1998) One of the girls? The changing gender of journalism, in C. Carter, G. Branston and S. Allan (eds) *News, Gender and Power*. London: Routledge.

Vares, T. (2002) Framing 'killer women' films: audience use of genre, *Feminist Media Studies*, 2(2): 213–29.

Whitehead, S.M. and Barrett, F.J. (2001) *The Masculinities Reader*. Cambridge: Polity.

Further Reading

Douglas, S. (1994) *Where the Girls Are: Growing Up Female with the Mass Media*. New York: Random House.

Macdonald, M. (1995) *Representing Women: Myths of Femininity in the Popular Media*. London: Arnold.

Lont, C. (ed.) (1995) *Women and Media: Content/Careers/Criticism*. Belmont, CA: Wadsworth.

Meyers, M. (ed.) (1999) *Mediated Women*. Cresskill, NJ: Hampton Press.

Ross, K. (2002) *Women, Politics, Media: Uneasy Relations in Comparative Perspective*. Cresskill, NJ: Hampton Press.

TEXTS IN CONTEXT

Understanding the power of mediated images to shape social perceptions about gender has been a central focus of feminist media scholarship for over three decades. Early researchers (during the 1960s and 1970s) examined media content in order to provide quantitative proof that the media typically rely on a stock of stereotypical images of women. Women, they found, were recurrently portrayed as being pretty, passive, nurturing and concerned with the domestic. Moreover, they argued, these reinforced sexist attitudes and behaviours toward women inhibiting women's full participation in public life (Epstein 1978; Tuchman 1978).

A second tradition in feminist media scholarship, one that developed approximately two decades ago, shifted the conceptual emphasis from the surface 'message' of media content to the ideological role of media texts in reproducing male dominance (Coward 1985; Winship 1987). Analyses of media representations of women sought to expose how patriarchal ideology structured their messages and contributed to the (re)production of hierarchical gender relations. Today, feminist scholars assume that it is not enough to examine media texts in isolation. Media texts must always be analysed within the contexts of both their production as well as the wider cultural circulation of gender discourses in society.

The first reading in this section, Myra Macdonald's 'From Mrs Happyman to Kissing Chaps Goodbye: Advertising Reconstructs Femininity', illustrates this new approach to textual analysis. Her history of the ways in which discourses around consumerism have constructed feminine identities over the past century argues that the advertising industry provided multiple forms of feminine identity in order to reach new markets and increase corporate profits. If women could be convinced to identify with a range of feminine subjectivities, advertisers reasoned, they might be tempted to devote more of their household budget to the ever-expanding range of consumer goods. Meanwhile, despite the number of feminine identities with which women might identify, Macdonald suggests, the range has been stagnant for more than 100 years. In our postmodern era, she concludes, advertising that ironically critiques earlier forms of feminine identities may seem progressive, but in the end it undermines neither the traditional devaluation of the 'feminine' nor women's secondary social and economic status in society.

Patricia Holland's 'The Politics of the Smile: "Soft News" and the Sexualization of the Popular Press' traces the heavily sexualized content of many British tabloid newspapers to the late nineteenth century, when increasing competition among newspapers for mass readerships spurred many publications to broaden their appeal to include women. To attract this feminine audience, at the time newspaper publishers and editors believed that all they needed to do was increase their 'soft' news content (for example, human-interest news, family, fashion, beauty, relationships). Some refer to this early attempt to appeal to women readers as a 'feminization' of the news. In the process, newspapers opened up public spaces for women to discuss issues closely related to their lives as women. Almost 100 years later, in the 1970s, increasing competition for dwindling newspaper readerships again contributed to a shift in newspaper content, argues Holland – from feminization to sexualization. Tabloid newspapers like the *Sun*, for instance, changed from being a 'serious' broadsheet newspaper with mostly 'hard' news to a sexualized tabloid regularly featuring a semi-naked 'Page Three Girl' and advice about sex life. The emphasis on sexualization (the increasing inclusion of sexual stories or sexual angles) has spread from these particular features to shape most of the paper's news stories. Holland concludes that the use of women's bodies and sexuality in the *Sun* undermines the democratic potential of the British popular press. Sexualized gender difference works as a form of discipline on women's speech and activities, inhibiting their full participation in the public sphere.

Sexualization is also a central theme in Saraswati Sunindyo's chapter, 'Murder, Gender and the Media: Sexualizing Politics and Violence'. Analysing news coverage of separate incidents of murder or attempted murder of three Indonesian women in the 1980s by well-known men who had been their former lovers, Sunindyo shows that coverage sexualized the victims. In each case, the press distinguished between 'good' women and 'bad'. Good women uphold a bourgeois ideology of motherhood – a woman who places the desires of her family before her own. A 'bad' woman is one who has sexual desires to which she yields. Their male attackers, nevertheless, were exclusively portrayed as 'driven' to violence to protect their family's honour. While condemned for their violence, each of the men was portrayed sympathetically. Their infidelity was treated as understandable because 'a natural man ... needs more than one woman to have sex with'. These men were represented as being 'normal'. Their female victims, however, were depicted as 'abnormal' – not at all like 'good', 'normal' women, who are asexual. The overall message, concludes Sunindyo, is that the victims deserved their fate – they brought it upon themselves because of their 'unnatural' sexual desires.

Sexuality also provides the focus for Marguerite Moritz's essay, 'Old Strategies for New Texts: How American Television is Creating and Treating Lesbian Characters', which looks at how lesbian identities have recently been constructed in US television. Acknowledging that the media are increasingly offering a wider variety of fictional lesbian characters, Moritz nevertheless argues that in the end, the visual and narrative codes of television restore these female characters to their 'proper place'. While some individual lesbian characters achieve personal or professional success, 'that victory is balanced out by other messages, both in the text and in the visual content'. As Moritz concludes, this suggests that 'these characters have a long way to go before achieving equal status with their heterosexual counterparts'.

While early feminist researchers concluded that women are stereotypically portrayed as pretty, passive and domestic, Sherrie A. Inness's chapter, 'Pretty Tough: The Cult of Femininity in Women's Magazines', confirms that today, images of tough and determined-looking women are now fairly commonplace. She has found evidence for this claim in her analyses of women's magazines, comic books, cartoons, science fiction films and television programmes. Yet the potential strength of these images is almost always discursively undermined, says Inness, because assumptions about 'natural' biological differences between men and women remain largely unchallenged. Magazines create a fantasy of toughness where women 'perform' toughness as a style of femininity. Moreover, women's toughness is almost always connected to sexual appeal. This reassures readers that even a tough woman remains sexually objectified and available for men. Inness concludes that the articulation of toughness and sexuality 'diminishes the threat that tough women pose to the dominant social order by suggesting that a woman's sexual availability and physical attractiveness will be in no way diminished by her tough actions and appearance'.

References

Coward, R. (1985) *Female Desires: How They are Sought, Bought and Packaged.* New York: Grove Press.

Epstein, L.K. (ed.) (1978) *Women and the News.* New York: Hastings House.

Tuchman, G. (1978) Introduction: the symbolic annihilation of women by the mass media, in G. Tuchman, A.K. Daniels, and J. Benét (eds) *Hearth and Home: Images of Women in the Mass Media.* New York: Oxford University Press.

Winship, J. (1987) *Inside Women's Magazines.* London: Pandora.

Further Reading

Carter, C., Branston, G. and Allan, S. (eds) (1998) *News, Gender and Power.* London: Routledge.

Davis, S.W. (2000) *Living Up to the Ads: Gender Fictions of the 1920s.* Durham: Duke University Press. Philadelphia: University of Pennsylvania Press.

Helford, E.C. (ed.) (2000) *Fantasy Girls: Gender in the New Universe of Science Fiction and Fantasy Television.* Lanham: Rowman & Littlefield.

Kitch, C. (2001) *The Girl on the Magazine Cover: The Origins of Visual Stereotypes.* Chapel Hill: University of North Carolina Press.

Mayne, J. (2000) *Framed: Lesbians, Feminists and Media Culture.* Minneapolis: University of Minnesota Press.

Stevenson, N., Jackson, P. and Brooks, K. (2001) *Making Sense of Men's Magazines.* Cambridge: Polity.

FROM MRS HAPPYMAN TO KISSING CHAPS GOODBYE

ADVERTISING RECONSTRUCTS FEMININITY

3

Myra Macdonald

> Shopping is to a woman what getting drunk is to a man.
> (Columnist Dorothy Dix, in *Daily Mirror*, 19 December 1935)

> A new traditionalism, centered on family life, is in the offing ... Romance and courtship will be back in favor, so sales of cut flowers are sure to rise ... A return to home-making will mean a rise in supermarket sales.
> (Jib Fowles, in *New York Times*, 1988, quoted in Faludi, 1992, p. 36)

Women, since at least the late nineteenth century, have been particularly associated with consumerism. The 1980s film *Pretty Woman* is only one in a long list of cultural celebrations of the link between shopping and women's sexual desires. If food is reputedly the route to the male heart, shopping, preferably on an unlimited budget, is the imagined pathway to a woman's. The French language makes the point succinctly: '*consommation*' refers equally to consuming and sexual consummation. As evidence grew in the early decades of the twentieth century that the developing arts of retailing and advertising were attracting a predominantly female clientele, marketers and advertisers became significant definers of twentieth-century women's desires and aspirations. The media's interest in attracting women as readers or viewers was often motivated first by their perceived commercial value as consumers.

This chapter will explore the part that consumer discourses have played in endorsing and reproducing particular models of femininity in the course of this century. As early as the interwar period, long before post-structuralism had been heard of, advertising was constructing multiple possible identities for women in an effort to enhance their spending power.

Women who saw themselves as self-sacrificing mothers *and* as occasionally self-indulgent pleasure-seekers were going to be better consumers than those who related to one persona only. Where consumerism saw increased purchasing potential, feminism saw the creation of a multifaceted and artificial feminine mystique. Anxious to explore instead the common experiences that united women, and, more gradually, the real political differences that separated them, such as class, sexuality and ethnicity, second-wave feminism in the 1960s and 1970s had little in common with consumerism. Postfeminism, in the 1980s and 1990s, has been hailed as an accommodation, however uneasy, between these two old enemies. The last part of this chapter will consider how persuasive this theory is.

Women, the Media and Consumption in the Interwar Period

With the growth in department stores, such as Macy's in New York (established as early as 1860) and Selfridge's in London (established in 1909), middle-class women were enticed out of their domestic cloisters and into the public sphere. Outings by bourgeois women had long been legitimate in the interests of finding a marriage partner, as Jane Austen's exquisitely detailed and witty early nineteenth-century accounts of balls and promenades as methods of feminine self-display demonstrate. Venturing out of the home was also allowed in the course of that century for the dispensing of philanthropy to the poor or the sick. Going out to indulge in the pleasure of looking and buying, with woman the surveyor rather than the surveyed, marked a revolutionary innovation (Bowlby 1985).

Women's supremacy in the field of consumption quickly had its effect on the emerging mass media both in Britain and the USA. 1930s advertising trade journals in the United States regularly attributed between 80 and 85 per cent of all consumption to women, and as early as the 1920s identified women as a coherent target group. The class-differentiated 'Colonel's Lady and Judy O'Grady' were, advertisers were pithily known to remark, 'sisters under the skin' (Marchand 1985, pp. 65–6). The growing band of press advertisers eagerly exploited opportunities to coax women out of their feminine caution into a desire to spend. By 1926, the high-selling *Ladies' Home Journal* was already devoting over half its 270 pages to advertisements (Marchand 1985, p. 7).

In Britain, Alfred Harmsworth (later Lord Northcliffe) was the first to capitalize on the attraction of women to advertisers. In the 1890s, he launched two popular women's weekly magazines, one with a title, *Home Chat*, which neatly encapsulated current thinking about the feminine sphere and feminine discourse. In 1903 he took the more pioneering step of setting up the *Daily Mirror* as a newspaper 'for gentlewomen'. The aim was commercial success rather than support for feminism, even though Northcliffe's entrepreneurial zest persuaded him to appoint a majority of female journalists. The failure of this project reputedly enhanced Northcliffe's disillusionment with women's intelligence and abilities: 'Women can't write and don't want to read', he is alleged to have 'growled' (Williams 1969, p. 93). The immediate result was the sacking of the female staff, and the transformation of the *Daily Mirror* into a successful general-interest picture paper.

This experience did not deter Northcliffe from including a women's section in his newspapers. He had initiated this in the *Daily Mail* in 1896, and by 1909 was warning its editor, Marlowe, to ensure the continuing femininity of the magazine page, as competition for women readers intensified from the *Daily Express* (LeMahieu 1988, p. 33). Their function as bait for advertisers encouraged women's pages (particularly in the more popular papers) to experiment with layout and typography ahead of the rest of the paper. Northcliffe's alleged claim that 'women are the holders of the domestic purse-strings. . . . They are the real buyers. Men buy what women tell them to' (quoted in LeMahieu 1988, p. 34) was to find many echoes as the twentieth century progressed, in the film as well as the press industry.

Charles Eckert (1978), Jane Gaines and Charlotte Herzog (Gaines and Herzog 1990; Herzog and Gaines 1991), amongst others, have documented the interaction between the selling of movies and the selling of goods in 1930s America. Women, again, were the principal target. Hollywood films acted as showcases for the latest feminine fashions, which, by the 1930s, were being promoted and sold in tandem with the film's opening. Newspapers and magazines, on both sides of the Atlantic, helped to promote the fashion of the stars by running features on their dresses or costume designers, and by treating female stars as the first source of glamour pictures. In the mid-1930s, the *Daily Mirror*, reviewing the fortunes of women over the previous 30 years, identified film stars as the most powerful influence. 'Here we are', commented the writer Cecile Leslie, 'thanks to the Dietrichs, Harlows, Garbos and Colberts. . . . For it is the film stars who are in great degree responsible for us of 1935. They have shown us how to make the best of whatever type of face and figure we possess'. Stars were, in the words of the article's introduction, responsible for defining the rules of 'that amusing game – the game of being a Woman' (*Daily Mirror*, 17 December 1935).

Films also helped to promote cosmetics and beauty products. Lux soap was the most widely publicized product in the 1930s to use star appeal to sell itself to admiring fans. Daily newspapers in Britain, as well as film magazines, carried a series of advertisements extolling the benefits of the brand to named actresses, including Bette Davis and Myrna Loy. The unrelenting rigours of the cinematic close-up were cited as evidence of the soap's ability to prove its qualities of gentleness and deep-cleansing softness. Film idols set standards of appearance that influenced many women's choices as consumers. Jackie Stacey's (1991) fascinating discovery of the extent to which female fans of the 1940s and 1950s identified with the stars beyond the screen, constructing them as objects of desire and imitating their hairstyles and clothes, would almost certainly have been true of the interwar period also.

Financial incentives prompted radio, too, to dream up ways of targeting women listeners, especially in the United States, where commercial motivation flourished earlier than in the regulated British environment. Soap opera was the most obvious result, combining the selling of the sponsor's products (Procter & Gamble toiletries) with a narrative structure designed to keep women compulsively tuned in. By the 1930s the custom of equating women with domestic consumption and control of the family budget was so well established that it was etched into most forms of media, and was almost single-handedly responsible for the burgeoning of the women's magazine press. It encouraged the establishment in Britain of two increasingly successful weekly magazines (*Woman's Own* in 1932 and *Woman* in 1937), while in the United States *McCalls* changed its format in 1932 to improve the visibility of its advertisements (McCracken 1993, pp. 65–6). Contemporary statistics about gender and purchasing decisions, taken together with the plethora of diverse products now being manufactured for domestic use, made women the obvious group to become the first holder of the successful 'market niche' award, even if marketing terminology had not yet evolved the term.

That Amusing Game of Being a Woman

Advertising discourses of the interwar period evolved a personal style of appeal, or personal mode of address, to their assumed readers. Whereas in everyday life we adapt the ways we talk according to our knowledge of the people we are speaking to, being playful or ironic with some and formal and serious with others, media modes of address have to rely on assumptions about their intended audiences. For this reason, they have been described as addressing an implied, rather than an actual, reader and as playing a significant role in *constructing* subjectivities for the audience or readers (Brunt 1990).

During the interwar period, three constructions of feminine identity dominated in advertising discourse: the capable household manager; the guilt-ridden mother: and the self-indulgent 'flapper'. These were not self-contained categories of actual women, but manufactured versions of feminine responsibilities or aspirations that had particular resonance for women of the period. While the first two principally spoke to women in the domestic sphere, they also had wider ideological influence in sustaining the importance of the home against the new libertarianism of the 'jazz era'. The pleasure-seeking 'flapper' most obviously addressed a generation of young women exploring the new leisure opportunities of the period, but it also provided a dream of escape for the housebound married woman. The modes of address, as we will see, were sometimes directed at men rather than women, but the constructions of femininity remained constant.

The capable household manager

In the interwar period, a number of developments conspired to redefine women's domestic responsibilities as a science or a skilled craft. Women had to be enticed back to the home, whether from their brief taste of industrial life during World War I, or from their pre-marriage employment in the professions, many of which operated a marriage bar. The growth of suburbia broke up women's traditional social networks, and turned sparkling new homes into potential shrines, just as domestic servants became increasingly hard to find. If this was not enough to motivate a new ideological status for household management, domestic chores were potentially shrinking because of the increasing production of labour-saving devices, and the growing availability of ready-made clothing and pre-packaged foods. While working-class women still juggled jobs outside the home with domestic responsibilities, unaided by either servants or electrical gadgets, middle-class women were ready to take a novel pride in managing their homes with minimum outside help.

Training for this new 'career' mushroomed during the period, with the growth of domestic science courses and a steady stream of manuals offering advice and instruction. Some of these made explicit links between the time and motion studies being carried out in the industrial sphere and the desirability of introducing similar principles of efficiency into the domestic realm (Lewis 1984, p. 116). Women themselves, still largely accepting their prime responsibility for hearth and home, applied pressure for better access to the new technologies and improved training through campaigning organizations such as the Electrical Association for Women, founded by

Caroline Haslett in 1924 (Davidson 1982, pp. 40–3). Women in Britain were conscious that they were not gaining maximum advantage out of the rapid spread of the electrical supply in the 1930s. While in the United States, refrigerators and vacuum cleaners were already well established, in Britain only relatively small percentages of the population owned these by 1939 (although the possibility of hiring equipment increased their distribution to some extent). Cookers (electric and gas) and small appliances such as irons were more widely available.

Analogies between women's domestic skills and the qualities expected in industry and the professions began to appear in newspapers and women's magazines as early as the 1920s. Helena Normanton, described as a law student and a brilliant young feminist, wrote in the *Daily Express* (6 September 1920) of the discipline and discrimination involved in cookery: 'The same gifts that enable a woman to be a methodical and balanced teacher, writer, doctor, or nurse will make her into a good cook if she wishes them to do so. Economy, plan, method, judgment, and proportion are all called into play'. Her view was echoed by a 1925 article in the same newspaper (this time on the women's page) entitled 'What is Household Science?' The writer, Mary Evelyn, comments that 'the kitchen is the cook's laboratory or place where experiments are made' (*Daily Express*, 17 June 1925). Housework had never before been awarded such a high status.

Advertising discourses caught the mood, using flattery to hail women as experts well versed in the finer points of household management. Advertisements for Electrolux vacuum cleaners turned the housewife into a scientific educator, able to interpret diagrams explaining the advantages of the Electrolux filter and dust-collection system:

> To the ordinary eye clean and dirty air look much the same. But science has proved, as you can see from these diagrams, what a difference there is – and the Electrolux made the difference! By means of its chemically-treated pad through which all the air in the room is passed, the Electrolux removes the dangerous germs and bacteria and leaves the air germ-free and wholesome.
>
> (*Daily Express*, 27 March 1930)

Science was evoked repeatedly in advertisements for new cleaning agents. 'Do you use Persil the right way?', advertisements asked, as the product's chemical properties were outlined: 'it's the oxygen set free by Persil which does the work' (*Daily Mirror*, 9 June 1925). Advertising also acknowledged that women shared information and ideas as well as gossip. Household tips from female friends, relatives or named experts were regularly included in women's pages and frequently used in advertisements to endorse products. Of obvious commercial value, these also suggested a bank of feminine knowledge and information which was recognized and valued in no other public discourse of the time.

Science in the kitchen became symptomatic of modernity. Advertisements for cleaning agents particularly stressed the connection between the modern and the scientific. Women, freed from 'drudgery' (the advertisers' favourite 'boo' word for domestic chores) could enjoy the modern pastimes of the age. Repeatedly, advertisements for labour-saving machines such as vacuum-cleaners and thermostatically controlled cookers implied that the woman released periodically from the kitchen would make a more exciting companion. Men were cajoled into purchasing (or hiring) vacuum cleaners to save their wives (often described, with a nuanced reminder of sexual delights, as 'brides') from the toil of housework. An advertisement for Goblin cleaners asked pointedly, 'SIR! Is your wife cheerful when you get home tired?' (*Daily Mail*, 14 March 1930). If not, the solution was obvious. Hoover enticed husbands, too, by claiming that leisure was what a woman needed 'to keep herself daintily dressed and up-to-date' (*Daily Record*, 15 December 1930). New World Regulo-controlled gas cookers allowed an elegantly dressed woman to provide her own testimonial: 'I used to spend half my morning in the kitchen (looked and felt like it, too ...). Now ... I can just leave the whole dinner to cook itself ... whilst I trot out and do my shopping or see my friends, or enjoy myself in lots of ways I never had time to do before'. The advantages were palpable: 'John says it's made a New Woman of me!' (*Scottish Daily Express*, 4 March 1935).

Redesigning housework as scientific management did not quite succeed in making it glamorous, but it did make it compatible with the spirit of modernism. The contrasting subjectivities of the 'housewife' and the 'New Woman' could be blended into one. 'Mrs Happyman' embodied the combination. She was the modern advocate for Electrolux, responsible as we saw earlier for demonstrating its scientific advantages, but her priorities were unashamedly conventional: 'Look, everybody', she exclaimed with delight, 'Homes transformed and beautified – the servant problem solved – and every husband a Happy man, like mine. That's what this really wonderful machine will do for you' (*Daily Express*, 25 March 1930).

As Christina Hardyment ruefully points out, the 'businesslike gloss' that discourses of household management put 'on the mundane matter of housework' helped to distract women from dreams of participating more fully in the public sphere (1988, p. 187). Management skills in women, and familiarity with science and technology were to be encouraged as long as they remained confined within the home. Although the time released by labour-saving foods, ready-made clothes or domestic appliances was frequently depicted as enhancing women's leisure opportunities, it was rarely seen as enabling women to combine the roles of homemaker and worker outside the home. A 1930 advertisement for Vim was an exception. 'Our Mothers', its advocate explained, 'could not have managed both housekeeping and business', but now it was possible to combine both with ease – and with a cleaning lady employed for only 'a couple of hours' (*Daily Mail*, 6 March 1930).

Guilty mothers

While technology reconstituted housework for modernity, women's roles as mothers invited a more traditional approach. Women's capacity for guilt was ruthlessly exploited by advertisers in the interwar period. Even when the problem to be solved by the advertised product was women's exhaustion, women were invited to take the blame. An advertisement for Wincarnis tonic stressed that a relaxed and stress-free atmosphere in the home was the woman's responsibility. Based on worries that female 'fatigue and anaemia' were capable of wrecking marriages, the first-person text repeatedly underlined this thesis. One 'young Mayfair wife' admitted, 'Although I didn't realise it, I was to blame. Nine times out of ten the woman is' (*Daily Express*, 6 December 1935).

In both Britain and the USA, advertisers homed in on mothers' insecurities about the quality of their childcare. Ruth Schwartz Cowan cites a content analysis of advertisements in the *Ladies' Home Journal* between the wars which demonstrated that appeal to guilt was a favourite tactic (Cowan 1983, footnote, p. 187). The tricky economic situation, together with the growing attention to child psychology, provided a fertile breeding ground for maternal anxieties. The quality of nourishment mothers were providing for their children was one of the worries advertisers encouraged, especially in advertisements for the new breakfast cereals and food supplements. What Roland Marchand refers to in the States as the parables of the 'Unraised Hand' in the classroom and the 'Skinny Kid' (1985, pp. 296–9) were echoed in British advertising, as women were urged to identify with the mother whose son was not 'good enough for the team' until she fed him Grape-Nuts (*Daily Mail*, 17 June 1925) or the mother whose baby did not look as strong as others (advertisement for Scotts Brand Emulsion, *Daily Mirror*, 6 December 1935).

Fears about hygiene were a second and potent source of concern. At a time when penicillin had not been heard of, and diseases such as tuberculosis claimed many young lives, this anxiety was readily evoked. Since germs, as advertisers frequently emphasized, were invisible, the housewife could never be totally sure that she had exterminated them. In Britain throughout the 1920s and 1930s, Lifebuoy soap advertisements vividly described dust as the 'invisible enemy', and graphically enacted domestic scenes where children were at risk from lurking microbes, while Vim piously declared 'it's not original sin but original dirt we have to fight' (*Daily Mirror*, 19 March 1930). The Victorian moral crusade had moved unceremoniously from the temperance hall to the kitchen floor. When motherly angst wore thin, fear of scorn from neighbours or friends could be equally effective. Harpic advertisements in the 1930s featured a pair of disapproving eyes, with a caption guaranteed to strike terror into the reader: 'Are you SURE your lavatory never offends? Friends won't tell you about your lavatory' (*Scottish Daily Express*, 7 March 1935). Shock tactics in advertising discourse were softened, however, by reassurance. Experts and advisers were frequently quoted within the advertisement, encouraging trust. Doctors and nurses (real or fictitious) were favoured sources of confidential advice. With such support, women could embrace the caring burden with confidence and enthusiasm.

Flappers invade the public sphere

For the new generation of cosmetic and luxury products coming onto the market in the interwar period, a thoroughly modernist version of femininity needed to be constructed. The unmarried 'modern miss', designated in the 1920s as the 'flapper' woman, loved to enjoy and indulge herself, participating in sport, dancing or driving open-topped motor cars. Her spending power was earned by working in the public sphere, most probably as an office employee, or sales assistant. With bobbed hair, and clothes which gave an androgynous look to her svelte figure, her sophistication was symbolized by her elegantly displayed cigarette. As Billie Melman (1988) observes, the term 'flapper' shared the history of other words that acquired pejorative connotations when applied to women. Although outgoing and lively, the flapper was also irresponsible and flighty. She occupied the public domain of the street or the dancehall while her married sister kindled the domestic hearth. Although a creature of modernity, the flapper was often caricatured as replaying the traditional characteristics of femininity in new garb. Her display of feminine manipulation, narcissism and coquettishness was a frequent theme in Haselden's cartoon strips in the *Daily Mirror*, published prominently on the editorial page. Her association with leisure pursuits rather than serious activities helped to devalue her social and, especially, her political status.

This process was particularly visible in the public discourses surrounding the introduction of votes for all women over 21 in late 1920s Britain. Pejoratively referred to in the press as the 'Flapper Bill' or the 'Rule-by-Women Bill', this long overdue extension of the franchise raised spectres of incompatibility between femininity and citizenship rights. The age-group to be enfranchised (21 to 29, women over 30 having already been given the vote in 1918) provided the excuse for forgetting about women's capacities and selflessness in the domestic sphere and for highlighting instead their fickleness and self-indulgent silliness. The disdain in which the new voter was held was typified by a cartoon in the Scottish *Daily Record* (18 May 1929) during the election campaign. 'Here is the latest election story', it quipped: 'A canvasser calling on a woman elector asked if she was interested in the Liberal Party. "Yes, of course!" she replied. "Where are they having it?"' (18 May 1929).

For the advertisers of the expanding range of cosmetic and beauty products, or of artificial fabrics such as rayon, the flapper was the ideal icon. The selfless concerns of the wife and mother were replaced by a self-directed attention to image. Soap advertising exemplified both approaches, with a clear dividing line between those brands (such as Lifebuoy and Sunlight) destined to offer protection to others by fighting household germs, and those (such as Lux or Knight's Castile) guaranteed to stimulate personal fantasies. Cartoon strips were frequently deployed in 1930s advertisements as a popular means of indulging desires already fanned by romantic fiction and women's magazines. Germs may have been the obstacle to utopia confronting the mature woman, but the obstacles to romance were more intimidating to the young, competing (because of the wartime toll on available men) for a marriage partner. Bad breath, body hair and body odours were graphically depicted as major hazards to be defeated by the array of chemical remedies being produced in the new light-industry factories. Blemishes bestowed by nature could also be masked by seductive lingerie, silk stockings or careful attention to dress.

The flapper image of the 'new woman' as playful, self-indulgent, sexually aware, and adventurous also suited the advertisers of cigarettes, perfume, chocolates, motor-cars and other luxury goods. Although many of these targeted male purchasers, the association of the product with women helped to enhance its seductive aura. Advertising for Nippy chocolates in newspapers of the 1930s featured female open-topped car drivers and female motor-cyclists. This daring outdoor image contrasted with the version of femininity on offer from Rowntree's advertisements in the run-up to Christmas in 1935. Addressed to men, the text focused on box appeal: 'Choose among the hundreds of delightful designs, knowing that Rowntree's Chocolates are those which a girl loves best, and that long after they have vanished the box will be used for her little personal knick-knacks' (*Daily Record*, 21 December 1935).

Although the flapper image accorded ill with women's increasing claims for political recognition, her outgoing modernity allowed advertisers to align her independence of spirit with women's rights campaigns. As an advertisement in the States for toothpaste suggested in the early 1930s, deciding which brand to favour could become a surrogate political act (Marchand 1985, pp. 186–7). Following a lead caption 'When lovely women vote', the text concludes that their inevitable choice is Listerine toothpaste. The woman romantically represented in the illustration is, we are told, 'charming, educated, well-to-do' and *'prominent in the social and civic life of her city'* (my italics). That her main concern should be her choice of an appropriate brand of toothpaste is not meant to surprise us. When the American Tobacco Company consulted Edward Bernays (nephew of Sigmund Freud and pioneer of public relations) about the best method of encouraging women to smoke, he suggested equating cigarette smoking with women's rights. With the support of feminist Ruth Hale, he negotiated the inclusion of ten cigarette-smoking young women in the 1929 Easter Parade in New York 'as a protest against women's inequality' (Ewen 1976, pp. 160–1). Equality might be co-opted as a device to sell goods, but it gained little practical support from the period's emphasis on female consumerism. As Christine Frederick, a contemporary home economist and advertising adviser, observed in *Selling Mrs Consumer* (1929), 'Woman is ... powerful in buying because of her secondary position to men' (Ewen 1976, p. 170).

In the interwar years, the different subjectivities constructed for women in consumer discourses coexisted without friction. The technology-freed housewife could become the 'new woman' in her newly discovered leisure hours, while the youthful flapper might mature contentedly into the caring, guilt-ridden mother. Modernity added excitement to the domestic role, without fundamentally disturbing its status. The Gramscian theory of 'hegemony' offers some help in understanding this process. Gramsci argues that dominant ideologies do not impose themselves coercively on our consciousness: instead, they dovetail into ways of thinking that we are comfortable with, that make sense to us and may even seem to acknowledge important truths about our lives. Women's role in the domestic sphere was given a new lease of life in advertising discourses that turned unpaid labourers into technologically sophisticated craft-workers with special competencies and skills. By redrafting discourses of domestic labour, advertising both brought them into line with modernity and flattered women into taking pride in their traditional place within the home.

That hegemony, given a further boost by the advertising and women's magazine discourses of the consumer boom years of the 1950s, was sharply challenged by the second wave of feminism in the 1960s and 1970s. Led by Betty Friedan's *The Feminine Mystique* (first published in 1963), feminism charged consumerism with constructing identities for women that were deeply conservative. Initially adopting Friedan's manipulative model of the media, feminists set up consciousness-raising groups to extend women's awareness of the relationship between their own experiences and the social structures underpinning these. By this means, they also extended politics to include the subjective and the experiential. With the slogan 'the personal is political', a new agenda was set to include personal relationships, sexuality, and even fashion and personal style. Throughout the 1970s, feminist and consumerist ideologies and discourses were ranged implacably against each other, sparring from time to time, but occasionally also learning each other's tricks.

Independent but still feminine

During the 1970s, feminists began to wage guerrilla war on advertising's sexism. Stickers accusing advertisers of degrading women appeared on the London Underground and graffiti slogans were sprayed on street posters, humorously and effectively parodying consumerism's masculine discourse. A Fiat advertisement, sporting an elegant woman lying on the car roof and exclaiming 'it's so practical, darling', attracted the riposte, 'When I'm not lying on cars I'm a brain surgeon' (Posener 1986).

Feminist appeals for change were less successful when channelled through the official advertising monitoring bodies. The Advertising Standards Authority, responsible in Britain for all advertisements other than broadcast ones, was unimpressed by feminist complaints in the 1970s. Retaliating with its own research, published in 1982 as *Herself Appraised*, the ASA demonstrated that most women were content with current representations. Although accused of bad faith for focusing solely on advertisements printed in women's magazines, which were least likely to cause concern, this report fuelled suspicions that feminists were paranoid whingers, totally lacking, despite their witty graffiti campaigns, in a sense of humour. Feminists were criticized for ignoring 'the existing facts of life, i.e. that the majority of women still see themselves as housewives *and that a high proportion of products are aimed at women in their traditional role rather than in their business role*' (ASA spokesperson quoted in *The Guardian*, 26 June 1978, my italics). The second part of this defence confirms that the prime motivation keeping the domestic emphasis alive was commercial rather than purely ideological.

Advertising in the 1970s was not, however, entirely impervious to the debate about women's changing roles and aspirations. Despite its reluctance to accede to feminist demands, the Advertising Standards Authority did clamp down on the most blatant abuse of women's bodies as sales gimmicks for products such as motor cycles or industrial tools. More subtly, advertising itself began to take stock of the evidence that women wished to be regarded as individuals rather than as roles. The tone was set by the up-beat modes of address in the new generation of 'liberated' young women's magazines (such as *Honey* (1960), *19* (1968) and *Cosmopolitan*, making its British début in 1972). Advertisers who addressed young women as unique in their style and aspirations encouraged wider consumption of cosmetics and fashion. By blending harmoniously with the environment and discourse of the new magazines, advertising also benefited from the intimacy and trust that these publications established with their readers.

Recognition of women's individualism began to feature in 1970s advertisements, although it became more pronounced in the following decades. In the 1970s, Triumph advertised bras 'for the way you are', but the images were still of feminine women, 'woman-shaped and proud of it' (*Cosmopolitan*, November 1978) or 'the very picture of serenity' (*She*, November 1978). By the mid-1980s, the caption remained the same, but the images identified a wider range of subjectivities, from tender mother, to sun-seeking holiday-maker, to art-loving sophisticate. The *Daily Mail*, in its campaign to woo more women readers, also exploited a varied set of identities to illustrate its caption 'behind every successful woman there's a *Daily Mail*'. In an odd inversion of readership expectations, an advertisement for that paper in *Cosmopolitan* (November, 1978) depicts a mother being applauded by adoring children as she bears a three-tiered birthday cake to a table already groaning with labour-intensive goodies; while in the same month, the more domestically orientated *She* features a young woman, with two male companions, participating enthusiastically in a yachting expedition. Perfumes, too, caught the individualistic fever. Cachet featured snap-shot images of eight different women to accentuate its caption: 'A fragrance as individual as you are' (*She*, November 1978). Max Factor's Blasé also featured a range of individualistic women to bear witness to its slogan: 'It's not what you wear: it's the way you wear it'.

The other hint that feminism was in the air came from the advertising agencies' sudden cultivation of stylistic androgyny. This began with Revlon's fragrance, Charlie, launched first in the United States in February 1973 and soon established as an international brand leader. 'Charlie' was clad in trousers, always striding confidently along, but aware of her own sexual appeal. On film or in still pose, her gaze was directed knowingly towards the camera. She was to be seen, as the caption instructed us, as 'gorgeous, sexy, young'. Revlon was careful to retain Charlie's feminine credentials: 'Independent and not needing a man, but still feminine, not into women's lib' (cited in Myers 1986, p. 77). Although Charlie wafted a breath of fresh air across Revlon's other creation of the period, the 'sensual, but not too far from innocence' woman of Jontue's cloyingly romantic campaign, her femininity was never in doubt. Other feminine women in masculine attire followed, most notably in Chanel No. 19's Gentleman's Club campaign, where the sophisticated young woman takes the male club by storm, literally letting her hair down as she capsizes into the traditional leather armchair to read her *Financial Times*.

This use of male dress was novel in advertising, but, in common with its appearance in the cinema, it worked to increase the sexual appeal of the woman rather than the reverse. It had little to do with a feminism that was already wary of trick suggestions that women's equality meant becoming more like a man. Feminism may ultimately have been more influential in the 1970s in encouraging advertisers to expand the product areas that were thought appropriate to female consumption. New arrivals included cars; drinks previously thought of as male; and banks, building societies and insurance companies.

With the eye-catching caption 'Sex has never been a problem for us', an advertisement for the British Leyland Mini in the mid-1970s makes heavy weather of the attributes of the car (such as stylishness, or the luxury that 'pampers the gentle sex') that cannot be talked about in an era conscious of 'sex discrimination' (*Observer Magazine*, 13 June 1976). Car advertisements in women's magazines often appealed to women as mothers, trying to pack the family shopping and baby gear into inadequately sized boots. A Citroën Estate advertisement used the image of a toddler with the caption 'she takes up more room than two adults' to catch the reader's eye (*She*, November 1978). Guinness was marketed for women who had already 'pinched' men's pullovers, aftershave and trousers (*She*, February 1974), or for women who could even 'look stunning dressed in a boiler suit' (*Nova*, September 1975). Money management advertisements used more traditional appeals either to women's concern about their families' well-being or to their romantic desires.

At the same time, many advertisements of the 1970s ignored feminism entirely, reproducing the caring images of good wives and mothers, or the sexually titillating images of women that were familiar from other media discourses of the decade such as the 'page three girls' in the Rupert Murdoch *Sun*. Although advertising had not yet caught up with the notion of the 'superwoman' identified in Shirley Conran's book of that title in 1975, it had begun to extend the repertoire of feminine subjectivities likely to encourage consumption. Advertising remained uncertain about the direction that women themselves wished to follow. Confident that feminism was not the favoured route, they toyed with a variety of contrasting identities.

Advertisers generally lagged behind women's magazines in the cultivation of new modes of address, even when the evidence suggested that commercial advantages could be gained from modernizing their approach. Shortly before the publication of the ASA's report in 1982, the Equal Opportunities Commission in Britain published its own research into women's thoughts on contemporary advertising (Hamilton et al. 1982). This research, humorously entitled *Adman and Eve*, compared women's reactions to four 'traditional' and four 'modern' advertisements for the same products. Its aim was to measure their relative persuasiveness in encouraging women to make a purchase. Including among the four test cases the *Daily Mail* 'birthday mother' advertisement, it found, not surprisingly, that women preferred the more up-to-date approach.

Advertisers were not persuaded. One of the campaigns tested as an example of the modern 'category' was the early 1980s television advertisement for Camay soap, in which a young, elegant and affluent woman steps from her Porsche into her executive flat, and ignores a ringing telephone to lavish attention on herself in the bath. This advertisement, written by an all-woman team, allows the answering machine to deal with her male friend's telephone call in the intermission between the two-part slogan, spoken by a male voice-over: 'rich creamy Camay ... for women who choose to please themselves'. Despite the finding of the EOC study that this was much preferred to an earlier, non-narrative, campaign, the advertising agency had by 1983 reintroduced a man to this advertisement, in response to their own market research findings that most women wanted its romantic connotations to be more explicitly articulated (cited in BBC2 programme, *Washes Whiter*, 22 April 1990). Pleasing oneself, if one was a woman, was still not acceptable within advertising discourse, especially if this involved rejecting a man.

Postfeminist Utopias

By the later 1980s and 1990s, consumer discourses were taking a new approach to feminism. Believing both that feminism's battles had been won, and that its ideology was now harmless by virtue of being out of date, advertisers invented 'postfeminism' as a utopia where women could do whatever they pleased, provided they had sufficient will and enthusiasm. The feminist's overburdened woman juggling the demands of career and childcare with the pleasures on offer in the gym or bedroom was magically transformed into the executive superwoman, always on the move and always in complete control. Jet-setting, caring for children, revelling in an exciting social life were all easily compatible. Yet another in the procession of twentieth-century 'New Women' had been born.

Pleasing oneself, freedom and self-sufficiency all moved up the copy-writing hierarchy. 'Making the most of oneself' became as mandatory a consumerist goal as looking after others. Those with goods and services to sell to women caught up with the message of freedom and self-fulfilment advocated by feminism and rejoiced, before the political implications of its demands could ricochet off the walls. Consumer discourses in both advertising and the women's monthly magazine press now eagerly absorbed the terminology of self-assertiveness and achievement, 'transforming feminism's challenging collective programme into atomized acts of individual consumption. For the new superwoman to combine career and home, cultivate independence while maintaining family relationships, remain sexually alluring but also convincingly businesslike, a panoply of material aids and services was required. From microwave ovens to massage oils, from linen suits to silk lingerie, from aerobics to assertiveness-training classes, her iconography depended on spending money. This new version of consumerism, claiming feminist credentials, undoubtedly strengthened many women's perception that feminism was an essentially middle-class movement. Advertisers' slogans which picked up surface aspects of feminist discourse muddied the waters of feminist campaigning.

Borrowing from an alternative discourse to add zest to your creativity is a regular trick in advertising and other forms of popular culture. Known in cultural studies as a process of 'recuperation' (Brunsdon 1986, pp. 119–20), 'co-option' or 'incorporation', this manoeuvre pretends to respond to the competing ideology but ignores its ideological challenge. Environmental and ecological concerns have been subject to similar treatment. Happy to incorporate 'green' issues when they aid consumption (whether of unleaded petrol or of eco-friendly toilet cleaners), advertising agencies understandably baulk at the more radical suggestion that we should all reduce our consumption or abandon our cars in order to protect the future of the planet. Ignoring counter-discourses such as those of feminism or ecology has never made good commercial sense, especially in media aimed primarily at young people: fully accepting and integrating their implications is, however, equally unsound financially. The compromise is to adopt the surface terminology, without taking on board the ideology that underpins it. As Charlotte Brunsdon claims, the effects of 'recuperation' are misleading: 'Not only do the oppositional ideas and practices lose their bite, but they can function to make it appear as if change has been effected' (1986, p. 120).

The concept of 'recuperation' is not universally accepted. Foucault rejected it as giving too concrete and definitive a form to the continuing process of struggle between discourses (Foucault 1980, pp. 56–7). His view is coloured by a misperception of the finality of the recuperative process. Recuperation is not a single action, but an ongoing process, subject to constant review. What Foucault does rightly suggest, however, is that recuperation may be viewed more ambiguously than Brunsdon implies. Co-opting even selective elements of feminist discourses might also be regarded as a gesture in their direction. 'Making the most of yourself' does begin to transform the passivity of narcissistic self-contemplation into the dream of active and dynamic self-fulfilment even as it reins that dream back into the feminine activity of 'going shopping'.

Although my own preference is for Brunsdon's position, I also accept that for many women feminism is now thought of as a historical rather than a current ideology, and their primary contact with its objectives may often be through the discourses of consumerism. If this is a distorted refraction, it may nevertheless be significant in stimulating debate about gender roles and expectations. Against this background, the remainder of this chapter will consider three forms of co-option of feminist ideas and ideology that emerged in consumer discourses in the 1980s and 1990s. These are as follows:

- the appropriation of quasi-feminist concepts;
- the redrafting of 'caring' to make it compatible with self-fulfilment; and
- the acknowledgement of female fantasies.

Freedom to kiss the chaps goodbye

Advertisers in the later 1980s and 1990s happily made use of concepts that had acquired new status thanks to the feminist and other civil liberties movements. 'Freedom', 'independence' and 'pleasure', all problematic terms within political and cultural theory, were reduced to matters of lifestyle and consumption. Women could now 'do their own thing', without worrying about male reactions, even though men often continued to hover anxiously in the background. The fast cutting of television advertisements was especially suited to capturing the panache of the latest 'new woman' in action. Supersoft hairspray proved its ability to protect and hold the hair against the elements as its owner jetted between Heathrow and same-day appointments in Berlin and Rome. Sunsilk styling mousse allowed women to 'take control' and put an end to 'wrestling' with their hair. Self-confident women dominated the action in both these commercials, but the voice-over was still distinctively male. Women were occasionally, however, granted the last word, as in the Volkswagen Golf 1980s advertisement where a jilted woman discards the jewellery and fur coat given to her by her lover, but keeps the car keys as her passport to independence.

In magazine advertising, connotations of feminist influence were more subdued, but being 'comfortable with who you are' (a caption on Hush Puppies shoe advertisements in 1994) was a common implicit injunction. The accompanying aspirational images made it clear that this was a command to fulfil your potential, not rest on your laurels. Men became commodities who could help or hinder progress, but they were not yet superfluous to requirements. A Boots 17 advertisement aimed at young women in 1992 teased its readers by running two images in sequence: one, a facial close-up of a beautiful young model with her lips pursed in a kiss, and the caption 'how to kiss chaps'; the second, an extreme close-up of her nose and mouth, with lipstick being applied nonchalantly to the lips, and the caption now reading, simply, 'goodbye'. Before the reader had time to wonder at a campaign advocating celibacy or lesbianism, the word-play on 'chapped' lips was revealed.

This advertisement offers alternative subjectivities to the reader. The immediate address is to the conventional heterosexual desires of young women, anxious to learn how to please their men. But over the page, we are projected momentarily into a contrary universe of independence, self-reliance and self-sufficiency. Before a blow can be struck for feminism, however, the joke takes over. The playfulness of this and other advertisements of the 1980s and 1990s encourages us to laugh at traditional versions of femininity, but stops well short of openly challenging them. Triumph adopted a similar strategy in the 1990s. Its 1993 campaign featured an ecstatically cheerful model, sporting an independently-minded new hairstyle, new look and new bra. Although the small print tells us that the black lace product is called 'Amourette', the main caption declares men to be part of the trappings of lifestyle that can be readily exchanged when desired: 'New hair, new look, new bra. And if he doesn't like it, new boyfriend'. This is more jocular and tongue-in-cheek than Triumph's earlier campaigns, but, while it departs from the commonly romantic or sexually servile discourse of lingerie advertising, the independence of spirit that is captured here still implies that *a* boyfriend is a necessary part of the image.

In the postfeminist era, traditional female preoccupations such as men or body-care were not abandoned, but women were now urged to travel light and indulge themselves, not others. This perspective also dominated in the health and fitness discourses of the period. While women of earlier decades were invited to spend hours in front of the mirror, the new instruction was, in the words of the Vidal Sassoon advertisements, to 'Wash and Go'. The encouragement to be oneself did, however, have limits. In contrast to feminism's dawning recognition of the importance of cultural difference, consumerism offered choices that were supposedly universal. Most of the models in British advertising remained white and young: in the United States, because of the greater commercial power of the non-white ethnic communities, there was somewhat greater diversity. Yet even in that country, the balance in the general women's magazine press was unevenly struck, and tensions often erupted between the white-look aspirations of beauty features and African-Americans' desire to celebrate their own appearance. In Britain, where black models were used, they tended to appear in advertisements for clothes, not beauty products. As in the shopping mall that promises to each and everyone that it will satisfy a variety of tastes, but is the most uniform transnational space that most of us will ever encounter, conformity is exciting only when it masquerades as difference.

Caring for me, too

In the interwar years, caring was still associated with guilt and self-sacrifice. Even though labour-saving advances in the kitchen released spare time for women, their new leisure activities remained firmly off-stage. In the 1950s, in the wake of World War II, official rhetoric encouraged women to desert the public sphere and devote their energies once more to being ideal wives and mothers. Advertisers and women's magazines, supported by more sophisticated market research and an economic boom that stimulated spending on the home, readily colluded with this campaign, even though its ideological hegemony bore little relation to the realities of life for many women, financially driven to part-time, low-paid work.

Feminist thinking questioned women's 'natural' talent for caring, and reconstructed it as a social imposition placed on women for men's con-venience. Feminists encouraged women to get out of the home to develop their full potential. While feminism's criticism was targeted at the structural and social roots of the problem, an unintended and paradoxical by-product was to lower yet further the status of the domestic sphere. Initially derided by feminism, the area of fashion has been recently integrated within a feminist perspective ... No similar reconstruction has been carried out on women's domestic role, cast too all-inclusively as the infection that stops the wound of male oppression from healing. In contrast to fashion, domesticity's subversive power appears restricted. Cake moulds mocking the phallus or celebrating the lesbian symbol do not form part of the average ironmonger's stock. If domestic activity is characterized solely as cleaning the toilet, doing the washing up, as endless cooking for unappreciative families or changing nappies on unresponsive babies, pleasure is easily omitted from the reckoning. But more creative aspects of domestic life do exist, and are seen by some women who have chosen to stay at home, or who find domestic chores a relaxing alternative to work outside the home, as rewarding and pleasurable. Baking, decorating and interior design, entertaining or gardening are amongst these.

French novelist and essayist Annie Leclerc was attacked by fellow feminists for arguing in the 1970s that the denial of the pleasures of domestic activity owed much to the power of a male-led language to devalue women's interests (1987, pp. 76–7). A similar point was made by British journalist Mary Stott, commenting on television quiz shows' readiness to include questions on male hobbies (such as sports or woodwork), but not on women-related domestic crafts such as embroidery or baking (*The Guardian*, 9 January 1992). The former, she claimed, were regarded as 'general knowledge'; the latter as too specific and esoteric. Christine Delphy, on the other hand, accuses Leclerc of ignoring the role of housework in sustaining women's oppression (1987, pp. 80–109). While this is an important argument, it is not incompatible with recognizing the possibility of pleasure in domestic activity when that is consciously chosen by women rather than structurally enforced. In recent years, women's creativity in crafts such as tapestry and weaving has been reclaimed by feminists (e.g. Parker 1984) anxious to ensure these achieve the same recognition and status as traditional male handiwork, but female creativity in domestic management continues to be seen as tainted by the pejorative connotations of the private sphere itself. In this sense, feminism and dominant ideology appear curiously united.

Partly because of this problem, feminism gained limited support from those women who identified positively with the domestic sphere. Mistaking its attack on structural inequalities for an assault on their interests and preoccupations, they felt doubly devalued: both by dominant ideology and by a movement purporting to support them. Advertising, still anxious to sell domestic products primarily to women, was able to exploit these feelings and offer its own compensations. The reinstatement of the home was achieved in part by filling it with rounded human beings, more emotionally complete than the stultified if glamorous models who, in the words of the L'Oréal Plénitude advertisements 'moved with the times'. In the United States in particular, this movement within consumer culture quickly infected other areas of popular culture. Dubbed 'new traditionalism', it has been seen as part of the backlash against women's advances (Faludi 1992).

In Britain, the Oxo family was recreated in the mid-1980s after market research suggested that the terms most women associated with the family were not 'love', 'peace' or 'harmony' but 'squabbling', 'isolation', 'fatigue' and 'drudgery'. Katie, whose tasty casseroles had been simmering on and off the boil since the 1950s, now held together a family prone to bickering and selfishness, who treated their home as a hotel and their mother as a piece of the furniture. Often harassed and constantly undervalued, Katie, granted a vaguely defined life of her own outside the home, constantly retains the sparkle in her eye, at least to share complicity with the viewer at home. Her pride in her lively but unregenerate family is at once deeply conservative, but potentially vindicated by audience memories of cardboard cut-out children from earlier commercials. In the manner of soap opera characters, the Oxo family has evolved, but left the ideology of the family intact.

The soap opera techniques of the Oxo narratives have also been adopted in other caring advertisements of the 1980s and 1990s. Allowed secret access to the mother's point of view, women viewers can identify with her frustrations as well as her triumphs. A Hotpoint advertisement for state-of-the-art domestic appliances presents a mother busy in the kitchen while her self-absorbed family leave one by one to pursue their own interests. Only then do we realize that she, too, is planning her escape to play tennis with her girlfriend while the preprogrammed machines get to work. This scarcely amounts to liberation, but it does allow a minute crack to appear in the self-sufficient pleasures of caring.

Mothers were beginning to ask to be noticed, even if the sound-level had barely risen above a whisper. Changes in Flora margarine advertising typify the trend. Its advertising campaign in the early 1980s became famous for persuading the public that polyunsaturated fats were much healthier than butter. It achieved this with graphic images of male torsos, and captions addressed to women, such as 'Is it time to change your husband?', or 'How soon will all your men be Flora men?' By 1986, however, Flora advertisements featured sensible-looking 'thirty-something' women photographed against a backdrop of fresh flowers. The verbal text now took a different tack: 'Of course, I like the light, delicate taste of Flora. My whole family does. But I have a much better reason for eating it. That reason is me.'

The 'reason that was me' was concurrently being shouted from the rooftops in cosmetics and body-product advertising. Within the domestic sphere, traditionalism seemed hardly to have been challenged sufficiently to be dubbed already as 'new'. If there was a noticeable change in 1980s consumer signifiers of caring, it came through the depiction of caring men, rather than through a redrafting of women's role. Young 'new men' were shown wheeling baby buggies and shopping trolleys, or popping Lean Cuisine menus for two into the microwave. . . . [I]t is worth noting . . . that when men became carers in advertisements, caring was suggested either to be beyond them, or to be so simple that anyone could do it. Even though the appearance of men in the kitchen was to be welcomed, it perversely rein-forced the belief that women complained unduly about their lot.

From secret gardens to women on top

When feminism declared that the personal was political, it triggered a new interest in women's desires. If psychoanalysis was the main tool in the cultural theorist's enquiry, a more populist approach was taken by Nancy Friday. Starting with *My Secret Garden* in 1973, she documented the hitherto unspoken evidence of female sexual fantasies, relying to a large extent on women's own accounts. Her first volume, as its title implies, found guilt a major obstacle to free expression, turning the dominant voice into that of the confessional. By her 1991 volume, indicatively titled *Women on Top*, confession and guilt have given way to celebration of women's right to sexual pleasure. Friday takes an uncomplicated and positive view of this, perceiving fantasy as a self-contained gold-mine waiting to be quarried.

Fantasies, and particularly women's fantasies, become more complex if we ask where they come from and who has shaped them. If the formation of our fantasies is linked, as the formation of our conscious thoughts is, to the culture in which we operate, then the ownership and origins of 'women's' fantasies become problematic. As Lisa Tickner points out, it is a mistake to argue that women's sexual feelings and desires were merely repressed by a dominant male culture, when their very articulation was conducted his-torically in male terms. After centuries of male definition, women have difficulty, for example, in reclaiming the discourse through which they have been encouraged to think about their own sexuality (Tickner 1987, pp. 237–8). This is also acknowledged, in stridently evangelical terms, in the attempts of Mary Daly (in, for example, *Gyn/Ecology*, 1978) to exor-cize the demonology of patriarchy and restore positive energies to the hags, crones, harpies, furies and amazons who have become embodiments of men's fears about women. While Nancy Friday believes in the value of unlocking fantasies repressed within the female psyche (even when these include the notorious accounts of 'rape fantasy'), Mary Daly argues that in order to reclaim metaphors and symbols for women's own self-expression we must first appropriate them.

Women's fantasies have historically been represented in advertising discourses as private, mysterious and incommunicable. Disembodied, and unknowable, these fantasies intensify connotations of the feminine woman as enigmatic and narcissistic, inhabiting a private universe that makes her a convenient repository for male rather than female imaginings. ... In recent years, women's fantasies played out in advertising mini-narratives, and indeed in the longer narratives of films such as *Thelma and Louise*, have incorporated more active revenge themes. Nancy Friday remarks on this shift in *Women on Top*, noting that the fantasies that women had in the 1970s of being seduced by strong powerful men (the controversial 'rape' fantasy) had given way increasingly to fantasies of female retaliation, including the scenario of the woman forcing the man to have sex with her. The degree to which these can be seen as a response to feminist discourses is less certain. The ambiguity of the revenge fantasy is indicated in two recent advertisements on British television. One (an advertisement for shoes) depicts a woman metaphorically castrating her boss: the other (for a bra) creates a micro-narrative around female vengeance classically produced by jealousy over a man.

The advertisement for K Shoes casts the avenger in smart office suit severing the balls on her boss's executive toy. This is a woman who hands in her notice with panache, style and a sardonic sense of humour. As she makes her final exit from the office, her triumph is momentarily undercut as a close-up focuses on her heel trapped in a grid in the floor. Unlike the film noir, where such an event would signal the beginning of the end for the woman, this dilemma marks the start of a further victory. Nonchalantly lifting the grid, detaching it from her shoe, and handing the offending item to her boss's secretary, she inspires revolt in her, too. In a striking blow for solidarity, the secretary grimaces in the direction of her boss, turns on her K Shoe heels, and marches out in dignified step with her new-found sister. If this narrative has a feminist moral, its humorous touches modify its threat to the masculine viewer. The excessively mimed reactions of the boss and his male partner, squirming when metaphorically under attack, smirking when appearing to triumph, act like the clown's extravagant gestures to deflect male pain and humiliation.

The Gossard Ultrabra fantasy rejects any feminist trappings. Here the heroine, distinguished by her striking cleavage, seeks her revenge on the woman who is trying to steal the affections of her boyfriend at a select party. Humiliation strikes the interloper when she is 'rescued' from an incipient sneeze by the Ultrabra woman reaching into her rival's bosom and extracting yards of tissue that have been used for artificial padding. Throughout, the complicity between the heroine and her boyfriend is maintained through his refusal to have his gaze distracted from her Ultra-bra-adorned cleavage. The fantasy is one of jealous bitchiness rather than feminist-inspired self-assertiveness.

In the postfeminist era, romantic fantasies are enacted, as here, with a new playfulness or with a new style and sophistication. Chanel No. 5 television advertisements resorted to hyperreal settings and enigmatic narrative structures in the late 1980s in a bold attempt to span the chasm between romance and postmodernism. Fantasies of doing without men entirely are rarer in consumer discourses, but exceptions are beginning to appear, particularly in car advertisements. Even in the interwar period, the car could symbolize escape for women. In the wake of *Thelma and Louise*'s box-office success, Peugeot's agency devised a campaign for its 106 model featuring two British women discarding the trappings of their consumer lifestyles and the security of their past for a carefree life on the open road in the American West.

In Conclusion

Postfeminism takes the sting out of feminism. The subjectivities of femininity, presented seriously earlier in the century, are reincarnated towards its end with a twist of humour and a dash of self-conscious parody. The outwardly caring woman willingly shares the lapses in her devotion, with a wink in the direction of the audience. The superwoman is so sophisticated that she looks poised to leave the planet and return as a *Blade Runner* replicant. Fantasies of taking our revenge against men, and getting away with it, are the most daring dreams on offer, but allying this with the selling of feminine heels undercuts the euphoria.

What this chapter suggests is that within advertising discourses, the range of what it means to be feminine has been surprisingly stagnant throughout the century, despite the profound cultural and social changes, and despite the commercial advantages to be gained from brand-differentiating the consumer as much as the product. What most clearly distinguishes the advertising discourses of the postmodern era from their modernist predecessors is the jokiness of their approach and their willingness to cast women as heroines of their mini-narratives. It is difficult to describe either of these as a postmodernist development. Woman's long history of acting as a depthless sign, responsive to masculine whim, makes her peculiarly resistant to sharp transformation from modernist meaningfulness to post-modern emptiness. The fantasies in which she appears may have become more exciting, less mundane, as special effects and visual tricks replace the heavy-handed techniques of early print advertising, but her kaleidoscopic ability to whet whatever appetite the viewer fancies stretches like a continuum from the 1920s to the present.

What is new, however, is the advertiser's recognition that the perception of the viewer, and especially of the female viewer, has undergone a radical transition in this time. No longer easily coaxed to believe that her life mission is to scrub grates or even to spend dreamy afternoons driving along country lanes, women, it is assumed, will now respond more favourably to constructions that collude, however superficially, with their upbeat, outgoing perception of their lives. Hence the wink and the joke, the refusal to take motherhood too seriously, that sets the gap between the 1950s Persil advertisements (risible to a contemporary audience in their zealous and class-bound moralizing) and the 1990s Oxo family.

Advertisers, too, always in tune with aspirational thinking, know that women increasingly want to be 'on top'. It is hard to imagine a contemporary advertiser choosing to replay in any straight form the romantic strip cartoon narrative favoured by toilet soap advertisers in the 1930s, with the woman in a purely passive role, awaiting male attention. Romance still features, but it has either been rendered exotic, or spiced with danger. Occasionally, as we have seen, women can step into the shoes of the heroine, and get the better of men; a safe strategy in selling products aimed uniquely at women, but deploying it in car advertising is more daring, and, as a means of changing the image of a traditionally masculine drink, bolder still. A recent advertisement for Tennent's Lager depicts four young women on a lunchtime outing sending up the amorous attentions of an Italian waiter. Although the stereotyping of the male allows the sensibilities of traditional Tennent's drinkers to be protected from the ridicule of the young women's laughter, this marks a new approach in lager advertising. Allowing women sporadic triumphs may have begun to blur the gender boundaries, but reversing femininity's value as a malleable sign is not readily accomplished.

Unsettling masculinity's stability as a sign might speed up the pace of change. To date, masculinity has been extended by men appearing foolish (usually in role reversal contexts), occasionally caring (especially of babies), or displaying virile bodies emphasizing their strength and carefully developed physique. If the last reverses the pattern of the 'male gaze', it does not reverse the status of masculinity. Mr Happywoman, delighting in his partner's pleasure, is still some way off.

References

Bowlby, R. (1985) *Just Looking*. London: Methuen.

Brunsdon, C. (ed.) (1986) *Films for Women*. London: BFI.

Brunt, R. (1990) Points of view, in A. Goodwin and G. Whannel (eds) *Understanding Television*. London: Routledge, 60–73.

Conran, S. (1975) *Superwoman*. London: Sidgwick & Jackson.

Cowan, R.S. (1983) *More Work for Mother: the Ironies of Household Technology from the Open Hearth to the Microwave*. New York: Basic Books.

Daly, M. (1978) *Gyn-Ecology: the Metaethics of Radical Feminism*. Boston: Beacon Press.

Davidson, C. (1982) *A Woman's Work is Never Done: a History of Housework in the British Isles 1650–1950*. London: Chatto & Windus.

Delphy, C. (1987) Protofeminism and antifeminism, in T. Moi (ed.) *French Feminist Thought: a Reader*. Oxford: Blackwell, 80–109. (First published 1976.)

Eckert, C. (1978) The Carole Lombard in Macy's window, *Quarterly Review of Film Studies*, 3(1): 1–21. (Also reprinted in Gaines and Herzog 1990.)

Ewen, S. (1976) *Captains of Consciousness: Advertising and the Social Roots of the Consumer Culture*. New York: McGraw-Hill.

Faludi, S. (1992) *Backlash: The Undeclared War Against Women*. London: Vintage.

Foucault, M. (1980) *Power/knowledge: Selected Interviews and Other Writing, 1972–1977*. Brighton: Harvester Wheatsheaf. Translated by C. Gordon *et al*.

Friday, N. (1973) *My Secret Garden*. New York: Trident.

Friday, N. (1991) *Women on Top*. London: Hutchinson.

Friedan, B. (1965) *The Feminine Mystique*. Harmondsworth: Penguin. (First published 1963.)

Gaines, J. and Herzog, C. (eds) (1990) *Fabrications: Costume and the Female Body*. London: Routledge/AFI.

Hamilton, R., Haworth, B. and Sardar, N. (1982) *Adman and Eve: a Study of the Portrayal of Women in Advertising Carried out for the Equal Opportunities Commission*. Lancaster: University of Lancaster marketing consultancy and research services.

Hardyment, C. (1988) *From Mangle to Microwave: the Mechanization of Household Work*. Cambridge: Polity Press.

Herzog, C. and Gaines, J. (1991) 'Puffed sleeves before tea-time': Joan Crawford, Adrian and women audiences, in C. Gledhill (ed.) *Stardom: Industry of Desire*. London: Routledge, 74–91.

Leclerc, A. (1987) Parole de femme, in T. Moi (ed.) *French Feminist Thought: a Reader*. Oxford: Blackwell, 73–9. (First published in 1974.)

Lemahieu, D. (1988) *A Culture for Democracy: Mass Communication and the Cultivated Mind in Britain Between the Wars*. Oxford: Clarendon Press.

Lewis, J. (1984) *Women in England 1870–1950: Sexual Divisions and Social Change*. London: Wheatsheaf.

Marchand, R. (1985) *Advertising the American Dream: Making Way for Modernity, 1920–1940*. California: University of California Press.

McCracken, E. (1993) *Decoding Women's Magazines: from 'Mademoiselle' to 'Ms.'*. London: Macmillan.

Melman, B. (1988) *Women and the Popular Imagination in the Twenties: Flappers and Nymphs*. London: Macmillan.

Myers, K. (1986) *Understains: the Sense and Seduction of Advertising*. London: Comedia.

Parker, R. (1984) *The Subversive Stitch: Embroidery and the Making of the Feminine*. London: Women's Press.

Posener, J. (1986) *Louder than Words*. London: Pandora.

Stacey, J. (1991) Feminine fascinations: forms of identification in star-audience relations, in C. Gledhill (ed.) *Stardom: Industry of Desire*. London: Routledge, 141–63.

Stuart, A. (1990) Feminism: dead or alive?, in J. Rutherford (ed.) *Identity: Community, Culture, Difference*. London: Lawrence and Wishart, 28–42.

Tickner, L. (1987) The body politic: female sexuality and women artists since 1970, in R. Betterton (ed.) *Looking on: Images of Femininity in the Visual Arts and Media*. London: Pandora, 235–53.

Williams, F. (1969) *The right to know: the rise of the world press*. London: Longman.

THE POLITICS OF THE SMILE

'SOFT NEWS' AND THE SEXUALIZATION OF THE POPULAR PRESS

4

Patricia Holland

'What Makes a Woman Smile?'

The *Sun* newspaper aims to make women smile. Where it has total control, in the photographs which give its pages such graphic impact, its success is, literally, spectacular. Smiling women appear on the news pages and the celebrity pages. They appear in the glamour pictures; the pictures of royalty and of television personalities; in the pictures of ordinary people whose everyday lives have brought them good fortune, and, above all, they appear on Page Three. The woman who proudly displays her breasts is almost always smiling.

The *Sun* gave a decisive twist to the very meaning of a popular paper when, following its purchase and re-launch by Rupert Murdoch in 1969, editor Larry Lamb set about exploiting entertainment values with unprecedented panache. He based the paper's appeal on irreverence, scandal, 'saucy' humour and sex. Above all he introduced the daily image of a half-clad woman. The Page Three girls, 'those luscious lovelies you drool over at breakfast time' (*Sun*, 20 September 1982), became a shorthand reference for all the paper stood for.

Popular newspapers seek to amuse as much as to inform, to appeal to the emotion as much as to the intellect. The smile has been established as part of a package which continues to reach out to real women and men in an invitation to buy the paper and engage with its informal address. Increasingly over the twentieth century the aim of the popular press has been to 'tickle the public' with entertainment values. Matthew Engel took the title of his book on the history of the British popular press from an anonymous verse that went round Fleet Street in the nineteenth century:

Tickle the public, make 'em grin,
The more you tickle the more you'll win.
Teach the public, you'll never get rich,
You'll live like a beggar and die in a ditch. (Engel 1996: 17)

From the 1880s and 1890s, the introduction of lightweight features and all types of trivia, including the domestic, as well as a move to a 'softer', more ticklish type of news, has been seen as a *feminization* of the new mass-circulation press, brought about by its desire for a broad appeal. In seeking out a mass audience, there was a need to recognize women as an influential segment of the potential readership, and the feminine had long been identified with the popular and accessible. But the changes initiated by the *Sun* in the 1970s pushed the meaning of 'popular' in a new direction. The *Sun* was no longer feminized, but *sexualized*.[1] Central to its appeal was the provocative image of a woman's body. Breasts were added to the smile. Instantly this implied a readership sharply divided along gender lines. Men and women readers were separately addressed, through a language and imagery that carried the full power of sexual, as well as gender, difference. The smile on the face of the Page Three girl conveyed a double message: 'After a lifetime of learning to establish eye to eye contact during conversation, the glamour girl has to learn to accept eye to breast contact' explained ex-Page Three girl Jackie Sewell (Wigmore 1986: 13).

A changing relationship between public and the private spheres of activity has been acted out in the pages of the twentieth-century press. Areas of life constructed as private in the nineteenth century were now drawn back into public view. At first, the new mass-circulation papers sought to make visible the domestic and the personal. They circulated gossip, scandal, human-interest stories and a wealth of material on household management, cooking, childcare and other domestic issues. 'Softer' news brought a more personal, more human face. Then, in the last decades of the twentieth century, the even more private world of sexual activity became uninhibited, publicized. Sexual material had long been part of popular imagery, but the nineteenth century and early twentieth century had taken for granted that this was something for men only, and it was concealed from general public view. Now sex brazenly invaded the news columns and dominated the entertainment pages. The concept of 'privacy' can no longer imply 'invisibility', although the terms of its visibility remain hotly contested.[2]

Women's democratic participation, and the role of a newspaper in furthering democratic involvement, is also at issue. A democratic press must also appeal to women and, by the end of the nineteenth century, women were already demanding the space to express their public concerns. Democratization *entails* feminization. By the 1970s, the *Sun* was claiming that the sexualization of the press also brought greater democratic freedoms – for women as well as for men. But the pivotal image of a woman's body brought those claims up against the boundaries of sexual difference. In 1986 MP Clare Short introduced a Parliamentary Bill to ban the use of the Page Three pin-up on the grounds that it was embarrassing and degrading for women. In the heated debates that followed – in Parliament, in the media and around the country – the relationship of women's sexualized image to women's public presence became an issue that divided feminists as well as the public at large. Many suggested that the circulation of the image made women less secure in all sorts of public arenas, from the daily experience of walking in public places to the wider sense of playing a role in public life (Tunks and Hutchinson 1991). Since women were ever more assertively establishing their presence in all spheres of public life, including journalism, it was clear that the movement from feminization to sexualization in the pages of the downmarket tabloids had a political dimension.

The shift in emphasis poses questions about the nature of women's presence in the public sphere of discourse and decision making in a new way. It also poses questions about the nature of news itself. Tabloid editors continue to ask, 'what makes women smile?', but *we* should be asking, how do women participate? What would it mean for the presentation of news to be properly 'engendered' – to use the term that Anne Phillips (1991) used of democracy – in order to achieve a popular media that would be equally potent and meaningful for both sexes?

Some years ago I wrote an article which looked at Page Three from the point of view of women readers, and suggested that its claims to address ordinary women in a new way had some foundation (Holland 1983). I now want to explore more fully the politics of those claims.

The Feminization of the Press

The evolution of the popular press has brought with it a changing relationship between readers and text. It has also, from its earliest days, helped to create an expanding sphere of public discourse which, of necessity, involved increasing numbers of women. As part of the mass audience, women were to make a public appearance on terms that had hitherto been denied (Benhabib 1994; Ryan 1996).

The new technologies of the late nineteenth century for the first time enabled daily newspapers to address a huge and varied readership spread across the nation. Editors and interventionist proprietors aimed to please a wider range of people, many of whom had little time and less inclination to plough through the convoluted metaphors and classical allusions that characterized nineteenth-century newspaper prose. Readers were now to be pampered and 'tickled' rather than challenged or patronized. This 'new journalism' moved away from writing that indulged in ponderous self-importance towards a clearer, more accessible use of language, seeking to eliminate the sense of strain between readers and text created by more demanding reading.

'We shall do away with the hackneyed style of obsolete journalism: and the men and women that figure in the forum or the pulpit or the law court shall be presented as they are – living, breathing and in blushes or in tears – and not merely by the dead words that they utter,' wrote the editor of the *Star*, T.P O'Connor in January 1888. (Engel 1996: 45)

For Evelyn March Phillips writing in the *New Review* (1895), the new journalism meant 'that easy personal style, that trick of bright, colloquial language, that determination to arrest, amuse and startle' (Hunter 1991).

Verbal attractiveness was accompanied by a move towards a more visual mode of presentation, led by the needs of advertisers. The new dailies depended on advertising revenue to keep their prices to a level their readers could afford (Curran and Seaton 1991). Advertising in itself was becoming an important new medium as the modern consumer-based, leisure economy began to get under way. The mosaic layout of a popular newspaper developed partly to accommodate illustrated and boxed advertisements, while the use of exclamatory and hortatory advertising slogans prefigured the use of striking headlines. There was a recognition that the newspaper purchaser 'doesn't read, he [sic] glimpses' (Engel 1996: 132; see also Allen and Frost 1981; Postman 1985).

It was thought that the less educated readers in the wider market would respond to a 'direct appeal to the eye'. The editor of the *Daily Illustrated Mirror*, the first British newspaper to use photographs, wrote, in January 1904:

Our pictures do not merely accompany the printed news, they are a valuable help to the understanding of it . . . the direct appeal to the eye, wherever it is possible, will supplement the written word, which is designed in a more cumbrous fashion to penetrate the mind. (Quoted in Wombell 1986: 76; see also Holland 1997a, 1997b)

Importantly, a more visual style was also thought to appeal to that other group of new readers, women. A contemporary commentator is on record as saying 'Men naturally think in abstract concepts, women think in pictures' (Ryan 1996).

Women found themselves at the heart of the new society. Their economic influence was growing, as the aspirant working and lower-middle classes gained more purchasing power. The 'new woman' of the turn of the century was more independent, more likely to have a job that would bring her enough money to follow fashion, to make trips to the seaside and to buy magazines and other reading matter. At the same time, women were at the centre of a consumer economy which was increasingly based in the home. A more comfortable domestic life was becoming possible for those lower down the social scale, and homes began to be furnished with labour-saving and leisure goods. Even if they did not control the purse strings, women were the home-makers, and advertisers were anxious to reach an ever larger number of them.

A permissive address to women as consumers helped to open up the space for their public participation as readers. At the same time, women journalists were campaigning for recognition. Barred from the raucous male world of the newsrooms, women who aspired to a journalistic career lacked the means to acquire a basic training. In response, *Atlanta* magazine ran a 'school of practical journalism' for women in 1896 and organized writing competitions. A Society for Women Journalists was set up in 1884 to challenge women's exclusion from the clubs and societies through which members of the journalistic fraternity built up their networks and secured their status. The Society had its own offices and a club in Pall Mall for the benefit of the 2,000 women estimated to be practising (Hunter 1991; Sebba 1994; see also Calhoun 1992: 115, 284).

The changes in editorial policy opened the way for women writers, who could now be valued for bringing a personal touch to the pages of a paper. The powerful editor W.T. Stead, proponent of the 'new journalism', was among the first to employ women writers, appointing a woman, Hulda Friederichs, as chief interviewer on the *Pall Mall Gazette* in 1882. It was a short step from the personal to the disreputable. In the 1890s, the American Elizabeth L. Banks became notorious for her scandalous reporting of her life as a maid 'in cap and apron' for the *Weekly Sun*. ' "Oh, but we do not want the ordinary sort of writing from you," the editors would say,' she wrote in her *Autobiography of a Newspaper Girl* (1902). ' "You've started this newer and more entertaining kind of journalism over here and you must keep it up!" '

The mass-circulation press began to explore ways of appealing to different strata of women. The pioneer *Daily Mail*, launched in 1896, sought out the middle-class wife in the expanding suburbs through its personality and gossip pages. Discreet and respectable in appearance, it was designed to attract the upwardly mobile – or at least upwardly aspirant – with features on homemaking and household management for 'intelligent women'. In 1908 the paper set up the *Ideal Home* exhibition as a celebration of the domestic values to which the paper still adheres. 'All the world and her husband' flocked to its displays of domestic goods and consumer fantasies (Ryan 1996).

Following the success of the *Daily Mail*, its proprietor Alfred Harmsworth, soon to become Lord Northcliffe, was ready to move into new territory. In 1903, he launched the *Daily Mirror* specifically as a women's paper. It had a woman editor, Mary Howarth, and an all-woman staff. The experiment did not last long, killed by what sounds very much like misogyny as well as by the failure of its narrow formula of tittle-tattle and gossip for wealthy women. 'Women can't write and don't want to read' was Northcliffe's sour comment. The paper was denied the opportunity to live through its teething problems, and the replacement editor described sacking the female staff as 'a horrid experience – like drowning kittens' (Engel 1996: 150; Allen and Frost 1981).

Northcliffe's impatience was symptomatic. The aim appears to be to include 'feminine' values without handing over any power to women. In a memo to the editor of the *Daily Mail* he once wrote, 'the magazine page is getting less feminine. It should be a woman's page without saying so' (Ryan 1996). But while the appeal of the popular press was opening up the democratic scope of news information and widening the base of public debate to women as well as men, a link between femininity and a low public status was already ingrained. Andreas Huyssen has described the 'notion which gained ground in the 19th century that mass culture is somehow associated with women, while real, authentic culture remains the prerogative of men'. Women were seen as readers of 'inferior literature, subjective, emotional and passive, while man ... emerges as a writer of genuine authentic literature – objective, ironic and in control of his aesthetic means' (Huyssen 1986: 47, 46). The 'feminine' remained linked to the visual, which seemed more easily accessible and less susceptible to rational thought than the verbal. Feminine discourse was not only outside the discourse of the educated classes, but was marginal to the universal claims of modernity and the political and public world.

The 'vulgar' tastes of a working class that was gradually acquiring facilities for leisure and cultural activities seemed equally separate from the masculine seriousness of the middle classes. For Huyssen, 'the problem is

... the persistent gendering as feminine of that which is devalued' (1986: 53). This judgement falls into the very trap that Huyssen is describing, since 'gendering as feminine' is seen to be a 'problem'. For us the reverse problem is of concern, not the 'gendering as feminine of that which is devalued', but the devaluation of that which is gendered as feminine and, indeed, the devaluation of any move towards the incorporation of women's concerns, especially if this is done under the control of women themselves.

At issue is not just the seriousness and authenticity of popular news media, but the nature of their address to the reader. The move towards accessibility in the new journalism developed along two parallel paths, as the split between fact and opinion, reporting and feature writing, accuracy and 'colour' began to gape more widely, dividing the 'serious' papers from the tabloids as well as marking divisions within each individual newspaper. An informational address which claimed to be gender-neutral was set against an entertainment address which developed as feminized, lighter, less demanding and more entertaining. For 'factual' reporting, 'hard news', a language that was clear and to the point came to replace rolling Victorian clauses and circumlocutions. This was a language that made plain its claims to truth, accuracy and universality. The 'soft news' of the entertainment sections and the feature pages was to be judged by different criteria. Yet, despite the claim that 'hard news' made for universality, the distinction remained gender-marked, with women providing the colour and the human touch and men seeking out the reliable facts (Sebba 1994).

More complex difficulties arose as the century progressed and increasing numbers of women insisted on their right to be part of the world of 'hard news'. In a quite different way, 'softer' entertainment values continued to invade the news pages.

The Sexualization of the *Sun*

'What I like to do first thing in the morning is to sit up in bed and have a really good look at Vanya,' wrote Colin Dunne in the *Sun* in September 1977. 'Sometimes she has a rose in her hair. Sometimes she wears a dainty necklace. Occasionally, the odd ribbon. Those apart she is always naked and I wonder how it is that she and Ena Sharples can possibly share the same sex.' A sea change in the very definition of a newspaper came about when Rupert Murdoch bought the *Sun* in 1969 and decreed that its selling points should now be 'sex, sport and contests' (Engel 1996: 253). A year later, editor Larry Lamb introduced the topless models, who became the paper's best-known feature. Its predecessor, the trade-union backed *Daily*

Herald, had endeavoured to create a sense of tough working-class community among its readers in the interwar years (Curran and Seaton 1991). From the 1970s, the *Sun* set out to create a different sort of communality by addressing the new working-class prosperity, in which pleasure was legitimized and the culture of deference put aside. The promise of uninhibited personal gratification was compatible with a rapidly expanding consumer-based economy, and went together with an open contempt for established authority and those who would keep you in your place (Holland 1983).

Larry Lamb decreed that sex in the pages of the *Sun* was to be linked not to pornographic images, nor to highly groomed models, not even, primarily, to celebrities, but to tastefully posed, ordinary young women, smiling at the reader and revealing their breasts. They must be 'nice girls', he is on record as saying (Chippendale and Horrie 1992). In those days of innocence, the *Sun*'s brash hedonism seemed to be sharing something of the freedoms argued for by feminism. Despite its unashamed commercialism, the change in style and content was in tune with the liberatory mood of the times. This was the era of *Cosmopolitan* magazine which opened up a public discussion of sex for women. Sex was explicitly dealt with in feminist magazines, notably *Spare Rib*, and even *Parents* magazine, which dealt with childcare issues, indulged in daring presentations featuring natural childbirth and a considerable amount of nudity. Rupert Murdoch was said to admire the 'serious' broadsheet, the *Guardian*, because of that newspaper's readiness to deal with issues of sexual behaviour on its women's pages. (The *Guardian* was later referred to by *Sun* writers as 'the World's Worst'.)

The *Sun*'s class and gender realignments echoed a wider set of social changes, resisting the 'discourses of sobriety', trade unions, BBC news and old-fashioned politics. It valued itself as a rebel, in reaction to the remnants of post-war stringency and narrow morality. Page Three was launched as an image of defiant liberation. Its message to men was age-old, but its message to women was that women are now free to be sexual. Generations of Page Three 'girls' encouraged women readers to join them, to be proud of their bodies and to have fun. The address to women, often in major features such as the amply illustrated adaptation of Joan Garrity's *Total Loving* (July 1977), was along the lines of 'loosen up, discover sexual pleasure'. Images of naked men joined those of naked women.

The brashness, visual excitement and downmarket appeal of the *Sun* meant that no newspaper that aimed for a mass readership could ignore it. It was imitated by the long-established *Daily Mirror* – which introduced Page Three-type topless models for a brief period – and the newly established *Daily Star* which determinedly scattered bulging breasts throughout its pages. Finally it opened the way for the *Sport*, a tabloid that claimed to be a newspaper but which dispensed with all pretence to offer anything but fantasy and soft porn. The 'softening' of the news had taken a new turn with the reassertion of the female body as spectacle. The sexualization of the popular press had brought a different set of alignments between public and private domains, and between masculine and feminine concerns in its pages.

On the one hand, sexualization could be seen as a logical development of feminization, continuing to draw into the wider debate issues of sexuality and sexual relations that had been hidden but which women themselves, not least in the feminist movement, now insisted were of public importance. On the other hand, there was a deep contradiction in the presentation. Although women were invited to enjoy themselves, to follow their desires and to drop their inhibitions, the divided address, accompanied by many a nudge and a wink, made it clear that *this* women's pleasure is above all a pleasure for men. In this context, the visual is no longer associated with women and with a less linear style of understanding, but with a masculine insistence on the inalienable right to a lustful gaze.

The *Sun*'s visible culture of sex invaded every part of the paper, including the pages it has from time to time run for women. In the paper's own version of its history:

> The *Sun* called its women's pages "Pacesetters" and filled them with sex. They were produced by women for women. But they were sub-titled "The pages for women that men can't resist", acknowledging that there are plenty of topics that fascinate both men and women. Like sex. (Grose 1989: 94).

But the sex remained male oriented. Chippendale and Horrie write of the 'laddish' culture among young women journalists on the paper, outdoing the men (1992).

As the years progressed, the *Sun*'s assertive vulgarity became differently aligned to the cultural and political map of the day. When Kelvin Mac-Kenzie took over the editorship in 1981 the paper became strident in its radical Conservative sympathies, expressed as two fingers to the estab-lishment and an insolent individualism. The Page Three image was part of a rightward move in a political and cultural consciousness confirmed by the years of Conservative government. The central image of the semi-naked 'nice girl' and her welcoming smile was developed as a politics of disen-gagement. 'Page Three is good for you' was the caption that headed a Page Three picture in 1984. 'P3's titillating tit-bits are just what the doctor ordered – as a tonic against the world's gloomy news. Research has shown that the *Sun*'s famous glamour pictures are a vital bit of cheer for readers depressed by strikes, deaths and disasters.'

'A London psychologist' is quoted as saying:

> When you think how gloomy and threatening most of the news has been lately – strikes, assassinations, hijacks, starving millions and the falling pound – you need Page Three as a shot in the arm. I am sure the *Sun*'s famous beauties are a vital safety valve for the country's men when things in general seem to be getting out of hand.

The embrace of the 'loadsamoney' culture, of jingo and bingo, was in tune with a mood that crossed the social classes. Other popular papers and the burgeoning magazine market had followed suit. The culture of sex-for-fun was echoed in advertisements and on television. By the mid-1990s, the *Sun* had lost its rebellious spice. Now its sexual obsessiveness had been overtaken by a host of 'laddish' magazines on the news-stands, and by raunchy imagery on the advertising hoardings. On television *The Good Sex Guide* (1993–94) had kicked off the schedules of the new ITV company Carlton, and inaugurated a genre of trash television which was partly youth-oriented, partly masculine sex fantasy. Kelvin MacKenzie himself left the *Sun* and launched *Topless Darts* (1996) on the cable channel Live TV. In the pages of the *Sun* the humour could all too easily harden into malice and the sexual fun into a leery, sneery soft misogyny.

A relaxation of restraint also came to mean less restraint on intolerance. It made possible the intemperate abuse of those whose sexuality and lifestyle does not conform. In the daily mosaic of the newspaper, the image of the sexy woman continues to be laid against female demons like single mothers, lesbian teachers and ugly women, such as Ena Sharples, the *Coronation Street* character whom Colin Dunne had thought could not possibly share the same sex as Page Three girl Vanya. Although the excesses of the Kelvin MacKenzie years are now rare, the obverse of the culture of hedonism remains a theatre of cruelty, which takes pleasure in the distress of the targeted individual.

Women's visibility in the public realm has involved repeated reminders that heterosexuality is always an issue between men and women, from the demand to see newsreader Angela Rippon's legs (Holland 1987), to a preoccupation with Prime Minister Margaret Thatcher's wardrobe. Which brings us back to the image of the smile and to the relationship between the body and the face in the iconic Page Three image.

Body and Face

Much has been written about the use of the female body as spectacle and as commodity (Mulvey 1989; Coward 1984). Carole Pateman has drawn the issue even more firmly into the political realm in the unlikely context of the theory of contract which, for liberal thinkers, secures the legitimation of civil society. The theory proposes that free social relations take the form of a series of contracts freely entered into between autonomous individuals. Contracts, such as those involving employment, are governed by law, and structure daily life. Pateman points out that women have been largely overlooked by classical contract theorists, and that, although a contract is seen as the paradigm for an equal agreement, in those contracts that are of necessity between women and men – as in marriage – the parties begin from an unequal position. Such contracts always imply a politicized *sexual* difference and reinforce what she describes as men's 'sex-right' over women's bodies (Pateman 1988: 3).

It is important for her argument that we should not lose sight of this potent *sexual* inequality, as its specificity can too easily be lost in a discussion of other categories of inequality less subject to taboo, such as those of power or gender. Men's sex-right is central to contracts, from marriage to prostitution and surrogacy, 'in which the body of the woman is precisely what is at issue' (Pateman 1988: 224). Despite the liberal doctrine that 'everyone owns the property in their capacities and attributes', men still 'demand that women's bodies in the flesh and in representation should be publicly available to them' (1988: 13–14). A fanciful analogy might pose the Page Three smile as a form of contract which reaches out to the male reader. It appears to secure an unproblematic agreement between men and women which promises access to a sexualized body.

There are many possible types of smile. The *Sun* specializes in the 'lovely to see you!' smile, one that comes straight off of the page, the gaze of the smiler entangling with that of the viewer. It is cheerful, commonplace and relaxed, and it aims to elicit smiles from the readers, men and women. 'Try to avoid a toothy grin or a Bardot pout. This sort of expression can make you look self-conscious. It's best not to copy anyone. Just be yourself,' was the advice given to aspiring Page Threes (*Sun*, 27 October 1981).

This smile is familiar from the snapshots of friends and family treasured by almost everyone in the Western world. Ever since the introduction of the Box Brownie in 1900, the domestic snapshot, taken 'as quick as a wink', has sought to capture a smile that builds a bond of companionship between photographer and subject, quite different from the confrontational tension created in formal portraits taken by a professional photographer (Holland 1997a; Parr 1997).

This pictured smile is part of the familial ritual, a family masquerade. It is a welcome convention which expresses a longing for happiness and togetherness even when, tragically, it may conceal the opposite (Williams 1994; Spence and Holland 1991). It is an affirmation of belonging and fitting into place, an acquiescence underpinned by pleasure. The work of the newspaper smile is to create an engagement with its own special public, built on the analogy of family warmth.

Much of the text of the *Sun* is organized around the presence and absence of such a smile. In the tradition of the popular press it seeks out good news in contrast to the 'gloomy and threatening' news of the 'serious' broadsheets. As an object lesson to its readers it offers contrasting images of women who will not smile – 'Mrs Misery', a betting-shop cashier, 'was sacked because she was so grumpy she drove punters away' (*Sun*, 3 September 1996). Such surly refusal on the part of spoilsports, moralists and the bad tempered deprives everyone else of their pleasure and undermines the security of the metaphorical family structure.

With this relaxed and familiar smile firmly in place, the *Sun* has gone on to forge an indissoluble link between the welcoming face and the revelation of women's breasts. 'Lovely to see you!' was the headline over a Portsmouth crowd greeting the fleet on its return from the Falklands in June 1982. A smiling young woman, an ordinary girl, just one of the crowd, pulls up her shirt to reveal her breasts. 'A pretty girl reveals how happy she is to see Britain's heroes home – by baring her charms for the delighted sailors', the text confirms (*Sun*, 12 June 1982). Sexuality is both affirmed and its danger defused in the ordinariness of the presentation.

For those who refuse the link between smile and female sexuality, the threat of humiliation is always present. When, in 1986, Labour MP Clare Short brought in a Parliamentary Bill to ban Page Three, the response was personalized abuse against 'killjoy Clare'. The *News of the World*, at the time edited by ex-Page Three caption writer Patsy Chapman, set out to find a picture of the MP in her night-dress (Tunks and Hutchinson 1991; Snoddy 1992: 110). This metaphorical attempt to undress Clare Short was symptomatic. Women who refuse to smile tend to be fully clothed, but once the clothes come off the message of the body cannot be denied. A face, even a smiling face, carries the potential of speech. The revealed body calms and defuses the challenge of that potential.

The Page Three image is an active, working image, layered with mythological resonance (Warner 1987). It displays a 'body that matters', to echo the title of Judith Butler's exploration of the discursive construction of real, material bodies. It works to reiterate the 'regulatory norms with which sex is materialised'. But, as Butler goes on to point out, 'sex is both produced and destabilized in the course of this reiteration' (Butler 1993: 10). The exposure of a woman's breasts needs strong legitimation, and that legitimation is achieved by the acquiescent smile. Page Three models repeatedly emphasize the point by speaking of the pleasure they take in the role.

Page Three has changed over the years. The models have become more knowing and the presentation has lost something of the exuberant celebration of the early days. Perhaps more importantly, the context in which it is to be understood is different. The women in the pictures are no longer timeless. The well-known models have grown older, and their public personae have developed. Some have had children; some, like Linda Lusardi and Sam Fox, have tried to build up show-business careers; others have become unemployed and disillusioned. Their personal accounts of their experiences, published from time to time in newspapers as diverse as the *News of the World* and the *Guardian Weekend*, range from the maudlin to the insightful. Many give a very different picture from that portrayed in the jokey features that fill the pages of the *Sun*.

The highly visible image of a sexualized woman has brought into question the role of the popular press as a potential space for the expression of women's democratic aspirations and public participation. And yet an army of invisible women, journalists, photographers, researchers and editors, has been steadily encroaching into hitherto-protected masculine preserves. Could it be that the reassertion of the irreducible differences on which *sexual* relations are based is partly a response to an increasing equality in *gender* relations?

Democracy, Women and the Public Sphere

Rozsika Parker and Griselda Pollock have documented the historic relationship through which the status of male painters has depended on a distinct role for women in the world of art. While women were excluded as artists – the eighteenth-century Royal Academy banned them from its prestigious life classes – their visible presence was necessary to the very concept of 'art'. The idealized image of 'woman' for centuries represented the archetypal subject for easel painting (Parker and Pollock 1981).

Just like the painted odalisque, the baroque visibility of women in the *Sun* is part of a fantastic excess with which the paper engages its readers. Repeating many similar ironies, the transformation of the popular press into a more accessible, more democratic medium – potentially more feminine – has been carried out through an image that works to temper women's equal participation in those public spaces. A vocal feminist opposition to Page Three has argued that the circulation of the image, as a fantasy for men, would put real women at risk in the physical spaces of the streets. My argument is that by reinforcing sexual difference, the nature of the democratic discursive space is brought into question. Democratic discourse, which needs to be feminized, reaches a different sort of limit when it becomes sexualized. This limit will always need to be negotiated, but negotiation is closed off if sexual difference is always presented in a way that reinforces sexual inequality.

It has been demonstrated in relation to a variety of historical contexts that the exclusion of women from public activities has been structural rather than a mere contingency. This means that the imbalance cannot easily be rectified by equal opportunities legislation or positive discrimination programmes, however important such initiatives may be. Carole Pateman has mapped out the ways in which the very concept of a liberal 'individual' implies a notion of sexual subordination, and 'civil freedom depends on patriarchal right' (Pateman 1988: 38, 219). In Hannah Arendt's account of the Greek polis, the private domestic base was needed to create a public space in which men could participate as citizens (Arendt 1989). For Nancy Fraser, the concept of a 'public sphere', which could make possible a free and equal exchange of views, was a masculinist ideological notion (Calhoun 1992: 116). Joan Landes argued that 'the exclusion of women was constitutive of the very notion of the public sphere' in the age of the French Revolution (Thompson 1995: 254).

It is consistent with these analyses that the 'serious' broadsheets, with their claims to objectivity and universal values, have excluded women even more firmly from positions of power. The first women to become editors of national newspapers (apart from the first, abortive, *Daily Mirror*) have run the most scandalous of scandal sheets, rather than upmarket papers with liberal credentials. Wendy Henry and Patsy Chapman, both editors of *News of the World*, learned their trade on the *Sun*. Hence the paradoxical position that women who lay claim to the exercise of power in the public arena of tabloid news must themselves oversee the fantasy image of a sexy woman.

The entertainment values that, in the popular press, now invade all parts of the paper, need to be reconciled with 'public sphere' objectives, where participation depends on the restrained statement of competing opinions, and where there is an assumption that all can contribute without regard to status or other identity factors (Calhoun 1992). A viable 'public sphere' would be a democratic space where, in the words of Anne Phillips, we can 'leave ourselves behind':

> We do want to 'leave ourselves behind' when we engage in democratic politics: not in the sense of denying everything that makes us the people we are, but in the sense of seeing ourselves as constituted by an often contradictory complex of experiences and qualities, and then of seeing the gap between ourselves and others as in many ways a product of chance. (Phillips 1991: 59)

The sexualized image of a woman is a constant reminder of the utopian nature of this goal.

Excess and the Politics of Fun

A consideration of the position of women in the popular press points to the need for an evaluation of the *political* implications of this interplay between fact and fantasy, 'information' and entertainment. This means that the visual presentation of a newspaper, the size of the headlines, the style of language used are never side issues. Hard news is always dependent on soft.

For that reason, rather than exploring the accuracy, bias or otherwise of the popular press, I have, in this chapter, been concerned with other aspects of its democratic role. Its role in circulating vocabularies, images and concepts with which to make sense of the contemporary world and the place of men and women within it, is of prime importance, but it also plays a role in offering a space in which people may see themselves, their views and their interests reflected, both as individuals and as groups. Bearing in mind these two aspects, rather than trying to isolate the informational content of the popular press from its entertaining presentation, a political critique would note the ways in which the news content is structured and shaped by entertainment values, while the information is itself filtered through the entertainment material (Curran and Sparks 1991). 'News' and 'entertainment' become ever more entwined as the entertainment matter colours the reader's understanding and itself carries important forms of information. James Curran has made this point in relation to the media in general, arguing that 'Media entertainment is one means by which people engage at an intuitive and expressive level in a public dialogue about the direction of society. Media entertainment is in this sense an integral part of the media's "informational" role' (Curran 1991a, 1991b: 102). Far from neglecting the political role of newspapers, this refocusing of attention is essential to an understanding of the downmarket tabloids as the most influential media of political communication.

The relentless push towards entertainment values has meant that the definition of what makes 'news' is itself constantly changing. The carefully established distinction between fact and opinion is now less easy to maintain. The need for accuracy has become dissolved into the excess of the headline, through a joke, an ironic exaggeration or an expression of outrage. It is part of my argument that, in the downmarket tabloids, the 'Page Three principle' has been a crucial element in this transformation. Images of women – seductive, spectacular yet naturalistic – have been central to a cultural and economic change which is also a political one. 'Samantha waving from the top of an armoured car as it was driven through the picket lines at Wapping was one of the defining moments of the 1980s', wrote journalist Peter Martin of Page Three icon Samatha Fox (Martin 1997:16).

The long association made by the *Sun* between spoilsports, sexual puritans and a Labour Party now rejected as 'old Labour' has been a highly political campaign, filtered through the association of sexuality and a hedonistic lifestyle. As part of its violently anti-Labour stance during the 1992 election, the *Sun* replaced its usual Page Three with a bulgingly fat 'flabbogram lady', captioned 'Here's how Page Three will look under Kinnock! Fat chance of fun' (Seymour-Ure 1995). Political discourse of this kind appears to transcend party politics. The *Sun* dramatically changed allegiance for the 1997 election, supporting the Labour Party in its 'modernized' form under Tony Blair. On that occasion, its latest Page Three 'superstar', Melinda Messenger, 'Blairs all' and tells readers why she backs Tony Blair. Clearly the party-political switch had had no impact on the 'Page Three principle'. A politics of sexual fantasy which opens up a gap between women and men by reinforcing men's 'sex-right' over women's bodies continues to imply a political allegiance which ultimately undermines democratic participatory rights, and which continues to link the feminine with the trivial.

The *Sun* continues to reiterate that women's bodies matter, and it repeatedly demonstrates that the materiality of those bodies will always subvert women's claims to seriousness in a world where they need not smile. And yet, in the spirit of a sexuality that aims to be less under male control, many ordinary women have made it clear that they value the right to smile, even if, for the moment, they cannot smile entirely on their own terms. In a 1987 television debate, ex-Page Three model Linda Lusardi asserted that she had turned the Page Three image to her own advantage. She used it as a sign of the proud independence it had brought to her, rather than a sign of subordination to men's fantasies (BBC Community Programmes Unit 1987). That smile continues to be directed at women, too, even if it is instantly recuperated into the service of a masculine framework of understanding (Norris 1997).

But while real, embodied – if invisible – women continue to have only minimal roles in the shaping of our popular media, the men who produce the pages will continue to build their power on the decorative excess of the women who are pictured on them – just like the eighteenth-century academicians and their voluptuous models. Interestingly, a debate in the pages of the serious broadsheets during June and July of 1997 on whether a lightening of the news content of those papers constituted a 'dumbing down' or a feminization, was largely conducted by women journalists and quickly took up the issue of women's writing. Smiling or not, the need is for participation on women's own terms. This, of course, will have consequences for the concept of 'news' and for that of 'entertainment'.

Notes

1. It is possible that 1998 will prove to be another turning point in the history of the *Sun* and the popular press in general. Following an underlying decline in the number of readers, which accelerated alarmingly from 1996, the *Sun* decided to change direction once again. It appointed a young woman, 29-year-old Rebekah Wade, as deputy editor, abandoned the Page Three pin-up and moved to a generally less laddish approach. The *Sun* felt the need to seek a new niche as, on the one side, magazines such as *Loaded* developed the raunchy style with spectacular success and, on the other, the mid-market *Daily Mail*, with its more serious journalism, increased its readership.
2. The Press Complaints Commission, the self-regulatory body which monitors the ethics of the British press, covers issues of privacy in its Code of Practice. The Commission responds to complaints from members of the public. Disputes regularly arise over the ethics of such issues as intrusive photography and intrusion on grief or shock. These issues are important, but the point that I am making here is a broader one about the general tenor of news values.

References

Allen, R. and Frost, J. (1981) *Daily Mirror*. Cambridge: Patrick Stephens.

Arendt, H. (1989) *The Human Condition*. Chicago: University of Chicago Press.

Banks, E.L. (1902) *The Autobiography of a 'Newspaper Girl'*. New York: Dodd, Mead.

Benhabib, S. (1994) Models of public space: Hannah Arendt, the liberal tradition and Jürgen Habermas, in C. Calhoun (ed.) *Habermas and the Public Sphere*. Boston, MA: Massachusetts Institute of Technology.

Butler, J. (1993) *Bodies That Matter: On the Discursive Limits of 'Sex'*. London: Routledge.

Calhoun, C. (ed.) (1992) *Habermas and the Public Sphere*. Cambridge, MA: MIT Press.

Chippendale, P. and Horrie, C. (1992) *Stick it Up Your Punter: The Rise and Fall of The Sun*. London: Mandarin.

Coward, R. (1984) *Female Desire: Women's Sexuality Today*. London: Paladin.

Curran, J. (1991a) Rethinking the media as a public sphere, in P. Dahlgren and C. Sparks (eds) *Communication and Citizenship*. London: Routledge.

Curran, J. (1991b) Mass media and democracy: a reappraisal, in J. Curran and M. Gurevitch (eds) *Mass Media and Society*. London: Arnold.

Curran, J. and Seaton, J. (1991) *Power Without Responsibility*, 4th edn. London: Routledge.

Curran, J. and Sparks, C. (1991) Press and popular culture, *Media, Culture and Society*, 13: 215–37.

Engel, M. (1996) *Tickle the Public: One Hundred Years of the Popular Press*. London: Indigo.

Grose, R. (1989) *The Sun-sation*. London: Angus & Robertson.

Holland, P. (1983) The 'Page Three Girl' speaks to women too, *Screen*, 24(3): 84–102.

Holland, P. (1987) When a woman reads the news, in H. Baehr and G. Dyer (eds) *Boxed In: Women and Television*. London: Pandora.

Holland, P. (1997a) 'Sweet it is to scan': personal photographs and popular photography, in L. Wells (ed.) *Photography: A Critical Introduction*. London: Routledge.

Holland, P. (1997b) 'The direct appeal to the eye? Photography and the twentieth century press', in A. Briggs and P. Cobley (eds) *Introduction to Media*. Harlow: Addison Wesley Longman.

Hunter, F. (1991) The society of women journalists, in G. Cevaso (ed.) *The Eighteen Nineties: Encyclopaedia of British Literature, Arts and Culture*. New York: Garland.

Huyssen, A. (1986) Mass culture as woman, *After the Great Divide*. London: Macmillan.

Martin, P. (1997) The sad tale of Mr Fox, *Observer Life*, 16 February.

Mulvey, L. (1989) 'Visual pleasure and narrative cinema', *Visual and Other Pleasures*. London: Macmillan.

Norris, P. (ed.) (1997) *Women, Media and Politics*. New York: Oxford University Press.

Parker, R. and Pollock, G. (1981) *Old Mistresses: Women, Art and Ideology*. London: Routledge & Kegan Paul.

Parr, M. (1997) 'August Sander: A personal perspective', talk given at the National Portrait Gallery, London (March).

Pateman, C. (1988) *The Sexual Contract*. Cambridge: Polity.

Phillips, A. (1991) *Engendering Democracy*. Cambridge: Polity.

Postman, N. (1985) *Amusing Ourselves to Death*. London: Methuen.

Ryan, D. (1996) All the world and her husband: the *Daily Mail* and women readers. Paper given at Institute of Contemporary British History Conference (September).

Sebba, A. (1994) *Battling for News: The Rise of the Woman Reporter*. London: Sceptre.

Seymour-Ure, C. (1995) Characters and assassinations: portrayals of John Major and Neil Kinnock in the *Daily Mirror* and the *Sun*, in I. Crewe and B. Gosschalk (eds) *Political Communications: The General Election Campaign 1992*. Cambridge and New York: Cambridge University Press.

Snoddy, R. (1992) *The Good, the Bad and the Unacceptable*. London: Faber & Faber.

Spence, J. and Holland, P. (eds) (1991) *Family Snaps: The Meanings of Domestic Photography*. London: Virago.

Thompson, J.B. (1995) The theory of the public sphere, in O. Boyd-Barrett and C. Newbold (eds) *Approaches to Media: A Reader*. London: Arnold.

Tunks, K. and Hutchinson, D. (1991) *Dear Clare ... This is What Women Feel about Page Three*. London: Radius.

Warner, M. (1987) *Monuments and Maidens: The Allegory of the Female Form*. London: Picador.

Wigmore, N. (1986) The Page Three Connection, *Guardian*, 27 March.

Williams, V. (1994) *Who's Looking at the Family?* London: Barbican Art Gallery.

Wombell, P. (1986) Face to face with themselves: photography and the First World War, in P. Holland, J. Spence and S. Watney (eds) *Photography Politics Two*. London: Comedia.

MURDER, GENDER AND THE MEDIA

5

SEXUALIZING POLITICS AND VIOLENCE

Saraswati Sunindyo

This paper focuses on three cases of wife and mistress murder that gained media and public attention in Indonesia in the 1990s. In contrast to some other, less publicized cases of the murder of women,[1] these three seemed to entail political scandal; the perpetrators were (or were rumoured to be) functionaries of a state commonly criticized for corruption and oppressiveness. It was this that drew attention to the cases and obscured the male violence against women that was involved. The media and public discourse in these cases, however, engaged representations of sexuality: the victims were 'sexualized' while the aggressors were somehow 'desexualized' by attributing their motives to a desire to protect their families.

I will argue that the representation of these three cases reconstructs gender ideology by attempting to control women's sexuality, distinguish 'good' women from 'bad' women, and exclude women who do not fit into the typology of a good mother. Such construction or reconstruction of gender did not take place in a political vacuum. It was linked to the substantiation of the bourgeois ideology of motherhood – that is, woman as nurturer of her offspring, her husband, and finally of the community and national spirit; that is, the woman's role that was officially sanctioned by the New Order state of Indonesia.[2]

The Political Context

Prior to 1980, Indonesian society was the site of persistent political dissatisfaction expressed in events such as the 1974 student protests known as the Malari Affair, a wave of student activism and the first mass protest during the New Order era. The students focused on the dependency of Indonesian economic development and foreign aid and investment (largely from Japan). In their analyses, such development was closely tied to the interests of the political elite and its business collaborators. The demonstrators demanded, among other things, the dissolution of the presidential panel of personal advisers and the eradication of corruption.[3] The student demonstration was followed by violent riots in Pasar Senen, one of the major commercial districts and shopping areas in Jakarta. The Malari Affair resulted in mass arrests of student leaders and the banning of eleven newspapers and one magazine, with five of the newspapers still under ban 20 years later.

Social dissatisfaction continued and another wave of student protests broke out in 1977–79, climaxing with the publication of a student manifesto known as *Buku Patih* (*White Book*). The book criticized the New Order government, again focusing on its abuse of power, corruption and economic inequities, with a very strong appeal for political changes. It was banned shortly after it appeared and the students' arrests and trials followed.[4]

In addition to the student protests, there were many other manifestations of a generalized protest consciousness. One of the major sources of dissatisfaction with the regime was the problem of corruption and the state's incompetence in handling it despite official claims to the contrary. The police were an obvious target for the public's general resentment. One of the expressions in everyday public conversation prior to 1980 was the phrase *prit-jigo*,[5] a derogatory expression for the police. Although a specific term, the meaning reflects a wider discontent, against the whole military and the regime in general.[6]

Corruption, commonly the eliciting and acceptance of bribes, had become a well-known attribute of public officials. Another way to influence an official was to offer him sexual companions. Hotels, bars, massage parlours and other tourist facilities were sites for such 'immorality' associated with corruption and bribery.[7] However, anti-corruption campaigns usually cling to the conservative position that women and sex are the main corrupting factors, rather than instruments of the main corrupting factor, the official abuse of power.

In 1979, a national newspaper, *Sinar Harapan*, published a series called 'Remang-remang Jakarta', a report on prostitution in Jakarta. The reports were published daily, and both the content and the character of the stories made the series (later published as a book) into a sensational subject of conversation.[8] The articles mixed sensation and sexual inquisitiveness with exposure of decadent and corrupt bureaucrats.

Among the articles were interviews with those involved in the prostitution business, providing information about the clients and the women, including some well-known figures identified only by initials. For example, the paper ran the confession of a pimp who had started out as an independent construction contractor. In order to win contracts, he had to provide women to government officials and businessmen. The story of a madam revealed that she had seven powerful men backing, or financially supporting, her (*backing* is also the term used in Indonesia).[9] The same series revealed that a popular magazine had served as a sales catalogue for high-class prostitutes during the 1970s.[10] This provocative series, however, even when published as a book, offered no in-depth analysis of prostitution.[11] As a result, the public reaction to the exposés remained rooted in moral puritanism and sexism.

The Politics of Gender

The New Order government more strictly enforced the ideology concerning the role of women; women's organizations and their voices were transformed into 'New Order fashion'. Shortly after the New Order took power in 1966, many existing women's organizations were banned, left-leaning women activists were jailed or had died in massacres, and the national women's organization Kowani (Kongres Wanita Indonesia, Indonesian Women's Congress) was paralysed. This last effect resulted from the fact that Kowani's leadership has been dominated by Gerwani (the leftist women's movement influenced by the PKI, the Indonesian Communist Party).[12] Consequently, many women's issues raised by the 'old' order women's organizations and activists, such as childcare and sexual harassment, were also seen as tainted and were dropped from all practical agendas.[13]

A new women's organization was formed in 1974 called Dharma Wanita (Women's Duty), a national organization headed by the First Lady of the republic, which functioned as an umbrella organization for women's organizations in all government offices. Dharma Wanita membership is mandatory for every woman working in a government office and for all wives of government employees. The leadership structure parallels the hierarchy of the husbands' offices and positions. The more outspoken women's organizations were paralysed, and Dharma Wanita clearly did not aim to articulate women's rights issues.[14] The New Order government also launched a programme for women described as the PKK or Family Welfare Guidance. Described as a movement to promote 'community well-being', the programme started by concentrating on women in rural areas. Every village head's office displays a poster listing the PKK programme and the five precepts or *Panca Dharma Wanita* (Five Responsibilities of Women): a wife is to (1) support her husband's career and duties; (2) provide offspring; (3) care for and rear the children; (4) be a good housekeeper; and (5) be a guardian of the community.[15]

Clearly the ideology of women as offspring producers, mothers and guardians of the national interest did not first appear when the New Order government took power, nor did it exist only because the state reinforced it through Dharma Wanita and its family welfare programme. The post-1965 state, however, put its weight behind these notions. While women's organizations that were concerned with women's rights issues were banned and their activities stigmatized as a result of the abortive coup of 1965, the PKK and Dharma Wanita were well placed, working from the top government offices to the grassroots level, promoting their creed and causes.[16]

The Supadmi Case

On 26 March 1981, the military high court of East Java sentenced two police intelligence officers, Lieutenant Colonel Suyono and Captain Bastari, to prison, the former for six years and six months, and the latter for five years.[17] Both were found guilty of attempting the premeditated murder of Mrs Supadmi.[18] Suyono, who was about to be appointed as a *bupati* (regent) in an East Javanese district, with the help of his subordinate, Bastari, botched an attempt to kill his mistress. The case attracted unrestrained media fascination.

Mrs Supadmi, a 'high-class' call girl, who was sitting beside her lieutenant colonel 'lover and protector' in the front seat of a police jeep, was first hit on the head by the captain from the back seat. Two shots were fired when she grabbed at the gun pointed at her head. When she realized that her 'protector' actually meant to murder her, she held her breath and pretended to be dead. The assailants took her out of the car and fired another shot at her throat. Stripped naked and thrown into a pit over 15 metres deep (the location is called Jurang Gupit, the deep pit), her body caught on some bushes before it hit the bottom. When she heard the car leave, she crawled back to the road.

Mrs Supadmi was found by a truck driver and a forest engineer. On the way to the hospital, fearing that she was going to die, she asked her rescuers to write down the names, titles, ranks and the office addresses of her two killers. She did not die, and the whole media craze began.

Media construction: contradiction

The first news concerning the matter broke four days later in *Sinar Harapan*, one of the major national newspapers, after a press conference by the East Java police command. The story stated that on 23 August 1980, the forest police of Bojonegoro, East Java, found a naked woman, bloody and wounded in the neck, both thighs and palms. The Police Command of East Java, accordingly, had arrested Lieutenant Colonel Suyono and Captain Bastari, who confessed to shooting the victim.[19] This news became a big and juicy issue – two police officers had attempted to murder a woman in a brutal way. However, the same story also released the police finding that the motive was extortion. 'Unexpectedly, the victim, who had been mistress of Lieutenant Colonel Suyono, had demanded a large amount of allowance, a house, and a car. If Suyono refused to give her all she asked for, she would tell his wife about their relationship. All of these demands could not be fulfilled by Suyono by any means.'[20] Thus four days after Mrs Supadmi was rescued and while she was still in the hospital, recovering from surgery to remove a bullet from her jaw, a statement was published attributing a very sympathetic motive to her assailant: a man in a high-ranking police department wanted to protect his family from an *anita tuna susila* (immoral woman, i.e. the formal term for prostitute) who threatened to 'destroy' his peaceful household.

This analysis parallels Cameron and Frazer's interpretation of the hegemonic construction of sex and serial murder cases: when a man kills a woman – especially one vulnerable to being labelled loose or immoral – the act itself is unforgivable, but the motive can be understood by society at large. The attempted murder by these two policemen was clearly condemned by Indonesian society, yet the motive – to protect one's family – was upstanding and therefore comprehensible. Two weeks after the event, an editorial 'analysis' of the 'scandal' appeared in *Berita Buana*, a Jakarta newspaper. The editor drew an analogy to the British political sex scandal involving Christine Keeler and Secretary for War John Profumo, ignoring the dissimilarities – the Profumo–Keeler affair ended with Profumo losing his important political position and had nothing to do with murder, or protection of family.[21] The editorial underscored the fact that in both cases the couple was in a relationship outside marriage, and that in the Supadmi case such behaviour presented a danger to both the police corps and the country. 'The lesson to be drawn from this is that personal relations, sexual and such, should not entangle us in extortion, and most importantly should not lead to the revelation of the country's secrets.'[22] The editors went on: 'We hope that the incident in Bojonegoro will remain confined to those who

committed the crime and will not contaminate the image of the Police
Department as the protector of the society, which we labored so long and
hard to achieve. Do not let one drop of poison ruin the whole jug of milk.'
Not only was sympathy denied to the victim because of her profession and
her way of treating 'our' man, but also the brutal assault she experienced
was submerged into 'just another sexual scandal between a state official and
a prostitute'. This, according to the media, could endanger not only the
persons involved, but also the country. The fact that the two assailants were
members of the police department contributed, on the one hand, to the
media's eagerness to cover the case. On the other hand, it obscured the
violence of the crime because it was felt necessary to protect the image of
the police corps and to ensure the people's continued 'trust'.

The media were eager to print any piece of information they could get on
this case. Soon after Mrs Supadmi was released from the hospital, journalists
crowded her house in her home town and interviewed her on what had
happened.[23] Stories appeared about the relationship, how she survived the
attack, and how she was the flower of her village, that she had an uncle who
was a retired military officer, that she had married more than once. Three
weeks after the incident, the national news agency Antara reported that Mrs
Suyono had hired a defence lawyer for her husband and Captain Bastari. In
a press conference, the lawyer appealed to the media not to further publicize
the case, 'to help reduce the suffering of the assailants' families'.[24]

The trial took place in March 1981. Seven months after the incident,
people had not forgotten the case – testimony to the media's tenacity. The
courtroom was full; people crowded the courtyard, listening to the proceedings, which were broadcast over loudspeakers. Mrs Supadmi was
cheered at her first appearance. The people came as spectators, to witness
the process of 'justice', but also to see in person their 'heroine', Mrs
Supadmi, who tried to hide her face during her first appearance but not
thereafter. She was a heroine when people needed a symbol of their desire
for justice,[25] but she seemed, at least at first, wary of the voyeurism that
drew the crowd to the court building. Pictures taken of her during the trial
were informally sold in the courtyard, different prices for different angles,
cheaper prices for black and white than colour. But, in spite of Mrs
Supadmi's function as a symbol for justice, her profession (and therefore
her gender and her sexuality) created contradictions. For example:

> Mrs. Supadmi showed up in a dazzling outfit and looked sexy. She was
> wearing a light brown *kebaya*, brown high heels, and a bun hairdo. An
> officer in charge commented, 'Mrs. Ludewiji is definitely an extra-
> ordinary beauty, better than a movie star.'

...

After the third day of the trial, the young and 'sexy' divorcée continued being guarded, but no longer covered her face as when she first entered the courtroom.

...

Many of the policemen's wives who attended the trial said, 'She knows how to dress herself up and be sexy.'[26]

The media, however, were not the only party who sexualized the victim: the people (mostly young men) who went to the trial fell into the same contradiction. Among the remarks addressed to Mrs Supadmi were 'Sister! Come on out and let's get acquainted!' and 'Salut! You can expose the POLRI main POLRI officer's womanizing!'[27] Mrs Supadmi was the prosecution's key witness and was the main attraction for both spectators and commentators. Her strength as a woman who had survived a brutal attack and was able to bring her attackers to court was repeatedly attributed to her 'difference' from women outside her profession; she was seen simply as a sensual and sexual being. When a case like this happens, again and again women's sexuality is constructed: the 'loose woman' category is filled with desire and sensuality; the 'good or ordinary women' category is totally emptied of sexuality.

As the trial progressed and the defence lawyer started to challenge Mrs Supadmi's credibility as a 'responsible witness', the characterization of the victim becomes clearer. She was depicted not only as a primarily sexual being, but also as a vengeful person who did not value love and devotion.[28] The two assailants, in contrast, were represented as asexual beings – men with no lust, respected, restrained and loving fathers and husbands.

While the victim was characterized as sensual and alluring, the assailants were depicted as ordinary men who happened to panic and get confused under overwhelming pressure. They were also pictured as asexual and upstanding – at least, Captain Bastari, who was not the lover of Mrs Supadmi, was:

The second defendant said that Mrs Ludewiji is bigger than he is, so instead of him pulling her, she was the one who successfully pulled him toward her.

Why didn't you let yourself be pulled to her lap? Don't you think it would feel good? asked the judge.

Well, she is not my wife. If she were my wife, I would just have fallen into her lap! said the second defendant.

The judge himself fell into sexualizing the courtroom by making the violent attack laughable and sexy, yet emphasizing the 'asexual' nature of the attackers. Even when the sexual relationship between the lieutenant colonel and Mrs Supadmi was acknowledged, the man was not viewed as having sexual desire parallel to that of Mrs Supadmi. Either Suyono's sexuality was taken for granted as a 'natural man who needs more than one woman to have sex with' or the sexual relationship between him and the victim was just *khilaf* (at that moment he was not himself and was carried away by evil persuasion).

Unfortunately for the defence, certain facts were clear: Mrs Supadmi was still alive and had brought her case to light. The judge, the media and the public were aware that the two assailants were guilty. Despite the defence lawyer's attempts to ridicule her and the media representation of her, in her testimony Mrs Supadmi rejected their monopoly of the moral high ground:

> JUDGE: If you felt terribly hurt, why didn't you cry?
> MRS SUPADMI: I pretended I was dead. If I cried I might have been dead by now.
> JUDGE: So this is a case of unsuccessful murder?
> MRS SUPADMI: It is not that it merely faded, but that God protected me.[29]

Her famous line 'God protected me' represented her resistance to the normative tone inside and outside the courtroom.

The Cases of Siti Rahmini and Dietje

Six weeks after the trial of Mrs Supadmi's assailants, Jakarta was rocked by another case. A murder took place about the time of the Suyono and Bastari trial, and involved Dewanto, a high-ranking official from Sekretariat Negara (the state secretariat). Dewanto was secretly married to a second wife, the victim, who was his former babysitter. This case was also widely publicized, and statements about the motive were released almost immediately:

> Siti Rahmini was murdered because she demanded 'equal rights' between herself and the first wife.[30]
>
> . . .
>
> According to the confession of Dewanto, Siti often undermined him by demanding this and that. She knew Dewanto's position, she knew

Dewanto's weakness in marrying her without his first wife's knowledge. She used this weakness to pressure him. His evil intentions sprang from his fear that his wife would discover what he had done.[31]

...

According to Police Lieutenant A. Tonang, Dewanto admitted that he was behind the murder of his second wife. The motive given by Dewanto was that he had always felt uneasy since he married her, that she often threatened to tell the whole affair to his first wife and the State Secretariat office. Furthermore, Siti was killed because she was too demanding. First she asked for a house and furniture, then she asked to be formally married, and finally she asked that he devote equal time to her – one night with his first wife, and one night with her.[32]

Both this case and the case of Mrs Supadmi involved 'respectable' and socially powerful men. Media coverage of both cases blamed the victim for her demands and threats to unveil the identity of the key aggressor. Both claimed that the defendants acted to 'save' the family. However, there was a major difference between the courts' handling of these cases. Mrs Supadmi's case was taken to the military high court, with a strong warning from the police commander of East Java that it was the accused persons who were to be held responsible and not the police corps. During the trial, the discourse was very much characterized by the desire of the military-dominated government both to clear itself of any blame and to show that there was justice to be had in Indonesia by holding the individual defendants accountable. The judge from the military high court even admitted that Mrs Supadmi's case gained the people's attention not just because of Mrs Supadmi's profession but because of people's yearning to see justice done to those who committed crimes.[33] The judge expressed concern that the two assailants were members of the police corps (and thus of the military), who were supposed to protect the people.

In contrast to Mrs Supadmi's case, the theme of sexual scandal was absent from press coverage of Siti Rahmini's murder, although it also involved violence against a mistress (except that Siti Rahmini was married to Dewanto under Islamic law). Rahmini's case did not celebrate a protagonist or involve sentiments of dissatisfaction with the state, military or police force. Although media coverage was extensive, crowds did not fill the courtroom. Whereas the judge in Mrs Supadmi's case condemned the two assailants for the immorality of stripping the victim after they thought she was dead, the judge in Siti Rahmini's case cautioned 'all second wives ...

housemaids, and especially all mothers to be cautious with their daughters and towards their maids' relations with their husbands – more so since narcotics are widely available in the underground market – [so as] not to repeat the same incident'.[34] Although Dewanto was prosecuted, it was women who were warned by the judge.

Another case that was equally dramatized by the media was the murder of Dietje, a well-known model and winner of several beauty contests. She was killed in 1986. Although her death generated rumours about her involvement with some politically and economically powerful men, she was not portrayed as a voluptuous being.[35] Her status as a mother and the wife of a respected man and her fame as an image of traditional Javanese femininity in her work appeared to shield her from the media effort to demonize her.[36] Still, like Mrs Supadmi and Siti Rahmini, Dietje was constructed as a 'natural' victim of male violence because of her 'profession' and the presumption that she had sexual liaisons with very important men. Contrary to the Supadmi case, the target of sensation in the media was the possible involvement of a powerful person in the killing.

Media and public attention was higher than for the previous two cases. Daily and weekly papers printed speculation and gossip surrounding the case. In the first week of the case, the media conjectured that this famous model might have had affairs with a respected Jakarta figure and pointedly mentioned that her husband was paralysed.[37] The media were eager to find any crumbs of information, and rumours about the reason for the murder and the person behind it spread rapidly. Letters to the editor, an important source of media democracy in Indonesia, urged the police to find the killer.[38]

Dietje's case involved questioning the police department's ability to solve the case.[39] In the Supadmi case, the wife of the assailant appealed to the media to stop the uproar that humiliated her family; in Dietje's case, both her husband and the police commander demanded that the media stop publishing sensational and speculative news, claiming that 'the consequences, obstructing the investigation, were too great'.[40] When the police found a suspect, the media ran numerous articles about the alleged killer. In response, the president of Dewan Kehormatan PWI (Persatuan Wartawan Indonesia, Honorary Council of the Indonesian Journalist Association) appealed to the press to keep the media attention objective and respect the right to presumption of innocence of the alleged killer until a guilty verdict was brought: 'Journalists are particularly warned to keep in mind the journalists' ethical code on presumption of innocence; so that it is assured that journalists will not just compound the errors committed by the legal system.'[41]

In comparison the most sympathetic analysis of Mrs Supadmi's case levelled a broader social critique and inquired whether the circumstances surrounding her attempted murder were not a sign of disappearing social responsibility in Indonesian society. 'It could be the reality of the very world of the intelligence agency which made it possible for a subordinate person to blindly follow the will of his superior.'[42]

Both cases, Supadmi's and Dietje's, involved appeals to the media to restrain publication of findings. The family of the main perpetrator in Supadmi's case did so to protect his and his family's image, and the victim's family in Dietje's case appealed for the same reason. Moreover, the Honorary Council of the Indonesian Journalist Association cautioned the media not to jump to conclusions about a particular suspect, somehow suggesting that the police might have found the wrong person.

These three cases are not the only ones of their kind, there are other cases which the police are still unable to solve.[43] These three, however, involved public discourse and were sensationalized by the media because they highlighted issues of corruption and social dissatisfaction toward the state. The murders or attempted murders of these women gained public attention not for reasons of gender but because of the involvement of public officials.

The Discourse of Sex, Courage and Family

The courts issued guilty verdicts in all three cases. Suyono and Bastari served prison terms. Dewanto was granted leave every Independence Day for his good behaviour in prison, where he taught English to the inmates and is once again a free man. Dietje's case was officially solved, but gossip prevails concerning the actual killer and the 'tangible' motive. However, these three cases show again and again the construction and reconstruction of female (and male) sexuality and the family.

In the Supadmi and Rahmini cases, the assailants were involved sexually with the victims. According to his testimony, Suyono had a sexual relationship with Supadmi for two years. During the whole media craze about his wrongdoing, he was not portrayed as an 'extraordinary man' in needing more than one woman to fulfil his needs. There was no question of his male sexuality. The underlying premise was that an affair such as his was natural for a man. Suyono, and to some extent his subordinate Bastari, were simply regarded as soldiers who happened to forget their Armed Forces oath,[44] so they could not be considered 'courageous' soldiers. The importance of the verdict, according to the judge, was that it gave a cautionary example to the police and military corps and to the society at large.[45]

Mrs Supadmi's actions, however, were not regarded as exemplary, even though her struggle to hold her breath, pretending she was dead, concealing the pain she experienced, and realizing that the two men she trusted wanted her dead, were acts of incredible courage. For Mrs Supadmi herself and for those who sympathized with her, her phrase 'God still protected me' was a means of resistance. However, this phrase gave credit to God rather than to her own strength. Because of her profession, her courage was not assumed to be something that people could learn from. After the trial was over, the Indonesian Film Artist Association (PARFI, Persatuan Artis Film Indonesia) successfully protested an attempt to have her play herself in a movie about her case. The association argued that by making Mrs Supadmi a movie star, the image of the police department would be devastated. Mrs Supadmi brought a lawsuit against PARFI through the LBH (Lembaga Bantuan Hukum, Legal Aid Organization) but to no avail.[46]

During the time when Suyono and Bastari were being sentenced, and the news broke about the murder of Siti Rahmini by her 'respected' husband, a woman activist came to me and asked, 'Don't you think we need to give a "family hero" medal ... to Suyono and Dewanto for protecting their families?'

In both cases – the attempted murder of Mrs Supadmi and the murder of Siti Rahmini – the perpetrators gained some sympathy for what they did to save the 'good family' from destruction. Subconsciously, violence against women and even the act of murder were in these circumstances thought to be understandable, if not justified. However, 'saving the family' seems to have been seen as solely a male motivation.

Helping, protecting and saving the family could well be the very reason that Mrs Supadmi, a village girl, became a call girl, why Siti Rahmini secretly married a man of high status and economic stability, and why Dietje was involved in modelling and planned to move into the real estate business. These women's sacrifices for their families were never mentioned nor credited. Instead, they were – to a lesser degree in Dietje's case – perceived as 'women who lusted to destroy the family'.[47]

As for Dewanto's devotion to family, there was a contradiction unexplored by both the media and the public. If he was understood to have plotted the murder of his second wife (the mother of two of his children) in order to protect his 'first' family, then there must be more than one category of family: one that is to be protected, and one 'that is not so important', regardless of the offspring.

Blaming the Victim and Beyond

The New Order government's policy on wives and women of civil employees emphasized and reformulated the role of women as mothers whose responsibility it is to conserve the order of the nation and its community.[48] The media never mentioned whether Supadmi and Rahmini were good mothers. Both fell into the category of 'the other woman', and both were daughters of poor parents from remote villages. In contrast, Dietje was represented as a feminine woman and wonderful mother and wife. Her alleged affairs with numerous powerful business and political figures did not taint the image that the media drew. In Dietje's case, her marital status and her own and her husband's class background protected her from a vicious media attack on her character. Supadmi was identified by judges, defence lawyers and the media as 'different' from other women. Rahmini's death was marked as a warning to wives of their husband's secret marriages with 'other' women. A new regulation barring polygamous marriage for all civil service men was enacted after this case. Although many women, among them members of Dharma Wanita and Kowani, supported the regulation, some found that it also made it harder for wives of government employees to file for a divorce. The lesson popularly drawn from Dietje's death, in contrast, concerned the dangers of ambition in a woman.

The three women were delineated as being outside the norm, women who have crossed the line drawn by tradition and the state's ideology of womanhood. In media representations and in public gossip concerning these three cases, women were again reminded that there are two distinct categories based on sexuality: the good and the bad. This parallels the finding of North American and European feminists who have examined themes in the cases of sex murders and serial killings: female prostitutes are portrayed as the 'natural' victims of their killers.[49] The acts of the killers are unforgivable, but their motivations are understood by society at large and are portrayed as not having anything to do with misogyny or patriarchy.[50] However, there are major differences between the construction of the killer in sex and serial murder cases and in the wife–mistress murders examined here.

The serial and sex murderers analysed in Western studies are depicted as half-beast, half-men – sexual deviants, not normal men. This is in sharp contrast to the way the accused in the cases discussed here were looked at; their normality was not questioned. The claim that their motives were to protect their families assumed that they were 'normal', even upstanding family men. In these cases, it was the victim who was demonized. The victim was 'abnormal' and different from respectable women. She was pictured as greedy, nagging, loose, over-sexual; always demanding the impossible, she was *kurang pasrah* (not submissive enough). This was true for all of the women in these cases except for Dietje who, because of her class, escaped this stigmatization.

Even though the media made the attempted murder of Mrs Supadmi an example of how corrupt a police officer could be and demanded a conviction to discourage similar crimes of corruption, it simply could not refrain from also blaming the victim. Although Dietje was not overtly portrayed as a 'bad woman'[51] her death was seen as containing a lesson: 'if she had been more like any other wife, she might still be alive today'. A myth was constructed that these women were in some sense deserving victims of male violence.

Anti-government sentiment and resentment against army and bureaucratic corruption fuelled the media's frenzied interest in the Supadmi and Dietje cases and to some extent the Rahmini case. Although there were other sex murder cases during this period, only these three attracted media attention. Because the defendants were politically prominent, the cases afforded the media a rare opportunity for covert criticism of the power structure. Yet precisely this focus acted to obscure the equally important issue of male violence against women.

Notes

1. There were some other cases, either solved or unsolved: the murder of Dewi, a career woman whose office was in the Sahid-Jaya Hotel, Jakarta; the murder of Julia Jarsin, a film actress, also in Jakarta; and that of an unknown woman in Makasar, Sulawesi. These three cases gained media attention when first discovered, but inspired less public discourse and political gossip than the three cases discussed in this chapter. In my opinion, this was because they lacked a political dimension with state officials as perpetrators. In 1989 there was another brutal killing in a style known as *mayat dipotong tujuh* (a corpse chopped into seven). The media sensationalized the case, the murderer was quickly arrested, put on trial and convicted. This case was a classic representation of violence against women: the victim's husband had a secret wife, and claimed that he had to kill his first wife because day in and day out she treated him with disrespect, i.e. she never cooked breakfast and made him clean her shoes every morning before she left for work. The victim was represented as a bad wife, although the husband was convicted.
2. The New Order is the term used by the military government to refer to its regime, officially established in 1966....
3. See Hans Thoolen (ed.) (1987) *Indonesia and the Rule of Law: Twenty Years of*

New Order Government: A Study, pp. 86–8. London: Pinter.

4. Ibid., pp. 90–1.

5. *Prit* is the sound of a whistle; *jigo* is a slang term, originally from Chinese, for 'five hundred'. '*Prit-jigo*' means that once a policeman blows his (they are mostly men) whistle, he extorts 500 rupiahs.

6. When René, a student from the Bandung Institute of Technology (ITB), was killed after a soccer match between the police academy and ITB, sentiment against ABTI (the Indonesian armed forces, which includes the police) increased. Among the banners carried by students of ITB during the funeral procession was 'Prit-jigo' and 'ABRI Mana Janjimu' ['ABRI, what about your promises?').

7. During the Malari Affair, for example, during the riot following the student demonstration, Jl. Blora, a street known for its steam-bath and massage parlour houses (covert prostitution operations), was one of the targets of mass anger for its sex business.

8. See Yuyu A.N. Krisna (1979) Menyelusuri Remang-Remang Jakarta, *Sinar Harapan*.

9. Ibid., pp. 42–4.

10. Ibid.

11. It adhered to the traditional distinction between male and female sex drives. The book's introduction by Indonesian novelist Ashadi Siregar merely offered some views about how prostitutes, in pursuit of their own dreams, exchanged sex for money and a glamorous life. He implies that such an exchange is unacceptable to 'normal' women.

12. See Sukanti Suryochondro (1984) *Potret Pergaraken Wanita di Indonesia*. Jakarta: Rajawali; Saskia E. Wieringa (1985) The perfumed nightmare: some notes on the Indonesian women's movement, Working Paper, Sub-Series on Women's History and Development, no. 5. The Hague: Institute of Social Studies.

13. This was especially true during the first decades of the New Order. In the beginning of the 1980s non-goverment organizations appeared voicing feminist issues. See Wieringa, op. cit.

14. According to the New Order government, the rationale for forming Dharma Wanita was to strengthen national unity, to secure the loyalty of government employees, to increase political stability, to concentrate the energy of the civil service on assisting the economic development plan, and to encourage the wives of government employees to support their husbands' careers and responsibilities. Other goals of this organization formulated by the New Order government included: giving guidance in promoting and strengthening women's consciousness and responsibility toward the nation, promoting the channelling of 'sisterly' sentiments under one national banner, mobilizing all wives' organizations in the direction of service to the nation. Kongres Wanita Indonesia (Kowani) (1978) *Sejarah Setengah Abad Pergerakan Wanita Indonesia*. Jakarta: Balai Pustaka; Suryochondro, op. cit.

15. See Wieringa, op. cit; Hardijto Notopuro (1984) *Pernan Wanita dalam Masa Pembangunan di Indonesia*. Jakarta: Ghalia Indonesia; Slamet Widarto Prodjohadidjo (1974) *Pengertain Gerkan P.K.K. dan Strktur Organisari*. Yogyakarta: DPRD-DIY.

16. The New Order state ideology concerning women is not without contradictions. In the late 1970s the government, through its Ministry of Women's Affairs, campaigned for a 'women and development' programme, and encouraged women to participate in the labour force through their *perain ganda wanita* (double roles of women). In the 1980s the New Order government promoted the sending of women to work in the Middle Eastern countries. Unmarried and married women were eligible for this employment opportunity, leaving their families for long periods. The *Panca Dharma Wanita* precept of being a good mother and caring for children was apparently irrelevant in this case.

17. They both had been jailed from the day they surrendered to the police until the day of the sentencing. The six-year, six-month period was counted from the first day they were jailed, not from the day of the verdict.

18. *Kompas*, 3 April 1981.

19. *Sinar Harapan*, 27 August 1980.

20. *Bedta Budnd*, 4 September 1980; *Kompas*, 8 October 1980; *Sinar Harapan*, 27 August 1980.

21. See *Bedta Budnd, 4 September 1980*.

22. Ibid.

23. See, for example, *Sinar Harapan*, 4 October 1980.

24. Antara, 12 September 1980.

25. On the other hand, her case was also useful for the state's campaign, showing its attempts to eradicate corruption.

26. *Sinar Harapan*, 15 March 1981. 'Mrs Ludewiji' is another name for Mrs Supadmi.

27. *Sinar Harapan*, 27 March 1981.

28. See *Kompas*, 12 March 1981.

29. *Kompas*, 12 March 1981.

30. Title of an article in *Suara Karya*, 8 May 1981.

31. *Kompas*, 3 May 1981.

32. *Sinar Harapan*, 17 May 1981.

33. *Kompas*, 24 March 1981.

34. *Kompas*, 7 December 1981.

35. Interviews with her relatives, families and people in modelling and the fashion business, conducted soon after her death, pointed out that she really loved her husband and children and was a very soft-hearted, sweet and hard-working woman. *Kompas*, 25 September 1986; *Sinar Harapan*, 1 October 1986; *Tempo*, 20 September 1986.

36. This might not be the case in terms of the rumours circulating around her death, but the media themselves did not represent her the way they sexualized Mrs Supadmi.

37. *Jakarta Post*, 3 October 1986; *Kompas*, 25 September 1986; *Merdeka*, 3 October 1986; *Tempo*, 4 October 1986.
38. See *Sinar Harapan*, 8 October 1986.
39. See Depari, 'Kasus Diege dan Ciltra Polri', in *Kompas*, 11 October 1986, *Merdeka*, 10 December 1986.
40. *Sinar Harapan*, 30 September 1986.
41. *Berita Buana*, 30 December 1986.
42. Soenarto Sukartono, 'Lagi tentang Kasus Mahmilti III di Surabaya', *Kompas*, 11 April 1986.
43. Other murder cases, such as that of Mrs Dewi, a professional woman who was killed in her office, and that of Julia Jarsin, a film actress, did not provoke as much media attention or public gossip as the three cases discussed in this chapter. They lacked the political dimension, as no state officials were implicated as perpetrators.
44. *Kompas*, 27 March 1981.
45. See *Kompas*, 27 March 1981.
46. See *Kompas*, 25 July 1981.
47. After the trial ended, a female journalist interviewed the wife of Suyono. She was being pictured as a soft-hearted, soft-spoken and understanding wife. About Mrs Supadmi, Suyono's wife said, 'I feel sorry for her. To have to live by disturbing the peace of other people's households and looking for a husband from door to door. Certainly there should be many ways to go to Rome.' *Sinar Harapan*, 14 July 1981.
48. See Wieringa, op. cit.
49. Jane Caputi (1989) The sexual politics of murder, *Gender and Society*, 3(4); Wendy Holloway (1981) 'I just want to kill a woman'. Why? The Ripper and male sexuality, *Feminist Review*, 9 October; Drew Humphries and Susan Carringelia-MacDonald (1990) Murdered mothers, missing wives: reconsidering female victimization, *Social Justice*, 17(2); Judith R. Walkowitz (1982) Jack the Ripper and the myth of male violence, *Feminist Studies*, 8(3). 'Sickness' (of the murderers) and 'sin' (of the victim) are the two discursive ingredients in the construction of victim, gender and sexuality.
50. See Deborah Cameron and Elizabeth Frazer (1987) *The Lust to Kill*, p. 14. New York: New York University Press.
51. There were no startling revelations, no sexual scandal with important people involved.

OLD STRATEGIES FOR NEW TEXTS

6

HOW AMERICAN TELEVISION IS CREATING AND TREATING LESBIAN CHARACTERS

Marguerite Moritz

In response to the women's liberation movement, Hollywood in the 1970s began producing what came to be called New Women's films. *Alice Doesn't Live Here Anymore* (1975), *Julia* (1977), *An Unmarried Woman* (1977) and *Starting Over* (1979) are among the most popular of that genre, which is generally characterized by its focus on women seeking new definitions of themselves and their personal relationships. Those movies and many more like them have been the centre of several important discussions among feminist critics who have demonstrated the many ways in which the visual and narrative codes of cinema have often worked to restore female characters to their 'proper place', often within the traditional family structure.

These film strategies have direct application to the portrayal of women on American television. Prime-time television programming, like Hollywood cinema, can be considered 'the limiting case, the ideal-type', so pervasive that it serves as a 'model for modes of production and modes of representation' all over the world (Kuhn 1982: 21). Just as dominant cinema relies on fictional characters playing out their roles in a narrative context, so too does American television find its entertainment value in storytelling. The similarities and connections between film and television are also clear from an institutional standpoint. Indeed, many Hollywood studios now routinely produce television programming while aspiring Hollywood film-makers often begin their careers in television. And most significantly, these industries share a long and well-documented history of being white, male, heterosexual and capitalist both in terms of what they produce and how they produce it (Kuhn 1982: 25).

Just as feminist film critics have demonstrated that the post-liberation women created by Hollywood are often not so liberated after all, this essay will show that lesbian characters created for prime-time American television may offer viewers little more than new texts created with old strategies in mind.

Recuperation and Ambiguity in Hollywood Cinema

Early Hollywood cinema in its classic era of big studio and big star films provided several stories in which strong women characters defy convention, only to be brought to the brink of ruin by their bold behaviour. Before the closing credits, however, they are rescued from their shaky precipice and repositioned in a more socially acceptable space. *Mildred Pierce* (1945), a melodramatic murder mystery starring Joan Crawford, offers perhaps the most analysed example of how this kind of recuperation plays out.

The main character, in the person of Crawford, is possessed of traits not typically associated with her wife–mother–homemaker status. She is ambitious, aggressive, determined and decisive. When her unemployed husband fails to provide sufficiently for her and her daughters, she asserts herself, proceeding to banish him from their home and to accomplish what he apparently cannot. Within a short time the uneducated but savvy Mildred builds up a booming restaurant business. But then success begins to take its toll. Mildred's personal life starts to unravel. Her youngest daughter succumbs to a tragic illness. Her oldest daughter is defiant and deceitful. And when it looks as though Mildred herself will be revealed as a murderer, the real culprit is uncovered and a devastated Mildred is taken back by her husband, presumably ready to retreat from her role in the outside world.

> Mildred's take-over of the place of the father has brought about the collapse of all social and moral order in her world. ... In the face of impending chaos and confusion the patriarchal order is called upon to reassert itself and take the Law back into its own hands, divesting women completely of any power they may have gained while the patriarchal order was temporarily impaired. This involves establishing the truth without a doubt, restoring 'normal' sexual relationships and reconstituting the family in spite of the pain and suffering which such repressive action must cause. (Cook 1978: 75)

The outcome presented in *Mildred Pierce* is seen by many feminist critics as prototypical of classical Hollywood films portraying strong female characters. 'Often narrative closure itself seems to necessitate the resolution of problems and ambiguities brought up by the desire of women characters to go to work, to be sexual beings, or both. The end of the story becomes the solution of that story when the woman is returned to her "proper" place, i.e., with her husband, at home' (Walker 1982: 167). While other narrative closures for these kinds of stories do exist, they run a narrow range. Kuhn suggests that recuperation is inevitable and is accomplished 'thematically in a limited number of ways: a woman character may be restored to the family by falling in love, by "getting her man," by getting married, or otherwise accepting a "normative" female role. If not, she may be directly punished for her narrative and social transgression by exclusion, outlawing or even death' (Kuhn 1982: 34).

Given that they were prompted by the women's rights movement and directed toward a more liberated female audience, it might be expected that the New Women's films of the 1970s would deal differently with narrative closure. But like history, Hollywood has a way of repeating itself. *Klute* (1971), starring Jane Fonda as prostitute Bree Daniels, is one of the first of this genre and, like *Mildred Pierce*, one of the most analysed. At the time of its release, some feminists hailed the film for its gripping portrayal of a strong woman by a politically active star. '*Klute* became a focus of critical attention because of the questions it raised about audience pleasure. It immediately attracted feminist approval for the powerful image of Jane Fonda's Bree Daniels. She seemed to be, at last, a positive Hollywood heroine, an "independent" woman for other women to identify with' (Lovell and Frith 1981: 15). But many other feminist writers developed a far different reading of the film. Gledhill argues that precisely because of its contemporariness, this film text is more able to mask its real message. For her, the Bree Daniel's role is simply an updated version of the evil woman created in 1940s film noir.

> The film is trying to articulate, within the ambience of the thriller, a modern version of the independent woman, conceived of as the sexually liberated, unattached, hip woman and without mentioning feminism or women's liberation arguably trying to cash in on these concerns to enhance the modernity of the type. (Gledhill 1978: 114)

I would argue that *Klute*'s production of the stereotype is no different in its ultimate effect, and that the film operates in a profoundly anti-feminist way, perhaps even more so than the 1940s thrillers from which it derives.

Not all of Hollywood's efforts to woo the New Women's audience relied on the restoration of male dominance. In fact, one of the marks of these films is their use of textual ambiguity. *Julia* is a case in point. The film is an account of writer Lillian Hellman (played by Jane Fonda) and her revolutionary friend Julia (Vanessa Redgrave). The film clearly raises a question as to whether the two women had a romantic sexual relationship, yet deliberately avoids answering it. 'While most reviewers agree that the relationship portrayed between the women is central to the film ... there are almost as many opinions as there are reviews concerning the precise nature of that relationship' (Kuhn 1982: 38). In *An Unmarried Woman* and *Alice Doesn't Live Here Anymore*, ambiguity itself becomes a form of resolution. By making the future of the female protagonist unclear, these texts provide a way in which the narrative can simultaneously appeal to audiences that want to see patriarchy challenged and those that expect to see it restored.

> It would be problematic for a cinematic institution whose products are directed at a politically heterogeneous audience overtly to take up positions which might alienate certain sections of that audience. Films whose address sustains a degree of polysemy – which open up rather than restrict potential readings, in other words – may appeal to a relatively broad-based audience. Openness permits readings to be made which accord more or less with spectators' prior stances on feminist issues. Julia illustrates the point quite well: while lesbians may be free to read the film as an affirmation of lesbianism, such a reading – just as it is not ruled out – is by no means privileged by the text. (Kuhn 1982: 139)

If strong female characters have typically been dealt with through recuperation or ambiguity by cinema in earlier decades, are the same strategies finding their way into American television portrayals today? The question is of particular interest when it is raised about stories with lesbian characters because these scripts might be seen as network television's most progressive efforts.

Homosexuality and American Television

During most of its history, American television effectively banned the portrayal of homosexuals. The three major networks were never legally bound to do so, but claimed instead that they were governed by what they termed matters of public taste. 'In the '50s, they couldn't use the word pregnant when Lucy was expecting a baby [on I Love Lucy],' explains Dianna Borri, NBC's manager of standards and practices in Chicago (quoted in Moritz 1989: 13). The networks contend that they reflect societal trends rather than set them. Therefore, as homosexuality has become more socially acceptable, so have gay characters.

It was only in 1973 that American television offered its first fictional portrayal of homosexuality with the made-for-TV movie *That Certain Summer*, starring Hal Holbrook as a gay father coming out to his son (Henry 1987: 43). A few other shows with homosexual themes followed, but that abruptly changed in 1980 when a more conservative national mood gave rise to the Moral Majority's campaign against television shows with too much sex and violence. ABC and CBS cancelled their plans for four separate productions with gay themes and NBC revamped its *Love, Sidney* sitcom to eliminate virtually any reference to the main character's homosexuality (Moritz 1989: 14). By the second half of the 1980s, network attitudes appeared to be shifting once again, this time toward a more liberal approach to both language and story themes. The emergence of AIDS, the relatively marginalized position of broadcast television brought on by increasing cable penetration and home video ownership, the demonstrated commercial viability of gay-themed material in other mass media, and the appeal of emerging social issues in general as a backdrop for broadcast productions all contributed to the creation of a climate in which homosexuality was once again permitted to emerge on American television. Lesbian characters, always a rarity in the past, were no longer invisible.

Starting in the mid-1980s, lesbian characters and story lines began their fictional coming out, the result at least in part of a changing institutional context in which what was once taboo had become potentially viable and sellable. *Golden Girls, Kate and Allie, LA Law, Hill Street Blues, Moonlighting, Hunter* and *Hotel* – some of the most popular shows on TV – all have had episodes (since 1985) with lesbian parts. *My Two Loves*, an ABC Monday Night Movie, explored in uncommonly explicit visual detail two women involved in a love affair. In addition, ABC introduced a series in the spring of 1988 that featured prime time's first regular cast member with a lesbian identity: *Heartbeat*, an hour-long drama about a women's medical clinic, presented actress Gail Strickland as Marilyn McGrath. Her role as an older woman, a nurse practitioner, a mother and a lesbian no doubt gave her considerable demographic appeal. After its initial six-episode spring run, ABC renewed the show and put it on its fall 1988 schedule. It was cancelled later that season because of consistently weak ratings.

Of course, the fact that lesbians are now being portrayed may simply reflect the industry's current attempt to give a contemporary look to its standard fare of sitcoms, cop shows and night-time soaps. In fact, if these portrayals do nothing more than extend negative stereotypes about women in general and about lesbians in particular, then they are neither indicators of pro-social programming nor of progressive politics at the networks. It is with that in mind that we look at how five recent prime-time American television shows construct and frame lesbian characters. They are *Heartbeat* (two episodes), *Hunter, Hotel* and *Golden Girls*. These episodes were selected because the lesbian characters in them are central rather than peripheral to the structure of the narrative.

Recuperation and Narrative Closure

The most striking case of recuperation to bring about narrative closure is seen in 'From San Francisco with Love', an episode of the detective show *Hunter* in which the macho Los Angeles cop for whom the show is named tries to unravel the murders of a millionaire and his son. As the story unfolds, Hunter goes to the scene of the first murder in San Francisco and meets Sgt Valerie Foster, who originally investigated the case. She is more than cooperative, sharing not only her police files with him, but her bed as well. She claims to be eager to help break the case and introduces Hunter to the millionaire's cool, cunning, very young widow. But Sgt Foster is really trying to throw Hunter off the track. She is also plotting to murder the millionaire's son and in fact we see her calmly shoot him in the head, her way of eliminating his claim to his father's fortune.

Why is Sgt Foster doing all this? Because she is the lesbian lover of the millionaire's widow and together they plan on getting away with murder and an $80 million fortune. Eventually Hunter uncovers the fact that the cop and the widow are actually lovers, but he still cannot prove that they are murderers. Hunter now prepares a plan in which he plays on the women's basic distrust of each other. The plan works, and the widow turns the cop in. But the cop has herself covered. She produces a tape recording she secretly made on the night that the women planned the killings. Both women are therefore implicated, both are caught, and both are guilty. The recuperation in this denouement is both unambiguous and complete. The women lovers prove to be their own undoing. They have, in fact, been cunning enough to get away with murder, but their deceitfulness and lack of trust is so total that they are doomed to fail in any venture that requires mutual reliance. Thus they have transgressed by being lesbians, murderers and disloyal lovers. They obviously are beyond restoration to a 'normative' female role. For these actions, they must and will be removed from society and properly punished.

This episode of *Hunter* was considered to portray lesbians so negatively that it drew a protest from the Alliance of Gay and Lesbian Artists (AGLA), an activist group based in Los Angeles which has been working to improve the image of homosexuals on television. 'The network realized why [we protested] and afterwards came to us and asked us to submit scripts [that would be acceptable],' ACLA member Jill Blacher says (Moritz 1989: 11).

The episode of *Hotel*, an hour-long drama about the people who work in a luxury San Francisco hostelry, takes a far different approach to its narrative closure, but the recuperation of its lesbian subjects is no less complete. Here the sexual involvement of hotel co-workers Carol Bowman and Joanne Lambert comes out only after Joanne tragically dies in a car crash. Carol is left not only to grieve her lost mate but also to deal with Joanne's father, who comes from the East Coast to take home his daughter's body and her personal effects. The father has no idea that his daughter has been living with a female lover, but he finds out when a hotel attendant brings him a package from his daughter's employee locker that is addressed to him. The package contains a videotape that he watches from his suite.

> JOANNE (ON VIDEOTAPE): Happy birthday, Dad. My gift to you this year is a heart-to-heart talk, at least my half of it. I know it's never been easy between us. ... I know you never meant to be so stern, so unapproachable. ... [Carol and I have] been together for six years now, Dad. Like they say, I guess it must be love.

Enraged, the father storms into the office of the hotel's top executive, Mr McDermott, and accuses Carol Bowman of corrupting his daughter.

> LAMBERT: My daughter was always a good girl. Unfortunately, she and I were not very close. At home, she was rather shy, quiet. I always felt she was too easily led, influenced by others. One of her friends, a member of your staff, took advantage of Joanne, corrupted her. ... Whatever our problems might have been at home, my daughter was not abnormal. She dated a great deal. She was not interested in other women.
> McDERMOTT: Why are you telling me this?
> LAMBERT: Good Lord, man, isn't it obvious? This Bowman woman works with the public every single day representing you and your hotel.
> McDERMOTT: What do you want me to do? Fire her?
> LAMBERT: You certainly aren't going to leave her in a position of being able to prey on other unsuspecting young women.

Given Mr Lambert's distinct disapproval, Carol Bowman decides that he can have everything; she will be satisfied with her memories. In the final scene, we see Carol and Mr Lambert packing up Joanne's things. The opening shot has the camera positioned high above them, shooting down, which both diminishes their presence and suggests that the deceased lover,

Joanne, may be looking on from above. When Mr Lambert finds a doll that he gave his daughter at age 5, he begins to cry and Carol comes to his side to comfort him.

> LAMBERT: Maybe you're right. Maybe memories are the most important things. I was always a better talker than a listener. ... Maybe it's time I started listening a little.
> CAROL: What do you mean?
> LAMBERT: You're the only one who can help me fill in all the blanks. Keep what's important to you. ... Just do me a favour. Just take me through them, tell me what they meant ... and maybe I can understand who Joanne grew up to be while I wasn't looking.

They embrace and the camera begins a long, slow pullback, again from the perspective of Joanne, looking on from above.

This narrative closure is ambiguous in that it does offer a degree of hope and acceptance for the lesbian lover. The irate father does, after all, admit that he wants and needs to know about his daughter's life, and that he will rely on her lover to give him that very personal information. Even though the daughter and her lover are both granted a measure of acceptance, that happens only after their relationship has been irrevocably terminated. The daughter is recuperated by virtue of her ultimate exclusion, and her lover is restored only now that she no longer is in the illicit relationship. In other words, the terms of their acceptance are based on their separation by death.

In two episodes of *Heartbeat* with lesbian themes, recuperation is achieved not through punishment or death but through the reaffirmation of patriarchy as it plays out in the lives of the other characters in the show. The fifth and sixth episodes, the final two programmes of the show's first season, were aired on two consecutive nights during the critical May ratings sweeps. The narrative involves four separate story lines, each one tracking a problematic relationship in which medical staff members are embroiled. One follows an impotent doctor and his impatient fiancée, a second involves the resident psychiatrist's efforts to deal with his life after his marriage falls apart, and the third deals with a jealous romance between two doctors on the staff. The lesbian story centres on nurse practitioner Marilyn McGrath and her unresolved relationship with her daughter Allison. Allison is coming back to California to be married in the home of her father, which her mother had left a decade earlier after revealing her lesbian identity. She makes it clear that she does not want her mother's lover, Patti, to attend the wedding, that she does not accept her mother's lifestyle, and that she is embarrassed by it.

ALLISON: Dad and Elaine [his new wife] would be more comfortable if you sat in the front row but didn't walk down the aisle.
MARILYN: I see. Is that what you want?
ALLISON: I want things to go smoothly.
MARILYN: So do I. Patti and I will do anything we can to help.
ALLISON: I don't want there to be any tension. I don't think it would be a good idea for you to bring her. I'm sure she's a lovely person but a lot of my friends don't know about you.

Marilyn agrees to her daughter's request but later feels guilty and upset. ('She doesn't want you to come to her wedding and I agreed,' she confesses to lover Patti. 'I don't want to go without you. I want to be with my partner.') Her lover, however, assures her that she has done the right thing.

It is Patti who urges Marilyn to make amends with her daughter ('It's your daughter and it's the biggest piece of unfinished business in your life. You've got to try to get through to her. Go and see her.') Marilyn indeed does go back to the family home she once left and has a painful exchange with Allison.

ALLISON: It's not that you're a lesbian. That's not what bothers me. It's, why did you marry Dad? Why did you have me?
MARILYN: I thought I could make a life with your father. I wasn't in love, but I liked him and I wanted children. And I decided I could keep those different feelings buried deep within me.
ALLISON: But you left me.
MARILYN: I didn't have a choice. It was the hardest thing I ever did, but believe me it would have been more devastating for you if I had stayed.

After Marilyn assures Allison that she will not turn out to be a lesbian too, the mother and daughter cry, embrace and apparently patch up their differences. Patti is allowed to go to the wedding, and it is here that all four story lines are resolved.

The scene opens with a shot of Marilyn and Patti seated next to each other in the front row, as the organist plays 'Here Comes the Bride'. After the ceremony, the story turns to the still impotent doctor and his increasingly uninterested fiancée as they line up at the buffet table. When she strikes up a conversation with another man, the impotent doctor asserts his proprietary rights and tells the man to 'take a hike'. At this, the fiancée stalks out but the doctor catches up with her in the bedroom where she has left her coat. They quarrel. She slaps him. He grabs her, kisses her, throws her down on the bed and begins making passionate love to her, his potency obviously restored. Thus ends one story line.

Next, we see the two doctors who have been having a difficult time with their newly established relationship. She has accused him of being secretly involved with Eve, the sexy blonde breast-implant surgeon at the clinic. Only now, as they dance cheek to cheek at the reception, does she accept his pledge of love and loyalty. He kisses her fingers, she strokes his hair; they smile lovingly and embrace. Thus ends the second story line.

The third narrative concludes with the psychiatrist waiting for his car to be brought around by the attendant so he can leave the reception. The seductive Eve appears, makes sarcastic note of his depression, and strikes a very responsive chord.

EVE: What's the matter Stan? No one to dance with?
STAN (THE PSYCHIATRIST): I don't feel much like dancing.
EVE: Wedding's a little painful, huh?
STAN: You really like to kick 'em when they're down, don't you?
EVE: You call this down? No, you've got a lot more room to drop.
STAN (LOOKING ANGRY): This must be your way of showing affection, right?

The camera cuts to a close-up of Eve looking at Stan alluringly. Then we see him grab her, wrap his arms around her and kiss her. At that moment, the attendant drives up with Stan's car. Stan opens the door and pushes Eve inside.

STAN: Get in.
EVE: So doctor, where are we going?
STAN: You'll know when we get there.

The show credits start to roll as he screeches out of the driveway, apparently off to a place where they can continue what they've started.

The narrative closure in *Heartbeat* is accomplished through the restoration of the patriarchal system not just once, but four separate times, beginning with the ceremony most symbolic of patriarchy: the wedding. In direct succession we see the three heterosexual couples who have shared the narrative's focus with the homosexual couple. In each case, the resolution of their problems revolves around an overtly sexual exchange in which the men exert their virility and dominance over the women in their lives. The impotent doctor rekindles his manhood by confronting another suitor, calling his girlfriend a 'slut', and having a sexual response to getting slapped in the face. The ever-collected and rational psychiatrist finally lets loose, getting physical and assertive with a colleague whom he treats like a young thing he has picked up at a party. Even Leo, the gentle pediatrician, makes it clear he is in charge as he tells his jealous mate on the dance floor, 'If you're looking for a fight baby, you ain't gonna find it here.'

While the heterosexual couples find resolution in romance, passion and drama, the lesbian couple is depicted as utterly prim and proper, completely self-contained and unobtrusive. The narrative closure of *Heartbeat* clearly shows that what does not happen to the lesbian couple is more important than what does.

The script is open-ended or ambiguous to the extent that the lesbian couple, after a considerable struggle, has achieved a victory. But even though they have obtained permission to come to the wedding, this narrative closure does not permit them to participate in the event. Marilyn has one line of dialogue ('I think I'm going to cry'). She and Patti are seen in one shot as the processional starts and in a second shot as the ceremony opens, then they become invisible. While the heterosexual couples exhibit an outpouring of desire as the wedding reception plays out, the lesbians are politely kept from our view, never intruding on the show's vision of what it is to be a couple or to be in a romantic relationship. They agree to accept a limited place, not walking down the aisle, apparently not dancing, eating or mingling with any one but nicely tucked back in the closet, out of view from the rest of the guests and from the audience as well. The overall effect is to reaffirm the patriarchal order and to tell the audience that what really counts goes on in the heterosexual world, the arena of passion, desire and drama.

It is interesting and perhaps not simply coincidental that the one situation comedy in the group of television shows under discussion is the one show in which the narrative closure does not rely on punishment, death or exclusion to bring about narrative closure. *Golden Girls* is a half-hour sitcom that regularly features four women characters – three friends in late middle age and one of their mothers who is in her eighties. All four women live together in an upmarket Miami home. This particular episode opens with Dorothy telling her elderly mother that she's expecting a visit from her college friend Jean.

The crusty old mother, one of the more knowledgeable of this group, immediately recalls Jean as a lesbian, astonishing Dorothy.

DOROTHY: How did you know?
MOTHER: A mother knows.

Now Dorothy and her mother have to decide whether to tell Rose and Blanche, the other women in the house, about Jean's sexual identity. When Jean arrives, Dorothy and her mother take up the topic with her.

DOROTHY: I wanted to make sure it was okay with you before I told them.

JEAN: If you think they can handle it, I prefer to tell them.

At this moment Rose walks in with a tray of her special 'clown sundaes', which she makes with raisin eyes and chocolate chip noses. The gesture epitomizes Rose's lack of sophistication and general inability to grasp what is going on around her and prompts Jean to deliver this aside to Dorothy: 'It'll just be our little secret.'

As the show unfolds, Jean finds herself increasingly drawn to the kind-hearted Rose. They both grew up on farms, and both like sad movies and staying up late playing card games. Eventually, Jean tells Dorothy that she thinks she has fallen in love with Rose. Dorothy passes on the information to her mother and together they reveal the story to Blanche. Now only Rose is unaware that Jean is a lesbian and that Jean is in love with her. When Jean tries to tell her how she is feeling ('I'm quite fond of you'), Rose finally begins to suspect something.

In the final scene, Jean asks to speak with Rose alone and she explains some of what she has been going through. Since her long-time lover died last year, Jean says, she has been in mourning.

JEAN: I thought I could never care for anyone again, until I met you.

ROSE: Well I have to admit I don't understand these kinds of feelings. But if I did understand, if I were – you know – like you, I think I'd be very flattered and proud that you thought of me that way.

As the two women put their arms around each other, the crotchety old mother enters and they hasten to explain lest she get the wrong impression. But she is still one step ahead of them.

JEAN: This isn't what it looks like.

MOTHER: I know. I was listening at the door.

ROSE: Why were you listening at the door?

MOTHER: Because I'm not tall enough to see through the window.

The camera cuts to Dorothy and Blanche, who have obviously been listening in at an open window all along. They give a sheepish wave, in effect admitting their intense curiosity over the Jean and Rose affair, and bring the show to its conclusion. This narrative closure exhibits little need for recuperating the lesbian character. Jean will go back home and go on with her life and her lifestyle and will be better off knowing that she is once again willing to take risks and to engage with people. Thanks to Rose, she now realizes she can have feelings for women other than her deceased lover.

Rose will also carry on with her life but will be enriched and enlightened by her experience with Jean. This is a story ending where differences are allowed to exist. The message to the audience is that a lesbian and a straight woman can have a friendship and can accept each other without finding fault or choosing sides.

Throughout the show, however, the subject matter is never treated seriously. Instead, lesbianism is represented as outside the experience of these women, something they do not even know about. One of them confuses lesbians with Lebanese people, saying they cannot be so bad because Danny Thomas is one. Another says she may not know what a lesbian is but she could look it up in a dictionary. Only the tough old mother, who often speaks of connections with the Cosa Nostra in her native Sicily, knows about women like that. Since the topic is never treated seriously, it cannot pose a serious threat and therefore does not require any serious redress. Like the rest of the show, the ending is permitted to be basically light-hearted and humorous.

Recuperation and Cinematic Structures

One of the chief contributions of feminist film scholars to cinema studies is their work on textual analysis. This approach attempts to uncover the ways in which cinema specifically creates meanings through its visual as well as its spoken story. The analysis therefore looks not just at character and plot but also at lighting, camera framing and movement editing, and other aspects of the visual, to see how it operates in conjunction with character and plot to create specific cinematic meaning. Textual analysis is pertinent in television studies because television has adopted many of its codes directly from Hollywood cinema. It is pertinent here since in both film and television texts, at least some aspects of recuperation and ambiguity are carried out visually, not simply in accomplishing closure, but in structuring and positioning the lesbian characters throughout the narrative. Feminist film theory asks how women are *not* represented in a script; it also asks how women are represented visually, what fixed images of women are appealed to, and how these images operate interactively in the story line and in the visual structuring (Kuhn 1982: 81). We now look at these same five television programmes with these questions in mind, examining specifically how television treats lesbian characters with respect to three significant areas of depiction: sexuality, personal rights and publicity or public disclosure.

Sexuality

With the exception of the conspiring murderers in *Hunter*, none of these lesbian characters is permitted to be sexual or even romantic. The contrast between the lesbian lovers and their straight counterparts in *Heartbeat* is stark. The lesbian couple never even approaches getting physical, but the male–female couples are frequently shown in close-up passionately embracing, kissing and alluding to their love-making plans. In one instance a couple is shown undressed in the bed where the guests have left their coats at an afternoon wedding reception. At the same time, in the entire two-hour course of the show, the lesbian lovers are limited to one medium shot in which they share a limp, passionless embrace. That comes at a moment when they are reassuring each other that their problems will work out. Thus when they embrace, rather than being sexual with each other, they really are consoling each other. In the final scene there is a close-up of their hands touching, one woman's hand resting on top of the other's. Again, the context of the story makes it clear that this also is not a sexual moment. It is a tender moment and a reassuring gesture, but sexual it is not. In *Hotel*, to cite another example, the lesbians are never shown together. The script uses a videotape as a device through which to bring the dead lover on camera. It could have used that same device to show the women together. Similarly, it could have used flashback to accomplish the same purpose. But it did not. The only shot of the lesbians together is in the still photos that remain in the apartment they shared and even here there is not a hint of sexuality or romance. We see close-ups of very innocent 'vacation' pictures; the two women might just as easily be companions and friends as lovers and partners for the previous six years. One photo shows the two women bicycling with two men, as heterosexual a depiction as possible given the story line. In *Golden Girls*, recuperation is carried out in the looks, dress and demeanour of the lesbian character. First, the lesbian part is played by Lois Nettleton, a well-known and respected actress. She is feminine, quiet, soft and soft-spoken. She wears pretty dresses and high heels. Like the Carol Bowman character in *Hotel*, like Marilyn and Patti in *Heartbeat*, she is depicted visually as distinctly feminine. This kind of visual rendering combines with narrative story lines that produce characters who basically are desexualized.

The exception are the lesbian killers in *Hunter*. These characters are clearly not drawn in the timid fashion used with the other lesbians. They are at the opposite end of both the visual and the emotional spectrum. These women are obviously sexual. They dress in sophisticated, revealing clothes. ('The way she's dressed,' says Hunter's partner of Sgt Foster, 'she's got herself a date.') Of all the lesbian characters under discussion, these two are the only ones who are shown expressing their sexual passion for each other. The following exchange, for example, takes place as we see a close-up of the two women, facing each other, their bodies touching as Casey runs her hand slowly down Valerie's cheek, throat and low-cut blouse.

> CASEY: It's cold out, Val.
> VALERIE: When do I get my mink?
> CASEY: As soon as the dust clears. But you will look better in sable.

They have been given narrative permission to be sexual because they are evil and willing to use their sexuality to achieve evil ends. The young widow, after all, ensnared the millionaire into marriage, not for his love, but for his money. Her lover, Sgt Foster, slept with Hunter to see what he would reveal about his investigation ('She thought I was going to be one of those after-sex talkers,' Hunter tells his partner.) The connection seems clear: if they are sexual then they must also be vicious, greedy, deceitful, cunning, and direct inheritors of the film noir genre.

Personal rights

In both *Heartbeat* and *Hotel* the lesbian characters discover that they have limited personal rights and go on to accept that limitation without challenge. Marilyn, for example, agrees to her daughter's demand that lover Patti stay away from the wedding. When she confesses that to her lover, Patti not only shows no anger or resentment but tells Marilyn that she should agree to whatever her daughter wants so as to seize this 'golden moment'.

At another point in the show, Marilyn recounts what happened when she revealed her identity to her husband several years earlier. He effectively banished her from their home and demanded that she give up any claim on custody of their daughter. She agreed because she had little choice. Now, years later, Marilyn is still agreeing and feeling as though she has little choice. Not once does she insist on having the same rights as her ex-husband, who is bringing his new mate to the wedding without hesitation. Indeed, Marilyn's demeanour throughout conveys her sense of responsibility for having caused heartache in the daughter. While she is continually agonizing over what she did in the past and what she should do to make things better in the present, it is the daughter who is given the right to be angry and enraged. If the daughter is mature enough to marry, one might argue that she is mature enough to accept her mother's choices. Yet her mother never makes that demand. Even though Marilyn admits that she is 'terrified' to do it, we see her returning to her ex-husband's home to find her daughter and once again apologize for being who she is. Marilyn is positioned as the person who is at fault, a position with which she never takes issue. Her daughter is positioned as the person who was injured or wronged and that gives her every right to vent her considerable anger both publicly and privately.

A similar kind of inequity of rights plays out in *Hotel*, only now it is the parent who is given the right to be angry and enraged and the lesbian daughter and her lover who must seek forgiveness for their transgression.

First we see, via videotape, the deceased daughter trying to explain to her father who she is and how she lives her life. It is an explanation she could never bring herself to make in person. As in *Heartbeat*, it is the lesbian whose appearance conveys nervousness and guilt, positions that carry over to the main character in the show, her lover Carol Bowman.

This character emerges as a person without power or knowledge. We see her proceed through a series of steps, all attempts at discovering the real limitations of her world, her situation, herself. Her first step is to seek advice and emotional support from a friend and co-worker. The 'tell me what to do, Julie' scene sets the stage for her encounters with the three individuals who really can determine her future and describe her personal rights. Carol goes to three men in succession to find out her fate. First, she meets with her boss, Mr McDermott, to ask if her job is in jeopardy now that he knows about her sexual relationship with Joanne.

CAROL: Will this affect my job? I know people can be, well, over-sensitive about ... [pause] ... things.
McDERMOTT: You should know by now: the only thing Miss Frances and I are sensitive about is the way our guests are treated.

Next Carol goes to her dead lover's father and briefly puts up her one fight. She tells Mr Lambert that his daughter never got up the courage to actually send him that videotape because she was afraid of his rejection. She accuses him of rarely phoning, never visiting, and now wanting to stake his claim on a daughter he barely knew.

CAROL: You think you can just sail in here and pick up the pieces. Well, some of those pieces belong to me and you can't have them ... I'm going to fight you on this.
LAMBERT: Don't do it, Miss Bowman. I will use the courts. I will use publicity, whatever it takes, and you will regret it. I swear you will.

Finally, she consults with a lawyer, but his advice is not encouraging.

LAWYER: It's not what you or Mr Lambert wants, but what state law dictates. In the absence of a will, Joanne's family becomes her sole heir. ... Realistically, the most you could hope for is some sort of nuisance settlement, you know, to make you go away.

CAROL: But it's not fair.

LAWYER: But it is the law. You know, my advice to you is to ask yourself whether a court fight would be worth it. The time, the money, and [he gives her a knowing look] the public exposure.

It is only after these three men have spoken that Carol knows what she can and cannot do, what her rights are. Her lack of power and control over her own fate is reiterated three times over. Even though she is a lesbian she is a character very much living in and dominated by a man's world. And this she is neither willing to challenge nor to fight. Rather than expressing anger at her lack of legal standing, she acquiesces. She not only agrees to give up any claim to her small, personal treasures, but she also helps the man who is determined to take them away from her. And when he experiences the grief that she has been dealing with all along, it is she who unhesitatingly comforts him, her subservience to him emphasized all the more by her kneeling at his feet.

Public disclosure

The idea of public disclosure appears in the scripts of all five shows. In *Hunter*, the killer cop assures her lover that the worst that can happen to them is a little bad publicity. In *Hotel*, the father threatens to use publicity to win his case and the lawyer cautions that a court fight might not be worth the 'public exposure'. In *Heartbeat*, the daughter will not allow her mother's lesbian lover at her wedding because she wants things to go smoothly and because some of her friends do not know about her mother's sexual identity. The idea of keeping the lesbian character's sexual identity secret comes up in *Golden Girls* as well. And indeed, the decision is made to keep that identity private, even though the character says she prefers to be open about who she is.

Implicit in each of these constructions is the idea that public disclosure is likely to result in public scorn. This has interesting parallels in *I Passed for White*, a Hollywood film in which a light-skinned black woman tries to keep her identity hidden in an effort to win social approval or at least to avoid social rejection. Why, if being homosexual is acceptable, is it necessary for any of these characters to keep their identities secret? Obviously, the implied message in all these scripts suggests that it is not socially acceptable to be a lesbian, that caution is always advised in revealing these matters. Just as the lesbian characters show little heart for fighting for their personal rights, they show little inclination to reveal their personal identities. That message is revealed as much in how they look as in what they actually do. In *Hotel*, when her lawyer suggests that she consider the public exposure, the camera cuts to a close-up of Carol to show her horrified countenance.

Conclusion

We began this examination by asking whether the same strategies that have been used in constructing strong women characters in both early and later Hollywood films are being used today by American television in its recent introduction of lesbian characters to prime-time television. Our examination makes it clear that the answer is yes. Except for *Hunter*, in which recuperation is total, these scripts employ a certain amount of ambiguity in that lesbian characters are permitted some degree of victory in their own personal battles. But in almost every instance, that victory is balanced by other messages, both in the text and in the visual content of the show, that suggest these characters have a long way to go before achieving equal status with their heterosexual counterparts.

When we ask a question that has become central to feminist film criticism – how are these characters *not* depicted? – several interesting answers emerge. They are not depicted as sexual or passionate, even when they are labelled as lovers in the script. They are not depicted as angry, even though their circumstances suggest that they have many reasons to be so. They are not shown as independent or assertive, particularly when it comes to securing their own personal rights. They are not shown making demands but rather are seen continually agreeing to the demands of others.

When we ask how they are depicted visually, the other part of the equation falls into place. In dress and manner both, they are shown to be feminine but not sexy, never daring. Any kind of physical exchange with a female partner is either omitted altogether or drawn in the most timid way (a hand resting atop another hand, a sweet but sexless hug). Close-ups of their faces often reveal an agonizing look, a repeated suggestion that their sexuality has caused others problems and for this they must take the blame and suffer the consequences.

These are not scripts that argue for the rights, legal or otherwise, of homosexuals. They are, instead, productions designed to attract mass audiences who will have varying degrees of willingness to accept any lesbian depictions in the first place. Just as Hollywood producers have been careful to incorporate a degree of polysemy into their cinematic texts, so too are American television producers careful to avoid alienating audience members by producing scripts that might be construed as too strident. While it may be argued that these scripts are by design relatively unconcerned with gay rights and more concerned with ratings, it is also true that once-taboo subjects in both cinema and television have gained acceptance only gradually. This may not be the first choice of feminists and lesbians, but it is a first step in working toward at least a small measure of social change.

References

Cook, P. (1978) Duplicity in Mildred Pierce, in E.A. Kaplan (ed.) *Women and Film Noir*. London: British Film Institute.

Gledhill, C. (1978) *Klute*: Part 2: Feminism and *Klute*, in E.A. Kaplan (ed.) *Women and Film Noir*. London: British Film Institute.

Henry, W. (1987) That certain subject, *Channels*, April: 43–5.

Kaplan, E.A. (1982) *Women and Film*. New York: Methuen.

Kuhn, A. (1982) *Women's Pictures: Feminism and Cinema*. London: Routledge & Kegan Paul.

Lovell, T. and S. Frith (1981) How do you get pleasure? Another look at *Klute*, *Screen Education*, 39: 15–24.

Moritz, M. (1989) American television discovers gay women: the changing context of programming decisions at the networks, *Journal of Communication Inquiry*, 13(2): 62–78.

Walker, J. (1982) Feminist critical practice: female discourse in *Mildred Pierce*, *Film Readers: Feminist Film Criticism*. Evanston: Northwestern University Press.

PRETTY TOUGH
THE CULT OF FEMININITY IN WOMEN'S MAGAZINES

7

Sherrie A. Inness

While thinking about the representation of toughness in American culture, I recently visited my local Barnes & Noble bookstore to peruse its extensive collection of women's magazines. Gazing at bank after bank of magazines with covers portraying nearly identical female models was an eerie experience. *American Woman, Glamour, Cosmopolitan, Self, Vogue, Vanity Fair, Mademoiselle, She, Seventeen, Allure, Redbook, Belle, Woman's Own, New Woman, American Cheerleader, Marie Claire, Elle, Black Beauty, Pride, Ladies' Home Journal* – some of these I recognized, others I did not, but all of the cover models looked remarkably alike, despite having a variety of hair styles and clothes, and sometimes different racial backgrounds. One attribute these models had in common was their lack of toughness. They were glamorous, beautiful, feminine, and graceful – but not tough. Studying the faces that stared back at me from the display racks led me to think about the role of toughness in today's women's magazines. Is toughness as completely excluded from the pages of these magazines as their covers would lead me to believe?

Flipping through the magazines, I discovered that despite the lack of tough girls on their covers, tough women do appear in the articles, advertisements, and photographs in these magazines – especially in high-fashion magazines such as *Vogue* and *Vanity Fair*. In one copy of *Vogue*, a heavily tattooed woman glares at readers from a Calvin Klein advertisement (To Be September 1996). In another issue of *Vogue*, a woman garbed in boxing gear confronts the reader, as if challenging her to a match (Evolution March 1996). In an article from *Elle*, androgynous models wear clothing that combines '[m]asculine tailoring and feminine touches'

('Masculine' 1997: 352). As I studied women's magazines from past years, I discovered numerous other images of tough women from the 1980s and 1990s. Obviously, tough women were not as rare as I had first assumed.

Examining these 'tough' women more closely, however, I identified a variety of ways in which their toughness was undermined. Although these magazines have recently begun to show more tough-looking women, this does not mean that they are questioning the innate biological differences between men and women and their 'natural' relationship to masculinity and femininity, respectively. The magazines present a fantasy of toughness. They create a Never Never land where models can present a performance of toughness – but it is only a performance. In this imaginary universe, which is clearly demarcated as a fantasy, women can appear dressed up with all the accoutrements of toughness, but the models' location in fashion magazines undermines their toughness, reminding readers that everything they see is a fantasy of style. In addition, the magazines perpetuate the notion that toughness in women is sexy, which assures the audience that women are not abandoning their traditional roles as sex objects for men just because they are tough. This equation between women's sexuality and toughness works in a similar fashion in *The Avengers, Charlie's Angels*, and *The Bionic Woman*. The relationship between toughness and sexuality diminishes the threat that tough women pose to the dominant social order by suggesting that a woman's sexual availability and physical attractiveness will be in no way diminished by her tough actions and appearance.

Women's magazines are an especially intriguing medium to study when reflecting on the essence of toughness because they play an important role in helping to formulate gender in our culture. Yet they are still typically viewed as unworthy of scholarly attention because they are popular reading material aimed at women. In her well-known study of women's popular literature, *Loving with a Vengeance: Mass-Produced Fantasies for Women* (1982), Tania Modleski discusses the typical critical response to popular women's texts: 'Women's criticism of popular feminine narratives has generally adopted one of three attitudes: dismissiveness; hostility – tending unfortunately to be aimed at the consumers of the narratives; or, most frequently, a flippant kind of mockery' (14). She wrote these words in 1982, but they remain germane today. This perspective is gradually changing as a greater number of feminist scholars have begun to recognize the importance of what Marjorie Ferguson calls 'one of the most significant yet least studied social institutions of our time' (1983: 1).[1]

Women's magazines are an important source of information for anyone interested in our society's changing gender roles. As Naomi Wolf writes, 'women's magazines are the only products of popular culture that (unlike romances) change with women's reality, are mostly written by women for women about women's issues, and take women's concerns seriously' (1991: 71). Because of this, women's magazines show how millions of women construct their identities according to the feminine norms touted by the magazines. It is difficult for *any* woman in American society to avoid these magazines: even women who argue that they never read them are still influenced by their omnipresent images. Because of their prevalence and popularity (many of the most popular ones have readerships in the millions), women's magazines hold a powerful position when it comes to negotiating the relationship between women and toughness because they prescribe how tough their readers and other women should look and act.

The advertisements that compose the bulk of most women's magazines are just as important as the stories and their accompanying photographs in determining the construction of gendered identities. Advertising in women's magazines plays an influential role in formulating, maintaining, and altering how readers understand the construction of socially acceptable gender norms. Advertisements function in a way similar to their surrounding text, but they also have different rules:

> Advertisements use the material of everyday life, but they draw upon this material in a highly selective fashion. That which is chosen for inclusion is reintegrated into the signifying system of advertising, where this material then provides the basis for the creation of new meanings. ... Advertisements do not, therefore, simply reflect the social world but re-create it, reconstitute it, and communicate this manipulated version to the audience.[2] (Budgeon 1994: 56)

Advertisements develop a unique universe that might contain different messages about gender than the articles and photo spreads that accompany them. We must study advertisements and their surrounding texts together, analyzing the concurrent and convergent messages they convey about the constitution of toughness.

Advertisements in women's magazines often seem most adventuresome about portraying challenging and controversial images of tough women because advertising is always happy to use controversy to sell underwear, perfume, cosmetics, women's suits, or other commodities. Advertising's 'very staying power derives from its ability to mimic the social. As society changes, advertising becomes the happy chameleon, always delighted to don spring's new colors' (Barthel 1988: 13). Advertising might act like a chameleon that follows social change, but we need to be alert to the ways that advertising can also lead to social change.

Not only advertisements, but women's magazines in general do more than alter how gender is constituted in American society. They can also change how gender is perceived. As Wolf observes, women's magazines have long been 'one of the most powerful agents for changing women's roles' (1991: 64). She suggests that the magazines can change what is considered acceptable or unacceptable behavior for women. As women's magazines are widely read, they have ample opportunity to convince millions that the views expressed by the magazines are just, fair, and truthful. The magazines depict a monolithic perspective on the world, presenting their contents as 'the truth', leading readers to believe that these texts present a mimetic view of the world; the magazines do not suggest that there is a world full of people with different perspectives. In *Subculture: The Meaning of Style* (1979), Dick Hebdige describes the importance of the media in changing how their audience members perceive the world: 'The media play a crucial role in defining our experience for us. They provide us with the most available categories for classifying out the social world. It is primarily through the press, television, film, etc. that experience is organized' (1979: 84–5). Women's magazines are very much a part of this process.

Women's magazines can deliver messages that encourage social change – either progressive or conservative (and often both). Because of the complexity of women's magazines and their various target markets, a magazine might convey many messages within a single issue. Thus, it should come as no surprise that a magazine might feature a picture of a short-haired woman astride a Harley and a decidedly feminine woman with long, flowing locks in the same issue. One critic writes, 'Women's magazines posit a collective and yet multivalent female subjectivity, which they simultaneously address and construct' (Ballaster et al. 1991: 172). We shall discover that many messages are contained in women's high-fashion magazines concerning women and their relationship to toughness, not all of them consistent. Although they play with tough images of women, women's magazines often use those images to affirm the desirability of femininity for women and to help maintain traditional gender divisions between men and women.

The Cult of Femininity

'Women must "perform" femininity, and fashion is part of that performance,' write Caroline Evans and Minna Thornton (1989: 13). To understand the role that women's magazines play in perpetuating femininity as the ideal for women, it is helpful to turn to Marjorie Ferguson's book *Forever Feminine: Women's Magazines and the Cult of Femininity*

(1983), in which she discusses the association between femininity and women's magazines. According to Ferguson, 'Women's magazines collectively comprise a social institution which fosters and maintains a cult of femininity. This cult is manifested both as a social group to which all those born female can belong, and as a set of practices and beliefs: rites and rituals, sacrifices and ceremonies, whose periodic performance reaffirms a common femininity and shared group membership' (1983: 184). If we concur with Ferguson, women's magazines (and also men's, such as GQ) are deeply invested in perpetuating the idea that femininity is aligned with women and masculinity is aligned with men. Women's magazines base their appeal on being the vehicles that provide the entryway into the mysterious world of femininity, providing 'the syllabus and step-by-step instructions which help to socialise their readers into the various ages and stages of the demanding – but rewarding – state of womanhood' (Ferguson 1984: 185). Ferguson describes the rituals women undergo to perpetuate the ideology of femininity: 'Individual members are socialised into their personal and collective identities through shared rites, rituals, parables, maxims, catechisms, badges and totems, in the same way that they are habituated into making the monthly or weekly dues they contribute towards the maintenance of the edifice itself' (186). The cult is kept alive by its millions of adherents and the social apparatus, such as women's magazines, that these women support.

As long as the primary purpose of women's magazines is to sell the many commodities that are essential elements in the creation of femininity, they will be hostile to women who too openly flaunt the fact that femininity is not the 'natural' and right state of women but is, instead, only one of many choices that a woman can make in creating her subjectivity and self-presentation is a dangerous notion to a magazine empire built on selling the products needed for a woman's endless pursuit of femininity.

Women's magazines offer a fantasy that fosters in their readers a desire for a state of being that can never be achieved. In their pursuit of the spectre of perfect femininity, women are encouraged to buy both the products that the magazines promote and the magazines themselves. Since toughness is strongly associated with a lack of femininity, tough girls are a threat to this capitalist edifice; thus, female toughness must be carefully controlled so that it poses little danger to the cult of femininity that women's magazines help to build and reinforce.

Women's magazines are also successful in strengthening the connection between femininity and women because they make femininity alluring to many readers. In her book *Decoding Women's Magazines From Mademoiselle to Ms.* (1993), Ellen McCracken provides an accurate description of how women's magazines persuade their audience that the magazines' vision of femininity is highly desirable and deserves to be emulated:

> Readers are not force-fed a constellation of negative images that naturalize male dominance; rather, women's magazines exert a cultural leadership to shape consensus in which highly pleasurable codes work to naturalize social relations of power. This ostensibly common agreement about what constitutes the feminine is only achieved through a discursive struggle in which words, photos, and sometimes olfactory signs wage a semiotic battle against the everyday world which, by its mere presence, often fights back as an existential corrective to the magazine's ideal images. (1993: 3)

In other words, entire magazines are designed to offer readers a highly enjoyable reading experience that functions to perpetuate femininity as the norm; even the cagiest reader finds it difficult to resist the fantasy world of femininity in these magazines. In a similar fashion, a men's magazine like *GQ* functions to heighten the appeal of conventional masculinity.

One may ask *why* tough women appear at all in women's magazines, if the magazines are intent on maintaining the notion that femininity is the norm for women. One would think that images and narratives about tough women would undermine the emphasis on femininity. We shall find that the opposite is actually true. Tough girls do appear, but typically women's magazines use toughness to reaffirm the connection between women and femininity. In addition, toughness is often associated with women's sexuality, which makes toughness less threatening to the dominant social order than it might first appear to be – a strategy already described in the previous chapter.

Another reason tough girls appear in women's magazines is because the magazines promote more than one version of womanhood. Today, perhaps even more so than in the past, no single representation of womanhood expresses what it means to be female, and women's magazines prosper from the growing complexity of what womanhood entails: 'The journal and fashion industries thriv[e] on the instability of the very idea of what a woman [is]: the "new" woman, the working woman, the sports woman, the family woman, the sexually liberated and educated woman [are] all as much created and exploited by the journals as by the advertising apparatus' (Griggers 1990: 96). The world of women's magazines has always been open to different depictions of womanhood – a strategy that helps to sell the magazines and the commodities that they advertise to the broadest audience possible. In creating a complex, multifaceted image of what it means to be a woman today, women's magazines have made room for many new images of womanhood, including those that apparently emphasize toughness. No matter how varied these images might seem, however, they must function within narrow boundaries. Thus, a 'tough' woman might appear, but she must be model-beautiful and slender.

These superficially tough images of women do not seriously endanger the dominant cult of femininity because tough women are only a minute percentage of the women who appear in the magazines. Studying hundreds of different magazines, I found that tough women were a tiny minority, despite their growing prevalence in recent years. The magazines I perused had dozens of pictures, advertisements, and articles that featured feminine women who did not appear remotely tough; women with teased manes of hair, long lacquered nails, and slinky dresses were impossible to miss. I had to search for tough girls; I went through many magazines that did not picture a single one. The more traditional magazines such as *Family Circle, Good Housekeeping, Ladies' Home Journal*, and *Woman's Day* rarely contained images of tough women. Even lifestyle and fashion magazines (*Cosmopolitan, Essence, Glamour, Mademoiselle*, and *Redbook*) portrayed few tough women. Not surprisingly, images of toughness were more apparent in *Elle, Vanity Fair*, and *Vogue* – magazines that feature daring, risk-taking high fashion – but this does not mean that these magazines necessarily have a more progressive attitude about women's roles. We need to recognize that high-fashion magazines are careful to distance the toughness they display from the reality of everyday. To gain a comprehensive image of the tough girl in women's magazines, this chapter studies a variety of women's magazines, concentrating on the high-fashion magazines because tough women appear more commonly in them.

The paucity of tough women in *all* of these magazines is disturbing because it suggests that little support exists in the popular media for women who dress and act in ways that are regarded as tough. Although some of their traits are portrayed as desirable, tough women are depicted as outsiders to the cult of femininity and are shunted to the edges of the fictional universe of the woman's magazine. This marginalization of the tough girl presents her as an anomaly. Tough women rarely appear in television advertisements, for instance, in contrast to the common appearance of tough men. Even the television commercials that could logically portray a tough woman generally do not. For instance, the endless advertisements for home gyms usually feature a man whose pumped-up pecs bulge impressively; his leotard-clad partner is far less muscular, and she often sports lipstick and carefully coiffed hair. The dearth of tough women is one of the most visible (or invisible) signs that tough women are not socially acceptable. This chapter primarily focuses on women who *appear* tough, and despite their increasing appearances in women's magazines, they still are marginalized and have in no way gained the same societal acceptance as more feminine, softer-looking women.

Women's magazines marginalize tough women by rarely depicting them. More commonly, the magazines depict women who adopt a few attributes associated with toughness. This lack of 'real' tough women is one sign of a magazine universe that is uncomfortable with the masculine coding of toughness. These magazines only represent tough attributes that can be toned down in one way or another, assuring readers that displays of toughness pose no serious challenge to the cult of femininity that the magazines uphold. The magazines present a feminized version of toughness, which is not genuinely tough. Instead, women's toughness is depicted as a masquerade. In some ways, the magazines present an inverse to the image of toughness presented in *Charlie's Angels* and *The Bionic Woman*, in which the central women acted (somewhat) tough, but did not look tough. In women's magazines, the women look (somewhat) tough, but it is clear that their image is only skin-deep. By exploring how women's magazines describe and portray leather fashions and mannish or masculine clothing for women, this chapter will offer readers a better understanding of how the popular media manipulates the signifiers of toughness.

Leather and Lace: Undercutting Tough Styles

To understand the depiction of women's toughness in fashion magazines, it is important to consider how they describe women's leather fashions.[3] Fashion magazines often portray women wearing leather attire and must in some way negotiate the aura of toughness associated with leather. In American culture, leather is strongly associated with masculinity and tough men. Mention the word 'leather' and images of motorcycle-straddling Hell's Angels are apt to spring to mind. Leather is tough and masculine. How, then, do women's magazines present leather fashions for women?[4] Does the bad boy image of leather make it too tough, too rough for the glamorous models who fill women's magazines?

The representation of leather is interesting because, like all clothing, leather does far more than keep a person warm. Leather signifies a great deal about its wearer. In 'Fragments of a Fashionable Discourse' Kaja Silverman (1986) discusses the multiple purposes of clothing: 'Clothing and other kinds of ornamentation make the human body culturally visible' (1986: 145). She observes, 'Dress is one of the most important cultural implements for articulating and territorializing human corporeality – for mapping its erotogenic zones and for affixing sexual identity' (1986: 146).

No form of attire makes a body more visible than leather, which suggests both toughness and sexuality. Valerie Steele writes about the appeal of leather, 'Many people find black leather sexy for both men and women. . . . Not only does leather have a certain tactile appeal as a "second skin," but it may also carry a variety of erotic connotations. From Marlon Brando's black leather jacket to Saint Laurent's black leather miniskirt, the message combines seduction and danger' (1989: 62). Steele adds that leather has acquired 'tough, even sado-masochistic connotations' (62). Leather signifies many characteristics, but it is always linked to toughness, particularly in men. Leather must be presented with care in women's magazines because it potentially threatens the magazines' dominant feminine imagery with its tough connotations.

Many articles and photo spreads explicitly tone down the association between leather and toughness. One article in *Glamour* entitled 'Leather or Not' states, 'Bikers, hit your brakes. The new leathers are coming through and they're miles from tough. This year's keepers are refined, tailored' (1995: 254). An article in *Seventeen* titled 'The Leather Report' assures its readers that leather is not as tough as they might assume, commenting 'Bye-bye, biker chick: Leather's new look is more tender than tough' (1995: 137). Calling into question the common linkage between bikers' culture and leather is one way that women's magazines try to reshape leather's image, making it kinder and gentler.

When leather does appear, magazines soften its tough image by posing leather-clad women with men, especially in what appears to be a romantic entanglement. An article in *Mademoiselle*, 'Zip! The Motorcycle Jacket – Truly Cool Again' (1988), depicts four women in motorcycle jackets. Three are portrayed in sexually suggestive poses with men, and one woman is photographed alone. In this article and others, the man acts as a signifier of heterosexuality and limits the toughness of the women models by disavowing the implicit linkage between toughness and lesbianism.

Another common technique for diminishing leather's connection to toughness is to emphasize the femininity of the woman wearing the leather clothing. For example, in an advertisement for Calvin Klein from *Vanity Fair*, a female model wears leather gloves and has a black leather biker's jacket flung over her shoulders (September 1992). She wears a low-cut black dress, has long hair, and is classically beautiful and feminine. In this interplay between masculinity and femininity, femininity is the dominant signifier. There is no suggestion that this statuesque beauty is threatening traditional gender roles, despite her masculine leather jacket. The masculinity of the jacket only heightens and accentuates her predominantly feminine appearance. In an advertisement for Calvin Klein jeans, a model wears a tough black leather jacket and rides a motorcycle, but her long hair and flawless face suggest that she is still all woman (August 1994). Similarly, in a story from *Vogue* that describes fashion trends, a model straddles a motorcycle and wears a black leather jacket that would make the Fonz envious, but the large gold earrings she wears and her makeup reveal that the model has not abandoned her femininity, despite her biker's garb ('Best & the Worst' 1996: 122). In another fashion spread from *Cosmopolitan*, a boyish model wears a biker-style leather jacket ('Runway' 1996: 223). She has a short boyish haircut, but her eye makeup is quite evident, as is her lipstick. In our society, makeup and lipstick are two important markers of hetero-femininity, undermining the model's potentially lesbian-masculine presentation. In another article from *Cosmopolitan*, a model wears leather pants, which come across as far more sexy than tough because she has a sultry, come-hither look ('Runway' 1996: 219). By stressing the femininity and heterosexuality of models who wear leather fashions, women's magazines convey to readers that leather attire, despite its tough tradition rooted in images of James Dean and other bad-boy heroes, only enhances a woman's femininity.

Another way women's magazines mitigate the toughness of leather attire is by frequently including pictures, fashion spreads, and articles that stress the importance of combining a leather item with a more feminine piece of clothing. In one picture, a frilly top accompanies a black leather mini-skirt with the reassuring caption: 'Bad-girl black leather looks sweet when it meets a tiny top or ruffled shirt' ('The Leather Report' 1995: 139). A fashion spread from *Vogue* suggests that even 'the traditional leather jacket softens up for spring' when made from white leather instead of black ('Pale' 1996: 316). In a fashion spread from *Vanity Fair*, a tough-looking leather bustier is combined with a silk skirt ('Funny' 1997: 91). Not only is the toughness attributed to the leather undermined when presented in the form of a bustier, a piece of clothing very much attached to femininity and sexuality, it is also undermined by associating it with the softness and femininity of silk. Combining styles associated with masculinity and femininity sends out a complex signal to viewers because the 'values of "masculine" and "feminine" in style are ultimately bound up with the values placed on actual male and female roles in social and sexual life' (Williamson 1986: 53). Masculine styles are connected with authority, prestige, and power – attributes associated with men. Feminine styles are connected with softness, delicacy, and powerlessness, which is why women in business often wear outfits that have masculine characteristics. Feminine and frilly outfits would typically be interpreted as wielding less power. Thus, combining the masculinity of leather with the femininity of other clothing is one way to diminish the masculine strength and authority that are often conveyed by leather.

Women's magazines frequently combine masculine and feminine styles, and not only with leather fashions.[5] For example, *Mademoiselle* contains a fashion spread that displays 'tough but pretty party clothes that wear as well as *West Side Story*' ('Stay Cool' 1995: 159). Another spread from *Mademoiselle*, 'White-Collar Cool,' portrays one model in a denim jacket combined with a frilly lace collar and another model in a leather jacket paired with big earrings and a flouncy blouse. The spread has semi tough headings such as 'Want to make something of it? Punch up a pastel shirt with a tight, streetwise skirt' ('Stay Cool' 1995: 161). In a photo spread entitled 'Pretty Tough' from *Seventeen* magazine, jean jackets are combined with bikinis to give a look that is attractive but cool. One model is dressed in a 'heat black' jacket that 'cruises over a pretty polka-dot maillot' (1988: 169). Another wears a 'bleached-out denim jacket (skimming the midriff) [that] toughens up a sweet peach bikini' (170). In a fashion spread from *Cosmopolitan* entitled 'Feminine Denim' (1993), a classic men's-style denim shirt is paired with high heels and bikini underwear (158). These examples show how customary it is for women's magazines to combine tough clothing with feminine, frilly attire – a sign of a culture that is ill at ease with women adopting too many characteristics associated with men and masculinity because of their association with lesbianism. The fashion styles that fill women's magazines suggest a great deal about how men and women have been segregated into separate spheres by gender. Even when tough fashions are not shown, their absence speaks as loudly as their presence, a sign that being tough is still not perceived as acceptable for women.

Being a Boy: Girls in Drag

Wearing men's clothing or severely masculine clothing is another signifier of toughness that women have adopted. For centuries women have worn men's clothing for many reasons: to travel more safely, to find employment, to express themselves, and for physical comfort and ease of movement. 'Women have opted periodically – and during certain periods with great fervor – to incorporate into their personas insignia of male status and masculinity' (Davis 1992: 33). Wearing men's clothing or very masculine clothing is also a fashion trend that has appeared and reappeared in women's fashion throughout much of the twentieth century becoming more popular than ever in the 1980s and 1990s.

When I initially began thinking about this subject, I assumed that magazines would be hostile to women wearing men's clothing or very masculine-style attire. After all, American culture has long been uneasy about cross-dressing for both men and women, and for centuries cross-dressing has been tightly controlled and policed.[6] Even today, a woman who dresses in extremely masculine attire is likely to meet with public ridicule. But women dressed in men's clothing or mannish clothing do make appearances in women's magazines, particularly those devoted to high fashion. Clearly, women's magazines allow for gender play and even gender bending. As the authors of *Women's Worlds: Ideology, Femininity and the Woman's Magazine* (1991) suggest, 'the women's magazine must be understood as a cultural form in which, since its inception, definitions and understandings of gender difference have been negotiated and contested rather than taken for granted or imposed' (Ballaster et al. 1991: 176). Despite the space that women's magazines devote to different images of womanhood, the same magazines make sure that cross-dressing and wearing mannish clothing are carefully contained. Women who garb themselves in masculine-style clothing are a distinct minority in women's magazines, and cross-dressing will probably never be more than an oddity.

In addition to challenging gender roles, one of the reasons mannish attire is potentially dangerous is because American culture assumes a strong correlation between lesbianism and masculine clothing for women. I am not arguing that women's magazines *always* wish to squelch the possibility of lesbianism. In 'Commodity Lesbianism', Danae Clark points out the relatively frequent appearance of women in the fashion industry who look like lesbians: 'In fashion magazines such as *Elle* and *Mirabella*, and in mail-order catalogs such as *Tweeds, J. Crew* and *Victoria's Secret*, advertisers (whether knowingly or not) are capitalizing upon a dual market strategy that packages gender ambiguity and speaks, at least indirectly, to the lesbian consumer market' (1991: 186). Clark discusses the ways that magazines use a strategy she refers to as 'gay window advertising' in order to appeal to a larger audience: 'Generally, gay window ads avoid explicit references to heterosexuality by depicting only one individual or same-sexed individuals within the representational frame. In addition, these models bear the signifiers of sexual ambiguity or androgynous style' (1991: 183). Clark builds a persuasive argument about gay window dressing and how magazines seek to appeal to the largest possible audience of consumers, whatever their sexual orientation might be. It is equally important to recognize that magazines that might sometimes, whether knowingly or not, use an image that could be interpreted as lesbian are also deeply invested in maintaining the heterosexuality of their focus. A few images that could be interpreted as lesbian do not interfere with the countless images that are strongly coded as heterosexual. In a similar way, mannish or masculine clothing can appear in women's magazines, but it is still overwhelmed by the more feminine attire that is far more prevalent.

Women's magazines must carefully negotiate how to present women in attire that appears mannish. In *New Woman*, one fashion spread featuring masculine-style clothing assures readers, 'Though inspired by classic menswear fabrics and tailoring, this fall's fashions are anything but mannish' ('Men's Department' 1995: 106). Being mannish must be avoided at all costs, which is why an article from *Essence* entitled 'My Style' suggests that a woman might soften up a man's suit by combining it with 'a lacy camisole and pretty jewelry' (1996: 142). Another article from *Harper's Bazaar* about menswear for women proclaims, 'Menswear influences are being seen again, now with distinctly feminine interpretations' (Lebowitz 1998: 208). This article also emphasizes the femininity of women by focusing on the makeup that a woman should have on while wearing men's clothing or clothing influenced by men's styles. Magazines walk a tightrope. They wish to feature clothing and styles commonly associated with men because this is one mildly scandalous way to sell a new look, but they do not want to suggest that women are usurping men's roles. Because women's magazines are built on maintaining femininity as the cultural norm, portraying women who appear too mannish, too masculine, or too tough is antithetical to the magazines' entire aim.

Dressing in men's clothing is such a delicate issue to negotiate that numerous fashion spreads in *Mademoiselle, Cosmopolitan*, and other women's magazines address the subject of how girls should wear boys' clothing. In the *Mademoiselle* article 'Full Pants Ahead' 1988 a photo spread is developed around women wearing masculine-style clothing, showing that such clothing need not interfere with a woman's femininity. The most peculiar story I have read on women wearing men's attire appeared in *Essence*. In this photo spread, the actor Mario Van Peebles, dressed as a private eye, tracks down a group of women who have been stealing suits from men's wardrobes. The last page of the piece features a photograph of Van Peebles wearing only his boxer shorts as he flees from the women he has been pursuing. They flaunt his clothing, which they have stolen. The caption reads: 'Seems the "game" had to teach Sonny a lesson. There's nothing wrong with women wearing menswear' ('The Great Suit' 1988: 91). Notice that the women, not the man, end up with the pants, which represent power and authority. This article suggests a great deal about society's fears concerning what happens in a topsy-turvy world where the girls wear the pants. Fifty years ago such a portrayal would have been unthinkable. Today, when a woman's magazine makes such a statement, it encourages readers to think about the significance of clothing and to rethink their relationship to it, perhaps even to wonder whether men's clothing is also acceptable for women.

When women in men's clothing do make an appearance in women's magazines, a variety of strategies are used to defuse the danger they pose to the divisions between men and women ordained by society:

> Notwithstanding fashion's frequent encouragement to women to borrow items and modes of men's dress, the norms of Western society demand that gender identity be grounded finally in some irreducible claim that is clearly either male or female, not both or some indeterminate middling state. ... It is characteristic, therefore, for cross-gender clothing signals, even the more common and variegated women's borrowings from men, to be accompanied by some symbolic qualification, contradiction, jibe, irony, ... that in effect advises the viewer not to take the cross-gender representation at face value. (Davis 1992: 42)

One way to assure readers of the femaleness of a subject is to include a touch of femininity to limit the toughness of men's clothing or mannish clothing worn by women. As long as the femaleness and the femininity of the models is evident, then the cross-dress attire becomes nothing more than a costume. For example, the women who model the male-style clothing in 'Full Pants Ahead' are all notably feminine. Though they are wearing such traditionally male clothing as ties, trousers, and pin-striped men's shirts, there is no possibility that a reader could mistake these women for men. A few of the models even flaunt clear signs of femininity, such as a purse. Similarly, a fashion article in *Essence* that describes 'suits with soldier chic' makes sure to inform its readers that girls will still be girls, even while wearing highly masculine attire: 'Whether military-inspired with epaulets, multiple pockets, gold buttons and an army green-and-khaki palette, or borrowed from the boys with tweeds and pinstripes in grays and camel, these new uniforms speak of power and a strong work ethic. A formfitting turtleneck sweater or a low-buttoning shirt becomes the perfect complement' ('What's New' 1996: 114). Women's magazines are masters at presenting an image or a description that both suggests and undermines masculinity and toughness.

Another way to reduce the threat posed by women dressing like men is to suggest that such behavior is sexy and fits neatly into a heterosexual context. A number of high-fashion magazines feature photographs and articles about cross-dressing women that acknowledge the sexual allure of such behavior. In one example, a fashion spread from *Cosmopolitan*, pantsuits for women that highlight the sexual desirability of the women are featured. The designer Ralph Lauren includes a picture of a woman model wearing a severely masculine blazer, complete with tie and handkerchief ('Runway' 1996: 224). There can be little doubt that Lauren and the other designers who create clothing for women are trying to attract an audience that finds such male designs appealing. Yet another example of an article that emphasizes the sexual allure of men's attire, from *Vanity Fair*, describes the Parisian fascination for 'girls with a penchant for dressing up in boyish attire. Their hair Eton-cropped, their legs trouser-clad, they stride along the boulevards with all the loose-limbed assurance of the young Kate Hepburn. This, too, is the tomboy spirit which informs the best of fall's fad for masculine-style women's clothes' ('Tailor' 1984: 68). Even a magazine like *Vanity Fair*, recognized for pushing the boundaries of what it can represent, is quick to reassure its readers: 'No matter how tailored, tweedy, or manly they are, one is always aware of the female beneath' ('Tailor' 1984: 68). Here, again, being perceived as too masculine or too mannish is the ultimate taboo. Even the most androgynous of cross-dressed women must be careful to reveal that they are biologically female.

Along with emphasizing the heterosexual desirability of cross-dressed women, women's fashion magazines diffuse the toughness and genderbending threat of cross-dressing by the very nature of their form. Because fashion magazines in our culture are closely linked with maintaining the myth of femininity, it is almost impossible to *avoid* reading the crossdressing segments as brief theatrical interludes between what the magazines represent as the 'reality' of femininity. The whole structure of the magazines prepares readers to recognize that anything other than femininity for women is only a theatrical display.

We also need to recognize that fashion magazines are able to take something potentially threatening (wearing men's clothing) and turn it into nothing more than the latest fashion of the week:

Because style is a cultural construction, it is easily appropriated, reconstructed and divested of its original political or subcultural signification. Style as resistance becomes commodifiable as chic when it leaves the political realm and enters the fashion world. This simultaneously diffuses the political edge of style. Resistant trends (such as wearing men's oversized jackets or oxford shoes – which, as a form of masquerade, is done in part for fun, but also in protest against the fashion world's insistence upon dressing women in tightly-fitted garments and dangerously unstable footwear) become restyled as high-priced fashions. (Clark 1991: 193)

Mainstream women's magazines appropriate the tough girl and turn her into an unthreatening commodity that can be bought and sold. Like the 1970s television shows examined in the previous chapter, women's magazines limit the threat posed by toughness in women by suggesting that toughness should not and does not interfere with a woman's adherence to femininity. Neither Charlie's Angels nor the leather-clad models that fill women's magazines like *Mademoiselle* and *Vogue* are going to overthrow the cult of femininity, because both the show and the magazines are deeply interested in perpetuating the mythology of femininity.

'Tough and Tender'

We have discovered how women's magazines use the imagery of toughness to create new fashions and to sell commodities ranging from leather jackets to silk shirts. However, these magazines are not suggesting that it is acceptable for women to be tough – rather, they repeatedly undermine the idea that women can be tough by linking toughness to femininity. An article in *Mademoiselle* describes the combination of toughness and softness that women should strive to achieve: 'Femininity used to be thought of as soft, frilly, and – all too often – ineffective. But nowadays there's nothing weak about it. In fact, some of the most admired women around are the ones who manage to combine qualities both tough and tender' ('Pretty' 1991: 168). *Mademoiselle* and other magazines do not want femininity to be reconceptualized too dramatically. These magazines demonstrate how the popular media create new images for women, yet simultaneously perpetuate traditional roles.

It is a mistake to perceive the images of tough women in magazines as *only* perpetuating stereotypical views of women. I [have] argued [previously] that Emma Peel, Charlie's Angels, and the Bionic Woman, despite the way that their toughness was undermined, could still be perceived as possible strong role models for women, particularly when they first appeared. Even the general societal reaction of the 1970s that the Angels were nothing more than bimbos did not prevent viewers past and present from understanding the Angels as positive models for women. Similarly, although I have argued that the majority of high-fashion women's magazines work to undermine the toughness of women, there is no reason that readers cannot carry away very different messages from these texts. It is entirely possible to read the magazines' portraits of non-traditional tough women as empowering to women. My interpretation of the magazines, I hope, reveals the complexity of the depiction of tough women in women's magazines and other popular sources.

Despite creating images of tough women that some readers might find empowering, women's magazines also maintain the gender status quo by insisting on obeisance to the cult of femininity. Women's magazines undermine toughness because it threatens the foundation upon which they are built, and they are not the sole media form that suggests toughness in women is merely skin-deep....

Notes

1. For additional critical work on magazines for women and girls, see Ros Ballaster, Margaret Beetham, Elizabeth Frazer, and Sandra Hebron, *Women's Worlds: Ideology, Femininity and the Woman's Magazine*; Shelley Budgeon, 'Fashion Magazine Advertising: Constructing Femininity in the "Postfeminist" Era'; Kerry Carrington and Anna Bennett, '"Girls' Mags" and the Pedagogical Formation of the Girl'; Kalia Doner, 'Women's Magazines: Slouching Towards Feminism'; Margaret Duffy and J. Michael Gotcher, 'Crucial Advice on How to Get the Guy: The Rhetorical Vision of Power and Seduction in the Teen Magazine *YM*'; Gigi Durham, 'The Taming of the Shrew: Women's Magazines and the Regulation of Desire'; Marjorie Ferguson, *Forever Feminine: Women's Magazines and the Cult of Femininity*; Elizabeth Frazer, 'Teenage Girls Reading *Jackie*'; Ellen McCracken, *Decoding Women's Magazines from Mademoiselle to Ms.* and 'Demystifying *Cosmopolitan*: Five Critical Methods'; Kathryn McMahon, 'The *Cosmopolitan* Ideology and the Management of Desire'; Angela McRobbie, *Feminism and Youth Culture: From 'Jackie' to 'Just Seventeen'*; Kate Peirce, 'A Feminist Theoretical Perspective on the Socialization of Teenage Girls Through *Seventeen* Magazine'; Jennifer Scanlon, *Inarticulate Longings: The Ladies' Home Journal, Gender, and the Promises of Consumer Culture*, and Janice Winship, *Inside Women's Magazines*.
2. Other studies of advertising and its influence include Diane Barthel, *Putting on Appearances: Gender and Advertising*; Stuart Ewen, *All Consuming Images: The Politics of Style in Contemporary Culture* and *Captains of Consciousness: Advertising and the Social Roots of the Consumer Culture*; and Judith Williamson, *Decoding Advertisements: Ideology and Meaning in Advertising*.
3. Additional articles on leather fashions in popular women's magazines include 'The Leather Forecast' and Nell Scovell, 'Leather Perfect.'
4. Leather is so potentially dangerous for women to wear because of its association with masculinity that articles in women's magazines spend a great deal of time discussing exactly how and when women should wear leather attire. See 'Do's and Don'ts.'

5. Combining a feminine style with a more masculine one is not the only way to limit the tough image of masculine clothing. Another tactic appears in an advertisement for Calvin Klein jeans in which a woman wears clothing associated with toughness and masculinity – ripped jeans, hiking boots, and a worn denim shirt. She has short hair and is standing in a rugged outdoor setting, but her tough image is reduced because her shirt is completely unbuttoned, revealing a glimpse of her breasts (Calvin Klein Jeans 3). As previously mentioned, emphasizing a woman's sexuality reduces her tough image.

6. Studies on the social anxieties aroused by cross-dressing include Marjorie Garber, *Vested Interests: Cross Dressing and Cultural Anxiety*; Corinne Holt Sawyer, 'Men in Skirts and Women in Trousers, from Achilles to Victoria Grant: One Explanation of a Comedic Paradox'; and Julie Wheelwright, *Amazons and Military Maids: Women Who Dressed as Men in the Pursuit of Life, Liberty, and Happiness.*

References

Ballaster, R., Beetham, M., Frazer, E. and Hebron, S. (1991) *Women's Worlds: Ideology, Femininity and the Woman's Magazine.* New York: Macmillan.

Barthel, D. (1988) *Putting on Appearances: Gender and Advertising.* Philadelphia: Temple University Press. 'The Best & Worst Looks of the '90s' (1966) *Vogue*, January, 122–31.

'The Best & Worst Looks of the '90s' (1966) *Vogue*, January 122–31.

Budgeon. S. (1994) 'Fashion Magazine Advertising: Constructing Femininity in the "Postfeminist" Era', in L. and A. Manca (eds) *Gender and Utopia in Advertising: A Critical Reader.* Lisle, Il: Procopian Press.

Carrington. K. and Bennett, A. (1966) 'Girls' Mags' and the Pedagogical Formation of the Girl, in C. Luke (ed.) *Feminisms and Pedagogies of Everyday Life.* Albany: State University of New York Press.

Clark, D. (1991) Commodity Lesbianism, *Camera Obscura* 25–6: 181–201.

Davis, F. (1992) *Fashion, Culture, and Identity.* Chicago: University of Chicago Press.

Doner, K. (1993) Women's Magazines: Slouching Towards Feminism, *Social Policy* 23: 37–43.

Duffy, M. and Gotcher, J.M. (1996) Crucial Advice on How to Get the Guy: The Rhetorical Vision of Power and Seduction in the Teen Magazine *YM*, *Journal of Communication Inquiry* 20(1): 32–48.

Durham, G. (1996) The Taming of the Shrew: Women's Magazines and the Regulation of Desire, *Journal of Communication Inquiry* 20(1): 18–31.

Ewen. S. (1988) *All Consuming Images: The Politics of Style in Contemporary Culture.* New York: Basic.

_____ (1976) *Captains of Consciousness: Advertising and the Social Roots of the Consumer Culture.* New York: McGraw-Hill.

Feminine Denim (1996) *Cosmopolitan*, August, 156–67.

Ferguson, M. (1983) *Forever Feminine: Women's Magazines and the Cult of Femininity*. London: Heinemann.

Full Pants Ahead! (1988) *Mademoiselle*, July, 102–7.

Funny Face (1987) *Vanity Fair*, July, 90–3.

Garber, M. (1992) *Vested Interests: Cross-Dressing and Cultural Anxiety*. New York: Routledge.

The Great Suit Caper (1988) *Essence*, November, 84–91.

Griggers, C. (1990) A Certain Tension in the Visual/Cultural Field: Helmut Newton, Deborah Turbeville and the Vogue Fashion Layout, *Differences* 2(2): 76–104.

Hebdige, D. (1979) *Subculture: The Meaning of Style*. New York: Methuen.

The Leather Forecast (1994) *Vogue*, October, 386–91.

Leather or Not (1995) *Glamour*, September, 254–9.

The Leather Report (Nov. 1995) *Seventeen*, 136–41.

Lelmiwitz, T. (1988) Genteel Dapper Dandy Appeal, *Harper's Bazaar*, April, 200–11.

Masculine Tailoring and Feminine Touches (Mar. 1997), *Elle*, 352–61.

McCracken, E. (1993) *Decoding Women's Magazines from Mademoiselle to Ms.* New York: St Martin's.

McMahon, K. (1990) The *Cosmopolitan* Ideology and the Management of Desire, *Journal of Sex Research* 27(3): 381–96.

McRobbie, A. (1991) *Feminism and Youth Culture: From 'Jackie' to 'Just Seventeen.'* Boston: Unwin Hyman.

Men's Department (1995) *New Woman*, November, 106–10.

Modleski, T. (1982) *Loving with a Vengeance: Mass-Produced Fantasies for Women*. Hamden: Archon Books.

My Style (1996) *Essence*, November, 142.

Pale Fire (1996) *Vogue*, April, 312–17.

Peirce, K. (1990) A Feminist Theoretical Perspective on the Socialization of Teenage Girls Through *Seventeen* Magazine, *Sex Roles* 23(9–10): 491–500.

Pretty, Powerful: The New Sexy is Strong (1991) *Mademoiselle*, March, 168–71.

Pretty Tough (1988) *Seventeen*, May, 168–71.

Runway (1996) *Cosmopolitan*, September, 213–25.

Sawyer, C.H. (1987) Men in Skirts and Women in Trousers, from Achilles to Victoria Grant: One Explanation of a Comedic Paradox, *Journal of Popular Culture*, 21(2): 1–16.

Scanlon, J. (1995) *Inarticulate Longings: The Ladies' Home Journal, Gender, and the Promises of Consumer Culture*. New York: Routledge.

Scovell, N. (1993) Leather Perfect, *Mademoiselle*, November, 94–6.

Silverman, K. (1986) Fragments of a Fashionable Discourse, in T. Modleski (ed.) *Studies in Entertainment: Critical Approaches to Mass Culture*. Bloomington: Indiana University Press.

Stay Cool, Girl (1995) *Mademoiselle*, March, 158–65.

Steele, V. (1989) Clothing and Sexuality, in C.B. Kidwell and V. Steele (eds) *Men and Women: Dressing the Part*. Washington, DC: Smithsonian Institution Press.

Tailor Maid (1984) *Vanity Fair*, July, 68–75.

What's New in Suits (1996) *Essence*, September, 114.

Wheelright, J. (1989) *Amazons and Military Maids: Women Who Dressed As Men in the Pursuit of Life, Liberty, and Happiness*. London: Pandora.

White Collar Cool (1988) *Mademoiselle*, October 126–19.

Williamson J. (1986) *Consuming Passions: The Dynamics of Popular Culture*. London: Marion Boyars.

Winship, J. (1987) *Inside Women's Magazines*. London: Pandora.

Wolf, N. (1991) *The Beauty Myth: How Images of Beauty are Used Against Women*. New York: Morrow.

Zip! The Motorcycle Jacket – Truly Cool Again (1988) *Mademoiselle*, November, 220–5.

(RE)PRODUCING GENDER

One of the major questions of concern to those interested in how media systems (re)produce gender concerns the social identities of media workers. As feminist standpoint theorists Dorothy Smith (1987) and Nancy Hartsock (1983) have explained, taken together, women's individual experiences of gender represent an historical accumulation of knowledge about social inequalities based on sexual difference. Those experiences are shaped not only by gender, though, but also by other forms of identity based on 'race', ethnicity, sexuality, class and nationality, among others.

Contemporary media research attends to the ways in which social identities change over time, in response to new experiences and a range of interactions, including those in the workplace itself. At least since the nineteenth century, for example, many women have experienced the newsroom as a hostile environment, one in which they often have been marginalized and patronized. Although the working conditions for women journalists has considerably improved in the past 30 years, historically women have been painfully aware that many of their male colleagues doubted their ability to do 'serious' journalism merely because they were women. Some also believed that any female journalist who achieved success did so primarily through her sexual availability (Stott 1973; Steiner 1996, 1998). The stated view now prevailing among many reporters and editors, both male and female, is that gender does not matter at all, although it is also clear that women are still rarely found in the most prestigious, influential jobs in the profession.

Institutional socialization occurs in journalism in much the same way as other media and non-media occupations. Every newsroom employs organizational and bureaucratic processes for selecting and assigning stories. News accounts are changed to fit legal standards, editors' and owners' prejudices, community culture, governmental pressure and advertisers' demands. This kind of internal gatekeeping has often worked against reporters who are trying to produce complicated stories; some researchers have argued that this is particularly true around issues related to race, class and gender (Cottle 2000; Dines and Humez 2003; hooks 2000).

Some workers resist socialization into what they view as the macho, middle-class, white culture of most newsrooms. African-American journalist Jill Nelson (1993), for example, claims that for four years she resisted socialization into the news culture of the *Washington Post* magazine section, but in the end resigned because she was unable to effect any changes that would make the culture more hospitable to her. Journalism studies researchers have argued that the combination of several years' university education and ongoing professional training and socialization teaches new reporters about their employers' standards, expectations, notions of the audience and professional routines (Rhodes 2001). New reporters learn and internalize the conventions of the workplace before they have a chance to challenge or contest them. As a result, increases in the hiring and promotion of women and people of colour have not necessarily transformed media organizations, especially as they have yet to reach critical mass or the top ranks of the editorial hierarchy. Indeed, whether because of the strong commitment of working journalists to the norms of the profession or the success of professional training and socialization, recent large-scale studies of US journalists have found few significant gender differences in styles of reporting (Lafky 1991; Weaver and Wilhoit 1996). The readings in this section illustrate both how production of texts is constrained by institutional norms and socialization processes and how some groups have managed to circumvent or subvert limitations in order to produce counter-messages.

For several decades, Margaret Gallagher has undertaken to monitor the international news media's employment of women as news reporters and anchors as well as the representation of women in the news more generally. The reading included in this section, 'The Impact of Media Monitoring', is from Gallagher's book *Gender Setting: New Agendas for Media Monitoring and Advocacy* (2001). In the essay, Gallagher summarizes the results of several international media monitoring projects in which she has been engaged, including the Global Media Monitoring Project where data were collected from 70 countries on a single day in 1995, and with a similar number of countries in 2000. Such international projects are remarkable; in 1995, for example, 15,000 stories were included in the analysis. Among the findings of the 1995 study was that women constituted only 17 per cent of the world's news subjects (this rose to 18 per cent in 2000). Women were least likely to be news subjects in stories about politics, government and business, and most likely to make the news in stories about violence, health and social issues, and in arts and entertainment news. Gallagher argues the case for global media monitoring because it provides a diachronic record of the differences and similarities of women's representation in the news and their employment as journalists around the globe.

Helen Davies's chapter, 'The Great Rock and Roll Swindle: The Representation of Women in the British Rock Music Press', shifts our attention from the news to the rock music press. Male rock journalists, Davies argues, are unable to take women seriously as musicians, as fans or as rock journalists. One result of this is that female musicians are rarely featured as serious artists. When they are the focus of a story, male journalists tend to define them in sexual terms, or, at best, as poor versions of male stars. She relates this point to women's subordinate status as rock journalists, arguing that they are similarly faced with an industry in which they are sexualized, marginalized and regarded as secondary to male rock reporters. In a final section of the original article which could not be reprinted here for reasons of space, Davies offers a highly detailed and sophisticated analysis of how the rock music press also trivializes and ridicules female music fans, especially so-called teenyboppers. The music press often refers to all women fans as 'groupies', consistent with the implication that women fans are merely motivated by their sexual attraction to the male performers.

Producing alternative media appears to be an important way in which women can address their subordinate status as media producers. In Carmen Ruíz's essay, 'Losing Fear: Video and Radio Productions of Native Aymara Women', she emphasizes how women can be empowered by participating in projects where they produced their own media content. Describing one such project, which she directed with a group of rural Bolivian women who had recently moved to the city of La Paz, Ruíz tells us how the women learned to produce radio plays, television dramas and educational videos around a diverse range of subjects, such as domestic violence, the prevention of cholera and environmental issues. Although women's voices, particularly those of indigenous women, were largely absent in the Bolivian media and in the wider culture (even in grassroots activist organizations), the Aymara women participating in Ruíz's project said after their training, 'Our throats came alive.' Apparently, this project continues to train women to produce their own media. Over the years it has enabled a growing number of Bolivian women to have a greater impact in political debates in the public sphere.

John Beynon's book, *Masculinities and Culture* (2002), looks at how ways of being a man are shaped by socio-historical forces, by specific institutional settings and by the media. In the chapter used here, 'The Commercialization of Masculinities: From the "New Man" to the "New Lad"', Beynon explains that the loss of certain manual labouring jobs in the 1970s and 1980s was mourned not merely for the loss of millions of jobs, but also because it marked the end of a particular form of British working-class masculinity. Several new masculine identities have emerged in the British media since this period – for example, the 'new man'. The 'new man' of the 1980s was represented either as a 'nurturer' – a pro-feminist man who admitted having feelings and rejected macho behaviour – or as a 'narcissist' – an effeminate man who celebrated high style and consumerism. In the 1990s, a 'harder' masculinity reappeared in the form of the football-playing 'lad' who rejected the feminized identity of the 'new man'. Today, the new young men's magazines such as *FHM* and *Loaded* are at the forefront in developing 'laddism', argues Beynon, promoting and exporting this form of macho masculine identity to sell consumerism to 'real' men.

The politics of gender, identity and access in cyberspace forms the focus of the final reading in this section, 'Women and the Internet: The Natural History of a Research Project' by Anne Scott, Lesley Semmens and Lynette Willoughby. The article begins by outlining the history of their study of women and the Internet. Initially, their thesis was that women have been relatively marginal in the development and use of the Internet. This, they argued, would have long-term negative consequences for equality in gender relations in the future. To understand which factors were limiting women's use of and access to the Internet, the authors surveyed women about their relationship to the Internet. Instead of supporting their original thesis, their findings made them realize that they needed to engage in some 'basic rethinking'. The women they interviewed interpreted their questions about Internet use in divergent ways and displayed a wide understanding of computer technologies. What the authors realized was that their initial assumptions about women's relationship to the Internet reflected a particular feminist predisposition in terms of telling the 'women and Internet' story – one that assumed that women were largely excluded or self-excluding from the development and use of computers. This turned out not to be the case with the women they interviewed. In rethinking the 'women and Internet' story, the authors concluded that any follow-up study would need to address two key questions. First, 'how are the new social geographies of ICT access being gendered?' Second, 'how can we [feminists] intervene to direct the shaping of new techno-social relations in more democratic, inclusive and neutrally gendered ways?'

References

Cottle, S. (ed.) (2000) *Ethnic Minorities and the Media*. Buckingham and Philadelphia: Open University Press.

Dines, G. and Humez, J.M. (eds) (2003, 2nd edn) *Gender, Race and Class in Media*. London, New Delhi and Thousand Oaks, CA: Sage.

Gallagher, M. (2001) *Gender Setting: New Agendas for Media Monitoring and Advocacy*. London: Zed Books.

Hartsock, N. (1983) The feminist standpoint: developing the ground for a specifically feminist historical materialism, in S. Harding, and M.R. Hintikka (eds) *Discovering Reality*. Dordrecht: Reidel.

hooks, b. (2000) *Where We Stand: Class Matters*. London: Routledge.

Lafky, S. (1991) Women journalists, in D.H. Weaver and G.C. Wilhoit (eds) *The American Journalist*. Bloomington: Indiana University Press.

Nelson, J. (1993) *Volunteer Slavery: My Authentic Negro Experience*. Chicago. Noble Press.

Rhodes, J. (2001) Journalism in the new millennium: what's a feminist to do?, *Feminist Media Studies*, 1(1): 49–53.

Smith, D. (1987) *The Everyday World as Problematic: A Feminist Sociology*. Boston: Northeastern University Press.

Steiner, L. (1996) Sex, lives, and auto/biography, *American Journalism*, Fall, 206–11.

Steiner, L. (1998) Newsroom accounts of power at work, in C. Carter, G. Branston and S. Allan (eds) *News, Gender, and Power*. London and New York: Routledge.

Stott, M. (1973) *Forgetting's No Excuse: The Autobiography of Mary Stott*. London: Virago.

Weaver, D.H. and Wilhoit, G.C. (1996) *The American Journalist in the 1990s: U.S. News People at the End of an Era*. Mahwah: Lawrence Erlbaum Associates.

Further Reading

Allen, D., Rush, R.R. and Kaufman, S.J. (eds) (1996) *Women Transforming Communications: Global Intersections*. Thousand Oaks, CA: Sage.

Beadle, M.E. and Murray, M.D. (eds) (2001) *Indelible Images: Women of Local Television*. Ames: Iowa State University Press.

Burt, E. (ed.) (2000) *Women's Press Organizations, 1881–1999*. Westport: Greenwood Press.

Christmas, L. (1997) *Chaps of Both Sexes? Women Decision-makers in Newspapers: Do They Make a Difference?* London: BT Forum/Women in Journalism.

Holmlund, C. and Fuchs, C. (1997) *Between the Sheets, In the Streets: Queer, Lesbian, Gay Documentary*. Minneapolis: University of Minnesota Press.

Shade, L.R. (2002) *Gender and Community in the Social Construction of the Internet*. New York: Peter Lang.

8 | THE IMPACT OF MONITORING MEDIA IMAGES OF WOMEN

Margaret Gallagher

> It's like riding a tiger: once you get on you cannot get off. This is a continuous
> process. You cannot stop it. There is no beginning, there is no end.
> (Manisha Chaudury, Centre for Advocacy and Research,
> in *Making a Difference*, 1999)

The results of the second Global Media Monitoring Project (GMMP),
carried out in 70 countries on 1 February 2000, suggested that the news
world might have been standing still for five years. On that day women
accounted for just 18 per cent of news subjects, compared with 17 per cent
in 1995 (Spears et al. 2000). The degree of concordance between the main
results from the two global monitoring projects was remarkable. Yet it was
hardly surprising. To have expected a perceptible shift in the world's news
over the time period would have been naive. The embedded nature of news
values and news selection processes is such that the overall patterns
detected by quantitative monitoring are unlikely to change appreciably even
over the medium term.

Indeed the apparent universality of prevailing news definitions obliges
advocates to question the extent to which it is realistic to expect a fundamental 'gender shift' in news agendas and priorities. Reflecting on their
1997 news monitoring experience, Red-Ada, a woman's organization in
Bolivia, posed a number of salient questions which highlight the constraints
on change. To what extent do journalists actually construct the news
agenda? Is it feasible to divert news values away from coverage of government and politics? To what extent is it really possible for other actors,
linked to aspects of daily life, to find a place in the news? Is it possible in the
short term for the press to reflect a gender perspective and to move away

from a masculine-as-universal vision of the world? To what extent can the press contribute to the construction of women as citizens, based on a vision of equality? For Red-Ada, the answer to this kind of question lies in the fact that in contemporary Bolivian society the press plays an important investigative and watchdog role on behalf of citizens – uncovering corruption, exposing people and events that contravene the law, and highlighting violations of human rights (Flores Palacios 1999: 129–30).

For advocates in many countries, this is the crucial link. In theory at least, it should be possible to turn that critical, investigative journalistic perspective onto the issue of gender. Critical journalists do not unquestionably accept the official line or the press release. They search for alternative sources of information not just as a check on reliability, but also to add texture and tone to their reports. It seems logical that gender – in terms of sources, priorities and perspectives – should be among the factors taken into account by journalists within this tradition. Yet it rarely seems to be. Media activists have begun to find ways of introducing this gender dimension into journalistic and indeed other media production routines. But the process is just beginning. As the experience of several media advocacy groups shows, change is likely to be achingly slow.

On the other hand, the media industries themselves develop at a vertiginous pace, posing ever more complex problems for gender monitoring and advocacy. Digitalization brings countless new channels to be kept in view. Mass audiences fragment into many smaller units, each with its distinct experience and interpretation of media content. Advertisers respond to video time shifting and consumer ad zapping by conceiving a radically different style of commercial that is interwoven with content, rather than separately identifiable. The Internet presents a seemingly limitless arena for new forms of imagery, as well as new channels for the transmission of traditional media content. And despite all the technological change, the same old patterns of gender representation apparently remain relatively intact. In that sense there is no sign of a radical break with the past, and there is no end in sight.

Riding the Tiger

> They keep us on our toes. A lot of times we take certain things for granted or we overlook them.
>
> (Editor-in-chief, *The Gleaner*, Jamaica, speaking of
> Women's Media Watch; Walker and Nicholson 1996: 100)

Riding the tiger of gender media monitoring and advocacy demands skill, nerve and determination. Spills and upsets are a constant threat, while there is rarely a sense of crossing the line or reaching the finishing post. Keeping media people on their toes means being able to keep them interested in the issues. This involves a constant search for new angles and discussion points. Progress is hard to measure, and even with the best planning, unexpected hazards can undermine gains already made.

As an essentially political activity, media monitoring and advocacy is almost inevitably affected by shifts in the wider political and economic environment. Sometimes these can overturn, almost overnight, painstakingly developed alliances. In a highly publicized meeting in January 1996 held in collaboration with the Indian Women's Press Corps, three years of effort by the then Media Advocacy Group were rewarded by a commitment from the Director-General of India's state television organization Doordarshan. He agreed to the development of gender guidelines or a programme code for television producers. But almost immediately afterwards, in anticipation of general elections to be held in May, the ruling party made critical changes in the leadership of Doordarshan. This had a tremendous impact on advocacy efforts. Not only was there no follow-through regarding the proposed guidelines, but the changes completely disrupted a complex set of relationships that had been built up over the previous three years.[1] This kind of setback can be devastating for small groups. The Israel Women's Network was jubilant when, after protracted discussions, it persuaded the Israel Broadcasting Authority (IBA) – the country's public service broadcaster – to sponsor courses on women's issues for its senior women. The agreement was regarded as a breakthrough (Sachs 1996). But only one course was ever held. Soon afterwards, changes in internal organization meant that the necessary will and commitment at decision-making level disappeared within the IBA (Sappir 2000).

The overall political framework can have both direct and indirect effects on media advocacy work. In the mid-1990s Australia's change of government signalled a move from a system that, broadly speaking, supported regulation in the community interest to one that favoured deregulation and free-market principles. This transformed the power relations between community and business groups, leaving little space for dialogue about solutions to community concerns and making it extremely difficult even to maintain the gains of the early 1990s in terms of gender-based media policies and codes. An organization like the National Women's Media Centre (NWMC) is affected by this kind of shift in political climate not just at the level of strategy – in terms of the available options – but also at the level of day-to-day practice. Like many advocacy groups, the NWMC depends on a high level of voluntary input. Much of this comes from media students. They learn something in return, so it is also a way of passing on the knowledge and skills that can bring about change. But the problem for the NWMC is that the brightest voluntary workers move into junior media jobs where they can no longer be active advocates – not because of lack of time, but because they must protect their career prospects. 'Whereas a few years ago there was often no problem, now even liberal media ask employees what affiliations they have. So for women wanting a media career, it's not viable to stay on in any "community activist" capacity.'[2]

For Women's Media Watch, Jamaica, dependence on voluntary effort also puts the organization in a vulnerable position. The country's deteriorating economic situation means that, to make ends meet, most people have two or more jobs. Inevitably, the volunteers are less involved than they used to be. Without a car, getting around Kingston is often difficult and dangerous at night for women. So the mere question of how to get home after an evening workshop with a youth group is a problem. 'People think we are a big agency, but we run with two part-time staff and a semi-paid volunteer. We have to struggle to run the programmes properly, because we can't pay qualified people. It's hard to raise seed money for capacity building, and the work (i.e. educational work) cannot generate income.'[3]

Finance is without doubt the most fundamental obstacle faced by most monitoring and advocacy groups. The battle to raise core funding for even a skeleton staff is constant. The NWMC in Australia currently relies almost entirely on member support to keep going. Funding cuts have forced Canada's Media Watch into an intensive restructuring process, cutting full-time staff from three to two and making changes to the way they work. The group began a fundraising strategy, including a direct mail fundraising programme, applications to foundations and private funding sources for various projects.[4] Organizations may spend endless time on funding applications, only to have them rejected. And without a clear fundraising policy, there is the risk that groups will allow their activities to become too dispersed by succumbing to 'donor temptation' (TAMWA 2000: 43). Project-based funding for specific monitoring activities can be useful, but it usually limits the amount of follow-up that is possible. Good work is started, but there can be no continuity. Projects tacked onto existing structures, or added to individuals' workloads, can result in burnout and wasted effort. Momentum is built up, and then there is frustration.[5]

The scarcity of funding makes partnerships crucial. Media Watch points out that funding for related activities such as media literacy or violence prevention can sometimes be obtained in association with another agency, on the understanding that gender portrayal issues will be a central part of the work. But partnerships are important in many other ways too. Media Watch has devoted much time to building partnerships with organizations that work in the areas of violence in the media, media literacy and diversity issues. This brings them in-depth information and resources that they would not be able to get with their own limited means. In return, Media-Watch can add a gender perspective to the work of partner organizations. China's Media Monitor Network for Women co-hosts meetings with other women's NGOs such as the Women's Health Group, East Meets West Group, the Women's Psychology Consulting Centre and the Women's Legal Assistance Centre of Beijing University. These activities not only provide new information and resources for women journalists, but also strengthen cooperation between the Network and other organizations.[6]

The Tanzania Media Women's Association (TAMWA) builds alliances through networking, the media and community outreach. Besides the media institutions themselves, TAMWA works with the Ministry of Community Development, Women's Affairs and Children, the Ministry of Constitutional Affairs and Justice and the police force, as well as other women's NGOs such as the Tanzania Women Lawyers Association, the Tanzania Gender Networking Programme and the Women's Legal Aid Centre. These and other partnerships with, for example, the Legal and Human Rights Centre and the Tanganyika Law Society, help TAMWA to meet its objectives: a wide cross-section of society is made to feel accountable, and thus gives support to TAMWA's activities. For its part TAMWA, through its access to the media, can play the role of 'mouthpiece' for the concerns of sister NGOs (TAMWA 1999).

Both the NWMC in Australia and Women's Media Watch (WMW) in South Africa work cooperatively with organizations with similar aims. As the only national women's voice on media policy and practice, the NWMC supports and networks with other local and state groups, trying to help them stay afloat and united during what has been a particularly difficult time to bring about change. The very different political climate of South Africa offers WMW more scope for intervention. WMW believes that regularly raising gender issues with media authorities such as the Independent Broadcasting Authority, the Advertising Standards Authority, the Press Ombudsman and the Broadcasting Complaints Commission of South Africa helps to keep gender on their agenda. 'It has a tendency to slip off when they are not actively confronted with it.'[7] Its links with interest groups can add weight to a complaint or action and can be a useful strategy in raising awareness. For instance, WMW works with NGOs such as the Network on Violence Against Women, and with national decision-makers including the Commission on Gender Equality, the Parliamentary Committee on the Improvement of the Quality of Life and Status of Women, the Parliamentary Women's Caucus and the ANC Women's Caucus. For WMW these contacts have proven helpful in putting pressure on media producers to make changes.

The issue of links and partnerships becomes even more central in the context of new technologies and the Internet. Many monitoring and advocacy groups already have websites, some of them interactive, often containing an enormous amount of information and providing links to other similar groups nationally and elsewhere. Through their websites media advocates can reach infinitely more people than ever before – both nationally and internationally. This area of activity is bound to increase, and groups need to be ready to manage the change. Canada's Media Watch found that with the rise of new technologies, the scope of their work increased dramatically. Yet they had fewer staff than ever in their history. To meet the challenge Media Watch has turned to the new technologies themselves for help. In 2000 it launched MOVE (Media Watch Online Volunteer Education), a pilot project to use online tools to train and support a nation-wide network of volunteers. Much of what Media Watch has achieved over the past two decades has been due to a dedicated network of volunteers who are involved in all aspects of its operations. The MOVE project is designed to allow this network to expand and flourish.

The Impact of Media Monitoring and Advocacy

> It is essential to remember that change is slow and takes time. Every success is important, no matter how small it might appear.
> (Melanie Cishecki, Media Watch)[8]

The specific achievements of gender media monitoring and advocacy are relatively easy to identify. The development of codes and policies, successful complaints procedures, workshops and discussions with the media industry, training in critical media analysis – there are many examples. However, it is more difficult to assess the impact of these efforts – the extent to which they have influenced practices and mentalities in an enduring way. Until now there has been little systematic research or evaluation, although with the passage of time groups themselves are increasingly in a position to reflect on their perceptions of change. The Centre for Advocacy and Research (CFAR) in India has watched exchanges between members of the Viewers' Forum and media professionals becoming sharper, and audience perceptions becoming keener. Looking back over almost a decade of debate, it seemed that gradually all the passion about how television was threatening Indian culture was largely forgotten. Instead, more down-to-earth discussion about media representations of the family, male–female relationships, the institution of marriage and the marginalization of specific groups in media content took over.[9] The extent to which viewers can in fact exercise control or influence media decisions may be unclear. But CFAR remains convinced that 'informed viewer opinion and activism is the only way to enlarge the area of viewer choice'.[10]

Assessing the extent to which feminist advocacy has succeeded in redefining media agendas is 'work in progress'. It requires retrospective study covering many years, and as yet few comprehensive analyses have been possible. However, some recently published research has begun to throw light on the impact of feminism over the past two decades. A detailed analysis of the media strategies of the National Organization for Women (NOW) in the United States between 1966 and 1980 concludes that the organization was able to transfer at least some of its key issues and frames of reference into the American news agenda. Over the 15-year period of the study, the issues that came to be taken most seriously by the media – for example, the Equal Rights Amendment and sex discrimination – 'did not begin as clear-cut public issues but were made into issues over time by feminist communications' (Barker-Plummer 2000: 153). Initially, for instance, journalists did not see the issue of sex discrimination as a legitimate framework for women's experiences and treated many claims of discrimination with ridicule. It was not until the mid-1970s that the work of NOW and other feminist strategists to persuade journalists that the general, systematic framework of 'discrimination' fit women's experiences, as it had fit those of minorities previously, could be seen in the 'institutionalization' of sex discrimination as a serious news topic. Similarly, media acceptance of sexual harassment as a political issue in the 1980s was the result of continual feminist communication and framing that moved the topic from 'personal' to 'political' over time. The overall conclusion of this study is encouraging for media advocates. Although news management fulfils an ideological function by 'sorting' and prioritizing issues for audiences – particularly in terms of a public–private categorization – 'the influence of other discourses and actors can move some topics from one of these categories to the other' (Barker-Plummer 2000: 147).

Some confirmation for this comes from a 12-country study of news coverage of the four world conferences on women, spanning 1975 to 1995. This also detected positive movement and change in the nature and content of reporting, with a marked reduction in simplistic, sensationalist and sexist coverage over the period. The sheer number of editorials published in 1995

(65, compared with 17 in 1975) is some indication of how far the issues of the women's movement had moved up the news agenda in the course of 20 years. The point was directly addressed in a 1995 *Washington Post* editorial describing the international women's movement as 'one of the striking social developments of recent decades. It has given voice and a measure of coherence to a previously neglected set of global and cultural concerns' (Gallagher 2000: 16). It would be difficult to find a better example of the shift – in both media perceptions and political reality – that had taken place since 1975.

Like the broad concerns of the women's movement, it takes time for issues raised by media monitoring and advocacy groups to gain legitimacy. When the NOS Gender Portrayal Department began its work in 1991 'gender portrayal in the media was widely seen as making a mountain out of a molehill, not something to fuss about in the emancipated nineties' (NOS Gender Portrayal Department 1996: 14). Gradually this perception changed. An evaluation carried out five years later showed that the department's research and presentations had been a revelation to most programme-makers. By 1996 the department could claim that 'the standpoint that "the way women and men are portrayed is one of the professional aspects that determines the quality of a programme" is now widely accepted.[11] The favourable reactions we have received from various quarters makes it clear that a process of change has been set in train' (NOS Gender Portrayal Department 1996: 15).[12]

It seems undeniable that, at the very least, the process of media monitoring has an impact on the way people 'see' or understand the media. According to one of the Canadian monitors in the 1995 Global Media Monitoring Project:

I'd been studying in this area for some time, but things really hit me that day that hadn't hit me before. A lot of news stories that could have included gender information didn't. ... Since that monitoring day, I've noticed myself looking at the media differently. I look at what's not there as much as I look at what's there, and I notice what makes for the gap between what's there and what's not. (Tindal n.d.: 11)

Or in the words of one of the young Dutch journalists involved in the 2000 GMMP: 'It's as if the news suddenly tipped on one side, as if you were reading the newspaper through 3-D spectacles' (in van Dijck 2000: 29).

Whether monitoring and advocacy initiatives have helped to bring about change in media performance itself is a much more difficult question to answer unequivocally. Reflecting on the first five years of the NOS Gender

Portrayal Department, Dorette Kuipers, the first head of department, put it as follows:

> We hope we've gained more gender portrayal awareness in pro-gramme-makers through our work, though it's hard to measure ... because we're working on a change of mentality. ... For instance, at a recent 50th anniversary celebration for the United Nations, the news presenter noted that there were 180 people in attendance from all over the world – of which only eight were women. Adding that sentence is becoming more a rule now than an exception, drawing attention to imbalance. ... We suspect we've played a role in this. (Tindal n.d.: 17)

Another example from the Netherlands points in the same direction. Amateur cyclist Rudi Kemna won the Dutch championship for the third time in a row. After the race, in an interview with senior journalist Jean Nelissen, he was asked whether he now planned to join the professionals. No, replied the cyclist. He was a 'househusband: I do the housekeeping and a bit of cycling'. 'So you do the cooking? ... And house cleaning as well?' Nelissen asked in astonishment. Back in the studio, the programme anchor joked gently that his veteran colleague was 'hearing for the first time that men also cook and clean' (*Screening Gender* 2000: video 1, item 9).

Such small gains – the addition of a sentence, a comment of appraisal – may seem negligible. But if they spring from an awareness that gender representation in the media is something to be questioned rather than taken for granted, they have the potential to transform public perceptions.

Gender is Not a Women's Issue

> *Gender is not a women thing.*
> (Placard used in 'Labels are rubbish' protest, Women's Media Watch,
> South Africa, 1998)

The example of the Dutch cyclist contains some lessons for gender media monitoring groups. How would an item like this be coded in a straight-forward monitoring exercise? No woman appears in the story. The news subject, reporter and studio announcer are all male. The story topic would be classified as sports, as would the occupation of the news subject. The standard coding grid would reveal an item with three men, in a story about sport. Yet this story is very centrally 'about' gender issues, and this is precisely what the coding fails to register. The fact that the cyclist describes himself as a 'househusband', the amazement of the reporter at the interviewee's preference for 'house cleaning' rather than professional cycling, and the wry comment of the studio anchor on his colleague's attitude (in turn implying that the anchor himself has a different point of view), are all hidden behind the numbers. Here we have an extremely clear example of the limitations of quantitative monitoring. Percentages and distributions may seem very clear and precise. In reality they usually hide a quite complicated pattern of gender representation, whose attributes are often extremely difficult to fit into predetermined categories.

This is not to say that the figures produced by quantitative analysis of media content are 'wrong' or that this kind of monitoring should not be carried out – on the contrary. As groups in many countries have discovered, these overall figures are invaluable in sketching out the broad parameters of gender portrayal. They provide inescapable evidence of the imbalance in media representations of women and men – in terms of status and authority, and indeed just sheer numbers. They can be extremely useful as a wake-up call, forcing those who maintain that 'things have changed' to face reality. Studies of this kind will always be needed, to keep track of general trends and patterns. But they are not sufficient to change media representations of gender.

Faced with the fact that only 18 per cent of news subjects are women, what can an individual media professional do? At best, she or he may make an individual effort to shift the balance in specific programmes. But numerical imbalance is only one small facet of the overall problem. Gender representation in the media is constituted in countless, more subtle ways – through the angle from which a story is approached, the locations in which women and men are shown, the choice of questions, the type of interview style adopted, and much more besides. Looking at the issue from this perspective, it becomes clear that the focus of research and action on 'women' as opposed to 'gender' is extremely limiting. It is in the comparison of how women *and* men are portrayed in the media that insights emerge, and change can ensue. 'Gender is *not* a women thing.' As a concept, it actually depends on an interpretation of the relationships between women and men. As an analytical tool, it needs to be applied to the study of both masculinity and femininity. As a platform for advocacy, men as well as women must adopt it.

From the perspective of gender media monitoring and advocacy, therefore, the old question 'do women make a difference?' – for instance, to media content – is not the most relevant one. More crucial is the question of how to involve the maximum number of citizens – women and men – in recognizing the imbalances in gender portrayal in media content. Most central of all is the question of how to persuade the maximum number of

media professionals – women and men – that fair and diverse gender portrayal will contribute to higher-quality output, which is likely to appeal to a
wider range of audiences. The involvement of men in gender monitoring
and analysis is important, not just in the sense of getting them 'on board'
but – more critically – because their readings and interpretations need to be
debated. Recent monitoring projects such as the Gender Media Monitor in
Trinidad and Tobago and the Women and Media Observatory in Italy have
made a point of including boys and young men on an equal basis with girls
and young women.

This seems an obvious next step for media advocates because, if gender
representation is to change, that implies the representation of men as well as
women. Male stereotyping is also an issue, as Justice Mlala of South Africa
has put it: 'We men are trapped in a dark and secret world called Men Talk,
where we swop tales of conquest and plunder but never of failure or perceived failure' (Le Roux 1999: 24). During the 1990s, within the academic
world a small field of men's studies began to explore issues of masculinity
and male identity. But as yet these questions hardly feature on the agenda of
media monitoring and advocacy groups, a matter of concern to the young
women in MediaWatch's 'tween' consumer literacy project: 'Like there is so
much stuff for girls. . . . That is great. But why don't guys have any stuff like
that? Why don't they say like you need help with *your* self-esteem? Like
guys aren't perfect. They don't have a wonderful life' (MediaWatch 2000:
13). Of course it is true that prevalent representations of femininity and
female sexuality maintain unequal power relations in a way that is particularly pernicious to women. But one way of ensuring that men, as well as
women, understand this is to analyse the construction of both masculinity
and femininity in media content and to debate the differences. As long as
'gender representation' remains synonymous with 'women's representation', gender media advocates will find it difficult to make the media
alliances that are necessary to bring about lasting change.

Alliance building with other public interest groups does not require the
abandonment of principles or objectives. But it may provide more leverage
in pursuing them. In mid-1998 NOW created a task force to research and
develop a Feminist Communications Network – a television, cable, radio
and web broadcast network – to deliver news, talk shows and content
delivered from a feminist perspective. A dream nurtured for decades, this
had proven elusive. After almost a year of deliberation and consultation, in
May 1999 NOW announced the launch of its Digital Broadcast Project.
The organization had concluded that the opening up of new channel space
through the digital spectrum offered 'an unprecedented opportunity to
make a dramatic change'.[13] Nation-wide access might at last be possible for

non-commercial, public service media such as the feminist communications network envisaged by NOW. But this access depended on a statutory requirement that the broadcasters already licensed to operate the digital channels should – by reason of their 'public interest' obligations – set aside channel space for public service media. The 1996 Telecommunications Act that had opened up broadcasters' access to digital television did reaffirm the 'public interest' principles of American broadcasting, but did not legislate on specific public interest obligations. When the Gore Commission, set up in mid-1997 to determine what obligations DTV owed the public, reported in December 1998, the report was excoriated in the press. 'Almost none of the debate about the report or the process that created it occurred in public view, because television stations – perhaps fearing regulation – kept the issue off the local and national news.'[14] Not surprisingly the broadcasters had no interest in sharing their channels, or in reducing their advertising revenue.

Through its Digital Broadcast Project NOW joined forces with People for Better TV (PBTV), a coalition of over 100 groups pushing for clearly defined and enforced public interest obligations for broadcasters in the digital television era. Although the Federal Communications Commission (FCC) had started issuing digital licences in 1997 and some operators began digital transmissions in late 1998, it had shown no signs of taking up the question of how DTV broadcasters were to be held to public service obligations. Throughout 1999 NOW and the other organizations involved in PBTV pushed hard – for example, via letters to Congress – for the FCC to be required to convene public hearings so that citizens could express their views. Finally in December 1999 the FCC announced that it would seek public comment.[15] Buoyed by their success in getting the attention of the FCC and of Congress, PBTV members planned a very extensive series of actions in the run-up to the 2000 national elections.

This promised to be a lengthy struggle. But whatever the outcome for NOW, the decision to link up with a broader social movement whose public interest goals could encompass its own was strategically sound. In the context of American broadcasting, it promised a better chance of success than might have been expected if NOW had single-handedly pursued an exclusively feminist agenda. As the business and commercial interests controlling the media continue to concentrate and coalesce, riding the tiger of gender media monitoring and advocacy will increasingly call for such alliances among public interest groups – not just within but also across national boundaries.

Notes

1. Media Advocacy Group, Consolidated Three-Year Final Narrative Report, 1995–1998: 8.
2. This and other information in the chapter: Helen Leonard, personal communication to author, July 2000.
3. This and other information in the chapter: Hilary Nicholson, personal communication to author, July 2000.
4. This and other information in the chapter: Melanie Cishecki, personal communication to author, July 2000.
5. Uca Silva, personal communication to author, July 2000.
6. Media Monitor Network (1999) Annual Narrative Report.
7. Women's Media Watch, *Final Report, 1999*: 4.
8. Melanie Cishecki, personal communication to author, July 2000.
9. Akhila Sivadas, personal communication to author, July 2000.
10. Understanding media: a training of the trainers, *Viewers' Voices*, November 1999: 6.
11. In 2000 the mandate of the Gender Portrayal Department was broadened to include ethnicity and age. It is now known as the NOS Diversity Department.
12. NOS is the national broadcast organization of the Netherlands.
13. NOW Foundation broadcast project: see www.nowfoundation.org/communications/tv/project.html
14. Mark Huisman (1999) Take back our TV; see People for Better TV website: www.bettertv.org/takebacktext.html
15. 'FCC begins proceedings to seek comment on public interest obligations of television broadcasters as they transition to digital transmission technology', FCC News release, 15 December 1999: see www.fcc.gov/Bureaus/Mass_Media/News_Releases/1999/nrmm9030.html

References

Barker-Plummer, Bernadette (2000) News as a feminist resource? A case study of the media strategies and media representation of the National Organization for Women, 1966–1980, in Annabelle Sreberny and Liesbet van Zoonen (eds) *Gender, Politics and Communication*, pp. 121–59. Cresskill, NJ: Hampton Press.

Flores Palacios, Patricia (1999) *La Mirada Invisible: La Imagen de las Mujeres en los Medios de Comunicación de Bolivia*, La Paz: Red de Trabajadoras de la Información y Comunicación RED-ADA.

Gallagher, Margaret (2000) *From Mexico to Beijing – and Beyond: Covering Women in the World's News*. New York: United Nations Development Fund for Women (UNIFEM).

Le Roux, Gabrielle (1999) The least-reported crime, *Rhodes Journalism Review*, December: 24–5.

Making a Difference (1999) Video produced by the Centre for Advocacy and Research, 10 mins, Delhi: Centre for Advocacy and Research.

Media Watch (2000) *Media Environment: Analysing the 'Tween' Market*, Toronto: Media Watch.

NOS Gender Portrayal Department (1996) *Getting Through: Five Years of the NOS Gender Portrayal Department*, Hilversum: NOS.

Sachs, Lesley (1996) The missing gender: the portrayal of Israeli women in the media, in Rina Jimenez-David (ed.) *Women's Experiences in Media*, pp. 62–7. Manila: Isis-International and World Association for Christian Communication.

Sappir, Shoshana London (2000) The Israel Women's Network: progress in the status of women in Israel since the 1995 Beijing conference. Paper submitted to the Beijing +5 conference, New York, 5–9 June.

Screening Gender (2000), audio-visual training toolkit produced by YLE (Finland), NOS (Netherlands), NRK (Norway), SVT (Sweden) and ZDF (Germany); videos (total 80 mins) and text; Hilversum: NOS Diversity Department.

Spears, George and Kasia Seydegart with Margaret Gallagher (2000) *Who Makes the News? Global Media Monitoring Project 2000*, London: World Association for Christian Communication.

TAMWA (1999) *Annual Report 1998*, Dar es Salaam: Tanzania Media Women's Association.

TAMWA (2000) *Annual Report 1999*, Dar es Salaam: Tanzania Media Women's Association.

Tindal, Mardi (n.d.) *A Day in the News of the World: A Study Guide for the Global Media Monitoring Project*. London: World Association for Christian Communication.

van Dijck, Bernadette (2000) Changing images: a long road, *Media Development*, XLVII(3): 28–9.

Walker, Melody and Hilary Nicholson (1996) Revisioning the Jamaican media: the experience of Women's Media Watch 1987–1996, in Rina Jimenez-David (ed.) *Women's Experiences in Media*, pp. 96–101. Manila: Isis-International and World Association for Christian Communication.

THE GREAT ROCK AND ROLL SWINDLE

THE REPRESENTATION OF WOMEN IN THE BRITISH ROCK MUSIC PRESS

Helen Davies

The British rock music press prides itself on its liberalism and radicalism, yet the discourses employed in music journalism exclude women from serious discussion both as musicians and as fans. In particular, the notion of credibility, which is of vital importance to the 'serious' rock music press, is constructed in such a way that it is almost completely unattainable for women.

The most important and influential part of the British music press was until recently its two weekly music papers, *Melody Maker* (*MM*) and the *New Musical Express* (*NME*), both published by IPC magazines. The *NME*, launched in 1949, contains reviews, concert information and interviews with performers and describes itself as 'a unique blend of irreverent journalism and musical expertise' (www.ipc.co.uk). *MM*, which started life in 1926 as a paper for jazz musicians, had similar content but a greater emphasis on rock, as opposed to pop, music. It was relaunched in 1999 as a glossy magazine, before ceasing publication or, as IPC put it, merging with the *NME*, in December 2000.

There are also a number of glossy, monthly magazines such as *Q* and *Vox*. It is to these weekly and monthly publications that I will be referring when I talk of the 'music press', but I will also occasionally refer to music writing in broadsheet newspapers such as the *Guardian* and the *Independent*, as this writing tends to share the same assumptions, and often the same journalists, as the dedicated music press. The type of music covered by the music press is constructed there as 'serious' pop music, to differentiate it from chart pop which, presumably, is not serious. Such a term illustrates the cultural capital (Bourdieu 1984) that accrues to fans of music viewed as cerebral. Despite these problems with the terms 'serious rock music' or 'serious pop music', I will use them here purely for the lack of a more suitable alternative. To describe this music as 'rock', as opposed to 'pop', is inappropriate as there is often little generic difference between artists viewed as 'serious' and 'not serious', and it is misleading and inaccurate to describe such music as 'alternative' or 'independent' since some of the artists covered by the music press sell hundreds of thousands of records, and many are signed to major record labels.

The vast majority of music journalists in Britain are male – men at *MM* outnumbered women by more than two to one – and female journalists are often relegated to the least important parts of the paper, such as reviewing readers' demo tapes. The music press assumes that all its readers are male as well, so that the situation is often one of male journalists writing for male readers, a fact reflected in the mode of address of much music writing.

It is therefore hardly surprising that much music writing tends either to ignore women entirely or to treat them in an extremely sexist way. It has been well documented that women are discouraged from becoming performers and from taking other roles in the music industry (Bayton 1997; Cohen 1997). I will mainly be looking at how the music press constructs concepts of credibility and authenticity that work to exclude women, and particularly feminist women, from the world of serious music.

Female Performers

The British music press employs a range of tactics to obscure and denigrate the work of female artists. Perhaps the most common way in which music journalists treat female performers is to ignore them completely. This attitude is particularly noticeable in retrospective writing on rock history, which often obliterates any trace of all but a token few women. This discourse has influenced other media coverage of rock and pop, including TV shows. For example, an hour-long ITV documentary on androgyny in pop, shown in 1999, mentioned only one female performer, Annie Lennox. She was mentioned ten minutes before the end, and was the only featured performer not to be interviewed ('Walk on the Wild Side', ITV, 17 February 1999).

As Davin (1988: 4) writes: 'The dominant version of history in any society will reflect the general assumptions and concerns of the dominant group.' The vast majority of music journalists are male, and it is unsurprising that they should tend to admire most the artists with whom they can most identify, i.e. other men. This exclusion of women from history means that, as Gaar (1993) puts it, 'there is little sense of an ongoing tradition of women in the music industry'. Women are a perpetual novelty, and each new group of successful female performers is heralded as the first. 'Breakthroughs' for women were declared in the 1970s, when Julie Burchill and Tony Parsons claimed that 'punk rock in 1976 was the first rock and roll phase *ever* not to insist that women should be picturesque topics and targets of songs' (Burchill and Parsons 1978: 79), and again in the 1980s, with Lucy Whitman declaring 'there has been a spectacular change on the popular music front over the last couple of years. There are more women in bands than ever before' (Whitman 1981: 6). More recently, *MM*'s review of 1996 stated that 'for years, Women In Rock was not really an idea taken seriously ... 1996 saw it finally happen' (*MM*, 21/28 December 1996: 41).[1]

'Taken seriously by whom?' is a question well worth asking. It should be noted that none of these writers is neutrally reflecting the situation as they see it. One reason that writers may continue to announce the 'new' opportunities for female musicians is to create images of themselves and their publications as liberal and non-sexist. The third quotation is particularly interesting, as it has been the music press itself that has refused to take women seriously. To write in this way obscures this fact and implies that some other agency has been responsible.

When women are mentioned, they are nearly always represented primarily *as* women, rather than as musicians. It is commonplace for awards ceremonies and readers' polls to differentiate between the 'Best Male Artist' and 'Best Female Artist', and women are often described as female versions of a male star. For example, an *MM* live review in 1998 referred to Courtney Love of Hole as 'Jon Bon Jovi with tits'. This was intended as a compliment. The Riot Grrrl movement has often been described as a female version of punk and its 'zines' equated to punk fanzines in a way that ignores the political elements of the movement and thus manages to defuse any threat that it may have presented (Kearney 1997).

Any threat posed by female artists is neutralized by their unfavourable comparison with men. At the same time, female artists, even those performing completely different styles of music, are treated as a homogenous group. Their very femaleness is deemed to give them something in common; an assumption reinforced by feminist rewritings of rock history (see, for example, Steward and Garratt 1984; Gaar 1993; McDonnell and Powers 1995). This marginalization as 'women in rock' is a way of keeping women as outsiders and of implying that there are many artists belonging to this genre. I have seen Alanis Morissette compared to Jewel, Meredith Brooks, Paula Cole, Suzanne Vega, Celine Dion, Joni Mitchell, Madonna, Alisha's Attic, Siobhan Fahey and many others. While in some cases the comparisons may be legitimate, most of the time they were a way of suggesting that one or other of the artists was superfluous or derivative: why would we need another female artist? This was made explicit in an interview with Natalie Imbruglia in the *Independent*, which began: 'You might have thought that after Alanis Morissette and Joan Osborne and Fiona Apple and Meredith Brooks the attraction of wailing troubled beauty would have worn ultra-slim. It seems not' (Compton 1998). Another common trend is for female artists to be asked about topics that stress their femininity. For example, whole articles have concentrated on women's experiences of motherhood, whereas I have yet to find more than a couple of sentences on male stars' experiences of fatherhood. Even these were inevitable in interviews with Kurt Cobain, who made a point of emphasizing the importance of his family to him.

Most offensively, female artists are insulted as women. In one singles review page of *MM*, the only women referred to or reviewed were described as, respectively, 'slappers', a 'hippy cow' and an 'old sow', while criticism of male artists was confined to their music (*MM*, 20 February 1999). This kind of casual misogyny appears to be acceptable: it was not criticized elsewhere in that issue of the magazine or in the letters pages of subsequent issues.

Writing about female artists as women first and musicians second has the inevitable outcome of a constant stress on their appearance and sexuality. An interview with a female performer will almost always begin with a description of her appearance and clothing. The following description of Natalie Imbruglia appeared without a trace of irony in a *Guardian* interview:

> She's yawning and rubbing her eyes. Those eyes. Along with those eyes come that skin, that smile, those lips, that cute accent. If anything she's too perfect – like a tiny toy person ... She doesn't sit still, but squirms about on the sofa like a playful kitten ... Winning me over takes about seven seconds. (Wollaston 1998)

Women are often described as being physically small and childlike – always 'girls', never 'women' – perhaps in order to further differentiate them from men. The sexuality of female artists is foregrounded. For example, articles on women in rock music are given suggestive titles such as 'Women on Top', Alanis Morissette is accused of 'sexual hysteria' (*Observer Review*, 16 February 1997) and Kylie Minogue is asked in great detail about her teenage sexual experiences (Heath 1991).

It is worth mentioning in this context the photographic representation of women. Critics aiming to illustrate the sexism of the music press have occasionally resorted to counting the pictures of male and female artists in a publication, expecting women to be hugely under-represented. However, although pictures of women are slightly less frequent than those of men, it is more important to examine how the women are represented. Cerys Matthews of Catatonia appeared on the cover of *MM* on 20 March 1999, then the cover of the *NME* the following week. The fact that a woman was on two front pages within two weeks could be hailed as a triumph for female performers, yet in both photographs she is portrayed in overtly sexual terms. In *MM* she is described as 'gorgeous' and is portrayed leaning forward in a low-cut top, while in the *NME* she is wearing a dress with an extremely tight and low-cut bodice. Although her sneer in the latter photograph is clearly intended to illustrate the 'ironic' nature of this representation, this does not alter the fact that this is still a photograph of a woman with most of her breasts exposed. Indeed, her breasts are the most eye-catching aspect of this photograph and, even when this is juxtaposed with an ironic sneer, the cover gives the impression that the most important things about this woman are her breasts. There is a great similarity between these photographs and the representation of women on the covers of men's magazines such as *Loaded* (which was, incidentally, founded by former NME journalist James Brown), particularly in *MM*'s description of Cerys as 'gorgeous' – again, her talent is less significant than her appearance.

A simplistic explanation for the highly sexualized representation of women would be that individual male music journalists are unable to view women as anything other than sex objects. However, female commentators also write and speak about female performers in terms of appearance and sexuality, perhaps illustrating that women seeking success in male-dominated spheres such as music journalism have to accept the assumptions and prejudices of these spheres. They must become 'one of the boys', identifying with their male peers rather than with the women on whom they comment. Sexist remarks can therefore not be viewed as demonstrative of the prejudices of individual journalists, but as part of what is regarded as the only appropriate discourse for pop music writing.

The exception to the rule of focusing on a female artist's sexuality occurs when there is a suggestion of lesbianism. Kearney shows how reports on Riot Grrrl failed to link it to lesbian feminism or to the queercore movement, and ignored the implications of the phrase 'girl love', preferring to define it as friendship, as 'childish play rather than adult sexuality' (Kearney 1997: 223). Although Kearney overstates the extent to which Riot Grrrl was a lesbian movement, it is true that the music press found this aspect threatening and therefore chose to ignore it. Similarly, Dusty Springfield's 'difficult' reputation can largely be explained by the fact that the music industry found her lesbianism difficult to accept.

The constant stress on women's attractiveness and sexuality is easy to identify and criticize. However, a more subtle form of sexism operates around issues of credibility. In the eyes of the serious music world, credibility is the most important factor in determining the value of a performer or piece of music. It can be equated with critical acclaim, and I will use the two terms interchangeably. As Chambers explains, the idea of 'a thinking person's rock music' emerged in the late 1960s, at the same time as the professional rock critic 'appeared to legitimate the whole affair' (1985: 84). Rock critics have been responsible ever since for deciding which artists are credible, and therefore good and valuable, and which are not, and therefore bad and worthless. It is unsurprising that credibility has almost always been denied to female artists. I want to examine exactly what constitutes credibility and why women can never fulfil this definition.

Whether or not the music press will grant an artist credibility depends to a great extent on whether she is viewed as authentic. The notion of authenticity is, of course, highly subjective, as some element of performance is always involved: as Frith and Horne (1987) point out, 'Eric Clapton didn't grow up black, American or poor and Bruce Springsteen long since ceased to be a working man' (1987: 74). However, the idea that some performers are 'fake' while some are not is an extremely pervasive one.

In order to be viewed as 'authentic', a performer's music must be seen as an accurate representation of him- or herself, produced for personal self-expression rather than financial gain, and it is for this reason that performers who do not write their own material are dismissed. Perhaps the most widely cited example of such performers are the female artists associated with Svengali figure Phil Spector in the 1960s, and female performers have been viewed with distrust ever since. For example, Kylie Minogue was hated by the music press in the late 1980s because her association with the song-writing and producing team of Stock, Aitken and Waterman meant that she was viewed as completely inauthentic. One factor in the granting of critical approval to Kylie was that she was perceived to have seized greater control over her music, in which light her earlier work was reassessed and gained a measure of credibility retrospectively.

However, a woman who insists on such control is often depicted, in the music press as in popular culture more generally, as a 'difficult', hysterical, insecure, control freak. Women who seize control of their careers – which can be defined, for example, as writing their own material, insisting on their choice of producer, or attempting to control their photographic representation – risk forfeiting their femininity. An article on Natalie Imbruglia portrayed her as completely unreasonable when she attempted to assert an extremely moderate amount of power over her image:

[T]he preamble to the shoot had been something of a farce. Effecting a control more suitable to someone with the stature of Barbara Streisand, Natalie wanted to choose the photographer, as well as her own hairdresser and make-up artist. She then requested a letter from the *Sunday Times* promising not to airbrush or tamper with the pictures in any way. Naturally, we didn't comply. (Jones 1998)

Magazines are often forbidden even to crop images without approval, so this refusal to comply is not in the least natural.

Linked to the idea of authenticity is the importance of the image of the performer as a unique personality expressing their own individual truth. It is for this reason that Natalie Imbruglia was so vehemently attacked when it emerged that her first hit was actually a cover version and had not been written by her.[2] If women are viewed as being manipulated by Svengali figures, then the performers are replaceable and dispensable, and therefore of no value. Women are traditionally assumed to be passive and so are constantly suspected of being the victims of such manipulation.

In order to be viewed as credible, a performer's music must also be viewed as intelligent and serious. The association of masculinity with the cerebral and femininity with the physical perhaps explains women's exclusion from credibility on these grounds. Women attempting to present themselves as intelligent are regarded as pretentious, with the music press's treatment of Alanis Morissette a case in point. She is criticized for 'sixth-form self-indulgence' (*Observer Review*, 29 October 1995) because 'her lyrics have the ring of a teenager who has just discovered Philip Larkin' (*Guardian*, 6 May 1996). When the Manic Street Preachers, an all-male band, quote directly from Philip Larkin in both their lyrics and on their album sleeves, this is taken as a sign of their high levels of intelligence and education.

Women are not felt to be capable of any deep thought or feeling, so are viewed as particularly pretentious when expressing any kind of pain or angst. When Natalie Imbruglia expresses feelings of depression, she is corrected and told that she has not been depressed but simply 'a bit down' (Wollaston 1998) and Alanis Morissette is instructed to 'fuck off and have some kind of life' (*Guardian*, 18 April 1997).[3] Again, a comparison with the sympathetic and serious treatment that Richey Edwards of the Manic Street Preachers received when speaking of his depression is relevant here, as is the image of the male rock star as a Romantic hero, discussed below.

The degree to which an artist's music is viewed as 'serious' is often inversely proportional to the extent to which their image is foregrounded.

Male bands wishing to be taken seriously almost without exception adopt the dowdy indie uniform of jeans and T-shirts, in order to imply that their music is the most important thing to them. This is in itself, of course, one type of image. However, it is unusual for female performers to take this approach, perhaps partly because women in general tend to put more time and effort into their appearance than men, and female musicians are as much a product of their society as anyone else. Also, as noted above, interviewers inevitably focus on the appearance of female performers anyway, so dressing down is likely to have little effect on the prominence of their visual image. Natalie Imbruglia's dishevelled look – no more or less contrived than Oasis's similarly unkempt appearance – is apparently 'rather like a young Marilyn Monroe ignoring her ample bosom and declaring, "Forget Hollywood, it's a career down the coal mines for me!"' (live review, MM, 14 November 1998)

The perception of an artist's talent is vital to her credibility, and it is here that women's traditional role as singers is extremely relevant. Singing is generally regarded as natural. Anyone can do it and it is wrongly perceived as not requiring practice and work, and therefore undervalued. As Coates (1997) points out, this does not explain why male singers are valued and female ones are not, but I would argue that it is generally assumed that singing is a feminine skill, and a female singer is therefore unremarkable, whereas a male singer is regarded as being exceptionally talented.

A final important element of credibility is the extent to which a performer is regarded as rebellious and differentiated from 'mainstream' entertainment. This often involves being seen as part of a subculture: 'authenticity is dependent on the extent to which records are assimilated and legitimated by a subculture' (Thornton 1995: 66). It is difficult for female performers to separate themselves from the mainstream because, as Sarah Thornton shows, the mainstream is often defined precisely as music associated with girls and women: 'the oft-repeated, almost universally accepted stereotype of the chartpop disco was that it was a place where "Sharon and Tracy dance around their handbags"' (Thornton 1995: 99). This association of the mainstream with women is not unique to rock music: Huyssen points out that 'pejorative feminine characteristics' have been ascribed to mass culture since the nineteenth century (1986: 193).

Frith and Horne illustrate how the emerging image of rock music in the 1960s was based to a large extent on its being 'unlike pop' and representing 'the usual bohemian rebellion against domesticity and the bourgeois family, the assertion that *the artist* is, by *his* nature, stifled by family life' (1987: 90, their emphasis). They point out that women were often taken to personify the conservative domesticity against which these men were rebelling.

However, the mainstream is not simply music for women, but music for working-class women, as is implied by the choice of the unmistakably working-class names 'Sharon and Tracy'. It is interesting that music journalists and male musicians almost universally attempt to project an image of working-class masculinity, to the extent that artists who deviate from this – for example, Suede or the Divine Comedy – do so extremely self-consciously and are seen almost in terms of rebellion. However, the female musicians of whom the music press approves do not project an image of working-class femininity but rather represent the same type of working-class masculinity that is appropriate for male stars. The clearest example of this is Cerys Matthews of Catatonia, who appears to be accepted by the music press largely because of her heavy drinking, frank discussion of sex and criticism of the English upper classes, with her Welshness adding to this image. The *NME* even went so far as to describe her as a 'Really Nice Bloke' (*NME*, 27 March 1999).

Subcultures do not generally welcome women, and those that have, tend to accept them only in very limited roles. This, coupled with the association of femininity with the mainstream, means that female artists can rarely hope to gain the sense of excitement, rebellion and therefore credibility that comes from an association with a subculture. Instead, perhaps from a realization of the unlikeliness of ever attaining credibility, women have tended to go to the opposite extreme, becoming family entertainers and gaining complete acceptance into the 'mainstream' so despised by the serious music press (Frith 1988).

The music press is only too happy to assist female artists with this move. Perhaps the reason that Natalie Imbruglia largely escaped the unpleasant and hysterical attacks reserved for Alanis Morissette was because she represented an incorporation of the image of the female singer–songwriter. This image has previously contained some threatening elements, particularly its association with feminism, and for it to become associated with a family entertainer and ex-soap opera star helps to contain this threat.

In order to be perceived as rebellious, it is helpful if a performer is seen as being angry, whether this be in political terms or just a generalized rage against the world. Anger is regarded as a masculine trait, so that even when women do dare to express their anger it is not seen in these terms: an angry woman is unreasonable or even insane, 'a gross caricature with no nobility, intellect or ethics' (Love 1993).

An angry image, with the hint of self-destructive tendencies that this implies, is viewed as heroic and exciting in a man, but women with such an image are pathologized. As Reynolds and Press put it: 'Where male artists who walk a high-wire over the abyss of self-destruction tend to present a spectacle of mastery, female performers who flirt with disaster tend to elicit different responses: a morbid mixture of voyeurism, pity and sadistic delight at the possibility that she might fall' (Reynolds and Press 1995: 269).[4] This could perhaps be due to the perception that angry women are usually angry because of things that have been done to them by men; for example, Riot Grrrl's emphasis on abuse and incest. As noted above, being in control is important to the attainment of credibility, and as Reynolds and Press point out, rebellious men are still seen to be in control of themselves while rebellious women are protesting at their own lack of control (1995: 329).

It would therefore appear that credibility is, in the eyes of the music press at least, a male trait, and one that women are rarely, if ever, able to live up to entirely. Natalie Imbruglia's attainment of a small measure of credibility was so remarkable that The Big Issue dedicated a whole article to detailing how she achieved it (Crossing 1998).

However, it is possible for female performers to gain some measure of credibility. First, a woman may be able to fulfil some of the criteria listed above. P.J. Harvey's perceived intellectualism means that she is regarded as a credible and authentic artist. Yet the fact that she is still not equal with male stars is illustrated by the continued stress on her appearance and sexuality.

A second approach is to gain credibility by association with a man, as Kylie Minogue is widely viewed as having done. Her relationship with Michael Hutchence enabled her 'SexKylie' image to be viewed as more authentic: 'One moment she was the brainless, sexless soap star, the next, after caressing the raging loins of INXS's wild man, she was the flirty sex goddess who was out to get what she wanted in the world' (Heath 1991: 48). More recently, she has gained credibility by working with men such as Nick Cave and James Dean Bradfield.

However, this can bring accusations that the woman is simply a puppet. Every early article on Natalie Imbruglia gave a list of the male musicians who worked on her album: 'She even managed to employ the services of Radiohead producer Nigel Godrich, Eels writer Mark Goldenber and Phil Thornalley, once of the Cure. And recently, she's been working with Dave Stewart. You don't get much more credible than that' (Wollaston 1998). The flippant tone of Wollaston's last sentence suggests the difficulty of including Imbruglia in the discourse of credibility. Attempting to gain status through working with 'credible' men can thus simply increase suspicion that the woman is being manipulated or is using her sexuality to further her career.

Female artists can also achieve credibility through men in another way, when stars who have been taken up for their camp qualities by gay men are viewed with a kind of ironic approval. Camp is defined by Richard Dyer as involving 'irony, exaggeration, trivialisation, theatricalisation and an ambivalent making fun out of the serious and respectable' (Dyer 1987: 178). A woman willing and able to make fun of herself in this way can gain an element of critical acclaim, as has happened recently with Kylie. It would seem that some female artists deliberately court such approval; for example, Madonna has incorporated images from gay culture into her videos, most notably that for 'Vogue'. This does, however, involve making sacrifices, as this type of ironic credibility means that the artist's work is not really taken seriously.

A third way for a woman to gain credibility is by becoming masculinized: 'one of the lads'. An *MM* interview with All Saints spoke very favourably of them because their continual swearing and joking meant that 'All Saints are – hold back the sneers – Just Like Us' (*MM*, 7 February 1998: 28). Such an approach can be remarkably successful. Charlotte, guitarist and only female member of Northern Irish indie band Ash, has been accepted to the extent that the band are continually referred to in interviews and reviews as 'the lads', with no reference to her femaleness being made at all. This could be seen as a positive development, but does involve the artist distancing herself from other women either implicitly or explicitly, and has been regarded by Riot Grrrl bands, for example, as 'assimilationist' and as 'selling out' – playing by the music industry's rules (Morris 1993).

Finally, a female artist can be granted credibility with time if she is no longer viewed as a threat. Madonna's recent, more conservative 'grown-up' image has certainly been viewed with less alarm than her previous incarnations, and the fact that she is now a mother is extremely relevant here. It would seem that in becoming a mother and wife, albeit a somewhat unconventional one, she has sufficiently conformed to acceptable feminine behaviour to no longer be viewed as threatening.

To summarize, when music journalism fails to exclude women from popular music history altogether it excludes them from the world of serious music by constructing a notion of credibility which is extremely difficult for a woman to obtain. The music press then attempts to play down the exclusion of femininity from rock music using the notion that 'the feminine' can be provided by men. The figure of the Byronic, bohemian, feminized man as a Romantic hero has been a staple of rock music since Jim Morrison in the 1960s, and its most recent manifestation has been Richey Edwards of the Manic Street Preachers. Men such as Edwards, Kurt Cobain of Nirvana and Brett Anderson of Suede are praised for their exploration of the feminine and, particularly in the cases of Edwards and Cobain, are described as emotional and tortured figures. Edwards was praised for his open discussion of his anorexia and self-mutilation, while the same topics were unpalatable when spoken of by female Riot Grrrls. If men can provide 'the feminine' then women are redundant.

Feminist Women

Given the intense sexism of the music industry and particularly of the music press, it is unsurprising that those women who do manage to become successful and/or credible are rarely willing to risk losing their position by making explicitly feminist statements. Female artists are continually asked about feminism in interviews, and this is one way in which they are spoken about as women first and as musicians second. However, very few female musicians openly declare themselves to be feminists.

Anjali of the Voodoo Queens, best known for the single *Supermodel Superficial* – a song with a specifically feminist agenda – said in an *MM* interview: 'I think we have something to say. Other people would probably call us feminists. It's a really difficult area. I mean, what does the word mean?' (*MM*, 29 January 1994). Such coyness could be explained by a lack of interest in politics in favour of concentrating on music. However, I would argue that such reluctance to talk about feminism is based on the way that the music press treats feminist women.

The music press places great emphasis on the discourse of 'coolness', which largely consists of a kind of adolescent world-weary cynicism and dictates that to become too passionate about any subject is potentially embarrassing. While journalists are able to waive these rules when they want to write enthusiastically about a new male band or artist, a major way in which feminists are ridiculed is by mocking them for having any form of strong belief. As Rumsey and Little put it, 'Rock's vocabulary dictates that being a feminist is not the way to be cool' (1985: 243).

The vitriolic abuse heaped on Alanis Morissette can only be explained by her openly feminist views, although this is, of course, never explicitly stated. More generally, women with overtly feminist beliefs are simply ridiculed. Sara Manning wrote in *MM*:

> The best thing that any Riot Grrrl could do is to go away and do some reading, and I don't mean a grubby little fanzine. When the topic of French feminist theory was raised in one of the discussions, there were blank looks and hostile reactions. Read Kristeva, Cixous, Irigaray. Read Freud's essays on sexuality and then come back with a reasoned

understanding of who the enemy may or may not be ... For now you can be a Riot Grrrl or you can be a feminist – you can't be both. (*MM*, 29 January 1994)

This untenable view illustrates the pressures put on women who define themselves as feminists and helps to further exclude the issue of feminism from music – few women could possibly meet such criteria, and therefore they cannot really be feminists. It is also an example of the music press employing a female journalist to criticize female performers with impunity, as well as of the music press using a self-consciously 'intellectual' discourse to suggest that forms of music of which it does not approve are inherently less intelligent. An equally common reaction of female journalists to Riot Grrrl was to assert that they personally 'don't need saving' (see, for example, Morris 1993: 11). Feminist musicians are both expected to speak for all women and asked to claim that they do in order that they can be repudiated.

However, the music press usually prefers to ignore feminism altogether. First-hand accounts of Riot Grrrl conventions make clear their similarity to the consciousness-raising meetings of 1970s feminists, yet writing on Riot Grrrl in the music press often ignores its specific politics, turning it into, as Kearney puts it, 'just another anarchic pose of youth' (Kearney 1997: 224). The *NME*'s 'Definitive guide to Riot Grrrl' managed to imply that the only thing people involved in the movement were 'rioting' against was boredom (Wells 1993). This cannot be justified by the argument that the role of the music press is to focus primarily on the music because male bands with outspoken political beliefs are praised. An edition of the *NME* carried the headline 'Ever Get the Feeling You've Been Cheated?' and featured a range of (almost all male) artists criticizing the government, and the Manic Street Preachers have been widely praised for taking the title for their album *This is My Truth Tell Me Yours* from a speech by Aneurin Bevan.[5]

To summarize, an admission of a feminist viewpoint can be extremely harmful to a female performer's career. This creates an absurd situation whereby performers whose lyrics and images are explicitly feminist have to repeatedly deny this in interviews. This helps to naturalize social relations in music, so that gender is not seen in political terms, but simply as part of human nature.

Female Performers: Conclusions

The music press abuses and trivializes female musicians in both explicit and more subtle ways. In recent years, there have been a number of attempts by female musicians to bypass the music press altogether. Most Riot Grrrl bands refused to speak to the music press after 1993 out of fear of misrepresentation, preferring to give interviews with small fanzines which they felt would give them a more sympathetic hearing. However, this tactic simply meant that whole articles on Riot Grrrl were devoted to the journalist's difficulties in obtaining an interview (see, for example, Wells 1993), so that the politics, and even the music, were even further sidelined.

This tactic of refusing to have anything to do with the music press has led to the recent creation of a number of magazines and fanzines written by women and devoted entirely to female artists. One British example of this is *Popgirls*. This was created by Manda Rin, lead singer with Bis, because she had been angered at the treatment she and other female musicians had received from the mainstream music press: 'I'm fed up of articles on girls in bands being purely descriptive of their looks rather than their attitude' (*Popgirls #1*: 4). While such publications are certainly a positive development, they tend to concentrate on obscure alternative artists, to have limited distribution, and therefore to remain on a very small scale, and so pose little or no threat to the male domination of the rock music press.

. . .

Conclusion

Julie Burchill (1998) writes of the staff at the *NME* in the late 1970s as a 'Boys' Club', and little has altered since then. The British music press uses its own very particular idiom, which differs little from that of more openly 'laddish' magazines such as *Loaded*. This means, for example, that a woman will always be referred to in terms of her appearance and described using sexist terms such as 'girl' – a term that the Riot Grrrl movement attempted to reclaim as positive – or 'bitch' – which can be used positively or negatively.

This distinctive idiom is internalized by aspiring music journalists – those writing in student publications, for example – who realize that they must write in the correct style to be successful. Such compliance and conservatism mean that the sexism of the music press is self-perpetuating, and that there are few differences between individual writers. It is ironic that an industry that regards itself as creative and progressive should reproduce such unoriginal and antiquated beliefs: 'the music press reflects the attitudes of most of the music world in being liberal, by and large, about racism, but densely reactionary as regards sexism' (Whitman 1981: 21).

Women wanting to enter this Boys' Club must conceal their femininity. They use the same sexist discourses as male journalists to distance themselves from the type of women whom the music press despises – working-class women or women perceived as some kind of threat. Of course, there are women who have resisted doing this, one prominent example from the UK being Julie Burchill. The occasional woman with a strong enough writing style can be accepted into the Boys' Club on her own terms, but examples of this are few and far between.

Journalism is a highly competitive career. Once a new journalist finds a job on a paper or magazine, they are quickly expected to learn to write in the style of that particular publication. It takes both courage and a great deal of writing talent to challenge such expectations successfully.

The sexism of the music press may discourage women from becoming musicians or music journalists, or from taking other jobs within the industry. However, it may also have effects outside the music business. *MM* had and the *NME* still has a relatively large circulation, with the majority of their readers being teenage boys. It is arguable that the sexism of such publications legitimates sexist views in their readers, especially as there are few alternatives to these two papers. Music fans who want to read interviews with performers and get information on new releases can turn to the Internet, but websites generally share the same discourses as the music press. Rumsey and Little point out the shallowness of the rebellious images of many male stars, noting: 'Feminists know that if rock/pop was really revolutionary, they would be embraced as the greatest rebels of all – real rebels, the genuine article, not just another piece in the jigsaw of popular ephemera' (1985: 244). However, the British music press prefers to concentrate on male bands following the same old tried and tested routes to success, and acting out a rebellion that usually just consists of a complete contempt for women. To admit women to the 'Boys' Club' would question the assumptions on which music writing has been based for decades.

Notes

1. The same article gives a list of 'those who paved the way', including Polly Harvey and Tanya Donelly, implying that there were no female pop musicians before the late 1980s.
2. However, it should be noted that the type of pop performance she had adopted

– the female singer–songwriter – certainly made the situation worse because the fact that she had not written the song appeared as a betrayal of this image.
3. The satirical 'Alanis Morissette lyric generator' on the Internet at www.brunching.com is an illustration of the fact that the image of her as pretentious and foolish created by the music press has largely gone unquestioned: there are no Manic Street Preachers or Nirvana lyric generators.
4. For an illustration of this phenomenon see, for example, the comments about Courtney Love in *MM* and *NME* during 1994. She was continually described as mad, pathetic and attention-seeking when expressing her anger at the death of her husband.
5. Minister of Health in Clement Attlee's government of 1945, responsible for establishing the NHS.

References

Bayton, M. (1997) Women and the electric guitar, in S. Whiteley (ed.) *Sexing the Groove: Popular Music and Gender*. London: Routledge.

Bourdieu, P. (1984) *Distinction: A Social Critique of the Judgement of Taste*. London: Routledge.

Burchill, J. (1998) *I Knew I was Right*. London: Pluto.

Burchill, J. and Parsons, T. (1978) *The Boy Looked at Johnny: The Obituary of Rock and Roll*. London: Pluto Press.

Chambers, I. (1985) *Urban Rhythms: Pop Music and Popular Culture*. London: Macmillan.

Coates, N. (1997) (R)evolution now? Rock and the political potential of gender, in S. Whiteley (ed.) *Sexing the Groove: Popular Music and Gender*. London: Routledge.

Cohen, S. (1997) Men making a scene: rock music and the production of gender, in S. Whiteley (ed.) *Sexing the Groove: Popular Music and Gender*. London: Routledge.

Compton, N. (1998) Natalie Imbruglio, *Independent on Sunday*, 8 February.

Crossing, G. (1998) Pretty vacant?, *The Big Issue*, 5–11 October.

Davin, A. (1988) Redressing the balance or transforming the art? The British experience, in S.J Kleinberg (ed.), *Retrieving Women's History*. Oxford: Berg.

Dyer, R. (1987) *Heavenly Bodies: Film Stars and Society*. London: Routledge.

Frith, S. (1988) *Music For Pleasure: Essays in the Sociology of Pop*. Cambridge:

Frith, S. and Horne, H. (1987) *Art Into Pop*. London: Methuen.

Gaar, G. (1993) *She's a Rebel: The History of Women in Rock and Roll*. London:

Heath, C. (1991) In bed with Kylie, *The Face*, 37.

Heath, C. (1994) Kylie's cool world, *The Face*, 69.

Huyssen, A. (1986) Mass culture as woman: modernism's other, in T. Modleski (ed.) *Studies in Entertainment: Critical Approaches to Mass Culture*. Bloomington: Indiana University Press.

Jones, D. (1998) Meet the fussiest pop star in the world, *The Sunday Times, Style*, 25 October.

Kearney, M.C. (1997) The missing links: Riot Grrrl – feminism – lesbian culture, in S. Whiteley (ed.) *Sexing the Groove: Popular Music and Gender*. London: Routledge.

Love, C. (1993) Revolution rebel style, in *Melody Maker*, 17 July.

McDonnell, E. and Powers, A. (eds) (1995) *Rock She Wrote*. London: Plexus.

Morris, G. (1993) Girls just wanna bait scum, *New Musical Express*, 20 March.

Reynolds, S. and Press, J. (1995) *The Sex Revolts: Gender, Rebellion and Rock'n'Roll*. London: Serpent's Tail.

Rumsey, G. and Little, H. (1989) Women and pop: a series of lost encounters, in A. McRobbie (ed.) (1989) *Zoot Suits and Second-Hand Dresses: An Anthology of Fashion and Music*. London: HarperCollins.

Steward, S. and Garratt, S. (eds) (1984) *Signed, Sealed and Delivered: True Stories of Women in Pop*. London: Palgrave Macmillan.

Thornton, S. (1995) *Club Cultures*. Cambridge: Polity.

Wells, S. (1993) The definitive guide to Riot Grrrl, *New Musical Express*, 6 and 13 March.

Whitman, L. (1981) Women and popular music, *Spare Rib*, June, 107.

Wollaston, S. (1998) The girl next door, *Guardian*, 15 May.

Internet Sites

IPC Magazines: www.ipc.co.uk.

The Almost Official Natalie Imbruglia Web Site: www.imbruglia.com.

What I did on my Summer Vacation: www.ernie.bgsu.edu/_ckile/rgomaha.html (no longer available). First-hand account of a Riot Grrrl convention.

LOSING FEAR

VIDEO AND RADIO PRODUCTIONS OF NATIVE AYMARA WOMEN

Carmen Ruíz

In both urban and peasant communities in Bolivia one frequently encounters groups of residents discussing and debating their affairs. Men form the closed part of the circle, expressing opinions, suggestions and disagreements. Women are often found in the open part of the circle, behind the centre of discussion, together, as if seeking protection; present, yet at the same time absent; listening, but without a public voice. 'I'm afraid,' say the women. 'Perhaps I won't use the right words, or maybe they'll laugh at me.'

Although half the membership of most of Bolivia's worker, merchant or neighborhood associations are women, these organizations are usually represented by men, not only in the executive but also in the public sphere. Organizations such as the guilds that represent street vendors and small businesspeople may have up to 80 per cent female membership, and yet the majority of their leaders are men.

It is not only in grassroots organizations in which the voices of women do not appear very often or are badly represented. Social, economic and political indicators of daily life in the country also demonstrate this absence. For example, the lack of women's representation is evident in the different expressions of formal political power, such as political parties, the government and the parliament as well as in diverse expressions of civil society and the mass media.

According to the indigenist position that recognizes the native population as a fundamental part of the nation,[1] Bolivia is a country unfinished as a nation. The native population has been marginalized economically, politically and culturally since colonization. According to politicians, Bolivia is a country facing the contradictions arising from poverty and from external and internal colonialism; and according to the different expressions of the women's movement, Bolivia is a country affected by gender-based oppression.

In this country of many and diverse faces, in the relations of everyday life, and in the mass media, the voice of women is not only one more absent expression but clear testimony of how silence and oppression coexist.

This chapter summarizes a project initiated in 1984 by the Gregoria Apaza Centre for the Advancement of Women (CPMGA)[2] called A Thousand and One Voices: Communication With Urban Aymara Women.[3] The project with Aymara women has three lines of action: training, production and reception of mass media, particularly radio and video. We use mass media to help bring about a change in the discrimination and subordination of urban Aymara women.

This project developed mainly with groups of Aymara women and residents of the different neighborhoods of the city El Alto, a region of predominantly Aymara immigrants located 15 miles away from the capital La Paz.[4] Our communication experience will be retold here in chronological order, including explanations of the groups involved and of the methodological criteria developed throughout the process.[5]

The communication programme of the centre consists of:

- a daily radio programme – *La voz de las Kantutas* – which broadcasts testimonies, interviews and dramatizations of the daily life of Aymara women who have migrated to the city
- educational video productions for a variety of campaigns such as violence against women, cholera prevention, reforestation of the neighborhood, and so on
- the popular reporters project, which trains Aymara women in reporting techniques for radio and television
- a community short-range radio station that is a key aspect of a local development plan for the enhancement of women and the defence of their rights.

Urban Aymara Women and Communication

Our throats come alive

The first time we evaluated the results of the communication project, it became clear that there were two different social actors, each with different expectations: the urban Aymara women and the group that worked at the women's centre.

Aymara women were interested in the processes of media production and in the possibility of training themselves in the use of modern and urban language: 'We lost the fear of speaking' was one of the most common expressions used in the self-evaluation of their participation. 'Our throats came alive,' said some. 'We ourselves direct our words, and in this way everyone knows that we can,' said others. The most succinct evaluation was given by a woman who had participated in various radio plays and in the presentation of a staged theatrical work in front of a large audience. She said, 'Now I speak better, I am more sure of myself in front of people from the city [La Paz] when I enter an office. I'm losing the fear of speaking.'[6]

The experience revealed a diversity of achievements. On one hand was the institutional perspective, closer to a communication strategy, in which the use of the radio as a mass medium was thought of as a way to achieve more social impact on larger numbers of listeners. On the other hand were the expectations of the trainees who were learning to use words, as instruments of new relations and communicative exchanges with the urban, modern and mestizo world.

To understand these two dimensions and the expectations held by each group of women, it is necessary to outline the social and cultural realities of El Alto and the history of the institution.

Impact of the national crises on poor women

Bolivia is experiencing a period of intense economic crisis for which no short-term solution is foreseen. This crisis, which has placed 80 per cent of the Bolivian population in a state of critical poverty, affects poor women in a distinct manner. Poor women are responsible for the administration of family income and are increasingly responsible for subsidizing a deteriorating household economy through diverse survival strategies.

This situation of crisis is felt in El Alto and particularly in Villa 16 de Julio, a barrio in the northern section of the city of El Alto. Since its creation in 1946, this barrio (with a population of 30,000 or 10 per cent of El Alto's population) has been a focal point of Aymara migration from rural areas to the city.

The conditions of scarcity force the population of Villa 16 de Julio to live by a logic of subsistence, for which the key phrase is 'survive day by day', and to put their energies into diverse activities that together form what has been called strategies of survival. The women of Villa 16 de Julio play an important role as administrators of scarce family resources. They work in the informal sector of the economy or participate in organizations seeking to increase family incomes. For example, women group together to accept donated food, to participate in educational programmes, to be in service activities and to be in labour unions. This participation of women in a diversity of organizations is combined with work in more strictly economic activities such as small-scale commerce, family enterprises and, occasionally, salaried work in small factories. More frequently, women are to be found working as housemaids in the center of La Paz.

The inhabitants of Villa 16 de Julio form a kind of small city, a mestiza society that draws sustenance – and not in a harmonious manner but rather in constant tension and conflict – from what is traditional Aymara and what is modern, urban and mestizo. Even if it seems easy to distinguish the various elements that feed it, the result of this mixture is a unique culture of conflicting codes.

The strategic proposal of the centre for a plan of local development based on the perspective of gender is the result of eight years of work in the city of El Alto. The proposal is based on the premise that there is no possibility of transformation in the situation of subordination of poor women if at the same time one does not fight against poverty. Equally, it will be impossible to eradicate poverty if simultaneously action is not taken to make substantial changes in the situation of subordination and oppression of women.

Identity: a game of mirrors and reflections

One of the distinctive characteristics of the community of Villa 16 de Julio is the strong relations maintained between residents and their originating communities (90 per cent of which are rural communities in the altiplano region of the department of La Paz). Links with the communities of origin are maintained through frequent travel to the countryside, participation in planting and harvesting, exchange of products, and through participation in festivals and rituals.

Consequently, the barrio of Villa 16 de Julio maintains a particular place in the urban world. The community's daily life evolves in a syncretic mix of two worlds that attract each other but that relate in a conflicting, sometimes antagonistic, manner: the Aymara and the Western/mestizo world.

Given its population density, El Alto has considerable importance in the spatial distribution of the altiplano region and its politics. This, however, has no correlation with the amount of attention given it in terms of necessities or urban services. As El Alto became a target for the different social and political expressions of local and central authorities, local outlets of the mass media and particularly commercial radio were established.

Daily language and expression

The living conditions of women in Villa 16 de Julio are characterized by economic and social subordination and the absence of political representation. Part of the living conditions are the 'conditions of expression'; those that are latent in daily verbal or non-verbal language as well as in the codes of mass media. In this sense, the silence of women can be seen simultaneously from various perspectives. One of these is that verbal silence is compensated by a non-verbal language expressed in the domestic environment.

The communicative expression of Aymara women is limited by their precarious mastery of the official language (Spanish), their migrant status, their use of traditional costume (skirt, shawl and hat), their low level of education and their condition of poverty. These factors inhibit them from establishing an efficient relationship with the public, urban, mestizo world. 'When they see that we're wearing a traditional skirt they ask: "What do you want!?" then they make us wait and leave us there for an hour. If a señorita [a woman dressed in modern, Western clothes] comes in they attend to her first' (Centro Para la Mujer Gregoria Apaza 1991). In this context, the use and control of words takes on vital importance, as vital as the satisfaction of basic needs.

Social silence

In El Alto as in La Paz, most women work for themselves in intermediary activities.[7] Reinforcing a circle to meet daily necessities, women do what they know best and what also permits the continuation of daily life: domestic labour. The fulfilment of domestic responsibilities constitutes for these women a reference point for their identity, which proposals for participation and social communication cannot afford to ignore.

Poverty and scarcity goes deeper than the obvious material conditions. They affect the most intimate construction of identity for urban Aymara women. Such notions as self-esteem, the exercise of power, representation and the carrying out of roles that give one a place in society are all profoundly marked by their contradictory position – the highly valued domestic role and function of motherhood on one hand and the discrimination and an overload of responsibility on the other.

The discourse of urban Aymara women about their own family and community roles and responsibilities is very sensitive to this contradiction. Overlaid with a profound experience of ethnic/cultural discrimination, the contradiction is expressed both in the relation between women and mass media and in women's mastery of public speech.

The Institutional Programme

The communication proposal of the CPMGA arose in 1985, with the idea of designing and carrying out a project that could respond to the critical period that Bolivia was facing. This was a period of deep economic and political crisis characterized by the emergence of diverse expressions of women's movements around the need to find solutions to the severe consequences of the crisis. During this period, a number of NGOs were created that were oriented to collaborating with the women's movement, while alternative communication proposals were promoted to recognize this movement. These programmes saw the use of communication media as an arena to discuss the situation of women, as a motivator of participation and as a denouncer of oppression. The communication proposal of the centre was generated on the following premises:

- the necessity of incorporating groups of women (their experiences, struggles, sentiments and daily lives), as the protagonists and broadcasters of an alternative message to the traditional images transmitted by the mass media
- the need for the use of radio as social communication, and as an alternative to the traditional radio practices in the history of both Bolivia and of popular organizations
- the implementation of a methodology that would combine group and mass aspects within an educational perspective for the promotion of women.

We began with a weekly 15-minute radio programme for women, called *La voz de las Kantutas*, which eventually became a twice-weekly 30-minute programme broadcast by three stations. Simultaneously, we worked on video programmes, educational pamphlets and articles in the press.

Radio production: *La voz de las Kantutas*

The CPMGA chose radio as the mass medium to initiate the project. Radio reaches virtually the entire urban and rural population, overcoming scarcities of infrastructure and electrical power. It corresponds to a strong oral tradition in Andean cultures and has played an important role in the struggles of Bolivian popular movements, such as the miners' stations,[8] the Educational Radio of Bolivia (ERBOL) and the labour union radio.

In Bolivia, traditional radio broadcasting has privileged the use of native languages. Its programming fits the schedules and habits of people's daily life, becoming a permanent companion in domestic spaces and with work outside the home. Its traditional uses have led to the development of unique formats based on Andean culture such as messages, greetings, congratulations and story telling. Finally, radio has lent itself to a strategic combination of group and interpersonal means articulated as a mass medium.

Initially, *La voz de las Kantutas* (named after the Bolivian national flower) had a radio magazine format. It included interviews, music and commentary by two hosts (a man and a woman), professional speakers, and sociodramas pre-recorded by groups of women and later edited to follow a central theme put together by the hosts.

The sociodramas were produced in workshops. They were seen as a connection between the educational work of the centre's development teams and the centre's communication production. Stories were later recorded following various forms of expression: from stories to dramatizations or, more simply, the recording of testimonies, commentary and opinion.

Radio production followed thematic cycles that were decided according to the thread of reflection in the work of the centre with different groups of women. The process of production began from the moment of data collection, through discussion with the community and organizations, to field recordings of radio dramas, debates, interviews and testimonies, script writing, processing of information, broadcasting, and finally to the moment of evaluation and planning.

Our starting point was the recognition of women's reality, through testimonies, stories, dramatizations, second-hand documentation and interviews. Following that, there was a reflection on the data or more qualitative information on the reality in which women find themselves. This debate was carried out with motivational elements such as games, paintings, sociodramas and simple conversations. Last, there was the design of a material proposal, its editing and broadcast.

During the design and execution of these steps, we took into account criteria such as the recognition of the principles and values of urban Aymara culture, the role of radio as a mass medium in the daily life of the urban Aymara population, the relationship between urban Aymara women and their consumption of radio as a mass medium, and the self-training of women in the use of radio. In this process, women became active broadcasters of their own discourse. This last element was intended as a way to subvert the traditional relationship that women had with radio by locating them as active broadcasters of their own world-view and using their own language.

However, this format did not identify the impact that our programmes were having on the audience. While in producing the programme there was a very close relationship with the participant women, the circle was artificially closed with the transmission of the programme. In the closing of the first cycle of radio programming we identified numerous conflicts regarding the relationship between our programming goals, the methods of participation and the relation with the audience. We referred to the goals guiding the practices of the institution, that is, the promotion of women and the focus on gender, culture and poverty.

The women participants perceived the programme as an opportunity for participation, training in expression, and the possibility of broadcasting their group experiences, advances and achievements. Their emphasis on practical gains reflects their strong feelings about the potential of becoming their own broadcasters of messages. This self-recognition means that these women value themselves as possible educators of other women. In conclusion, the perception of the programme held by these women was very much related to their participation, and from that a sense of ownership developed. They recognized themselves as broadcasters and educators of other women.

For the centre, the educational potential of radio broadcasting was related to the possibility of orienting the community's thoughts and attitudes about the demands of daily life and the possibility of establishing a connection between the domestic and the community's public activities. However, various difficulties hindered a more widespread continuation of the programme.

A conventional analysis of the programme's impact
Our impact analysis had not gone beyond what is conventionally analysed in mass communication (i.e. audiences, tendencies and opinions). We did not take into account the impact of participation (as producers or audience) on the daily behaviour of women, on attitudinal change and on social relations. The focus of this alternative approach is on evaluating less measurable effects and intangible achievements, such as the increase in self-esteem, the development of creativity and the opening of opportunities for pleasure, or, in short, the evaluation of women's experience of moments that are rare in lives dominated by the need for survival. For the urban Aymara women, the project has stimulated and strengthened their self-esteem. There is no doubt that the project has achieved an improvement in the expressive capacities of the popular women involved. The project has trained them to control resources better, incorporating them in the production of materials that adequately describe their daily problems.

The planning and evaluation of the objective of influencing public opinion
We identified an excessive emphasis on activities designed for strengthening individuals and groups, and a relative disregard of proposals directed at public opinion and the mass media. We can say little about achievements in terms of social circulation of ideas or of the institution itself, where the success of a project of communication must also be measured.

The emphasis of the project on the personal growth of small groups of popular women presented a number of concerns. To what extent was such production and broadcasting under-utilizing a mass medium? To what extent was the absence of institutional mechanisms for following up the audience reception ignoring an important dimension of the project? Was this disjuncture a result of a flaw in the design, or a result of how the communication proposal found a place in the institutional proposal?

In part the answers to these concerns can be found in the theoretical contributions of those who underline the importance of examining social uses and consumption of mass media. They refer to the fundamental role that the use of mass media, in a strategy of development, can have in the construction of collective identities and in linking the strategic interests of various popular groups (Alfaro 1988; Mata 1985, 1990).

From magazine to drama

One of the most important practical recommendations by the women participants in *La voz de las Kantutas* was to increase and improve the space given to radio dramas. As a consequence, we set up a drama workshop. The format of radio dramas breaks with the academic tone that dominated the magazine style and responds to the demands of the women.

The workshop focuses on the construction of collective stories that reflect the lives of the participants. The goal is to look critically at these stories with the intention of discovering the causes of problems and to propose concrete actions to resolve them. The content of the dramas presents a wide range of events from daily life; women are the protagonists, but also examined are their most intimate family relations, their desires, their expectations and their problems. In the workshops, the following steps are incorporated: brainstorming to select a theme, a round-table discussion to relate stories based on the selected idea, the determination of the central message, plot construction, the selection of characters, the division of the story by chapter and scene, direct lineal recording, the recording of the narration, editing, adding music and effects, and the broadcast. These radio dramas are fictitious narratives that represent the scenarios and situations of daily life in El Alto.

The principal achievement in the production of radio dramas is the method developed for plot construction. It puts emphasis on participation, on the Andean narrative, and on the expression of feelings, while at the same time it makes spaces for pleasure, reflection and spontaneity. However, in the evaluation, participants noted that the themes are not developed enough in terms of drama. They were seen to be superficial, both in terms of content and in the format itself. Their perception was that the radio drama is slow and linear and that it does not produce a sufficient degree of empathy with a mass audience. Another important element is that the expectation of production with a competitive quality (in commercial terms) has not been reached. The production is by amateurs and has the logic of a workshop formation or production.

The second stage of La voz de las Kantutas

Beginning in 1988, and as a consequence of the evaluation of *La voz de las Kantutas*, it was decided to put more emphasis on both participation and training in specific skills. This was the origin of the workshops on radio drama production that allowed for the production of messages more relevant to the problems, interests and forms of expression of the target audience.

In 1989, the same principle was applied to the production of *La voz de las Kantutas* through the training of a group of popular reporters. The intent was to promote a format that responded better to the language of the audience, facilitated greater participation and met the demands of the audience, all through the creation of spaces for information, advice and open discussion.[9]

We intensified activities in this period, moving from two to four hours of programming a week. This was accompanied by a diversification of format, by adding radio drama to the radio magazine space. At first the recording studios, technicians and announcers of Radio San Gabriel were contracted to produce the programme. With the purchase and installation of a studio in El Alto, production passed into the hands of the Communication Programme of the centre, which allowed for popular groups' participation. From 1989, the services of an Aymara announcer and a radio operator were contracted part-time. During the last three years, there were a total of 120 broadcasts of *La voz de las Kantutas*. A total of 89 hours were broadcast through the Aymara-language radio station Radio San Gabriel. The radio magazine was also broadcast through commercial radio stations such as Avaroa, Mendez and Chusquisada, doubling the number of hours broadcast. To date, four radio soaps have been produced, with an average of 20 episodes of 15 minutes each. There have also been 12 drama series.

By the number of spontaneous visitors to the recording studio in the first half of 1990, it is clear that there is growing interest in radio and television production. Many women and youths interested in educational programmes offered by the centre indicated that they had found the information through the radio magazine. Furthermore, the Research Center on Health (the organization that collaborates in the development of health issues for the radio magazine) has in four months dealt with 240 patients who arrived at the clinic as a result of information received on the radio. Surprisingly, we have even received Aymara visitors from the Peruvian border region of Puno.

La voz de las Kantutas also contributed to the diffusion of the health and educational goals of the centre. This occurred through the devotion of air time to practical advice and information on the care and stimulation of children, on maternal and infant health, and nutrition. The central theme of the programme approaches aspects of the living conditions of urban Aymara women in much the same way as outlined by our institution.

After six years, the project has achieved a close relationship between the communicational proposal and that of gender and neighbourhood development. This goal is strongly influenced by the notion of participatory democracy. During these years mass media (radio and television) have been used to communicate experiences of women. In making more powerful the expression of Aymara women, the training is designed to maintain a fluid circulation between the different components of communication, always reinforcing the incorporation of an Aymara perspective in the process of communication.

As a result, a communication programme was designed and incorporated into the 1990–93 plan for the centre. Its general objectives focused on the strengthening of the expressive capacities of urban Aymara women, the formation of public opinion on women's issues, and the systematization and broadcast of debate on the subordination of urban Aymara women.

Video: a mirror of ourselves

There is one television channel per 150,000 inhabitants in Bolivia. In La Paz, with a population of approximately 1 million, there are nine channels. As one can see from advertisements in the daily press, 75 per cent of the programming on these nine channels are foreign produced. The 25 per cent that are nationally produced are generally news and debate programmes or musical variety shows.

The genres that have been developed in that small percentage of national production are very limited. The most elaborate tend to be news shows. Other programmes, such as those directed to children, limit themselves to a series of video clips produced in the USA or in other Latin American countries such as Mexico, Brazil or Venezuela.

What does this mean for women such as the urban Aymara in a city such as El Alto, where practically every household has a television set and the consumption of this medium is part of daily life? It means watching daily 19 *telenovelas*, mostly of Mexican origin, with the remainder from Venezuela and Brazil. From this massive consumption of melodrama these women are exposed to certain models of family relations, expectations of social ascent, and happy endings.

Video production at the CPMEA began in 1986. Video was introduced as an educational tool in small groups to review aspects of the history of the women's movement in the country. At the end of 1989, the centre began to produce video reports along with documentary dramas. The programmes, made by the women themselves, have a documentary frame that transcends anecdotal situations by presenting them as social facts. They represent situations in the women's own reality.

Upon initiating video production the centre also began training Aymara women as video reporters (popular reporters) for participation in the documentaries. The programmes began to be broadcast on commercial stations on a weekly basis.[10]

Video continues the communicational process begun by the centre with radio, that is, a combination of the individual (in participation), the group (in reflection) and the mass (in broadcast). In this way, each stage in production can be used as an educational opportunity. Each moment of production has been of mutual learning for both actors and producers. The production of news and fictional video has allowed the centre and groups of urban Aymara women the possibility of showing real images of themselves to the population.

The characteristics of the news genre permit women to examine the realities of their daily lives, while at the same time giving a space where they themselves are in the leading roles. The form taken by the videos incorporates codes from Andean culture: the language (Aymara), music, narrative rhythm, construction of text and articulation of sequences.

The systematic broadcast of the reports has awakened much interest in the urban Aymara population, not only because of the themes but, more important, because the actors are barrio women. Yet a key point remains to be evaluated, as in the case of radio production: the reception.

The CPMGA does not have current and rigorous data about the effect of these television reports, other than through occasional visits, telephone calls and letters that the audience sends to the centre or broadcast station. Undoubtedly, as in the case of radio, an unbridged distance exists between the two components of our communication project. On one hand is the active participation of groups of women and individuals that learn and become empowered during the process of production, and on the other is the mass audience that receives the finished product through the media or in group session. This distance should be resolved from the point of design to the point of practice in the strategic communicational project being carried out by the women and the centre. We can trust, as we have from the beginning, that mass is not opposed to popular.

Popular reporters

The *pollera*[11] women are divided into hierarchies based on their economic situation and the extent to which they have integrated into the city. There is a difference between a woman with a *borsalino* hat, silk shawl, nylons, a gold *topo* and a long skirt, and a woman from the countryside with a flannel skirt and leather hat and who speaks only Aymara.[12] This stratification, which originated with the Spanish conquest, is conserved in various economic and social ways.

Such is the case with popular *pollera* women, who through participation in some popular media have achieved fame as social communicators. Some have found political positions as councillors and deputies. The numbers of these women remain small, but these women have become much-emulated role models.

For more than three decades, the radio has broadcast programmes in the Aymara language with men and women from the popular sector as literacy workers, community promoters and announcers. This has facilitated the formation of associations of popular communicators in native languages. In contrast, television gives little coverage to the urban Aymara woman. If it does, it is from a conventional perspective, through *telenovelas* and programs that reaffirm their traditional roles as housemaids, ornamental objects, symbols of abnegation and sacrifice.

To assist the participatory and popular direction of national radio broadcasting, the centre supported the creation of a network of popular reporters, initially for *La voz de las Kantutas* and later for the programme *Warmin Arupa*.

The team of popular reporters is made up of urban Aymara women from the northern zone of El Alto who have attended seminars at the centre on basic orientation and training in the use of radio and television and in the strengthening of expression. This group of reporters consists mainly of single mothers who are daughters of immigrants from the province. Their ages range from 34 to 41. They have varied education levels and work in domestic and informal activities. Links with other community organizations are strong: all are members of organizations related to parishes, literacy projects, food distribution or merchant associations. The reporters have said that their involvement in television aids them in acquiring useful knowledge for expression and participation in public events. One woman said, 'It's helped me a lot because I've been trained. In my own group of women they say they would like to be like me. I'm strong-willed, now I'm motivated for anything, I'm self-assured and I say how things should be.' The reporters also identify a more community-oriented result of their experience. They feel themselves to be spokeswomen for the demands of the zone and for the aspirations of other Aymara women: 'It is we who make known the necessities of the zone on television. Other women like to see discussion of their problems on television.'

There is a recognition of the undeniable increase in self-esteem and of the role that these women can play not only in their own organizations but also in the barrio, the city and society in general. There is also the recognition and empathy that the reporters awake in the audience. The messages received from a woman 'of the people' is given a greater degree of acceptance: she is part of reality, of daily life, and for that reason is seen to be legitimate.

Communication is vital in a city like El Alto where the emergence of new social actors blurs the values of representation, power relations, alliance, contradiction and leadership. Communication can affect the flow of these social elements which, depending on the situation, join together on the force of electoral alliances and the possibility of political promises. In these conditions the assumption is that by strengthening the role of popular reporters we also strengthen female leadership in the city. But this is difficult to prove in the short term.

From the communicational process in which the centre participates we are left with another concern: what is the potential of the popular reporters to affect change? It must be remembered that we are only speaking of a group of 20 women – out of a population of 30,000 – who are in the process of claiming their own words. We also speak of a conflict that continuously appears throughout the process: are individual achievements the engines of social change? In what way can the experience of communication include both dimensions – the individual and the collective, the public and the private?

Participation: Myth and Reality

The point of view of women participating in the production of radio and video has been assessed in two different evaluations.[13] According to a survey of Radio San Gabriel, the 59 women who had participated in the centre's projects perceive it as an educational programme that allowed them to understand various aspects of their reality and that reflected facets of their own daily lives: 'It makes you realize what the reality is.' 'It shows things from our lives.'

Participation in the programme is highly valued, underlining not only the importance of self-expression and making known their reality but also the possibility of entertainment and losing the fear of speaking: 'We ourselves direct our words.'

They recognize the effect on both individual and group affirmation, with phrases such as 'let's teach ourselves to respect ourselves' and 'let's value our work'. There is a consciousness of the need for social affirmation: 'We know that we can do it.' These perceptions are based on knowing themselves to be broadcasters of a message, educators of other women who, it is hoped, will 'realize what their situation is and organize'.

Participation in the programme represents a social space for recreation, reflection and sharing among women. They confirm that they learn to speak openly, gain knowledge of the experiences of other organizations from other zones, and achieve a greater knowledge of their own situation through the search for themes and information for the radio dramas. At the same time, they consider their activity as an incentive for the development of women in general, to whom they try to reveal different aspects of their lives as Aymara women with few resources. In the case of radio dramas, the reflection about real lives and their own experiences is considered educational and exemplary. The aspect of self-affirmation is constantly mentioned: they say they feel secure and proud of their work, of the fact that their voices are heard on the radio, and of their ability to express ideas and life experiences.

In general, we observe that women have a sense of ownership of the communication programme. In the evaluation of 1988, the women declared how badly they would feel if *La voz de las Kantutas* disappeared. In 1990, they declared they would find the means to continue the project on their own, organizing and negotiating with the media.

Participation is a part of the myths and utopias much beloved by projects of communication and popular education in Latin America. In its mythological dimension it has been seen as a panacea, an infallible remedy and an unquestioned necessity. In its utopic dimension it is an evasive dream, a winning ticket, but with a trick.

In the case of the project involving the CPMGA and the women from the Villa 16 de Julio, a basic certainty is that participation will be impossible if both groups of actors do not identify and practise common territory of participation, one that does not exclude actors such as women and youth.

A minimal agreement on a discourse that incorporates the strategic demands of women must be made along with the recognition that the interests of women are affected primarily by the well-being of the community.

Challenges and Perspectives

In a general sense, our project of communication supports grassroots organization and the community, contributing to a democratization of the mass media and the development of popular expression. Special emphasis is given to the expression of women, yet without exclusion of other ages and men. Two essential conditions for the achievement of this impact are participation through multiple training activities and the activity of selecting formats and genres that permit openness, flexibility and an accurate picture of the present.

The open forum of *La voz de las Kantutas*, for example, contributes to popular expression and the democratization of media, permitting the spontaneous participation of those who have no other channel of communication. While the radio drama has no direct relationship to grassroots organizations or the community, it is an important vehicle for the reinforcement of popular values and expression. This is because of the diversity of experience among its participants and because they do not lose sight of the problems faced in daily life.

Consequently, the themes explored by the programme refer to, among other things, the rights of women; the cultural and gender identity of Aymara women migrating to the city; and poverty, work and other conditions of daily life. The work of communication serves as an antenna that provides useful information to the institution about the social context in which it works. This channel of communication is fed by the reporters, actors and visitors to our programmes. They give information on events and on the problems and aspirations of the population. They provide the elements that help to understand better the values of urban Aymara culture.

However, the positive aspects and benefits of this communication project should not make us forget the challenges yet to be met. Throughout the process, we identified elements that cannot be dealt with overnight, especially in a small project carried out by an NGO with limited resources and reach.

A simple enumeration leads us to projections such as the necessity for links between production, broadcast and reception, a link generally clearer in theory than in practice. Another challenge is the incorporation of cultural aspects in every part of the communication process. If one understands culture to be a series of material facts that daily alter the physiognomy and habits of a social space such as the city (Savaria and Sandoval 1991), it is without doubt that the reconstruction and strengthening of the voice of women goes beyond training in expression and coherence of discourse. It goes beyond this because such a process must blend with ways of relating, the manner in which alliances are constructed, and conflicts declared. In short, it must blend with the basic and the daily relating of human beings, their common sense, and the ways they establish the rules of the game.

These challenges, together with the objective of establishing meaningful links between the impact of this process on women as individuals and social persona, give the communication experience a subversive dimension that goes beyond the physical use of words. In this sense, the possibility of expressing feelings, desires, nonconformity and demands is not only an effect of exchange between women and the state but also, and primarily, a dialogue that women can establish with themselves and their reality.

Notes

1. The 'indigenist position' proclaims the political proposal of the possibility of an Indian government and state – in Bolivia, a Quechua and Aymara state.

2. The CPMEA organizes activities for the promotion of women in the areas of training, economic production, services, research and communication. The centre works with various groups of women but always with immigrant Aynim women in the popular barrios of La Paz.

3. The Aymaras are indigenous inhabitants of the Andean areas of Bolivia. They were first conquered by the Incas and later colonized by the Spanish. Bolivia has almost 7,000,000 inhabitants, of which 1,156,000 are Aymara, according to the statistical projection from the 1976 census. From this number, more than 800,000 are bilingual (Aymara/Spanish) and almost 300,000, mostly women, are monolingual Aymaras.

4. El Alto developed as a suburb for workers, acquiring city status in 1976. It is located at 4,000 metres on a highland plain at the foot of snowy peaks; geographically it dominates the larger city of La Paz. Like many Latin American cities, called variously 'young towns', 'villas of misery' or 'land invasions', El Alto consists of numerous barrios (208 registered), of which many are squatter settlements in the process of legalization. The majority lack basic services such as running water, sewage systems and conditions of basic hygiene. El Alto is a

youthful city, as 66 per cent of its people are below the age of 25. The number of children and youths that work is significant, as is the number of young women that work full-time.

5. The diverse self-critical and analytical elements used to describe the experience are the fruit of the labour of many people, including the Aymara women, the residents of El Alto and the people who work at the women's centre. Through reports, evaluations, articles and commentaries, they have facilitated the reconstruction of the process as well as identified the possible strategies for its enrichment.

6. Aymara women face discrimination because they do not use the Spanish language well. Most of the time their knowledge of Spanish is so limited that they cannot effectively communicate for daily survival – asking for addresses and speaking in government offices (see Ruíz 1987).

7. The economic activity of most Altiplano women is non-contractual (73.5 per cent). The rest of the women (26.6 per cent) work under a contract. A total of 97 per cent of working women are involved in commerce, services or informal industry.

8. The miners' radio stations are located in the main refining centres of Bolivia. These stations function as support to the miners' social movement and are considered a model of the relationship between alternative media and the popular movement.

9. The changes also followed the recommendations of the external evaluation of 1988, which signalled the need to reach beyond the small groups connected with the institution. This challenge implied more involvement in shaping public opinion than with the education of closed groups.

10. The production of each weekly 10-minute report has the following steps: (a) training workshops for urban Aymara women, generally community leaders or those interested in the social issues of their community; (b) pre-production, which includes research and collection of information on selected themes and the writing of a tentative script; (c) production and filming of the images and pertinent interviews; (d) post-production, which includes editing, final research and delivery to television stations for broadcast; and (e) broadcast to a mass audience by a television station. The video is used as educational material to aid in the work of assessment and reflection among different small groups.

11. The *pollera* is the traditional Aymara skirt.

12. The division and stratification of popular sectors are complex problems with roots in the Spanish Conquest. The conquistadors struck alliances with some of the defeated, who in turn enjoyed a series of privileges.

13. The first set of data is from 1988, making reference only to *La voz de las Kantutas*. The perceptions of women from small factories and day-care centres and groups connected to the centre are examined. The second evaluation, carried out in early 1990, looks at the radio magazine and radio drama and reflects the impact of the project on the participants of the workshops.

References

Alfaro, R. (1988) *De la conquista de la ciudad a la apropiación de la palabra. Una experiencia de educación popular y communicación con mujeres.* Lima, Peru: Calandria.

Alfaro, R. (1990) *Cultura de masas y cultura popular en la radio peruana. Diagnóstico para construer una alternative radial.* Lima, Peru: Calandria.

Centro Para la Mujer Gregoria Apaza (1991) *Informe evaluación taller de radio novella.* La Paz, Bolivia: CPMGA (unpublished).

Mata, M. (1985) *Radio Enriquillo en diálogo con el pueblo* (Serie Investigaciones No. 3). Quito, Ecuador: ALER.

Mata, M. (1990) Radios popularizes: Pensando en los receptors, *Media Development*, 37(4).

Ruiz, C. (1987) Palabra de mujer, *Cuadernos de Communicación Alternativa*, 5: 23–40

Savaria, J. and Sandoval, G. (1991) *Jacha Uru¿ La esperanza de un pueblo?* La Paz: ILDIS, CEP.

THE COMMERCIALIZATION OF MASCULINITIES
FROM THE 'NEW MAN' TO THE 'NEW LAD'

John Beynon

Introduction: Masculinity from the 1980s

If the 1990s was the decade in which masculinity was extensively decon-
structed by academics world-wide, then the 1980s was most certainly the
decade in which it was extensively reconstructed. What do I mean by this?
Masculinity was more extensively transformed by economic and commercial forces in the 1980s than at any previous time. This postmodernist
transformation of masculinity has been extensively documented by three
writers in particular, Frank Mort (1996), Sean Nixon (1996) and Tim
Edwards (1997). I refer to each repeatedly throughout this chapter and
record my debt to them at the outset. Let me emphasize that this chapter is
effectively theirs, not mine. I can only hope that I do their work justice. I
proceed as follows. First, I place the 'new man' in a brief historical context
before examining the 'nurturer' and 'narcissist' strands. Second, I explore
the narcissist strand of new masculinity by drawing upon Nixon's threefold
model of analysis of the commercialization of masculinity in the 1980s by
reference to menswear, visual representations (including advertising) and
the men's style press. Third, I label the 1980s as the 'hello and goodbye'
decade, specifically 'hello' to the yuppie and 'goodbye' to the 'old industrial
man'. Fourth, I then move into the 1990s and on to the present time and
examine the further commercialization of masculinity, this time in the form
of the 'new lad' and laddism, a project particularly associated with the
magazine *Loaded* and the advent of 'lad television'. Fifth, I then trace the
new lad's ancestry and the considerable barrage of criticism that has been
levelled at him. Finally, a question is posed, namely: who was (or is) the

'new man'? I draw upon the views of three influential commentators, Chapman (1988), Mort (1996) and Edwards (1997). I conclude by arguing that a generalized 'new manism' has now emerged in which elements from both the nurturer and the narcissus strands have been scrambled together.

'How "new" is the "new man"?' is a pertinent question to ask. He has been around in various guises for some considerable time. For example, George Bernard Shaw was musing about what form he could assume in the twentieth century as early as 1903! Also, the term has often been used by historians to indicate past shifts in masculinity. Two examples are the new man of the Renaissance (epitomized by Leonardo and Michelangelo) or, more recently, someone like the ecclesiastic Edward White Benson, the subject of John Tosh's (1991) fine biographical cameo. In spite of comparatively humble origins, Benson had, through iron discipline and hard work, risen to become one of the most respected public figures of his time. He epitomized the new man of the latter half of the nineteenth century in that a self-made meritocracy was slowly beginning to emerge in which social position was earned through effort rather than being dependent on family background and inheritance. However, the term 'new man' belongs firmly to the 1980s and can be both a term of opprobrium (signifying a new and improved version of masculinity cleared of some, if not all, of the less endearing attributes of traditional, patriarchal masculinity) and one of jocular dismissal and humour (in which some of the alleged features of the new man, such as connecting with his inner self, are mercilessly lampooned). Some argue that there is little 'new' about the new man and that under the veneer he is the very same 'old man'. Some would even argue that he has never existed. Such a view is trenchantly expressed by Moir and Moir (1998), who maintain that the new man is nothing more than the creation of intellectuals and that he does not exist outside the academic mind and Gucci perfume ads! I now turn to the origins of the new man which is approached in terms of two strands, the nurturer and the narcissist.

Strand 1: The 'New Man-as-Nurturer'

The first strand in new man's heredity is allied to men's reactions to social change and the changing role of men in the 1970s and 1980s, particularly men's reactions to first-wave feminism. In the UK and USA pro-feminist men, sensing justice in the feminist movement and eager themselves for social change, attempted to raise both their own and their fellow men's consciousness and foster a more caring, sharing, nurturing man. They willingly supported the women's movement and taking a full role in the domestic arena (particularly in respect of child-rearing). These men were usually middle-class, well-educated intellectuals: an example in the UK would be Seidler's (1989) early work and contributors to the magazine *Spare Rib*. Feminism attacked patriarchy and pathologized patriarchal masculinity as arrested development and, as Chapman (1988) makes clear, equated it with rape, war, incest, pollution and much else. Changing patterns in family life, with men marrying later or not at all, along with a willingness to take on a supportive role in a woman's career, resulted in the emergence of the new man as an ideal. He was the riposte to vilified 'old man', his father, and a refugee from the hard-line masculinity epitomized by the paranoid, macho men with stifled emotions. They were enacted on the screen by Wayne, Bogart, Bronson and Stallone, with Stallone's Rambo character memorably depicted as 'bare-chested and alone, wading through the Vietcong swamp with not even a tube of insect repellent for comfort' (Chapman 1988: 227). Others reacted differently to the social changes taking place. One of the most lampooned images is of the new man as a tree-hugging, back-to-nature figure desperately searching for his real 'masculine self'. He will always be associated with Robert Bly, the American poet whose *Iron John* (1981) is still the subject of considerable debate and controversy. In it he calls on men to journey into nature, the great outdoors and engage in rituals in male-only groups to release long-suppressed emotions. Thereby, he feels, men can reclaim their souls and reclaim true manhood. He laments the decline of the father's influence in inducting the son into the ways of the world and argues that young men need older male mentors to help them connect with the wild, innate masculinity inside them. This is something with which modern man has lost contact but which is preserved in ancient myths. Many read the book as part of an anti-feminist backlash, accused Bly of blaming women for alleged male emotional distress and discontent, feared it would distract anti-sexist men as they struggled against gender oppression and argued that Bly had failed to distinguish between gender and sexuality.

Although Christian's (1994) is a small-scale study, its outcomes, given the paucity of empirical evidence of any kind, are noteworthy. He interviewed some 30 men (non-macho and mostly non-gay, in the age range 21–54) who were attempting to live non-sexist lifestyles because they believed in the justice of increased equality between the sexes. Moreover, many of these men were aware of sensitive and vulnerable feelings which they believed helped them have better relationships with women and children as well as with other men. Among the key early influences in these men's lives were:

- non-identification with traditional fathers and strong identification with nurturing fathers and parents who did not conform to conventional domestic roles
- a rejection of macho behaviour in school and a preference for the company of girls
- the generalized influence of feminism but, often, a relationship with one feminist in particular.

Christian (1994) reveals some apparent contradictions concerning the male breadwinner role. Since the 1960s women have become less prepared to accept dependence and there has been a widespread erosion of the male breadwinner role. However, many of the men in the study believed that a commitment to it was still compatible with a non-sexist lifestyle and aimed for a mixed breadwinner–homemaker role with their partners. Christian depicts pro-feminist men as a minority who may not be active in anti-sexist groups. Their importance lies in their attempts to relate to women in non-oppressive ways and try to be their allies in the struggle against gender oppression. Similarly, Kimmel and Messner (1992) depict anti-sexist men as active supporters of women's demands for equal opportunity, education, political participation, sexual autonomy and family reforms. Such men are clearly the product of recent economic, cultural and demographic changes which have rendered traditional masculinity less and less sustainable. As Christian (1994: 3) puts it, 'many men's experience and expectations of life and traditional ideas of masculinity have been seriously called into question in the late twentieth century'.

Widely criticized as being middle class, elitist, Western-centric and remote from the lived experience of most men, the stereotypical image of the anti-sexist, caring, sharing man nevertheless gained credibility and strength throughout the 1980s. But how deep or widespread was the change? Was it no more than a media-driven illusion of change or, in fact, a genuine change in the consciousness and behaviour of men? What evidence there is would indicate that, in spite of his survival into the new century of the 'new man-as-nurturer', men's involvement in domestic labour has not significantly changed. Christian argues that the situation has been compounded by the increasing work demands of employers which have made it even more difficult for men to change long-established masculine routines and expectations.

Strand 2: The 'New Man-as-Narcissist'

Before exploring this topic further, let me acknowledge again my indebtedness to Mort (1996), Nixon (1996) and Edwards (1997). This second strand of the new man is associated with commercial masculinity and the spectacular expansion of consumerism since the end of the Second World War (Shields 1992). The 'new man-as-narcissist' is clearly the son of his father's 1950s and 1960s rock and hippy generation, with its interest in clothes and pop music and far removed from the 'demob-suited', carbolic soap and Old Spice-scented generation. Although the commercialization of masculinity accelerated in the 1980s, the trend had its origins in late 1950s pop culture, especially in the United States, with the emergence of Elvis Presley and others who dressed to be looked at and admired. Mort (1996) pinpoints 1953–54 as the time when class-based masculinities started to be replaced by style-based ones as a series of take-overs and mergers set in motion a gradual erosion of the status quo of mass male (Burton's) fashion. Meanwhile, Ehrenreich (1983) identifies the 1950s playboy as the ancestor of the 1980s yuppie. In the 1950s early marriage and the subsequent support of a wife and children were visible proof of 'normal masculinity', any deviation from this preordained route rendering the individual vulnerable to imputations of homosexuality. Hugh Hefner's *Playboy* magazine's heterosexual hedonism avoided this while still rebelling against the dominant norms of 1950s masculinity. Whereas mainstream 1950s masculinity was antithetical to the feminine aspects of consumerism, the 'playboy' revelled in the acquisition of fancy clothes, fast cars and beautiful women. It was this utopian vision that was to be picked up and exploited by 1980s consumerism.

If the 1960s set the scene for the fragmentation of a hitherto relatively uniform masculine text, the 1970s, which Hunt (1998) terms 'the decade that taste forgot', took it a stage further. The 1970s witnessed a disintegration of the relatively unified youth culture of the 1950s and 1960s and, as a result, male fashion, propelled by creative advertising, became what Mort (1996: 25) terms 'a hydra' and stimulated a 'desire to play about with masculinity, to re-arrange traditional icons of maleness' (Mort 1996: 203). York (1982) captured this when he observed the proliferating expressions of young masculinities on the streets of west London. Hunt (1998) notes that the young male icons of the time (like the footballer Charlie George and the singer Rod Stewart) displayed a 'hard-soft' masculinity which was easily copied. 'Rodness', for example, was readily available in that all a young man had to do to acquire it was to drink, sing, pull girls and like football. For Hunt the strike-strewn 1970s rather than the peacock 1960s marked the emergence in Britain of more varied, mobile masculinities. The rampant commercialization of masculinity that was to follow was founded on a number of 1970s stereotypes ranging from the traditional ('Old Spice Man', 'Tobacco Man', 'Bitter Beer Man') through to the new kids on the block (the permissive, swinging 'Safari Man', 'Hair Spray Man', 'Lad Fop' and 'The Gay'). As the 1980s got under way the commercial exploitation of men-as-sex-objects became very big business. The voyeuristic sexualization of the female body, its packaging as visual erotica, was now transferred to the male body with the same ultimate purpose in mind – to sell, sell, sell. Menswear shops proliferated, full of broad-shouldered 'body armour' suits, with loud ties and flamboyant shirts; the male body became the peg on which to attach new fashion codes in an unprecedented way. Meanwhile, Ross (1999) describes how football and fashion began, at least at the mass end of the market, to be brought closer together, making more concrete a link already evident in the colourful career of the 'fifth Beatle', the foot-baller George Best, in the 1960s and 1970s. He describes how the football terraces became catwalks: 'The football fan of the early Eighties was no longer a rattle-waving, scarf-wearing wally or a toothless skinhead grunt, but a mass of label-wearing, style-coded casual wear freaks' (Ross 1999: 29). The 1980s witnessed a change in the politics of looking as the 'male-on-male' gaze joined the 'male-on-female' (along with female-on-male and even female-on-female) as socially acceptable, especially among young, fashionable metropolitan men with high disposable incomes. Nixon (1996) employs a threefold model to analyse how this came about:

- *Clothing outlets for men* Male retail outlets proliferated in the 1980s, ranging from the exclusive, designer outlets to the merchandizing of cut-price labels. The middle-ranging Next chain was one of the great mar-keting successes of the decade, their clothes 'speaking' aspirational lifestyle rather than class. In Next's hands the outmoded suit made a spectacular comeback, wreaking 'a vengeance against all forms of soft-focus effeminacy' (Edwards 1997: 21).
- *New visual representations of men* In the 1980s new visual representa-tions of masculinities appeared in advertising and on television. The male form began to be eroticized and objectified in ways that had pre-viously been applied to the female body. In the hands of photographers (for example, Ray Petri and Kevin Brody), advertising agencies (like Bartle Bogle Hegarty) and in cards and posters (for example, those by Athena) a narcissistic new man emerged, self-confident, well groomed, muscular, but also sensitive).
- *Style magazines for men* The emergence of the style press for men was

arguably among the most notable features of 1980s popular culture. In their pages diverse and mobile masculinities were created: as Edwards (1997) puts it, in both layout and content these were new kinds of magazines for new kinds of men. They constituted a new commercial project and were 'lifestyle manuals ... offering new ways of experiencing the city' (Nixon 1996: 155), in the process placing men-in-the-mirror, to borrow a term from Edwards's (1997) book. He documents the growth of style magazine publishing and the clever crafting of a range of visually sophisticated masculinities for the first generation to be brought up on colour television, one more visually literate than any before. Both Mort (1996) and Edwards (1997) are of the opinion that 1980s men were not changing because of sexual politics, but through commercial pressures. In fact, the style magazines had 'a lot more to do with new markets for the constant reconstruction of masculinity through consumption'. (Edwards 1997: 82)

Gay men, predominant in the image and fashion industries, were at the forefront of these changes and were blamed for what some perceived to be the 'feminization' of men's fashion. These critics strongly objected to what they held to be the prioritization of the 'gay look' in fashion, including the sending up of macho masculinity in terms of hyper-masculinity. Conversely, some gay men resented what they regarded as the cheapening of their own distinctive visual style by the fashion industry. It is easy to overemphasize the significance of these skirmishes for the general British male populace, most of whom live outside London and for whom such metropolitan lifestyles are light years away from their own daily experiences. Indeed, Nixon (1996) concludes:

> Whilst it is true to say that the boundaries between gay and straight, or even between male and female, are becoming more blurred in terms of media representations, the marketing of up-market fashion and the consumption patterns of some affluent and professional groups, this barely marks a sea change in the entire population where the categories of male and female, straight and gay, black or white, remain remarkably stable. (Nixon 1996: 117)

The 1980s were characterized by two masculine archetypes:

- The ostentatious City and Wall Street yuppie, at his most triumphant a Donald Trump-like character, famously portrayed on screen by Michael Douglas in *Wall Street* (1985).
- Old industrial man, rendered redundant by the decimation of heavy

industry, forever symbolized by the angry figures of miners confronting lines of police during the pit closures of the mid-1980s.

It is to these that I now turn in order to provide a picture of the 1980s as the 'hello and goodbye' decade.

'Hello' to the 'Yuppie'

Although the term 'yuppie' was also applicable to women, its connotations were (and remain) essentially masculine. At his heart was conspicuous consumption and a ruthless, cut-throat determination to be seen to be successful, all 'driven by an excessive desire to spend money. Whether it was property, cars, clothes or personal artefacts, consumption was a dominant feature of the yuppie lifestyle' (Mort 1996: 172). Following financial deregulation, the City of London became an economic and style centre and his was an overtly commercial masculinity, which Edwards (1997) captures vividly:

> The yuppie was not only a product of the economic expansion of the financial sector, he was an advocate of the most striking conspicuous consumption since the Second World War, posing, parading and swaggering around the City in his pinstripe and power-look suits, ties and accessories, swinging his attaché case, talking animatedly on his mobile phone, endlessly flicking the pages of his Filofax, sticking his hair and using every excuse to get into and out of his suit, his tie, his striped shirt and, of course, his Porsche. (Edwards 1997: vii)

If he worked in the City, the yuppie lived (at least during the week) in the redeveloped fantasia of the London Docklands (Hall 1998) and patronized the chic new restaurants and café bars of the refurbished (some would say divested of character) Soho, newly invaded by a wave of young media and advertising executives. Mort (1996: 163) recreates *The Great Gatsby* ambience of this controversial 'regeneration' when referring to the transformation of the old Welsh Nonconformist chapel in Shaftesbury Avenue into an up-market nightclub where yuppies could show off their new-found wealth:

> Decorated with murals and with a strong emphasis on art and architecture, the Limelight enshrined its own caste-like hierarchy within the spatial environment. The VIP suite restricted access to celebrities or to those able to buy into celebrity status. From an elevated gallery the elite could either look out across London, or gaze down from a position of superiority on the dance floor below. (Mort 1996: 162)

London's Soho became the location for two distinct constituencies of 1980s 'imaged masculinity', namely yuppies and gays. In this 'heterotopic world' young men engaged in what Mort (1996) terms as 'experiments in masculinity': 'For the most part these were organised along an axis separating heterosexual from homosexual behaviours. However, at moments more hybrid forms of identity were generated, as ways of being and acting mutated from one group to another' (Mort 1996: 182). Outside London 'yuppiedom' was comparatively thin on the ground. Yuppies, however, had their poor relations, what Edwards (1997) terms their 'underclass counterparts', who wore a uniform of trainers and down-market labels and counterfeits. Edwards (1997) recalls two dominant lifestyle images of 1980s yuppie masculinity, resonant with virility, sexual prowess and masculine sensuality:

- *The corporate power look*: the image of the aspirational yuppie in his wide-shouldered, double-breasted suit, striped shirt, braces, personal phone and BMW, shot against a background of a Docklands studio apartment.
- *The outdoor casual look*: the image of a muscular torso, stripping off his white T-shirt, or in an English gentleman's weekend clothes shot against his rural retreat far from the cares of city life.

Similarly, Nixon (1996) identifies two variants of the above, 'Edwardian Englishness' and 'Italianicity':

- *Edwardian Englishness* This was an image of masculinity associated with the urbane, aristocratic Englishness of Empire, of class, colonial domination, prestige and power. This nostalgia for a colonial past and an Englishness tied to the Edwardian era was particularly strong in the 1980s, with a string of nostalgic films like *A Passage to India* (1985), *Room with a View* (1986) and *Maurice* (1987) and a number of television series, notably *Brideshead Revisited* (1981) and *Jewel in the Crown* (1982).
- *Italianicity* This encapsulated the swaggering bravado of macho Italian masculinity, celebrated in numerous gangster movies and fashion photographs.

'Goodbye' to the 'Old Industrial Man'

Millions of men in the advanced economies lost their jobs and economic authority in the succession of recessions throughout the 1980s and early

1990s. The message was clear: loyalty, faithfulness and dedication to employers no longer counted for anything when it came to the operation of raw capital. The turning point in Britain was the 1980s Thatcherite deregulation of the economy, her adoption of market-led policies and a refusal to provide state hand-outs to halt the all-too-evident decline of heavy industry. These policies reached their apotheosis in Chancellor of the Exchequer Nigel Lawson's 1988 budget in which he slashed the top rates of income tax and reduced the basic rate. This fuelled consumption and led to the mushrooming of out-of-town shopping malls, retail parks and the promotion of shopping as a primary 'leisure–pleasure' activity. The new man-as-narcissist rode on the back of this post-industrialism and bur-geoning 'image industries' like advertising, media, promotion and public relations. As Mort (1996: 113) puts it, he was the logical outcome of the 'commercial narrative of gender', established through 'the sexual politics of advertising'. For the ordinary working man in areas of heavy industry (like the North East of England and South Wales) the pact between employer and employee based on mutual loyalty to a company was finally broken in the increasingly global marketplace. The traditional male career was attacked at all levels, but at least down-layered executives enjoyed high redundancy packages. The shift from manufacturing to servicing, and from industrialization to electronic technology, was immensely damaging for working-class men. The old industrial labourers, along with skilled and semi-skilled workers, were rendered obsolete by the technological advances they had helped to implement. Jobs that depended upon physical strength vanished in their millions and in their place came, at best, short-term contracts and part-time work.

Why was the loss of often inhuman, exploitative jobs (like coal mining) so mourned? First, these were not just jobs, but benchmarks of working-class masculinity. Economic and social changes destroyed these patterns of employment and, in the process, 'status, self esteem and the old moral authority which men used to have just by being men' (Coward 1999: 86). Second, this was not just a temporary 'laying-off' as in past industrial disputes: it was, rather, the end of the UK as a major venue for heavy manufacturing (for example, shipbuilding). Contracting out, downsizing and de-layering meant the end to stable patterns of working-class employment (Coward 1999: 48). By the mid–1980s a rise in suicide figures and increasing male homelessness was evident. As Coward says of these men:

> Feminism had given the women the confidence to move into masculine
> areas, combining work and motherhood, seeing new opportunities in

new work patterns. Men, by contrast, were experiencing their work changes, this so-called feminization of labour, more like a smack in the eye. (Coward 1999: 51)

What was going on in fashionable Soho was a million miles away from the lives and experiences of such economically and socially marginalized men. While shifting masculine scripts have impacted on all men, they did so unevenly. Increasingly style marked off young men from old, rich from poor, powerful from powerless, gay from straight. What emerged was a hierarchy of masculinities based on appearance and which abolished more traditional masculine divisions based upon work roles, ownership and sexual orientation. It became clear that men do not participate equally in the consumer society. Indeed, since the 1980s:

> wealthy, good-looking and well-located young men [have been] increasingly socially valorised over older, uglier or poorer men ... those with the looks, the income and the time on their side have never had it so good in terms of the opportunities which the expansion of men's style and fashion have to offer them.... But those without the luck, the looks or the time have never had it so bad and are consigned to looking and longing, or even exclusion and castigation for not playing the game. In this sense fashion is fascism: conform in the mirror of judgements, or else take the consequences. (Edwards 1997: 133–4)

Welcome to the 1990s: 'The Lads are Back in Town'

We have seen how in the 1980s the male body was treated as an 'objectified commodity' (Healey 1994), much as the female body had long been. Appearance and possessions became vehicles to give off meanings. It was the growth point for a renewed consumerism and the niche marketing of a sensuous imagery of young, affluent masculinity. The new, glossy men's style magazines were the principal vehicles for this commercial project based on male narcissism. As we shall now see, the 1990s marked something of a reversal, with an attack on the self-conscious gentility of the 1980s mags and the projection of a far harder and distinctly 'laddish' masculinity (Alexander 1997). What they had in common were that they were both overtly commercial ventures, carefully calculated to open up new markets and generate profits. Men's magazines in the 1990s toned down the masculine sensuality of the 1980s, although *Attitude* has tried to retain something of the sexual ambivalence opened up in the 1980s. Both *Arena* and *GQ* cast the 1980s aside by reintroducing a strong heterosexual script and stylish, soft-porn shots of women. But the great 1990s men's magazine success was undoubtedly *Loaded*, a publishing phenomenon, conjured up by James Brown and Tim Southwell in 1993 as an antidote to what they regarded as the effete style-based men's mags.

In Southwell's (1998) lively and entertaining account of the *Loaded* story he talks of its genesis. In Barcelona with Brown for a European Cup match, Southwell writes:

> We'd just emerged from a fancy nightclub full of very attractive and very accommodating Spanish nurses. We were delirious with the joys of life. We were also very drunk. Rambling down the Ramblas, I began a high octane recounting of the night's amazing events ... Suddenly James comes over all unusual, grabs me by the arm and fixes me in the eye with a strange, cold stare. 'Wait a minute,' he says, 'What you just said. There should be a magazine like this, moments like this ... it should be all about the best moments you ever had.' (Southwell 1998: 2)

As the dust cover of Southwell's book puts it, *Loaded* celebrated the fact that 'the boys from the bike sheds were running riot all over the school'. It was, claims Southwell (1998: 255–6), about capturing 'the best time of our lives for readers'. He denies it had any political or social agenda, resented the way in which charges of 'laddism' were levelled against them and is still angry that what started out as 'blokes being honest' became confused with yobbish behaviour and football violence. He continues:

> There was no specific concept like 'let's abolish the "new man" and replace him with the "new lad" ...' [The magazine] existed to celebrate what it was like to be a bloke in Britain from 1993 onwards ... I've never ever met a 'new lad' and the reason is quite simple: they don't exist. (Southwell 1998: 107)

However, it is left to Ross (1999) to attempt to explain *Loaded*'s popularity. He asserts that by the 1990s the high living that had been at the heart of the lifestyle of the elite and celebrities from the 1960s onwards was now available, albeit in a less lavish form, to everyone, whatever their means, on the streets throughout Britain and the magazine captured this:

> men's lifestyles were [now] more concerned about good times than the stiff, fake 'new man' crap that the other titles had been peddling in the Eighties ... Britain was learning how to party ... *Loaded* was the men's mag that walked it like it talked it. It spoke the language of the bars and clubs of the UK. (Ross 1999: 41, 44–5)

As the 1980s moved into the 1990s, booming London continued to dress up, while depressed Liverpool and Manchester dressed down. He continues: 'everyone was on a blag, selling a lot of knock-off here, a bit of drugs there, robbing this and fiddling that. There was a huge black market economy going on ... [this was] a million miles away from the cosy world inhabited by Thatcher and her Tory cronies' (Ross 1999: 31, 33). *Loaded* left the needs of narcissistic new man to its competitors, turned its back on metropolitan chic and returned to basics: 'Lads into football, beer, rock and talking about birds were hardly marking a new demograph ... It was just that it had been ignored by the mass market mags for years' (Ross 1999: 23). Moreover, as Calcutt (2000: 271) observes, *Loaded* was 'the ideal format for boys who did not know how to grow up and so acted out a pantomime version of traditional masculinity'.

Ross (1999) places *Loaded* at the very forefront of young men's culture in the 1990s, claiming nothing less than that the *Loaded* effect has been one of the key cultural influences of the decade. Sales figures certainly appear to substantiate this assertion. In summer 1997, for example, the main 'lad mags' had between them a combined readership of some 1.5 million, as follows: *FHM* (504,959), *Loaded* (450,000), *Maxim* (185,000), *GQ* (148,574), *Esquire* (92,907) and *Aretia* (77,107). *Loaded*'s popularity and sales figures climbed steadily at first from an average of 60,000 a month and then rocketed, making magazine publishing history in the process. In October 1996, it was selling 300,000 monthly; in summer 1997, it was 450,000; by January 1998, this was up to an astonishing 500,000; and the fiftieth anniversary number in May 1998 topped 600,000, with *FHM* as its nearest competitor some way behind. By the summer of 1994 *Loaded* was synonymous with irreverence and faddishness was in the air as a backlash against 1980s over-dressed, narcissistic new man. But this was not solely attributable to *Loaded*. Lads' programmes dominated television ratings, most notably *Men Behaving Badly*, with its two male lead roles played by Neil Morrissey and Martin Clunes, and Fantasy Football League. Then there was 'Brit Pop' (in particular, Oasis, Pulp and Blur), Chris Evans, Gazza, David Baddiel and Nick Hornby's (1992) eulogy to football obsession, *Fever Pitch*.

The 'New Lad': His Ancestors, Friends and Enemies

The new lad was a throwback to a time when men had been able to behave badly and not worry about censure. Laddism was a reaction both to the 1980s men's style press and to the growing assertiveness of women. His distant ancestor was the George Best and Stan Bowles working-class hell-raisers-made-good of the 1960s and 1970s, while his more immediate relative was the 1980s 'lager lout', the yuppie's lower-class alter ego who, as Hunt (1998) notes, quickly moved from a folk devil into a consumer category. Another immediate ancestor from the 1980s was the 'toyboy', a sexualized young man happy to be the sexual plaything of older women. Of him Mort (1996) writes:

> By Christmas, 1986, it had all got too much for the tabloids. Lumping [these] disparate male markets together, they came up with the 'toyboy'. Pics and tales of young, stylish lads snapped in their boxer shorts, the supposed playthings of older women ... After all, if forty eight year old 'rock granny' Tina Turner could 'boogie the night away' with her 'German hunk', so could any ordinary woman. (Mort 1996: 205)

The new lad had his origins in pop music and football and, as Edwards (1997: 83) comments, the link is hardly surprising 'as football has historically always been a bastion of blow-drying, smut-swaggering, sharp-looking English laddism'. The link between football and laddism was further strengthened in 'football fiction' by, for example, Nick Hornby and John King. While the former is football for family consumption, the latter's version is about machismo, violence and hooliganism. But although the new lad may be objectionable, selfish, loutish, inconsiderate, building his life around drinking, football and sex, he was just as concerned with consumerism and labels as his new man elder brother:

> If the 'new man' sold muscles and scent, Armani and Calvin Klein, the 'new lad' sells t-shirts and trainers, Hugo by Hugo Boss and Prada ... the style may have altered, yet the drive to consume remains the same ... 'new lads' are just as much a phoney marketing phenomenon as 'new men'. (Edwards 1997: 83, 249)

The success of *Loaded* was about selling magazines through the exploitation of working-class machismo. In fact, the whole 'lad phenomenon' was a profit-driven, middle-class version of the archetypal working-class 'jack-the-lad'. Calcutt (2000) also points out that 'the lad' was not on his own. By his side was the 'ladette', girls behaving just like lads and, like Zoë Ball, 'willing to play ball with the New Lad culture if it will advance their celebrity' (Calcutt 2000: 263). There was also a 'yobocracy' of celebrity lads made up of such 1990s luminaries as Paul Gascoigne, Danny Baker and Chris Evans. Laddism was not just a reaction to constraints placed upon male behaviour by feminism but, certainly in the hands of *Loaded*, a counterblast to the stifling metropolitan chic of the 1980s men's style press.

Many saw the attraction of laddism and *Loaded* (and the two have become synonymous) lying in the fact that young men were suddenly sanctioned to display the errant side of masculinity, a return to unreconstructed basics like flesh, fun and unselfconsciousness. As Southwell (1998) puts it: '*Loaded* had clocked on to the fact that there was another kind of Britain other than the Beefeater, f***ing around in Florence, that kind of high-brow Britain. *Loaded* clocked on to what we all knew anyway: there was another England, but no one had ever championed it' (Southwell 1998: 61). *Loaded* writers famously engaged in 'capers' by going out into the provinces or travelling world-wide in order to find out what was happening on the streets and in the clubs:

> It was about having a laugh ... about self-deprecation ... what *Loaded* was really saying was that all those things that people like doing, things like getting drunk, they were all right. *Loaded* was all about being honest ... we weren't trying to sell a lifestyle, we were having a laugh ... If we did anything it was to make berkish behaviour acceptable. It was a big celebration ... We were constantly receiving letters of thanks from people who'd followed the *Loaded* path after reading articles about travelling to the world's greatest festivals and cultural happenings. (Southwell 1998: 73–4, 98, 175)

Laddism was a celebration of the irresponsible, of unreconstructed young-men-running-wild reduced to their crude basics and promoted in *Loaded* through jockstrap humour and 'bikini-style' photography. As Benwell (2000) shows, irony is at the heart of the 'new lad' discourse, an 'unrelenting omnipresence of a certain knowingness, self-referentiality and humour'.

Inevitably, the whole lad culture in general and *Loaded* in particular was charged with gross sexism, a charge hotly rebutted by Southwell (1998):

> We like football, but that doesn't mean we're hooligans. We like drinking, but it doesn't mean that as soon as the pub shuts we turn into wife-beating misogynists. We like looking at pictures of fancy ladies sometimes, but that doesn't mean we want to rape them ... Men like looking at pictures of attractive women. Big Deal. Get over it ... It's a class thing. *Loaded* portrayed women in a very mainstream way and had no shame about the fact that this basic element would appeal to our readers, most of whom would be men and most of them would, if they were anything like us, appreciate the inclusion of such pictures. (Southwell 1998; 101, 212)

Critics were numerous, as Southwell recalls:

clubby-pubby, all lads together hedonism and a healthy disrespect for pretension and anything Soho ... [a magazine] not for men-in-arms, but for men who are reverting to type and getting drunk on the profits. (Helen Birch, *Independent*, quoted in Southwell 1998: 99)

There's a feeling with lads that girls are fun; sex is great; and everyone is having a good time ... sod the politically correct. (Rosie Boycott, *Daily Express*, quoted in Southwell 1998: 105)

In 'ladworld', feminism and homosexuality barely exist. (Suzanne Moore, *Guardian*, quoted in Southwell 1998: 206)

The choice facing men today is between simpering cissy and unreconstructed lout. (Tony Parsons, quoted in Southwell 1998: 209)

[Loaded is] a regression to an infantile state of 'behaving badly' by fetishising the behaviour and culture of their adolescence. (Michael Bracewell, *Guardian*, quoted in Southwell 1998: 209)

As the 1990s drew to a close the criticisms levelled at 'laddism' increased in intensity. For example, David Baddiel (1999), himself a leading 'telly lad', attacked the culture that he had in no small part helped to create, dismissing *Loaded* as 'unreadably passé'. Others, for example Margolis (1995), objected to the way in which television has allowed itself to be engulfed by the vulgar and attacked the Tony and Gary figures in *Men Behaving Badly* as irresponsible, stupid, slovenly and disgusting. Indeed, all the 'celebrity lads' (Paul Merton, Frank Skinner, David Baddiel and Chris Evans, among others) have allowed themselves to be trapped inside laddist personas to such an extent that they have become depressing, even tragic figures. Yet others attacked the banality of the mags that both feed and feed off laddism. Early in 2001 the announcement that an all-party committee of Members of Parliament was to examine the rising rate of young male suicides in Britain led to the claim that the 'culture of laddism' was largely to blame because it fed young men a diet of excitement that they could not possibly replicate in their own mundane lives (BBC1, *Breakfast*, 7 March 2001). Surprisingly, one of the co-founders of *Loaded*, James Brown, appears to concur with many of his critics: '*Loaded* was like being on tour with the Rolling Stones ... We were young and ... irresponsible and we were having the time of our lives. And when you're having that you don't think of the moral implications' (Jenkins 2000: 25). However, if for most laddism is just another clever way of making money out of young male consumers by resurrecting the appeal of the working-class jack-the-lad, hell bent on having a good time, others still regard it as a genuine rebellion, a reassertion of something 'fundamentally masculine'. But no one can deny its continuing influence, especially since it has been successfully exported to the USA. In August 2000, the American edition of *Maxim* broke the 2 million circulation level, making it the most successful magazine launch ever in the USA. Given their subject matter, it was appropriate that Goodwin and Rushe (1999) adopted a distinctly laddish tone to record the launch of the *For Him Magazine* in the USA:

> The troops are being assembled, the invasion plans are well advanced and the general is in place ... to launch if not a full-frontal assault at least a semi-naked one, to liberate the sensibilities of the all-American male ... For Uncle Sam, the count down to the acceptable face of totty-time has begun ... a guy's a guy, wherever he lives ... A testosterone-charged British sperm is swimming across the Atlantic ... If the American 'new man' was ever house-trained by feminism to be considerate, sensitive and interested in women's minds rather than their bodies, he is about to be led wildly astray. (Goodwin and Rushe 1999: 32)

Who is (or was) the 'New Man'?

The 'new man-as-nurturer' was a response to feminism, to male consciousness-raising and the activities of men's groups and the influence of both male and female intellectuals. Widely criticized as being middle-class, elitist, 'Western-centric' and remote from the lived experience of ordinary men, the stereotypical image of the anti-sexist, caring, sharing man nevertheless gained credibility and strength throughout the 1980s. But how deep or widespread was the change he initiated? Was it a media-driven illusion of change or genuine change in the consciousness and behaviour of men? Similarly, if some saw 'new man-as-narcissist' as an upholder of individualism and a bright new future for a more diverse masculinity, others dismissed him as little more than a gullible clothes horse. Indeed, there are sharply divergent views concerning the degree of actuality of the new man. Many, for example, would agree with York and Jennings's (1995) opinion that he was nothing less than the advertising industry's dramatization of its own self-image and driven primarily by commercial greed. Meanwhile, Polly Toynbee (quoted in Mort 1988: 17) is of the opinion that the new man is 'not here and it does not seem likely that we shall see him in our lifetime'. Nixon (1996: 197) tends to concur, describing him as nothing less than a 'regime of representation'.

...

Conclusion: The Emergence of 'New Man-ism'

. . .

In March 1998, Jeremy Paxman, one of the presenters of BBC2's *Newsnight* programme, included an item on the 'new man' in the programme which revealed much about the media's fascination with categorizing and labelling of contemporary masculinity. Four men appeared, each fitting into a narrow stereotype:

- An angry 'old man', who vociferously argued that men had come off badly in the changes to the divorce laws and the activities of organizations like the Child Support Agency.
- A 'new man', Mark 1, circa the 1960s and 1970s, who talked of his efforts to tap into his inner masculinity and feelings
- A 'new man', Mark 2, a child of the 1980s, responding to the changing roles and responsibilities of men in the consumer society.
- A 'new lad', who expressed the view that the new man did not exist in real life but was little more than a ruse by men to get women into bed.

New 'types' of men are constantly being invented by the media. In the lead-up to January 2000, 'Millennium man' was constantly mentioned, along with the 'dad lad' (that is, the 'lad' grown up and settled down). As I write this (in February 2001) I hear on the radio and read in the press of 'Colditz man', who wants to escape from 'dragon woman' and the onerous and stifling pressures of contemporary family life. ... [T]hese journalistic generalizations, while they guarantee their inventors a string of media appearances and might even put a finger on an element of truth, usually have very little evidence to substantiate them. It is also salutary to remind ourselves of the possible disjuncture between discourse and actuality. Easthope (1986) perceptively pointed out in the mid-1980s that the relationship between 'the discursive' and 'lives-as-lived' will always be ambiguous because 'men do not passively live out the masculine myths imposed by the stories and images of the dominant culture' (Easthope 1986: 167). However, he then went on to say: 'But neither can they live completely outside the myth since it pervades the culture. Its coercive power is active everywhere, not just on screens, hoardings and paper, but inside [their] heads' (1986: 167).

While there is widespread acknowledgement that masculinity has changed considerably during the 1980s and 1990s, there is, I believe no longer any clear consensus as to what the new man actually stands for. It is my contention that these two hereditary (in some ways antithetical) strands have been woven together in the public mind into a pot-pourri, nebulous new man-ism. The only defining feature to which we can point with any degree of certainty is that he is certainly not 'old man', his father. The present-day young have all been touched by this new man-ism in one form or another. Conveyed by television, film, pop songs, radio, advertising and the press, as well as in everyday social interaction, new man-ism remains a highly pervasive and masculine 'message' (Harris 1995), one that bombards men in various forms from all angles.

. . .

References

Alexander, J. (1997) Half a million men can't be wrong, *You*, 12 October.

Baddiel, D. (1999) Come on, you lads, it's cool to grow up, *The Times Weekend Supplement*, 6 November.

Benwell, B. (2000) Ironic discourse: masculine talk in men's lifestyle magazines, in Posting the Mael conference abstracts, John Moores University, Liverpool, August.

Bly, R. (1981) *Iron John*. Rockport, MA: Element.

Calcutt, A. (2000) *Brit Cult: An A to Z of British Pop Culture*. London: Prion.

Chapman, R. (1988) The great pretender: variations on the 'new man' theme, in R. Chapman and J. Rutherford (eds) *Male Order: Unwrapping Masculinity*. London: Lawrence & Wishart.

Christian, H. (1994) *The Making of Anti-Sexist Men*. London: Routledge.

Coward, R. (1999) *Sacred Cows*. London: HarperCollins.

Easthope, A. (1986) *'What a Man's Gotta Do': The Masculine Myth in Popular Culture*. London: Paladin.

Edwards, T. (1997) *Men in the Mirror: Men's Fashions, Masculinity and Consumer Society*. London: Cassell.

Ehrenreich, B. (1983) *The Hearts of Men: American Dreams and the Flight from Commitment*. New York: Anchor-Doubleday.

Goodwin, C. and Rushe, D. (1999) Drool Britannia, *Sunday Times*, 1 August.

Hall, P. (1988) *Cities in Civilization*. London: Weidenfeld & Nicolson.

Harris, I. M. (1995) *Messages Men Hear: Constructing Masculinities*. London: Taylor & Francis.

Healey, M. (1994) The mark of a man, *Critical Quarterly*, 36(1): 86–93.

Hornby, N. (1992) *Fever Pitch*. London: Gollancz.

Hunt, L. (1998) *British Low Culture: From Safari Suits to Sexploitation*. London: Routledge.

Jenkins, D. (2000) It's a man's world, *Daily Telegraph*, 10 December.

Kimmel, M.S. and Messner, M.A. (eds) (1992) *Men's Lives*. New York: Macmillan.

Margolis, J. (1995) Last orders for the 'new lad' fad, *Sunday Times*, 23 April.

Moir, A. and Moir, B. (1998) *Why Men Don't Iron: The Real Science of Gender*

Studies. London: HarperCollins.

Mort, F. (1988) 'Boys Own?' Masculinity, style and popular culture, in R. Chapman and J. Rutherford (eds) *Male Order: Unwrapping Masculinity*. London: Lawrence & Wishart.

Mort, F. (1996) Cultures of consumption, *Masculinities and Social Space in Late Twentieth Century Britain*. London: Routledge.

Nixon, S. (1996) *Hard Looks: Masculinity, Spectatorship and Contemporary Consumption*. London: UCL Press.

Ross, J. (1999) *The Nineties*. London: Ebury.

Seidler, V.J. (1989) *Rediscovering Masculinity*. London: Routledge.

Shields, R. (1992) *Lifestyle Shopping: The Subject of Consumption*. London: Routledge.

Southwell, T. (1998) *Getting Away with It: The Inside Story of 'Loaded'*. London: Ebury.

Tosh, J. (1991) Domesticity and manliness in the Victorian middle class: the family of Edward White Benson, in M. Roper and J. Tosh (eds) *Manful Assertions: Masculinities in Britain since 1800*. London: Tavistock.

York, P. (1982) *The Official Sloane Ranger Handbook*. London: Ebury.

York, P. and Jennings, C. (1995) *Peter York's Eighties*. London: BBC Publications.

WOMEN AND THE INTERNET
THE NATURAL HISTORY OF A RESEARCH PROJECT

Anne Scott, Lesley Semmens and Lynette Willoughby

We are three academics – a software engineer, a social scientist and a neuroprocessor engineer – in the early stages of a research project on women's relationship to the Internet. We wish to explore means of increasing the access of ordinary women to some of the most powerful of the new information and communication technologies (ICTs). We also wish to discern why previous efforts to improve women's ICT access have been less than successful. We are feminists, and all three members of our group have a history of involvement in projects to improve women's access to technology, to education and to social power.

This article is a reflection on the pilot stage of our questionnaire-based study. It was expected that the pilot study would generate, primarily, methodological refinements and empirical data, but the results presented a rather unexpected set of outcomes. Rather than generating answers, it was found that the study was generating questions. In analysing the preliminary results, we began to reflect on the assumptions we had brought to this project, and on the way these assumptions are embedded in a story that is becoming established as *the* feminist account of women's relationship to the Internet and other new ICTs. This narrative then became the primary focus of our attention.

It is, perhaps, unsurprising that the 'facts' for which we were looking could not be disentangled from a narrative in which we were deeply, if rather unreflexively, embedded. Feminist epistemologists have established that all knowledge, including our own, must be contextualized (Lloyd 1984; Harding 1991; Code 1995; Alcoff and Potter 1993). As Haraway (1986: 79) has noted: '... the life and social sciences ... are story-laden;

these sciences are composed through complex, historically specific story-telling practices. Facts are theory-laden; theories are value-laden; values are story-laden. Therefore, facts are meaningful within stories.' In this article, we would like to begin describing and deconstructing the political and academic story – a story we have entitled 'women and the Internet' – which we brought to this research project. We believe that this story has become familiar to feminists with an interest in gender and information technology; it is becoming – to borrow another of Haraway's terms – an 'origin story' (Haraway 1986). We will be representing 'women and the Internet' as a story with a fixed beginning, a contested centre and an open ending. It was an engagement with this origin story that catalysed our research interests, and which informed our questionnaire design in the study's pilot phase. A lack of firm results then inaugurated a process of reflection which has highlighted the dissonant constitution of that story. It is those reflections, and consequent rethinking of 'women and the Internet' as a narrative, that will be the subject of the rest of this article.

Women and the Internet: A Women-and-Technology Origin Story

'Women and the Internet' is a story that – notwithstanding a few feminist attempts to highlight the nineteenth-century activities of Ada Lovelace (Plant 1997a; Toole 1996) – generally begins with the military-industrial complex. Numerous histories describe the development of the first computers, during the Second World War, to crack enemy codes and to calculate missile trajectories. Large main-frames later began to be used for scientific research and in business for payroll and databases. The linked network now known as the Internet is also described as having had its origins in the US military (Salus 1995; Panos 1995; Quarterman 1993). During the early days of the space race the US Department of Defense created the Advanced Research Projects Agency (ARPA). Part of ARPA's remit was to improve US military communications and, in 1969, four ARPANET computers were connected; these four nodes constituted the origin of the Internet.

Supported by the National Science Foundation in the USA (Loader 1997: 6), academics and industrialists began connecting to the network. By the time NSF support ended in 1995, the commercial potential of the Internet in the form of the World Wide Web was beginning to be realized, and the Internet had emerged as a globalized communication system (Harasim 1993a; Castells 1996). It was catalysing new means of engaging in politics

(Tsagarousianou et al. 1998; Castells 1997; Schuler 1996; Wittig and Schmitz 1996), of constructing identity (Stone 1995; Turkle 1995), of managing business, and of organizing criminal networks (Castells 1996; Castells 1998; Rathmell 1998). Within the feminist tale of its origins, this world-changing technology has been said to have had its origins in a male world with four roots: the military, the academy, engineering and industry (Harvey 1997). Differing versions of this historical account have been used to underpin analyses of the exclusion of women and other minority groups from the Internet via, for example, search engine operation, Internet culture and the netiquette that governs acceptable on-line behaviour (Morahan-Martin 1998; Harvey 1997; Wylie 1995; Holderness 1998; Spender 1995).

Empirical surveys have consistently suggested that women are under-represented as users of the Internet. The numbers world-wide using the Internet have been regularly surveyed by the Graphics, Visualization and Usability Centre (GVU 1994–98). Table 1 shows the percentages of women participants over the period January 1994 to April 1998. The early figures show a very low participation rate which rose, stabilized at about 30 per cent, and is now rising again. The USA has the highest numbers of women on the Internet; European women, by contrast, represent only between 15 per cent and 25 per cent of Internet users while, according to Morahan-Martin (1998: 3), only 5 per cent of Japanese and Middle Eastern Internet users are female. Other surveys have tried to get a picture of the 'average' user. *Which?*, in its 1998 annual Internet survey, claimed that UK users have a distinct profile: 'They tend to be male, under 35, living in the South, more affluent, employed, with no children living in the household.' These data have played a pivotal role in grounding this tale of women's relative exclusion from the electronic networks.

Table 1 Women as percentage of users (GVU 1994–98)

	Europe	*USA*	*World-wide*
Jan. 94			5
Oct. 94			10
Apr. 95	7	17	15
Oct. 95	10	33	29
Apr. 96	15	34	31
Oct. 96	20	32	31
Apr. 97	15	33	31
Oct. 97	22	40	38
Apr. 98	16	41	39

While 'women and the Internet' has had a wide variety of re-tellings, the themes noted here tend to make repeated appearances. The resulting narrative has acted as a coherent and motivating origin story for feminists with an interest in the new information and communication technologies. In it, these technologies – with enormous potential to diffuse information more widely, to increase democracy, to overturn the modernist conception of the sovereign (male) individual and to improve women's everyday lives – seem to have been misused, misappropriated and squandered. The point that the ICTs are reinforcing the very inequalities they should be combating is hammered home. As Spender argues in her influential *Nattering on the Net* (1995), the ICTs represent the new literacy, therefore many women are being rendered as twenty-first-century illiterates.

What Should Be Done?

As noted in the introduction, we have been thoroughly immersed in this story. As feminists, committed to democracy and to women's full inclusion in the contemporary socio-technological revolution, we have been involved in practical efforts to change this situation ... We have all been involved in efforts to develop more women-friendly forms of ICT education.[1] We have put our energies into these projects in the belief that, without positive action by interested feminists, the electronic networks will soon be, as Wylie put it, 'no place for women' (1995).

Like others working in this area, we have used actor network theory and social constructionist analyses of technology to argue that technological development is, in itself, a social process; it is an endogenous part of the wider development of society. The shape of technological artefacts is, in both subtle and not-so-subtle ways, influenced by cultural expectations, legal frameworks, institutional imperatives, global finance markets, implicit models of potential users and social beliefs (Pool 1997; Franklin 1997; Cockburn and Ormrod 1993). Historically, if new technologies are to gain acceptance they must, in some way, have acted to construct a social and cultural context in which they 'make sense', and in which they are needed (Latour 1993; Cockburn and Ormrod 1993; Callon 1991).[2] Thus, to be successful, new technologies must be produced in conjunction with new social practices, new social forms and new social networks which are able to receive and utilize them. We have been committed to the construction of new socio-technical practices which are as gender-sensitive as possible.

As interrelationships between the actors developing the 'information society' become denser and more complex, the shape of the new actor network developing around the ICTs (Callon 1991; Latour 1993) will become less malleable and less reversible; a new techno-social reality will have been created.

If women do not 'fit' well within the new technological standards now developing, they will find themselves being marginalized within developing social practices and social forms. As Haraway has noted, 'not fitting a standard is not the same thing as existing in a world without that standard' (1997: 37–8). The gender and ICT problem thus seems to be an urgent one; once this new socio-technical reality has become firmly established, people who fail to fit well within it must either adapt to it or accept margin-alization.

'Women and the Internet', as a narrative, is thus a story suffused with anxiety. New technological standards, protocols, products and structures are being developed at an incredible speed. New legal frameworks, social practices, economic models, organizational structures, institutional forms, cultural traditions, educational practices and forms of discourse are emer-ging to provide a context for them (Hills and Michalis 1997; Loader 1997; Castells 1996). The process of development currently under way will thus have direct and far-reaching material consequences. Like many other feminists working within this area, we have seen it as imperative that women are not excluded from full involvement in the design, use and adaptation of the ICTs during this formative phase of their development.

So this story forms a context in which we believe it important to learn *why* women seem to be relatively excluded from the electronic networks. It was decided that we needed to ask women themselves how they felt about the Internet, about their preconceptions and, after trying the Net for themselves, their perceptions. This was the starting place for the pilot study 'women coming to the Net', in which women attending short courses on the Internet or related subject areas were asked to complete a questionnaire. The shape of the pilot study drew heavily on a bid to the ESRC's virtual society programme, which had been submitted earlier by two of the authors.

Story? Which Story?

While 'women and the Internet' opens in a reasonably cohesive fashion, this feminist tale then splits into at least three, semi-competing, versions.[3] At the risk of over-simplifying and caricaturing a very complex literature, we might designate these accounts as follows:

- the webbed utopia
- flamed out, and
- locked into locality.

These three versions of the 'women and the Internet' narrative differ sharply in the way they perceive women's relationship with the Internet. They range from an optimistic celebration of women's subversive activity via the electronic networks to tales of exclusion, harassment and violence. Indeed, these competing stories might be said to belong to different genres entirely.

Account 1: 'the webbed utopia'

Drawing on examples such as the famous case of the PEN network in Santa Monica (Wittig and Schmitz 1996), Light argues that the electronic networks offer women new possibilities for networking and for participative democracy. Light (1995: 13) insists that this vision is not 'a feminist Utopia like the science fiction worlds of scholars such as Sally Miller Gearhart (1983). Rather, it is realistic and practical; at its core is the concept of seizing control of a new communications technology.'

Whether, in fact, Light's assessment of practicality can carry the tale 'women and the Internet' all the way to its conclusion, she has correctly identified her genre. 'The webbed utopia' is heavily influenced by the recent flood of feminist science fiction and fantasy. Sadie Plant (1997b: 503), for example, recently stated that the 'doom' of patriarchy is inevitable, and that it 'manifests itself as an alien invasion, a program which is already running beyond the human'.

The optimism of the webbed utopians has been reinforced by a number of contemporary examples in which activists have successfully employed the Internet for political ends. Systers, cyber-grrls and other feminist networks, for example, have worked to open up women-friendly spaces on the electronic networks (Wakeford 1997; Camp 1996). Political networking – primarily via electronic mail – was successful in influencing the outcome of the Fourth World Conference on Women in Beijing; the campaign influenced both the conference's primary agenda and the scope of its associated NGO forum (Gittler 1999; Huyer 1999). Mexican Zapatistas have used the Internet to elevate a local dispute into a national and international political issue (Castells 1997). Political activists in China and Malaysia have used Internet-based communication to push the authorities into a corner, thus generating a political backlash (*Independent*, 1998a: 15, 1998b: 18, 1998c: 18). Computer-mediated communication has been used to revitalize urban democracy in a number of cities (Brants et al. 1996; Day and Harris 1997; Tsagarousianou et al. 1998). The ease and cost-effectiveness of publishing on the World Wide Web has also made it possible to develop an international women's listing magazine (Burke 1999). The use of the electronic networks has clearly enhanced both local and global networking, thus opening up new social and political possibilities.

'The webbed utopia' is an account that can, however, remain wilfully blind to dramatic differentials in access to, and control of, the electronic networks. Plant's claim (1995) that the networked organization of the World Wide Web inherently supports feminist and democratic styles of working seems, in this utopian tale, to give her epistemological logic of networking a precedence over the more material logics of economic and industrial power. While utopian feminists are busy eulogizing the wonders of women-only alternative public spaces, they are failing to challenge the contemporary use of cybertechnology – by industrial giants, global criminal networks, military strategists, wealthy financiers and international racists – to evade social regulation, entrench political control and concentrate economic power (Castells 1996, 1998; Loader 1997; Panos 1995; Fischer-Huebner 1998; Lyon 1998; Capitanchik and Whine 1999).

Account 2: 'flamed out'

If 'the webbed utopia' belongs to the genre of science fantasy, 'flamed out' belongs to the horror genre, complete with invisible lurkers, menacing intimidation, pornographers and even cyber-rapists (Spender 1995; Herman 1999; Hilton 1996). Even in feminist discussions of the ICTs that are primarily devoted to other concerns, references to unprovoked sexual aggression on the Internet form a recurring theme. In a passing reference to pornography on the Net, two authors recently suggested that:

> In these cases, new communication technologies not only help to immortalize the product of a distorted view of sexuality within patri-archal societies, but also help predators to find new victims, creating a reverse civil society, a community of the predatory violent. Rapists or paedophiles can connect with their like-minded friends and together they can create a virtual world in which the 'abnormal' becomes normal ... (Inayatullah and Milojevic 1999: 81)

In one study of 35 days' worth of contributions to an e-mail list, both men and women reported 'being intimidated by the bombastic and adversarial postings of a small minority of male contributors who effectively dominated the discussions' (Herring et al. 1992: 225). Moreover, a two-day discussion of a feminist topic – during a five-week period in which the other 33 days had been dominated by men – resulted in angry accusations from some of the men that they felt silenced. In fact, according to those narrating this version of 'women and the Internet', it is women who are being silenced. Studies by Kramarae and Taylor (1993), Herring (1996) and Ferris (1996) suggest that men tend to monopolize on-line communication, even when the topic of discussion relates closely to women's interests and experience. Clem Herman (1999) argues that sexual harassment on the electronic networks has the effect of silencing women users. These studies of on-line communication suggest that, to paraphrase Kramarae and Taylor (1993), computer-mediated communication is more a male monologue than a mixed-sex conversation.

The tactic of flaming – directed at those who infringe a masculinized netiquette' (Sutton 1996) ؛ con be used to harass and victimize women in cyberspace. Spender (1995) discusses at some length the hostile environment created for women by flaming on the Net and by the highly masculinized atmosphere existing in some computer labs; these issues have also been highlighted by Kramarae and Taylor (1993), Brail (1996), Wylie (1995) and Herring (1994). 'Flamed out' is by no means, however, a story told exclusively by women. Rheingold (1994), Miller (1996) and Seabrook (1997) have all pointed to the destructive influence of 'flaming' on women's – and men's – ability to participate in computer-mediated communication. These concerns have catalysed the creation of women-only spaces which can act as a 'sanctuary on a hostile net' (Camp 1996: 121).

'Flamed out' highlights the fact that the use of male violence to victimize women and children, to control women's behaviour, or to exclude women from public spaces entirely, can be extended into the new public spaces of the Internet. This powerful and engaging story, however, is also rather one-sided. Within the genre of horror, women are often presented as helpless victims of violence; in this respect, 'flamed out' is true to its literary roots. Such portrayals can be politically paralysing. Furthermore, they are highly misleading; most Net users do have some means to control or avoid intimidation and violence (Hamilton 1999; Newey 1999). Helpless victimization is not the experience of most women, in cyberspace or elsewhere. This version of 'women and the Internet' can be counter-productive for feminists; if cyberspace is so dangerous, women might well come to believe that their daughters would be safer spending their time somewhere else.

Account 3: 'locked into locality'

The third version of 'women and the Internet' central chapters might well find a home in the genre of domestic drama developed by nineteenth-century feminist novelists. Like these novels of historical realism, 'locked into locality' is suffused by a melancholy awareness that, while the social, political and economic action is taking place in a distant public space, most women are still shut away at home.

The electronic networks have been repeatedly described as a 'new public space' or even as a new 'public sphere' (Samarajiva and Shields 1997; Harasim 1993b; Schuler 1996). Women, however, are said to be underrepresented in these spaces, trapped in a shrinking 'private' sphere of print and of proximate, face-to-face contact:

> After five hundred years, women were just beginning to look as though they were drawing even with the men. They have reached the stage in countries like Australia where, for the first time, more women than men have been gaining higher education qualifications. But this success has been achieved in an education system still based on print. ... And just when it looks as though equity is about to be realized – the rules of the game are changed. The society (and soon the education system) switches to the electronic medium. (Spender 1995: 185)

In the nineteenth century, the world of print allowed geographically isolated feminists to connect with each other, and thus build nation-wide political networks (Alexander 1994; Lacey 1987). By turning inwards with a pen, Victorian feminists could upturn the constraints of the private sphere, and make an impact on the public world of ideas. They could subvert the geographies of public and private. ICT – by dramatically redefining contemporary notions of public and private (Rich 1997: 226; Gumpert and Drucker 1998) – may offer similar opportunities to twenty-first-century feminists.

The heroines of 'locked into locality' must do battle with the prejudices of their contemporaries regarding women's place, women's capabilities and women's desires. They must struggle to acquire necessary material resources: not a 'room of their own' (Woolf 1929), but a computer of their own and the software, education, training, time and space needed to use it. Women are often identified with local identities and the particularity of place (Castells 1997; Enloe 1989). As these geographies of place and locality are subverted by new geographies of information flow, women face a double challenge: they must defend their local spaces against the threat posed by a disembodied globalization, and they must also create spaces within the new electronic media for their own voices (Escobar 1999).

'Locked into locality', as an account, is thus highly sensitive to the material constraints of time, space, money, educational background, cultural expectations and employment opportunities, which act to limit women's opportunities and aspirations in relation to the ICTs. Research conducted by those constructing this tale suggests that the obstacles that women must overcome to gain full access to these networks are still substantial. Grundy (1996) points out that men are more likely than women to be in jobs providing access to the Internet; Adam and Green (1997) further note that constructions of women's work as 'less skilled' can be used to justify the granting of lower levels of autonomy in women's use of ICTs at work. The use of ICTs at work can reinforce expectations of accessibility and flexibility, which are often imposed on women (Markussen 1995; Wagner 1995). Boys tend to dominate computer clubs and gaming networks (Haddon 1992; Spender 1995). During the Internet's recent growth spurt, there has actually been a decline in the numbers of women studying computing in universities (Wright 1997). In a study of the use of domestically owned PCs, Wheelock (1992) found that wives/mothers made less use of the machines than other family members. In an international survey of women's groups and individuals (Farwell et al. 1999), the most frequently cited barriers to women's ICT access were lack of training and the cost of equipment. Respondents also mentioned problems relating to equipment accessibility, lack of time, information overload, language constraints, lack of privacy and security, fear of backlash or harassment, skill deficiencies and alienation.

Victorian feminists pushed for an extension of opportunities, so that a few women might be able to overcome the many obstacles in their path and forge public careers. Similarly, 'locked into locality' is, as a narrative, closely associated with the equal opportunities discourse of the WIT, the WISE and the GIST programmes.[4] By working to create social support networks, to institute cultural changes, and to induce higher expectations of, and by, girls and women, these programmes have been notably successful in enabling some women to pursue scientific and technological careers (Swarbrick 1987; Whyte 1986). They have also, however, been criticized for their individualism. In assisting individual women who wish to 'make it' in the male worlds of science and technology without first problematizing economic and social structures, the public/private division and the gendered cultures of contemporary technology, they run the risk of reducing structural issues to problems of individual deficiency (Cockburn 1986; Swarbrick 1997; Whyte 1986; Kelly 1985).

In spite of the problems associated with it, it is in the tale of 'locked into locality' that we have felt most at home. In its steady focus on material factor, both the dangers and the opportunities posed by the Internet are placed in perspective. Its historically and socio-economically sensitive individualism is highly usable within an educational context. As a narrative it is both practical and flexible. Our own research project was embedded in this version of 'women and the Internet'.

Women and the Internet: Questioning the Tale

'Women coming to the Net': a pilot study

Some time was spent putting together a questionnaire for the pilot stage of this project. We attempted to frame the questions in a way that was sensitive to the problems of time, space and material constraint which we believed would most affect women's experiences of the ICTs. In addition to addressing a number of demographic variables with relevance to the structure of many women's lives, our questionnaire asked respondents to discuss their perceptions of enabling and disabling technologies. We differentiated individual access and household, community-based and work-based access; questions were also asked about the control and ownership of ICT equipment and software, in practice. Respondents were asked to identify their preferred environments for using the Internet, their preferred contexts for training, and their preferences regarding types and quantities of external support. We also asked our respondents to tell us for what purposes they used their computers and for what purposes they would like to use their computers.

As we started distributing our questionnaires, we felt that we had developed a pilot research instrument of some sophistication. The questionnaires were distributed on three short courses aimed at women with differing levels of ICT ability and confidence. When analysis began, however, we found to our chagrin that we had almost no data that we could directly use. The answers on completed questionnaires reflected widely divergent readings of the questions, as well as a wide divergence in women's basic conceptualizations of ICT. There did not seem to be any patterns emerging at all.

Researching gender and IT

At this stage, some basic rethinking was required ... Problems seemed to stem from the fact that the question, as we had originally framed it, was unanswerable. The pilot study had been designed to address the question 'What are the factors that limit and constrain women's access to the new ICTs?' This is a question that emerges naturally from 'locked into locality', the version of the 'women and the Internet' story we favoured. It assumes that women are a relatively homogeneous group, who have been prevented by material and cultural factors from gaining full access to an unproblematized, electronic 'public sphere'. However, there are at least three problems hiding in this question. What do we mean by access? What do we mean by 'the Internet'? And *which* women? We would like to address each of these in turn.

What do we mean by *access*?

We began our study with a conceptualization of 'access' which challenged the notion that ICT users are – first and foremost – consumers . . . As long as 'access' means, as Wylie put it, access to 'the right to clerk and consume' (1995: 3), it is hard to counter the argument that greater equality of ICT opportunity can best be generated *after* a working network has been established by the more dynamic private sector. By contrast, we have tended to configure ICT users as citizens – as social, political and cultural agents.[5] Our conceptualization of 'access' thus owes a great deal to the actor network analysis of technology, discussed previously. The question we have been asking might thus be rephrased as follows: are women to be admitted to the electronic public sphere as workers and producers, or as full citizens and social agents?

Our conceptualization of 'access', however, has also been blind to concerns that do not fit naturally into this narrative. Dutton (1998) argues that we cannot think about ICT access in a manner that simply adds it to people's existing capacities and resources. Instead, we must think about geographies of access: to what are people gaining access, and for what are these new connections substituting? People might surf the web instead of going to their local public library, for example; instead of putting their money in the NatWest on the High Street, they might do their banking with First Direct; instead of spending their time chatting with a neighbour, they might build a close friendship with an e-mail user in Tokyo. In short, social, economic and political networks that were once heavily based on geographic proximity are being replaced by a new 'space of flows' – networks based on affinity or the provision of specialized services (Castells 1996). However, since not everybody can afford 'tele-access',[6] this will result in holes being punched in communities of physical locality, while more socially and economically exclusive 'virtual' communities are created. These segmented communities will be less able to maintain a shared culture (Escobar 1999: 35). The meaning of 'community' is thus changing with those people fortunate enough to have access to the Internet now being able to create (in effect) privatized, fragmented and geographically dispersed communities.

The question of access, therefore, cannot be addressed on an individualized basis. Rather, it must be transformed into a question about the social relations of technology. As May puts it, 'technologies do not necessarily bring with them specific social relations antagonistic or co-operative. It is the use to which technologies are put that develops their social relations' (1998: 253). How will the new ICTs be integrated into everyday life? What new social networks will be created? Who will those networks include, and who will be excluded? How will everyday activities be transformed? How will people with varying levels of ICT equipment, software, training and interest find, or create, a way to manage the micro power relations which have been thrown into some level of flux by the need to integrate these new techno-social forms? These questions cannot easily be addressed within the 'locked in locality' narrative, with its 'equal opportunities' focus on socially created material constraints that act on an individual level.

Moreover, our analysis of the data in our questionnaires suggests that the question of 'access' – even if we could develop an appropriate narrative frame for it – is simply too complicated to be usefully addressed via a short survey. The question of 'ICT access' must be embedded in a larger set of questions about ICT use which are, in turn, embedded in a set of questions about social institutions, social practices and social networks. Asking the respondents about the features on their computers told us little, for example, because we did not have contextualizing information relating to their reasons for having those features, the use they made of them, their conceptualizations of that use, and the way these practices were embedded in the larger structures of their lives.

What do we mean by the Internet?

Our questionnaire included a number of questions about the features that respondents had on their computers, the features they wished to have, and the use they made of their computers. These questions were designed to differentiate between active and passive use of the Internet. In keeping with the emphasis in 'women and the Internet' on enrolling women into an active construction of new socio-technical relations, they were designed to differentiate cyber-consumers from cyber-citizens. The data collected, however, came aground on a simple but thorny problem. Most artefacts begin to carry a multitude of meanings as they are appropriated by users and incorporated into their daily lives (Silverstone et al. 1992). This multiplicity, however, is greatly magnified in the case of both the personal computer and the Internet, whose very *raison d'être* is the manipulation and communication of symbolic meaning. We had fallen foul of the 'black box' fallacy (Grint and Woolgar 1997) – proceeding as if the Internet, and the equipment used to access it, could be conceptualized as 'things' with a single, coherent and accessible meaning.

As we began to analyse our data, we realized that we really could not make sense of the personal computer, or of the Internet, as a single thing. The respondents were clearly conceptualizing both the PC and the Internet in dramatically varying fashions; perhaps the PC is not a single thing. Our reflection and analysis leaves us with the uncomfortable conclusion that the computer/Internet remains, at least, five different things. Politicians and employers tend to think of the computer/Internet as a tool to keep track of money and stock, assist in marketing and publicity, transfer software and data, and improve management and administration. 'Locked into locality' draws heavily on this conceptualization of the computer/Internet. Artists, musicians and writers, by contrast, think of the computer/Internet as a publisher. All three versions of 'women and the Internet' have analysed the implications of the fact that people can publish on the web at little cost, and without going through publishers. This makes public platforms available to more people and catalyses the development of more democratic epistemologies; however, it also allows pornography and hate literature to be produced and disseminated via the Internet. In most homes, the computer/Internet is, first and foremost, a *toy*; it is primarily used for playing games (Haddon 1992; Wheelock 1992). As the computer/Internet-as-toy tends to be male dominated, with violent and misogynistic games, this conceptualization plays a key role in the 'flamed out' discourse. To teachers, academics and parents, the computer/Internet is often conceptualized as a library, with uses in information storage and dissemination, technologies of learning, and academic publishing. The implications for educational practice make this conceptualization of key interest to the progenitors of 'locked into locality'. The computer-as-tool conception – which reigned almost undisturbed during the 1970s and 1980s – has come under pressure from a newly hegemonic understanding of the computer/Internet-as-*social-centre*. The astonishing development of lateral communicability – via fax, e-mail, conferencing, electronic bulletin boards, discussion groups, multi-user domains, chat groups and the electronic transfer of large files – has, to a large degree, generated the optimism of the 'webbed utopian' discourse.

. . .

Which women?

The story of 'women and the Internet' is, at its core, a narrative about the restricting of Internet access to men (and some women) of certain social groups. It highlights the problems created by the fact that Internet users tend to be male, white, younger than average, and to have high average incomes. Even within these restricted social groups, however, there are major demographic issues – bearing particularly on the way that women organize their lives – that have been inadequately investigated. Are women, for example, with school-age children more or less likely to independently use the World Wide Web than other women? Do women living in same-sex households/relationships have more confidence with the new technologies than do those living with men? Are women more likely to engage with the new information technologies if they are also involved in community activities and/or in paid work? Are women Internet users more or less likely to be disabled than non-users, and are their impairments clustered within certain categories? In mixed-gender households, who loads software, organizes the desk-top and engages in other cyber-based nest-building tasks?

The 'locked into locality' narrative, with its deep sensitivity to the problematic construction of public and private in women's lives, is an ideal starting place from which to address these semi-demographic questions. We began our research in the belief that a large survey might usefully address such issues and indeed we found that these questions worked quite well on the questionnaire. A more widely distributed questionnaire that has come to terms with the other difficult issues raised above could be invaluable in this respect.

A more fundamental issue relates to our very choice of the Internet for study. Why has the 'women and the Internet' discourse focused on the Internet? As Dutton (1998) noted in his recent study of pager use, there are some ICT technologies with a much more even demographic spread of users, in relation to gender, social class and ethnicity. His research showed that these cheaper and less glamorous technologies are being creatively used by women to reshape local social structures, reorganize social geographies and recreate social institutions. This informal activity, however, has been little studied; it has been tucked away into the more peripheral corners of the information revolution. If we are serious about exploring women's ability to remain socially and politically effective in an information age, we cannot narrow our attention too severely. We need to think more carefully about the geographies of the information revolution itself.

Conclusion: A Retelling of the Tale

The story of 'women and the Internet' has served as something of an origin story for feminists working in this field. Although it has been deeply contested – in genre as well as detail – this story has acted as a coherent and persuasive motivating myth. We began our research project from a standpoint firmly embedded within it. In the course of our analysis, however, we have come to question the way this story has been framed. A number of questions have occurred to us:

- How much have the Internet's military–industrial origins actually influenced women's current and future relationships with this technology?
- What does it mean to say that women have been excluded from this new medium?
- Is there any point in talking globally about women's relationship to the Internet?
- Why has this tale focused so closely on the Internet (as well as virtual reality and other 'sexy' new technologies) while tending to ignore cheaper, more pervasive and perhaps more democratic technologies such as the pager and the mobile phone?
- Can we conceptualize the Internet as a single thing?
- How can we integrate the complex and seemingly incompatible threads of discourse from which this story has been woven?

It may be necessary to begin formulating a more reflexive and variegated origin story in relation to women and ICT. This new tale should address two key questions:

- How are the new social geographies of ICT access being gendered?
- How can we intervene to direct the shaping of new techno-social relations in more democratic, inclusive and neutrally gendered ways?

Although this new story should be extremely gender-sensitive, it might not begin with women – as a homogeneous category – at all. The 'locked into locality' narrative is fundamentally concerned with the way that citizenship is materially structured in relation to time, space and economic resources. A women and technology story that is adequate to its task should analyse the changing shape of these material geographies in the information age.

The story of 'women and the Internet' has catalysed wide-ranging research and valuable developmental work. Thus, rather than abandoning this narrative, we would suggest embroidering it with new texturing and a new reflexivity. We need to problematize the recurring themes that have shaped this narrative. The narrative logic drawn on in our research matters greatly; it acts to shape the conclusions to be reached for, as noted at the beginning of this article, facts have meaning only within stories.

Notes

1. East Leeds Women's Workshop, Women into Technology (Open University), Curriculum–Women–Technology project (EU), 'Community Development and the Internet' short course and module (Bradford University).
2. For an example of the way that this necessary process can be deliberately utilized to achieve social ends, see Randi Markussen's discussion (1996) of the Scandinavian participatory design tradition.
3. In fact, there are surely more than three competing versions of this tale. However, some of its strands – such as those arising from studies of the impact of IT on women's work, of international development and IT, or of the participatory design tradition – have tended to be rather peripheral to the early formulation of our research project, and are thus not discussed in this article.
4. Women into Technology, Women in Science and Engineering, Girls into Science and Technology.
5. This conceptualization has found some expression in national ICT policy, where it has come into conflict with the dominant, more conservative conceptualizations (LIC 1997; DCMS 1998). The Libraries and Information commission's *New Library* document (LIC 1997) emphasizes that access must be free at the point of use if the ICTs are to be used to increase social inclusiveness and to strengthen representative democracy.
6. Or desires it: see, for example, Umble's discussion (1992) of the Pennsylvania Amish communities' response to the telephone.

References

Adam, A. and Green, E. (1997) Gender, agency, location and the new information society, in B. Loader (ed.) *The Governance of Cyberspace: Politics, Technology, and Global Restructuring*. London: Routledge.

Alcoff, L. and Potter, E. (1993) *Feminist Epistemologies*. London: Routledge.

Alexander, S. (1994) *Becoming a Woman, and Other Essays in 19th and 20th Century Feminist History*. London: Virago Press.

Brail, S. (1996) The price of admission: harassment and free speech in the wild, wild, west, in L. Cherny and E.R. Weise (eds) *Wired Women: Gender and New Realities in Cyberspace*. Seattle: Seal Press.

Brants, K., Huizenga, M. and Van Meerten, R. (1996) The new canals of Amsterdam: an exercise in local electronic democracy, *Media, Culture and Society*, 18: 233–47.

Burke, K. (1999) AVIVA: the women's World Wide Web, in Liberty (ed.) *Liberating Cyberspace: Civil Liberties, Human Rights and the Internet.* London: Pluto Press.

Callon, M. (1991) Techno-economic networks and irreversibility, in J. Law (ed.) *A Sociology of Monsters: Essays on Power, Technology and Domination.* London: Routledge.

Camp, L.J. (1996) We are geeks, and we are not guys: the systers mailing list, in L. Cherny and E.R. Weise (eds) *Wired Women: Gender and New Realities in Cyberspace.* Seattle: Seal Press.

Capitanchik, D. and Whine, M. (1999) The governance of cyberspace: racism on the Internet, in Liberty (ed.) *Liberating Cyberspace: Civil Liberties, Human Rights and the Internet.* London: Pluto Press.

Castells, M. (1996) *The Rise of the Network Society.* Oxford: Blackwell.

Castells, M. (1997) *The Power of Identity.* Oxford: Blackwell.

Castells, M. (1998) *End of Millenium.* Oxford: Blackwell.

Cockburn, C. (1986) Women and technology: opportunity is not enough, in K. Purcell et al. (eds) *The Changing Experience of Employment: Restructuring and Recession.* London: Macmillan.

Cockburn, C. and Ormrod, S. (1993) *Gender and Technology in the Making.* London: Sage.

Code, L. (1995) *Rhetorical Spaces: Essays on Gendered Locations.* London: Routledge.

Day, R. and Harris, K. (1997) *Down-to-Earth Vision: Community Based IT Initiatives and Social Inclusion.* London: IBM Corp.

DCMS (Department for Culture, Media and Sport) (1998) *New Library: The People's Network, The Government's Response.* London: HMSO.

Dutton, W. (1998) *Society on the Line: Information Politics in the Digital Age.* Oxford: Oxford University Press.

Enloe, C. (1989) *Bananas, Beaches and Bases: Making Feminist Sense of International Politics.* London: Pandora.

Escobar, A. (1999) Gender, place and networks: a political ecology of cyber-culture, in W. Harcourt (ed.) *Women@Internet: Creating New Cultures in Cyberspace.* London: Zed Books.

Farwell, E., Wood, P., James, M. and Banks, K. (1999) Global networking for change: experiences from the APC Women's Programme, in W. Harcourt (ed.) *Women@Internet: Creating New Cultures in Cyberspace.* London: Zed Books.

Ferris, S. (1996) Women online: cultural and relational aspects of women's communication in online discussion groups, *Interpersonal Computing and Technology*, 4: 29–40.

Fischer-Huebner, S. (1998) Privacy and security at risk in the global information society, *Information, Communication and Society*, 1(4): 420–41.

Franklin, S. (1997) *Embodied Progress: A Cultural Account of Assisted Conception.* London: Routledge.

Gearhart, S. (1983) *The Wanderground: Stories of the Hill Women.* London: Women's Press.

Gittler, A. (1999) Mapping women's global communications and networking, in W. Harcourt (ed.) *Women@Internet: Creating New Cultures in Cyberspace*. London: Zed Books.

Grint, K. and Woolgar S. (1997) *The Machine at Work: Technology, Work and Organization*. Cambridge: Polity.

Grundy (1996) *Women and Computers*. Exeter: Intellect.

Gumpert, G. and Drucker, S. (1998) The mediated home in the global village, *Communication Research*, 25(4): 422–38.

GVU (Graphics, Visualization and Usability Centre: Georgia Tech University) (1994–98). On-line. Available: http://wwwgvu.gatech.edu/user-surveys/survey–1998–041#exce (17 January 1999).

Haddon, L. (1992) Explaining ICT consumption: the case of the home computer, in R. Silverstone and E. Hirsch (eds) *Consuming Technologies: Media and Information in Domestic Spaces*. London: Routledge.

Hamilton, A. (1999) The net out of control – a new moral panic: censorship and sexuality, in Liberty (ed.) *Liberating Cyberspace: Civil Liberties, Human Rights and the Internet*. London: Pluto Press.

Harasim, L. (ed.) (1993a) *Global Networks: Computers and International Communication*, London: MIT Press.

Harasim, L. (1993b) Networlds: networks as social space, in L. Harasim (ed.) *Global Networks: Computers and International Communication*. London: MIT Press.

Haraway, D. (1985) A manifesto for cyborgs: science, technology and socialist feminism in the 1980s, *Socialist Review*, 80: 65–107.

Haraway, D. (1986) Primatology is politics by other means, in R. Bleier (ed.) *Feminist Approaches to Science*, Oxford: Pergamon Press.

Haraway, D. (1997) *Modest_Witness@Second_Millenium. FemaleMan@_Meets_OncomouseTm: Feminism and Technoscience*. London: Routledge.

Harding, S. (1991) *Whose Science? Whose Knowledge? Thinking from Women's Lives*. Milton Keynes: Open University Press.

Harvey, L. (1997) A genealogical exploration of gendered genres in IT cultures, *Information Systems Journal*, 7: 153–72.

Herman, C. (1999) Women and the internet, in Liberty (ed.) *Liberating Cyberspace: Civil Liberties, Human Rights and the Internet*. London: Pluto Press.

Herring, S. (1994) Politeness in computer culture: why women thank and men flame, in M. Bucholtz et al. (eds.) *Cultural Performances: Proceedings of the Third Berkeley Women and Language Conference*. Berkeley: University of California.

Herring, S. (1996) Posting in a different voice: gender and ethics in computer-mediated communication, in C. Ess (ed.) *Philosophical Approaches to Computer-mediated Communication*. Albany: SUNY Press.

Herring, S., Johnson, D. and De Benedetto, T. (1992) Participation in electronic discourse in a feminist field, in K. Hall, M. Bucholtz and B. Moonwomon (eds)

Proceedings of the Second Berkeley Women and Language Conference, University of California, Berkeley.

Hills, J. and Michalis, M. (1997) Technological convergence: regulatory competition: the British case of digital television, *Policy Studies*, 18(3/4): 219–37.

Hilton, I. (1996) When everything has its price, *Guardian*, 27 August.

Holderness, M. (1998) Who are the world's information poor?, in B. Loader (ed.) *Cyberspace Divide: Equality, Agency and Policy in the Information Society.* London: Routledge.

Huyer, S. (1999) Shifting agendas at GK97: women and international policy on information and communication technologies, in W. Harcourt (ed.) *Women@Internet: Creating New Cultures in Cyberspace.* London: Zed Books.

Inayatullah, S. and Milojevic, I. (1999) Exclusion and communication in the information era: from silences to global conversation, in W. Harcourt (ed.) *Women@Internet: Creating New Cultures in Cyberspace.* London: Zed Books.

Independent (1998a) China fires first shot in Internet war, 4 December.

Independent (1998b) China uses jail threat to keep control of Internet, 13 December.

Independent (1998c) Malaysia losing fight against cyber protest, 13 December.

Kelly, A. (1985) The construction of masculine science, *British Journal of the Sociology of Education*, 6(2): 133–54.

Kramarae, C. and Taylor, H.J. (1993) Women and men on electronic networks: a conversation or a monologue, in H.J. Taylor, C. Kramarae and M. Ebben (eds) *Women, Information Technology and Scholarship.* Urbana, IL: Center for Advanced Study.

Lacey, C. (ed.) (1987) *Barbara Leigh Smith Bodichon and the Langham Place Group.* London: Routledge & Kegan Paul.

Latour, B. (1993) *We Have Never Been Modern.* Hemel Hempstead: Harvester Wheatsheaf.

LIC (1997) *New Library: The People's Network.* London: Department of Culture, Media and Sport.

Light, J. (1995) The digital landscape: new space for women?, *Gender, Place and Culture*, 2(2): 133–46.

Lloyd, G. (1984) *The Man of Reason: 'Male' and 'Female' in Western Philosophy.* London: Methuen.

Loader, B. (1997) *The Governance of Cyberspace: Politics, Technology and Global Restructuring.* London: Routledge.

Lyon, D. (1998) The world wide web of surveillance: the internet and off-world power flows, *Information, Communication and Society*, 1(1): 91–105.

Markussen, R. (1995) Constructing easiness: historical perspectives on work, computerization and women, in S.L. Star (ed.) *The Cultures of Computing.* Oxford: Blackwell.

Markussen, R. (1996) Politics of intervention in design: feminist reflections on the Scandinavian tradition, *Artificial Intelligence and Society*, 10: 127–41.

May, C. (1998) Capital, knowledge and ownership: the 'information society' and intellectual property, *Information, Communication and Society*, 1(3): 246–69.

Miller, S. (1996) *Civilizing Cyberspace: Policy, Power, and the Information Superhighway*. New York: ACM Press.

Morahan-Martin, I. (1998) Women and girls last: females and the internet. Bristol: IRISS '98 Conference.

Newey, A. (1999) Freedom of expression: censorship in private hands, in Liberty (ed.) *Liberating Cyberspace: Civil Liberties, Human Rights and the Internet*. London: Pluto Press.

Panos (1995) *The Internet and the South: Superhighway or Dirt Track?* London: Panos.

Plant, S. (1995) The future looms: weaving women and cybernetics, *Body and Society*, 1(3–4): 45–64.

Plant, S. (1997a) *Zeros + Ones: Digital Women + The New Technoculture*. London: Fourth Estate.

Plant, S. (1997b) Beyond the screens: film, cyberpunk and cyberfeminism, in S. Kemp and J. Squires (eds) *Feminisms*. Oxford: Oxford University Press.

Pool, R. (1997) *Beyond Engineering: How Society Shapes Technology*. Oxford: Oxford University Press.

Quarterman, J. (1993) The global matrix of minds, in L. Harasim (ed.) *Global Networks: Computers and International Communication*. London: MIT Press.

Rathmell, A. (1998) Information warfare and sub-state actors: an organizational approach, *Information, Communication and Society*, 1(4): 488–503.

Rheingold, H. (1994) *The Virtual Community: Finding Connection in a Computerized World*. London: Secker & Warburg.

Rich, B.R. (1997) The party line: gender and technology in the home, in J. Terry and M. Calvert (eds) *Processed Lives: Gender and Technology in Everyday Life*. London: Routledge.

Salus, P. (1995) *Casting the Net: From IRPANET to Internet and Beyond*, Wokingham: Addison-Wesley.

Samarajiva, R. and Shields, P. (1997) Telecommunication networks as social space: implications for research and policy and an exemplar, *Media, Culture and Society*, 19: 535–55.

Schuler, D. (1996) *New Community Networks: Wired for Change*. New York: ACM Press.

Seabrook, J. (1997) *Deeper: A Two-year Odyssey in Cyberspace*. London: Faber & Faber.

Silverstone, R., Hirsch, E. and Morley, D. (1992) Information and communication technologies and the moral economy of the household, in R. Silverstone and E. Hirsch (eds) *Consuming Technologies: Media and Information in Domestic Spaces*. London: Routledge.

Spender, D. (1995) *Nattering on the Net: Women, Power and Cyberspace*. Melbourne: Spinifex.

Stone, A.L. (1995) *The War of Desire and Technology at the Close of the Mechanical Age*. London: MIT Press.

Sutton, L. (1996) Cocktails and thumbtacks in the old west: what would Emily Post say?, in L. Cherny and E.R. Weise (eds) *Wired Women: Gender and New Realities in Cyberspace*, pp. 169–87. Seattle: Seal Press.

Swarbrick, A. (1987) Information technology and new training initiatives for women, in M.J. Davidson and C.L. Cooper (eds) *Women and Information Technology*. Chichester: John Wiley.

Swarbrick, A. (1997) Against the odds: women developing a commitment to technology, in M. Maynard (ed.) *Science and the Construction of Women*. London: UCL Press.

Toole, B. (1996) Ada Byron, Lady Lovelace, an analyst and metaphysician, *IEEE Annals of the History of Computing*, 18(3): 4–11.

Tsagarousianou, R., Tambini, D. and Bryan, C. (eds) (1998) *Cyberdemocracy: Technology, Cities and Civic Networks*. London: Routledge.

Turkle, S. (1995) *Life on the Screen: Identity in the Age of the Internet*. London: Phoenix.

Umble, D. (1992) The Amish and the telephone: resistance and reconstruction, in R. Silverstone and E. Hirsch (eds) *Consuming Technologies: Media and Information in Domestic Spaces*. London: Routledge.

Wagner, I. (1995) Hard times: the politics of women's work in computerized environments, *The European Journal of Women's Studies*, 2(3): 295–314.

Wakeford, N. (1997) Networking women and grrrls with information/communication technology: surfing tales of the world wide web, in J. Terry and M. Calvert (eds) *Processed Lives: Gender and Technology in Everyday Life*. London: Routledge.

Wheelock, J. (1992) Personal computers, gender and an institutional model of the household, in R. Silverstone and E. Hirsch (eds) *Consuming Technologies: Media and Information in Domestic Spaces*. London: Routledge.

Which? (1998) On-line. Available: http://www.which.net/nonsub/special/ispsurvey/executive.html (17 January 1999).

Whyte, J. (1986) *Girls into Science and Technology*. London: Routledge.

Wittig, M. and Schmitz, J. (1996) Electronic grassroots organizing, *Journal of Social Issues*, 52(1): 53–69.

Wright, M. (1997) Women in computing: a cross-national analysis, in R. Lander and A. Adam (eds) *Women in Computing: Progress from Where to What?* Exeter: Intellect.

Woolf, V. (1929) *A Room of One's Own*. Harmondsworth: Penguin.

Wylie, M. (1995) No place for women, *Digital Media*, 4(8): 3–6.

AUDIENCES AND IDENTITIES

For much of the twentieth century, media scholars were primarily concerned with demonstrating how the media affected people's behaviour. 'Effects' researchers assumed either that media messages had powerful, direct effects or that quantifiable effects were very limited. In this tradition of social science research, feminist mass communication scholars sought to provide empirical proof of the media's direct, negative effects on people's attitudes toward women.

By the late 1960s, some researchers were beginning to express dissatisfaction with the idea of direct, immediate media effects, even though they continued to believe that mass media are powerful. US media scholar George Gerbner and his colleagues at the Annenberg School for Communication at the University of Pennsylvania, for example, developed 'cultivation analysis' as a new approach to studying the cumulative impact of television on viewers' perceptions of society and its cultural values. Cultivation theorists argue that the plots and characterizations presented in the media, whether or not they are representative, encourage audiences to adopt views about society that are in line with what they have seen in the media. Perhaps not surprisingly, these views are typically associated with people who hold powerful positions in society. Cultivation scholars also argued that the more people watch television, the more likely they are to adopt those ways of thinking. This explains why, for example, the more people watch violent television, the more violent they think the world 'really' is. More to the point, cultivation theorists emphasize the 'mainstreaming' or homogenizing impact of television watching. Over time, regardless of one's political views or political identity, people who watch a lot of television adopt views consistent with conservative platforms. Various feminist scholars have used this conceptual approach to explain how sexism is cultivated over time (see Carter and Weaver, 2003).

At least since the 1970s, UK media and cultural studies scholars have focused on the ideological role played by the media in maintaining inequalities based on class, gender, 'race' and sexuality, among others. Here the media are seen to be central to the reproduction of a system of domination. At first, feminist scholars largely implied and asserted that patriarchal ideology was an important influence on audiences, but few attempts were made to demonstrate such claims empirically. Certainly, Stuart Hall's (1980) 'encoding/decoding' model of communication has had an enormous impact on ideology research in the UK and elsewhere. This model emphasizes the need to acknowledge the complex and contradictory ways in which audiences make sense of media messages, sometimes accepting, partially accepting or indeed rejecting the 'preferred' meaning of a media text. This critical model of communication prompted a number of scholars to undertake field research with audiences. For example, Charlotte Brunsdon (1981) interviewed women who watched the UK soap opera *Crossroads*. One of the findings of her study was that women took pleasure in the soap's explicit acknowledgement of the value of the feminine and women's knowledge and skills in the home. Soap opera texts, Brunsdon argued, played a contradictory role in women's lives, simultaneously providing an interpretative position that gave them pleasure while at the same time reproducing their subordinate status.

Sexual subordination forms a central focus in the first chapter in Part III, Robert Jensen's 'Knowing Pornography', which examines the place and significance of pornography in US culture and in its construction of male sexuality. Exploring both his own exposure to pornography and that of his male interviewees, Jensen argues that the sexual charge of pornography for heterosexual men is connected to an ideology of male dominance and female subordination. Men's use of pornography sexualizes and naturalizes this control over women. What men find arousing about pornography, he claims, is the power dynamic of male dominance. Moreover, pornography does not need to be violent to reproduce and naturalize this domination. Says Jensen, 'once male dominance is eroticized, male violence becomes at least potentially erotic'. If male dominance is erotic, he adds, extending that dominance to violence against women must be erotic. Jensen's embodied, personal approach to the impact of pornography on men's sexual imagination takes into account the actual experience of its users and testifies to the harmful impacts of pornography.

Elizabeth Hadley Freydberg's chapter, 'Sapphires, Spitfires, Sluts and

Superbitches: Aframericans and Latinas in Contemporary American Film', continues with this theme of representing men's dominance over women in her exploration of the textual distinction between 'good' and 'bad' women historically found in Hollywood cinema. She says that Hollywood has typically portrayed Aframericans and Latinas as white men's sexual play- mates, concubines or prostitutes. Only very rarely are they good enough to marry a white man. Such stereotypes of women equate dark skin with 'lustful debauchery' and associate white skin with being pure, chaste and moral. Following this line of argument, Freydberg historically traces the careers of several Aframerican and Latina actresses from the 1930s to the 1990s. She concludes that despite some recent positive developments in the portrayal of Aframericans and Latinas in US cinema, few positive (non-stereotypical) roles are available to them. The problem, as Freydberg sees it, is that the white people who run Hollywood are primarily interested in making entertainment for other white people. Moreover, the people who dominate Hollywood do not care if minority women are limited to negative stereotypes if money can be made from such images. In contrast, she agues, the independent film-making of Aframericans and Latinas continues to document the otherwise untold and diverse stories of minority women.

Women's voices also form a central focus in Mary Ellen Brown's chapter, 'Resistive Readings', which examines how women may use discussions about soap operas as a way of connecting with other women and creating discursive spaces in which to share their experiences of gender subordina- tion. As such, soap operas may offer women a means through which they are enabled to find ways of resisting the often restrictive media repre- sentations. The female fans whom Brown interviewed enjoyed soaps because they depicted characters that the fans perceived as being powerful and active women – ones who stand up for themselves at home and in the workplace. Moreover, Brown adds, members of soap gossip networks produce a kind of critique of hierarchical gender relations. As such, feminist media researchers might consider rethinking what constitutes feminist political action in order to recognize that soap opera gossip networks may offer women an accessible way of engaging with mainstream (patriarchal) culture in politically subversive ways.

The construction of gender identity is also a central focus of Jane Shat- tuc's book *The Talking Cure: TV Talk Shows and Women* (1997) which is a study of daytime television talk shows in the USA. The chapter from her book included here is 'Freud vs. Women: The Popularization of Therapy on Day-time Talk Shows' in which she analyses how these programmes encourage the formation of a collective feminine identity based on the recognition of a shared experience of women's subordinate status in society. Talk shows are potentially radical and subversive, argues Shattuc, when they offer public spaces for the voices of women rarely heard in society – working-class women, women of colour and women of various sexual orientations. Yet they are also potentially restrictive and exploitative when such voices are used as a source of audience amusement or condemnation in the name of corporate profit. Public confession, she suggests, has not only become a sign of power and control; it also affirms the 'active individual within a shared community'.

Part III ends with 'What Girls Want: The Intersections of Leisure and Power in Female Computer Game Play', in which Heather Gilmour argues that most computer software now being developed for girls helps reproduce hierarchical gender difference between boys and girls rather than breaking it down. In most computer games, 'girls continue to be essentialized as emotional, highly social, neo-Victorian subjects while males are defined as competitive and technologically inclined', Gilmour insists. New technologies, old binaries. Such assumptions about gender difference are not based on any essential differences between boys and girls, but instead illustrate the 'ideologies and assumptions of researchers and developers'. Having surveyed 180 students (90 boys and 90 girls) about their genre preferences, Gilmour found that the differences between boy and girl gamers are primarily matters of 'cultural gendering of leisure and play', rather than inherent biological differences. While game software developers address girls as a homogeneous, gendered group, girls maintain a certain heterogeneity of game preference and use. Gilmour calls on computing experts to go beyond conventional notions of femininity as a monolithic category, which inevitably work to restrict feminine behaviour, pleasure and self-definition.

References

Brunsdon, C. (1981) Crossroads: notes on soap opera, *Screen*, 22(4): 32–7.

Carter, C. and Weaver, C. K. (2003) *Violence and the Media*. Buckingham and Philadelphia: Open University Press.

Hall, S. (1980) Encoding/decoding, in Centre for Contemporary Cultural Studies (ed.) *Culture, Media Language: Working Papers in Cultural Studies*, 1972–79. London: Hutchinson.

Further Reading

Bobo, J. (1996) *Black Women as Cultural Readers*. New York: Columbia University Press.

Brunsdon, C. (2000) *The Feminist, the Housewife and the Soap Opera*. Oxford and New York: Clarendon.

Currie, D. (1999) *Girl Talk: Adolescent Magazines and Their Readers*. Toronto: University of Toronto Press.

Kinder, M. (ed.) (1999) *Kids' Media Culture*. Durham and London: Duke University Press.

Ross, K. and Nightingale, V. (2004) *Media and Audiences*, Maidenhead: Open University Press.

Seiter, E. (1999) *Television and New Media Audiences*. Oxford: Oxford University Press.

KNOWING PORNOGRAPHY

Robert Jensen

History gets written with the mind holding the pen. What would it look like, what would it read like, if it got written with the body holding the pen? (Berman 1990: 110)

In this essay, I want to let my body hold the pen. I have spent much time in the past few years trying to be in my body as I have researched and written about pornography.[1] I have concluded that, in conjunction with many other sources of information, I-in-my-body have insights into the role of pornography in the construction of male sexuality in contemporary US culture.[2]

Part of the authority for that claim comes from a simple observation: I get erections from pornography. I take that to be epistemologically significant; my body understands the charge of pornography. Because I was raised in a sexist culture with few (if any) influences that mitigated that sexism, I am in a position to explore how that sexual charge is connected to the ideology of male dominance and female submission that is central in contemporary commercial pornography (Jensen 1994).

I have focused on this embodied, personal approach partly in reaction to the scholarly literature on pornography, so much of which is written by men and is distinctly disembodied (for exceptions, see Abbott 1990; Baker 1992; Kimmel 1990). Political tracts, law review articles and reports of social science studies written by men rarely include any acknowledgement of the position of the author in a pornographic world, let alone an examination of what it means for how one comes to know about pornography. That kind of embodied exploration is rare because, as feminist theorists have long pointed out, in all those areas – philosophy, law, social science – emotional detachment and objectivity are seen as virtues. But that stance actually has repressed much of what we might know about pornography.

As Berman puts it, 'to leave your body and believe that you can still know anything at all is quite literally a form of madness' (1990: 110). In that sense, many of the scholarly works on pornography are quite mad – misguided attempts to sever mind and body, reason and emotion – that lead to less, not more, trustworthy knowledge.

This article investigates the following question: does mass-marketed commercial pornography play a role in the formation of a heterosexual man's sexual values and practices? My hypothesis is that men's use of pornography is one way in which men's dominance over, and control of, women is sexualized and naturalized. My narrative method does not 'prove' this, but attempts to explain how it has worked in my body. I conclude that my life provides support for the radical feminist critique of pornography summarized below. From there, I go on to discuss the value of embodied narratives, describe my own pornography use, and offer observations on pornography's effects on me and men. The chapter concludes with some thoughts on the value and limits of such work.

The Feminist Critique of Pornography

The radical feminist anti-pornography critique views pornography as a kind of sexist hate literature, the expression of a male sexuality rooted in the subordination of women that endorses the sexual objectification of, and sexual violence against, women. In the 1980s, this view was written into an anti-pornography civil rights ordinance that was successfully passed in some cities but rejected by the federal courts (see *American Booksellers Association v. Hudnut* 1985). In that ordinance, pornography is defined as the 'graphic sexually explicit subordination of women through pictures and/or words' and identified as 'a practice of sex discrimination' and a 'systematic practice of exploitation and subordination based on sex that differentially harms and disadvantages women' (Dworkin and MacKinnon 1988: 138–42).

The harms caused by pornography can be summarized briefly as (a) the harm to women in the production of pornography; (b) the harm to women who have pornography forced on them; (c) the harm to women who are sexually assaulted by men who use pornography; and (d) the harm to all women living in a culture in which pornography reinforces and sexualizes women's subordinate status (Itzin 1992; Russell 1993a). My claims do not hinge on establishing a direct causal link between pornography and sexual violence; rather than talking of pornography as a cause, we can identify it as one important factor in sexual abuse and misogyny in general (Jensen 1995b, 1994).

This view of pornography comes out of a more encompassing critique of male sexuality in patriarchy which suggests that male domination is the central dynamic in sexual relations between men and women, and sometimes between men and men or women and women (Cole 1989; Dworkin 1981, 1988; Jeffreys 1990; MacKinnon, 1987, 1989). This critique argues not only against the most offensive violent pornography in which women are clearly abused, but also asserts that 'normal' male sexuality is rooted in male dominance. From this perspective, cultural products such as pornography work to naturalize male control, rendering a system of power and abusive practices less visible.

The feminist anti-pornography critique has been the subject of extended debate for two decades, with both civil libertarians and anti-censorship/pro-pornography feminists raising objections to underlying assumptions and empirical claims (e.g. Burstyn 1985; Christensen 1990; Segal and McIntosh 1993). While I do not want to minimize the intensity and complexity of the debate, I do not find the pro-pornography position compelling in intellectual, personal or political terms, and it is important for me to anchor my work clearly in the radical critique of pornography.

For the purposes of this discussion, I adopt the MacKinnon/Dworkin definition of pornography, which includes most of the pornography that is marketed as pornography – that is, sexual material sold in adult bookstores that uses women for the purpose of sexually exciting men. The focus of this chapter is heterosexual pornography. Much of the radical critique can also be applied to gay pornography, but I will not pursue that here (see Kendall 1993). While the MacKinnon/Dworkin definition has been widely criticized, especially in the legal world, it is more than adequate here. It is also valuable to break away from the quest for a bright-line definition and talk instead about the pornographic continuum, which includes some images in mainstream media. I find elements of the pornographic – varying levels of hierarchy, objectification, submission and violence (Dworkin 1988: 265–7) – in everything from the *Sports Illustrated* swimsuit issue to snuff films.

Embodied Narratives

This paper attempts to honour the feminist commitment to 'the trustworthiness of your own body as a source of knowledge' and the possibility of 'intersubjective agreement' (Frye 1990: 177). Consciousness raising for men is loaded with potential problems if done in isolation from women, a problem that can be seen in various parts of the contemporary men's movement, especially the mytho-poetic wing, where a focus on the personal often impedes social analysis and liberatory politics (Jensen 1995a; Kimmel and Kaufman 1993). For men, that intersubjective agreement must include women; that is, we have to pay attention to feminist criticism to help us make sense of our experience. This need not require an inflexible commitment to feminist standpoint epistemology. But at the very least, I would argue that women have some sort of epistemic privilege – the idea that 'members of an oppressed group have a more immediate, subtle and critical knowledge about the nature of their oppression than people who are nonmembers of the oppressed group' (Narayan 1988: 35) – that men must honour. My goal in this chapter is to examine my life and compare it with the narratives of other men, using feminist insights to make sense of it all. This chapter is an attempt at the 'critical story-telling' that Hearn calls for in the project of 'collective self reflective theorising' (1987: 182). Such work is difficult to do with integrity, but my hope is, following Boone (1990: 12), that 'if the male critic can discover a position from which to speak that neither elides the importance of feminism to his work nor ignores the specificity of his gender, he may also find that his voice no longer exists as an abstraction, but that it in fact inhabits a body: its own sexual/textual body'.

Well-articulated defences of the value and limits of narrative method have been made, such as Stivers's (1992) discussion of 'postpositivist' social science. My goal is not to contend that my experience with pornography can be generalized to all men. Instead, I view this as a contribution to an ongoing conversation about pornography. If I examine my body and its pornographic history from a critical stance informed by feminist theory and practice, I can make claims about men, sexism, sexuality and sexually explicit material, and those claims will be more valuable than the so-called 'scientific' research about pornography (Jensen 1995c). The task is not finding the answer, but, in Frye's terms (1990: 179), perceiving patterns:

> The experiences of each woman and of the women collectively generate a new web of meaning. Our process has been one of discovering, recognizing, and creating patterns – patterns within which experience made a new kind of sense, or, in many instances, for the first time made any sense at all. Instead of bringing a phase of enquiry to closure by summing up what is known, as other ways of generalizing do, pattern recognition/construction opens fields of meaning and generates new interpretive possibilities. Instead of drawing conclusions from observations, it generates observations.

As introduction to my story, I need to explain my own journey to this position. My early work on legal aspects of the pornography debate used traditional methods, which allowed me to distance myself from my personal experience with pornography. But a growing sense of dissatisfaction with that work led me to a project designed to confront the content of pornography through an analysis of 20 pornographic paperback novels. I read the books, taking detailed notes about scenes, themes, portrayals and language used. In the role of detached investigator, I tried to move through the books using my 'rational' faculties but found my body getting in the way; I kept getting erections.

Before I started that project I was aware that pornography still could produce intense sexual reactions in me, even though at that time it had been several years since my last contact with pornography (I stopped using pornography after returning to graduate school and coming into contact with the feminist critique). Yet, in my pursuit of intellectual knowledge I had detached from the emotional, embodied knowledge of my past experience with pornography; the scholarly endeavour insulated me from those other ways of knowing about pornography. The deeper I got into the academic work, the further I got from that embodied knowledge until, finally, I was forced to confront it through the reaction of my body. As I read the books, intellectually I was able to identify and analyse the misogynistic images and messages. But physically, my body responded the way it had been trained.

That reaction threw into question assumptions with which I had been smugly comfortable. This had, and continues to have, an important effect on my sexuality and my personal life. My concern here, however, is with the equally important effect that experience has had on my scholarly work. I realized that could no longer deny that part of what I knew about pornography was personal and embodied, and that I would have to explore those questions if I wanted to be a competent and ethical researcher. As I planned a project to interview pornography users, I knew I would have to write my own narrative as well as theirs.

A Personal History of Pornography Use

I begin this account with the understanding that my interpretation of my experiences can be challenged. Clearly, I have a kind of access to my emotions and sexual reactions that others do not. But in any person, there can be a host of personal and political roadblocks to a clear understanding of self. My interpretations have changed over time, and what I offer is the best reading I have of them at this time, a reading that others may have grounds to challenge.

The analysis that follows relies heavily on my experience, but is constructed in conjunction with other men's stories, which come from three main sources. First, I have spoken informally with a variety of men as I have worked on this issue, and have learned much from those conversations. I also draw on published accounts of men's pornography use cited above. Finally, I have conducted interviews with self-identified pornography users and convicted sex offenders (Jensen 1995b). Although I refer to those men rarely in this paper, my analysis of my pornography use is heavily influenced by those men, who had a variety of experiences with, and opinions about, pornography and its potential harms and benefits.

From those sources, I believe that my use of pornography is fairly typical for a male born after the Second World War, what I call the post-*Playboy* generation. My exposure to pornography began around second grade. I have hazy memories of a soft core biker magazine, which included pictures of women naked from the waist up, that a friend had found and hid in his backyard. Viewing the magazine was always a group project; we would pass it around and comment on the women's bodies. After that, someone in my circle of friends almost always had a copy of *Playboy*, *Penthouse* or some similar magazine that had been found, stolen from a store or taken from dad. One friend had a hiding place in his attic, where we occasionally would go to look at them.

By the time I was in junior high, I had found my father's hiding place: *Playboy*, *Penthouse* and *Hustler*, in his dresser, in the second drawer, under the T-shirts on the right. At least one of my two brothers, I found out later, also knew the spot, although we never looked at them together. In my first year of high school, I was a friend of a boy who had perfected the art of getting into movies through exit doors. Usually we went into mainstream films, but when we felt bold we made a run at X-rated movies. I also remember having access to pornographic novels in my high school years and finding them as intense an experience as the visual material.

In college I saw a few X-rated movies with friends (both all-male and mixed groups) who treated the outings as campy fun, and went to a couple of those movies on my own. When I would go with friends from our college in a smaller town to Minneapolis, we often would stop at pornography shops to see what the big city had to offer. In my twenties, my use of pornography was episodic. At various times I would feel drawn to X-rated movies, and in a six- or seven-year period, I probably saw 10 to 15 of them, once or twice with someone else, but usually alone. I saw some of these movies at mainstream theatres, but more typically at adult theatres and bookstores, where I would browse among other material. The movies were what is most often called hard-core pornography: graphic sex scenes built around a contrived story line. I typically stayed for no more than 15 to 30 minutes; after the initial excitement wore off, feelings of guilt and shame made it uncomfortable to be in those theatres.

I typically did not purchase pornography to use at home, although through the years I occasionally bought magazines such as *Playboy* and *Penthouse*. I never showed pornography to women with whom I was involved, with the exception of one trip to an adult theatre with a girlfriend in college. I never made home-made pornography or recorded sexual activity.

Although I did not use pornography in an active way with partners, pornography was central to my sex life at various times. From grade school on, I masturbated to pornographic images, either those on paper in front of me or those retained in my mind from earlier consumption. I focused on certain kinds of images (women performing oral sex on men, men penetrating women anally, group sex involving a woman and more than one man), and I could summon up those images easily.

Although I always found pornography attractive, my heaviest use as an adult came during periods when I was not involved in a relationship with a woman. The last time I remember visiting a pornography shop was about 1987. I returned to graduate school and began my study of the issue in 1988, and since then I have seen pornography only in the context of my academic and political work, and I have kept that viewing to a minimum (the main exception to that is one trip to a gay pornographic movie after coming out). I have also viewed an anti-pornography slide show, which includes explicit examples, and which I have helped to present a number of times to school and community groups.

Although this brief summary of my own pornography use leaves out details that are too painful to recount in a public forum, it still was difficult to write. In my anxiety and fear is a lesson about pornography. At the macro level, pornography works to create, maintain and reinforce a system of male control. But for each individual who uses pornography, the story is more complicated and not just an expression of the desire to control women. I continue to feel guilt and shame over my past use of it, even though I realize that most men have had similar experiences. Some of the pornography users I interviewed expressed the same feelings. Others expressed no regrets over their use and were proud of what they saw as a transcendence of sexual inhibitions. While it is difficult to generalize about these emotions, I believe that, like me, most men who use pornography struggle with the mixed messages from society. On the one hand, pornography is widely accepted and can be used for male bonding; in other situations, a man's use of it can be turned against him with the charge that he can't get a 'real woman'. Men who were raised in sexually or emotionally repressive families, again like me, may use pornography but then confront those early internalized proscriptions.

Although I have been arguing for the importance of narratives, these differences in men's reactions to their own pornography use highlight how important it is to remember that no single narrative is the whole story. Men's accounts of their own use, including my own, must be weighed against each other, against the accounts of women,[3] and against the ideological content of pornography. Men's use of pornography, and their interpretations of that use, vary greatly. That does not mean that no coherent account of pornography in this society can be constructed. It need not be shown that all men use pornography in exactly the same way for pornography to be a key component of a system of male dominance. In this case, for instance, whether a pornography user feels guilt and shame or is proud of his use, the result is generally the same: the use of pornography continues.

Pornography and Me

I focus now on the effects that pornography had on me. Based on my experience, I argue that:

1. Pornography was an important means of sex education.
2. Pornography constructed women as objects, which encouraged me to see women in real life in that same way.
3. Pornography created or reinforced desires for specific acts, most of which focused on male pleasure and can cause female pain.
4. Rather than unlocking sexual creativity, pornography shaped and constrained my sexual imagination with its standardized scripts.
5. Race was an important aspect of pornography, reinforcing my view of women of colour as the 'exotic primitive'.
6. Viewing a large amount of overtly violent pornography was not necessary for pornography to have the effect of eroticizing violence for me.
7. That eroticization of violence had a tangible effect on my sex life.
8. Pornography is most centrally about control, and I was attracted to it by my need for a sense of control over women and their sexuality.

Sex education

Sex was not openly discussed in my home and, at the time I was growing up, sex education in the schools was limited or non-existent. So, most of my

sexual education came on the streets with peers and was rooted in pornography. It was in that material that I first saw nude adult women and
figured out the mechanics of sex.

There is nothing inherently problematic about learning about sexuality
from a publication. The problem is when those publications construct
sexuality in a male-dominant framework and present women as sexual
objects. These images were incredibly powerful for me and my childhood
friends. They helped plant in me some basic assumptions about sex: that a
certain kind of female appearance was most desirable, that women could be
used for sex in ways portrayed in the magazines and movies (as well as
through my use of those materials), that women's resistance to certain kinds
of sexual activity was the result of prudish inhibitions that could, and
should, be overcome. Those messages were transmitted by other cultural
products and institutions as well, but it was in pornography that I found
them most explicitly expressed.

Objectification of women

Assuming that most people will not contest the assertion that pornography
objectifies women, I want to examine in more detail what that means to men.
A female friend of mine once told me that one of the things that infuriates her
at work is walking into a business meeting and watching men in the room
size her up as she moves to her seat. She said she knew that I did it, that her
husband did it, that men in general do it. I told her she was right. I do it.
Even after several years of study of feminist theory and pornography, I do it.
I don't do it as often as I used to, and I catch myself almost immediately.
But it happens, even after coming out as a gay man. And sometimes when I
realize I am doing it, I choose not to stop, which is a difficult admission to
make. It is those times especially that I realize how thoroughly women are
constructed as objects in this culture, how powerful that construction is,
and how it still has a strong hold on me. Although I believe that the way in
which men apprehend women visually is a central part of the sexual subjugation of women, on the street I always have the option of ignoring my
own convictions and using a woman for my own fantasy.

Is this really an act of male supremacy, or simply an appreciation of
beauty or an acknowledgement of our sexuality? I do not mean to suggest
that sexual attraction is inherently corrupt; to raise these issues is not to
advocate a prudish repression of sexuality. But it is crucial to examine the
power at work in sexual situations. Heterosexual men's sexuality in this
culture is constructed around the domination of women. In some other
world, one not tainted by sexism, my concerns perhaps could be minimized.

But in a culture that for centuries has defined woman as object, it is essential that men be aware of, and honest about, the way in which we see women.

Again, pornography is not the only element in this construction of women. But my use of pornography was a central component of it. In my case, I have seen women on the street and created sexual scenes with them that were taken directly from pornography I had seen. That has not happened in some time; it is one thing I no longer allow myself. But the fact that it was once a routine part of my sexual imagination tells me something about how pornography has affected my view of women.

Although some commentators have suggested that such objectification is unavoidable, even natural, I believe that resisting it is a fundamental step for men trying to avoid sexist behaviour. As Kappeler (1986: 61) writes:

The fundamental problem at the root of men's behavior in the world, including sexual assault, rape, wife battering, sexual harassment, keeping women in the home and in unequal opportunities and conditions, treating them as objects for conquest and protection – the root problem behind the reality of men's relations with women, is the way men see women, is Seeing.

Desire

As the testimony of women has pointed out, men's desire for certain kinds of sexual activity can be taken directly from pornography. There will always be a causation question: do the desires exist independently and then get represented in pornography, or does pornography help to create the desires? One convention of pornography leads me to think that in some ways, pornography can construct desire. Since the mid–1970s, the 'money shot' or 'cum shot' – showing the man ejaculating onto the woman's body – has been a standard of explicit pornography to provide visual proof of men's pleasure (Williams 1989). As a veteran pornographic movie actor put it: 'The cum shot in the face is the stock-in-trade of orgasms. It's the ejaculation into a woman's waiting face that gets the audience off more than anything else' (Bill Margold, quoted in Hebditch and Anning 1988: 31).

Some of the men I interviewed said they enjoyed that type of climax, and I can recall similar desires in the past. Consider this comment from a man's response to a sex survey (Hite 1982: 781): 'Nude pictures from men's magazines turn me on, and when I finally ejaculate, I aim right at the girl's breasts, pubic hair, or buttocks, whichever pleases me most. The more copious my output of sperm, the more satisfied I am.'

Did that desire arise from some 'natural' source? From the social construction view of sexuality that I take, the concept of authentic sexual desire is problematic; there is no pure, natural sexuality that is not mediated by culture. Here I simply contend that pornography is a force that can shape desire and that we should be concerned with how men may be conditioned to desire sexual acts that are humiliating, degrading and painful for women.

Scripting sex

Several men I interviewed argued that sexually explicit material helped open up their sexual horizons. For me, pornography constricted rather than expanded my sexual imagination. Looking back on my experiences, I see no evidence that pornography fuelled sexual creativity or sparked creative fantasies. Fantasy implies a flight of imagination, a letting go of oneself, the possibility of transcending the ordinary. For me, pornography did none of those things. It constrained my imagination, helped keep me focused on sexual activity that was rooted in male dominance, and hindered me from moving beyond the ordinary misogyny of the culture. Instead of my imagination running wild, my imagination was locked into a film loop, reproducing scripts and scenes from pornography. Pornographic sexuality – as reproduced in pornography and throughout our culture – crippled my erotic imagination, and I have only recently begun the long project of recovering the erotic, in the expanded sense in which it is used by Heyward (1989) and Lorde (1984).

A validation of this view comes, ironically, from the actor Margold, who saw no harm in pornography but understood the way it restricts the erotic. In discussing why people need pornographic films, he said: 'We're drowning in our own sexual quicksand because there's a lack of imagination' (quoted in Hebditch and Anning 1988: 27).

Race

For me, racial differences had erotic potential. Some of the men I interviewed, all of whom were White,[4] said that they did not like pornography that used women of colour and that they would fast-forward past it or pass over it in magazines. There was no pattern to these judgements; some men liked Asian women but not Black women, while for others the opposite was true. Some men only wanted to watch White women. In the pornography market, there are publications and films that cater to all these tastes.

Those two responses – fascination with or distaste for women of colour – are flip sides of the same racist coin. For White consumers, women of colour can be even more sexually stimulating. For some, such as me, that connected to the stereotype of the 'exotic primitive' and conjured up images of a wild sexuality. So I found pornography that used women of colour especially attractive and have specific memories of pornographic magazines that featured Black women and Asian women. That reaction, of course, is hardly progressive. The pornography that highlighted non-White women played on stereotypes of the subservient Asian woman, the hot-blooded Latina and the sexually promiscuous black woman. Although I did not consider myself racist at the time, my interest in such material grew out the racism I had learned (and am continuing to unlearn), just expressed in a manner less overtly racist than those men who told me they found women of colour in pornography to be unattractive to them.

Violence and pornography

I use the terms 'violent' and 'non-violent' hesitantly, because there is no clear line between the two categories in a misogynist culture. But in the common use of those terms, violent pornography is usually taken to mean depictions of sexual activity that include overt violence, such as physical abuse, the use of restraints, the presence of weapons or strong verbal coercion. Non-violent pornography usually describes depictions of sexual activity without those elements. The feminist claim that pornography fuses sex and violence is often rejected by men who say they do not use or enjoy violent pornography. But pornography does not need to be overtly violent to be part of a process by which violence is eroticized. I was never interested in violent pornography, yet I was conditioned by 'non-violent' pornography to accept violence as erotic. Again, this is one of those claims that is difficult to prove because we live in a culture that in general sexualizes violence; no one can say for sure what specific images or influences create an appetite for sexualized violence. But pornography plays an important role.

I realized that violence had been eroticized for me when reading the novels previously mentioned. At the time, I would have vigorously denied any claim that I found sexual violence erotic. But as I read those books, I was aroused by descriptions of sexual violence, such as a description of a man's sexual torture of a woman with whips and other paraphernalia. No matter what I thought about sexual violence, the eroticization of violence had taken place in my body; it worked on me. I responded sexually not only to the descriptions of sex, but also to those portions that used explicit violence and coercion. I found myself becoming sexually aroused by material that violated what I thought was my own sense of what was appropriate and healthy sex. I wanted to reject any experience of pleasure from those images, but my body accepted them.

What I had learned to find arousing was a basic power dynamic of male dominance and female subordination,[5] which is much the same in violent and non-violent pornography. Once male dominance is eroticized, male violence becomes at least potentially erotic. I could have denied that, as I think many men do, but my sexual reaction to the novels uncovered the reality of my erotic imagination. I heard strands of this same story from some of the men I interviewed. For example, one man who was convicted of sexually abusing young girls said that he never sought out violent porno-graphy, but that when he found himself watching such material by accident, he found it arousing and he 'got more into it'. He had learned that male dominance was erotic, and so the extension of that dominance to violence was also erotic.

Sex and violence in the world

In defence of pornography, Christensen (1990: 41) argued that 'the exis-tence of violent sex in no way impugns nonviolent sex or its portrayal'. I disagree. When the sex depicted in pornography is conditioned by male dominance, the line between the violent and non-violent is not nearly as crucial as many would like to believe. The hierarchical structure of non-violent pornography trained my body to understand the erotic potential that this culture has assigned to rape. During my study of pornography I learned that rape was sexy to me. That reality had been living in my body for some time, but it was disturbing to have to admit. It led to the ines-capable conclusion that I am capable of rape, even if I cannot imagine ever committing such an act. The simple truth is that in this culture, men have to make a conscious decision not to rape, because rape is so readily available to us and so rarely results in sanctions of any kind.[6]

I believe that pornography is implicated in – that is, not a direct cause, but a factor in – some men's acts of sexual violence.[7] And, as I have made clear so far, I do not see myself as exempt from being influenced by images that shape the sexuality of others. So, if that claim about violence I just made is true – that both I and the sex offenders I interviewed learned to eroticize violence – then why have I never committed a sex crime? First, it is not my contention, nor the contention of anyone in the feminist anti-por-nography movement, that pornography alone causes rape or that all pornography users commit rape. A complex network of factors lead a man to rape, and while pornography is an important component, it is obviously not the only one.

But it is also important to remember that while I say I have never committed a sex crime, all I can really say is that I have not committed a sex crime under the male-defined sexual standards of this culture, which are similar to the standards set out in pornography. My own sexual definitions were framed by my use of pornography, and according to those definitions I have not raped. Yet, I do not know if that is an opinion that would be shared by every woman I have known (Jensen 1995a). After trying to examine my sexual history from a non-pornographic perspective, I still come to the conclusion that I never crossed the line into coerced sex. But the final answer to that question would have to come from those women.

Control

The single most important thing I have learned from analysing my own history and from the interviews is how central the concept of control – by men over women – is to pornography. In my life, that is most clear from the period in which I used pornography the most heavily. It came in my midtwenties after the break-up of an intense relationship with a woman. One reason that I found the relationship so troublesome was that I was not in control. In most of my intimate relationships before and after that one, I retained most of the power to make basic decisions about the nature of the relationship. But in that situation, for a variety of reasons, I gave up control to the woman. That left me in a particularly volatile emotional state after the break-up, which I believe made pornography even more attractive.

In pornography, control remains in male hands in two ways. First, the magazines and movies that I can recall seeing depicted sexual encounters in which men were in control, guiding women's actions to produce male pleasure. The images that stay with me from that period are those in which the woman was completely subordinate, performing sexual acts on and for the man. Second, by making female sexuality a commodity, pornography allowed me to control when and where I used it, and therefore used the women in it. Brummett (1988: 209) makes this point in his analysis of pornographic movies viewed on a home VCR, pointing out how the control offered by the text is reinforced by the control offered by the medium (the ability to fast-forward and rewind to play back): 'VCRs never say no to their users; neither do characters in pornographic films. People agree to requests for sex with the same instant and uncritical willingness shown by the television and the VCR.'

Brummett's point also applies at least partially to other forms of pornography. For me, retreating to a pornographic world allowed me to regain an illusory sense of control over female sexuality that I had lost in real life.

I return now to my reference in note 1 to a shift in sexual orientation. This paper is about pornography marketed to heterosexual men, and at the time that I did the research and the majority of the writing, I lived and identified myself as heterosexual. As I revise this paper for publication, I identify myself as a gay man in the process of coming out. Or I may be bisexual. Or I could go back to being heterosexual. Or I may choose to live my life as a celibate gay man (or bisexual, or heterosexual). My point is that, at this time, I have no need, and no way, to fix my sexual orientation in stone; perhaps I never will. While this is not the place for an extended discussion of the extent to which sexuality is determined by socialization and/or biology, certainly my own life is an example of how one's behaviour is shaped by social norms and expectations. My use of heterosexual pornography was one way in which I, with the help of a heterosexist culture, made myself heterosexual. No matter what kind of desire I felt for men during that time (and I did at times feel that desire), I 'was' heterosexual in a very real sense of the term. This change in my life is, of course, relevant to an autobiographical paper, but I have left a discussion of it until the end because the change does not undermine my analysis of heterosexual pornography.

My increasing openness to my own gayness does provide one important additional insight into my pornography use. From discussions with other men and my own experience, it seems clear that one of the attractions of explicit heterosexual pornography for some men is the presence of naked male bodies and erect penises. Such pornography is one place where men can indulge homoerotic feelings without social sanction; after all, we are there to see the women. Although I would have denied such a motive at the time that I was using pornography, I have a clear sense that I was looking at the men in pornography in that way. This homoerotic feeling was no doubt compounded in situations where I viewed the pornography with other men (either in public theatres or private groups) by the knowledge that around me were men with erections.

Conclusion

The feminist anti-pornography critique has been tagged with a variety of negative and unwarranted labels: prudish, repressive, simplistic, theoretically totalizing, politically naive. I hope this chapter answers some of those criticisms. My reflections and arguments are not based in prudishness or disgust for sexuality. My goal is not to repress sexuality or deny people's erotic potential. I am not arguing a simplistic pornography-causes-rape position. I do not believe that my experiences and perspective can explain all men's use of pornography. And I am fully aware of the practical political problems in implementing the feminist critique through law. Most importantly, as a man, I am not trying to tell women how to feel about pornography; this chapter is not an attempt to settle the debate over pornography and sexuality within feminism.

So I do not claim to have proved anything about pornography in any definitive sense. My intention was to argue for an expansion of what counts as knowledge about pornography and to explain how and what I have learned about pornography in those ways. If I have been successful, I have given men an account against which they can compare and explore their own experience with pornography, which may or may not lead them to conclusions similar to mine. And I have offered men and women possible explanations for why men use pornography and assertions about pornography's effects.

When I discuss this kind of work, I often am accused of shaping my account of my experience to fit the anti-pornography theory that I have endorsed. I agree that the theory has affected how I think about, remember and understand my experience. I would also point out that everyone's account of their experience is shaped by such theoretical commitments. No knowledge is pre-theoretical; no one has access to an account of their behaviour (or anyone else's behaviour) that has not been refracted through ideology. A pro-pornography advocate's account of his experience is shaped by the ideology of sexual and expressive freedom, the idea that any sexual activity is by definition liberating. My work is 'tainted' by my commitment to radical feminist ideology, but only to the degree that the work of people who take an opposing view is tainted by their sexual ideology. The question is not whether one has gone beyond ideology to get at the real truth, but whether one has constructed the account with integrity and offered a compelling interpretation.

In my early work on pornography, when I confined my investigation to more traditional modes of inquiry, I wrote a very different account of pornography's role in the world. I believe that account was incomplete and misleading because of what I concealed, both from myself and others. Our experiences, especially with things as powerful as sexuality and pornography, affect our view of the world; that is one of the fundamental lessons of feminism. Ignoring or repressing those influences does not bracket them out of our research or politics, but simply hides them and impedes our inquiry.

Notes

1. The potentially relevant facts about who 'I' am include, in no particular order: White, born in 1958, Midwestern born and living in the south, raised in the lower-middle to middle class and now residing in the middle class, married for five years until recent separation, father of a 3-year-old boy, living as a heterosexual most of my life until recent coming out (more on that later), anti-sexist/pro-feminist, the third of four children from a typically dysfunctional American family.

2. I did not do this work, of course, in isolation. This article reflects the contributions of a number of friends and teachers, including Nancy Potter, Naomi Scheman and Donna McNamara. And a special note of appreciation to Jim Koplin. After seven years of friendship and collaboration, I am not always sure which ideas are mine and which are Jim's. Happily, neither of us worry much about that. I am sure, however, that my life would be far less rich, and my scholarship less valuable, if I did not know him.

3. For such narratives, see Organizing Against Pornography (1983). The transcript of the Minneapolis hearings was also published as a book in England (*Pornography and Sexual Violence*, 1988). Also see Attorney General's Commission (1986). That report was published commercially as McManus (1986). Excerpts from the testimony before the commission have been published in a book edited by Schlafly (1987). My citation of the Meese Commission report, which was rooted in a conservative view of pornography, is not intended as support for its politics.

4. The interview subjects were not all White by design. The work was done in Minneapolis, which is predominantly White, and I received responses to my requests for interviews from White men only.

5. This is not meant to absolve the genre of pornography that casts women as dominant over men. The eroticization of power in that way does not give women real power in the world, and it does nothing to help us in the search for egalitarian models for sexuality that eroticize equality (a goal that, I realize, not everyone shares).

6. This idea is taken from comments made by Donna McNamara, then the community education director for the Hennepin County Sexual Violence Center, at a college programme on pornography that she and I presented.

7. I prefer not to talk about direct causation in such questions of human behaviour, but instead rely on narrative accounts of women and men for evidence of the relationship between, in this case, a cultural product and behaviour. Some anti-pornography feminists are more willing to identify pornography as a direct cause, often citing experimental research (Russell 1993b, 1988).

References

Abbott, F. (ed.) (1990) *Men and Intimacy: Personal Accounts of Exploring the Dilemmas of Modern Male Sexuality.* Freedom, CA: Crossing Press.

American Booksellers Association v. Hudnut [1985] 771 F.2d 323.

Baker, P. (1992) Maintaining male power: why heterosexual men use pornography, in C. Itzin (ed.) *Pornography: Women, Violence and Civil Liberties*, pp. 124–44. Oxford: Oxford University Press.

Berman, M. (1990) *Coming to Our Senses: Body and Spirit in the Hidden History of the West.* New York: Bantam.

Boone, J.A. (1990) Of me(n) and feminism: who(se) is the sex that writes? In J.A. Boone and M. Cadden (eds) *Engendering Men: The Question of Male Feminist Criticism*, pp. 11–25. New York: Routledge.

Brummett, B. (1988) The homology hypothesis: pornography on the VCR, *Critical Studies in Mass Communication*, 5(3): 202–16.

Burstyn, V. (ed.) (1985) *Women Against Censorship.* Vancouver: Douglas & McIntyre.

Christensen, F.M. (1990) *Pornography: The Other Side.* New York: Praeger.

Cole, S. (1989) *Pornography and the Sex Crisis.* Toronto: Amanita.

Dworkin, A. (1981) *Pornography: Men Possessing Women.* New York: Perigee Books.

Dworkin, A. (1988) *Letters from a War Zone.* London: Secker & Warburg.

Dworkin, A. and MacKinnon, C.A. (1988) *Pornography and Civil Rights: A New Day for Women's Equality.* Minneapolis: Organizing Against Pornography.

Frye, M. (1990) The possibility of feminist theory, in D.L. Rhode (ed.) *Theoretical Perspectives on Sexual Difference*, pp. 174–84. New Haven: Yale University Press.

Hearn, J. (1987) *The Gender of Oppression: Men, Masculinity, and the Critique of Marxism.* New York: St Martin's Press.

Hebditch, D. and Anning, N. (1988) *Porn Gold: Inside the Pornography Business.* London: Faber & Faber.

Heyward, C. (1989) *Touching our Strength: The Erotic as Power and the Love of God.* San Francisco: Harper & Row.

Hite, S. (1982) *The Hite Report on Male Sexuality.* New York: Ballantine Books.

Itzin, C. (ed.) (1992) *Pornography: Women, Violence and Civil Liberties.* Oxford: Oxford University Press.

Jeffreys, S. (1990) *Anticlimax: A Feminist Perspective on the Sexual Revolution.* New York: New York University Press.

Jensen, R. (1994) Pornographic novels and the ideology of male supremacy, *Howard Journal of Communications*, 5(1 & 2): 92–107.

Jensen, R. (1995a) Feminist theory and men's lives, *Race, Gender & Class*, 2(2): 111–25.

Jensen, R. (1995b) Pornographic lives, *Violence Against Women*, 1(1): 32–54.

Jensen, R. (1995c) Pornography and the limits of experimental research, in G. Dines and J.M. Humez (eds) *Gender, Race and Class in Media: A Text-reader*, pp. 298–306. Thousand Oaks, CA: Sage.

Kappeler, S. (1986) *The Pornography of Representation*. Minneapolis: University of Minnesota Press.

Kendall, C.N. (1993) 'Real dominant, real fun!' Gay male pornography and the pursuit of masculinity, *Saskatchewan Law Review*, 57(1): 21–58.

Kimmel, M.S. (ed.) (1990) *Men Confront Pornography*. New York: Crown.

Kimmel, M.S. and Kaufman, M. (1994) Weekend warriors: the new men's movement, in H. Brod and M. Kaufman (eds) *Theorizing Masculinities*, pp. 259–88. Thousand Oaks, CA: Sage.

Lorde, A. (1984). *Sister Outsider*. Freedom, CA: Crossing Press.

MacKinnon, C.A. (1987) *Feminism Unmodified: Discourses on Life and Law*. Cambridge, MA: Harvard University Press.

MacKinnon, C.A. (1989) *Toward a Feminist Theory of the State*. Cambridge, MA: Harvard University Press.

McManus, M.J. (1986) Introduction, *Final Report of the Attorney General's Commission on Pornography*. Nashville, TN: Rutledge Hill Press.

Narayan, U. (1988) Working together across difference: some considerations on emotions and political practice, *Hypatia*, 3(2): 31–47.

Organizing Against Pornography (1983) *Public Hearings on Ordinances to Add Pornography as Discrimination Against Women* (transcript). Minneapolis, MN: Organizing Against Pornography.

Pornography and Sexual Violence: Evidence of the Links (1988) London: Everywoman.

Russell, D.E.H. (1988) Pornography and rape: a causal model, *Political Psychology*, 9: 41–73.

Russell, D.E.H. (ed.) (1993a) *Making Violence Sexy: Feminist Views on Pornography*. New York: Teachers College Press.

Russell, D.E.H. (1993b) *Against Pornography: The Evidence of Harm*. Berkeley: Russell Publications.

Schlafly, P. (ed.) (1987) *Pornography's Victims*. Westchester, IL: Crossway Books.

Segal, L. and McIntosh, M. (eds) (1993) *Sex Exposed: Sexuality and the Pornography Debate*. New Brunswick, NJ: Rutgers University Press.

Stivers, C. (1992) Reflections on the role of personal narrative in social science, *Signs*, 18(2): 408–25.

Williams, L. (1989) *Hard Core: Power, Pleasure and the 'Frenzy of the Visible'*. Berkeley: University of California Press.

14 | SAPPHIRES, SPITFIRES, SLUTS AND SUPERBITCHES
AFRAMERICANS AND LATINAS IN CONTEMPORARY AMERICAN FILM

Elizabeth Hadley Freydberg

The American film industry continues to produce films in which Aframericans and Latinas are cast in degrading roles, irrespective of the vehement protests of these two groups. The roles to which it most often relegates members of the two largest minority groups in America are unquestionably negative stereotypes. *Stereotype* as defined here 'is an imitation, a copy of something or someone that is, by means of the media machinery, held up first as THE symbol or symbols to the exclusion of others; and then repeatedly channeled out to viewers so often that in time it becomes a "common" representation of something or someone in the minds of viewers' (Blackwood 1986: 205).

Stereotypes may be either positive or negative; for example, *some* Black people are excellent singers and dancers, but not all Black people are endowed with these talents. Whether the image that a stereotype projects is positive or negative, however, it always limits the range of human behaviours and emotions that viewers are willing to ascribe to a stereotyped group. In the language of fictive or imaginative media, stereotype creates 'flat' characters.

Stereotypes in many contemporary films reinforce preconceived notions of the status quo about people outside mainstream society. Moreover, the majority of stereotyping found in films is negative: it portrays the individuals in the stereotyped group as having personal qualities that are undesirable. This negative stereotyping fulfils a social function: it is through stereotype that the ruling majority rationalizes its maltreatment of people whom it has designated as inferior.

Images of Aframericans and Latinas have a long history of deformation and distortion because of racism – a byproduct of colonialism, and sexism. 'Racism is the subjugation of a cultural group by another for the purpose of gaining economic advantage, of mastering and having power over that group – the result being harm done, consciously or unconsciously, to its members' (Anzaldúa 1990: 225). Sexism in many ways resembles racism in that its dynamic can be expressed largely in terms of social and economic power. Although racism may create social structures in which the dominator and dominated can be almost entirely separate in terms of social contact, sexism requires contact between dominator and dominated. In addition, dominating cultural groups have long used sexism in the service of racism by using the sexual terrorism of rape as a weapon to punish and control both genders of the subjugated group.

The 'exaggerated images' depicted in film as representative of Blacks and Latinas are those of prostitutes – women who sell their bodies for monetary profit; concubines – women who are kept, usually by a White male; whores – sexually promiscuous women who do not profit financially but who appear to enjoy sleeping around; and bitches – sexually emasculating, razor-tongued and razor-toting, hostile, aggressive women who will fight man or woman at the slightest provocation. A critical analysis of films and the use of historical and sociological data demonstrate some rationale for why these stereotypes persist in American society. Such analysis also reveals that these stereotypes originate with and are maintained by the racism and sexism of those who control America's film industry specifically and media in general.

Aframerican and Latina women have historically been treated as demoralized sex objects by White men. Black women were brought by White men to America to work in the agrarian South and to breed a larger slave population to supplement the workforce with free labour. White men not only appropriated the labour and the children of Black women under slavery, but they also appropriated Black women's bodies through rape. And, when the colour of their mulatto offspring bore silent witness to rape, these men profited from the unholy harvest by selling their own children and justified their violent subordination of Black women by labelling them promiscuous seducers. White women to some extent accepted the rationale offered by their husbands and brothers. Although their acceptance of the rationale of promiscuous Black women may have been motivated by the need to repress an unpleasant truth, White women had an even more compelling reason to believe: profit. Like White men, White women profited from the economics of slavery. After emancipation and the failure of reconstruction, White women as well as White men retained a system of beliefs about Black people that was fundamentally identical to what they had maintained during the slave era – for the same reason, profit.

Although Latina women were not brought to America for breeding, they were perceived as members of a 'conquered' people, and as such were accorded the same lack of respect by Anglo men. (The term *Anglo*, in Latina discourse, refers to Caucasians not of Hispanic descent; although context can create a negative connotation, it is not used in this chapter derogatorily.) Mexicans were defeated by the USA first in battle at San Jacinto in 1836, then their final ruination was precipitated by the loss of the majority of their land to the USA with the annexation of Texas in 1845; the signing of the Treaty of Guadalupé Hidalgo in 1848 – the acquisition of California, Nevada, Utah, Arizona, New Mexico, and even parts of Colorado and Wyoming; and finally the Gadsden Purchase of 1853 (Brinton, Christopher and Wolff 1964: 510). The attitude of Whites toward Hispanics was infused with biological and militaristic superiority based upon the same pseudo-scientific rationalizations that had nurtured the most sophist defences of slavery. Such ethnocentricity is manifest in Arthur G. Pettit's (1980: 12) observation:

> The issue by the early 1840's was not whether the Mexicans were inferior to the North Americans but whether the Mexicans as inferiors ought to be left alone or conquered. Southerners, speaking with the 'voice of experience' in dealing with another dark skinned race, were simultaneously loudest in asserting brown inferiority and strongest in affirming the risks of racial pollution. John C. Calhoun, standing firm on the Old Testament conviction of Ham's degeneracy, argued that the true misfortunes of Spanish America involved the fatal error of placing colored races on an equal footing with white men and maintained that the alternative to racial separation was economic stagnation, political chaos, and genetic pollution.

And in reference to Anglo attitudes regarding the Puerto Ricans, Luis Mercado (1974: 153) states, 'Puerto Rico was governed through the U.S. Department of Interior and the U.S. Navy and Army Departments. The ruling officials usually were men who strongly reflected the plantation mentality, customs, and folkways of the Deep South, with its preoccupation with race, class, and religion.' Puerto Rico was annexed in 1898 with the signing of the Paris Treaty, and its people became US citizens with the enactment of the Jones Act in 1917 (Kelley 1986: 443, 568).

The dehumanization of Black and Latina women was maintained in stereotypes in literature created by White people that were eventually to surface in film during the early twentieth century and that continue in contemporary film as the century draws to a close. The images of Latinas have their origins in the dime-store novels of the nineteenth century, but the images of African American women are derivatives of sentimental apologists for slavery in the plantation novel genre and their successors in the wave of nostalgia for a way of life 'gone with the wind' after 1865. Even D.W. Griffith consulted the rabidly racist novels of Southerner Thomas Dixon to 'authenticate' the controversial images of Black people reflected in *The Birth of a Nation* (1915). All the Black characters, male and female, are abnormally lustful and are performed by White men in 'black face', except the 'tragic mulatto' played by Madame Sul-Te-Wan.

Similarly, the Latina of conquest fiction is portrayed as the half-breed harlot whose purpose is to pique the male sexual appetite and whose mixed blood elicits similar behaviour to that of her Black counterpart, the mulatto. Both Black and Latina women may be used as White men's sexual playmates, as concubines or prostitutes, but neither possesses the necessary matrimonial attributes assigned to the characters of virtuous White women. Their 'coloured' blood precludes such unions because it activates capricious behaviour (also characteristic of the 'tragic mulatto'):[1] These stereotypes are conceptualized according to a racial hierarchy in which purity, chastity and moral virtue are equated with light skin, and lustful debauchery is equated with darker colouring. The Latin 'dark lady' is often a promiscuous, short-tempered, miscegenated bitch who will curse, stab, or poison her love interest in a jealous rage; whereas her Castilian sister, of aristocratic ancestry, is the lady. The well-bred Castilian lady of literature and film is permitted these characteristics not because Anglos respect her ancestry, but because she is usually cast as whiter than her darker Latina sisters of Mexican, Puerto Rican or Brazilian descent.

Before turning to analysis of specific films, it is important to acknowledge that stereotypes of Black and Latina women do have their counterparts in images of White women in film. White women have been maligned, stereotyped and derogated. White women, however, have the privilege of a more diverse palette of images. In some cases, White women have exercised the prerogative to change their images through the Hollywood 'star' system, through 'power-behind-the-throne' roles off screen; and finally through their own work as film-makers, producers, directors and writers. Black and Latina women have had nominal access to the informal routes to genuine power; thus they have had less opportunity to redefine their own images.

African American women continued to appear in films as maids and mammies throughout the 1930s, which culminated in Hattie McDaniels receiving an Oscar for her role as a mammy in *Gone with the Wind* (1939). Hollywood musicals became the popular fare of the 1940s because they were a necessary diversion from the Second World War. Hollywood musicals that launched the careers of both African American and Latin women (leading many to believe that this was their chance to escape the traditional stereotypes in entertainment) were short-lived and spawned new stereotypes.

Lena Horne, initially mistaken for a Latina in her film debut in which she briefly sings and dances in *Panama Hattie* (1942), received accolades for her singing of a Latin song. She subsequently appeared in *Thousands Cheer* (1943); the all-Black *Cabin in the Sky* (1943) as seductress Georgia Brown; and in the all-Black *Stormy Weather* (1943) as Selina, whose rendition of 'Stormy Weather' is renowned. MGM, however, did not know what to do with a beautiful African American woman who refused to pass and who rejected scripts that she considered negative to African American images. Although the studio attempted to make her a sex object even in the latter two films, her poise and sophistication transcend the stereotype. Horne was continually cast in limited musical scenes 'that Southern distributors, who objected to seeing a black woman on the screen could neatly excise from the films' (Kakutani 1981: 24D).

Although her Latin sisters may have been cast in more films, the 1930s and 1940s images were either zany caricatures or carnal playmates for Anglos. Mexicana Lupé Velez (1908–44; née Maria Guadalupe Velez de Villalobos) and Brazilian Carmen Miranda (1909–55; née Maria do Carmo Miranda da Cunha) exemplify the former, and Del Río, discussed later, represents the latter. Velez, whose fiery harlot depiction began with the silent film *The Gaucho* (1928), became famous as the zany Latina in *Hot Pepper* (1933), *Strictly Dynamite* (1934), *The Girl From Mexico* (1939), *The Mexican Spitfire's Baby* (1941), *The Mexican Spitfire's Elephant* (1942) and *The Mexican Spitfire's Blessed Event* (1943). Miranda's Hollywood musical films include *That Night in Rio* (1941), *Weekend in Havana* (1941), *Springtime in the Rockies* (1942) and *Copacabana* (1947). Characterizations of women generally became more derelict after the Hollywood Production Codes, established during the 1930s, were relaxed around 1951. White women played the harlot, the heroine, and also during this era and successive eras appeared as African American and Latina women. But the African American and Latina women were limited to the injurious images – frequently used to demonstrate the contrast between them and the superior White women on the screen. The focus here is on African American and Latina women who have had a reasonable amount of longevity in film and those who have starred in films that are financial successes.[2]

Black people have arduously opposed the demeaning images of their race presented in films since the appearance of D.W. Griffith's *Birth of a Nation* (1915). Now, as then, representatives of the commercial film industry respond to criticism through the assertion that they are reflecting 'real life' (Dempsey and Gupta 1982: 68). During the 1950s, however, Black people in 'real life' were engaged in the struggle for racial equality and Civil Rights in every American institution. Although African American women such as Rosa Parks, Ella Baker, Daisy Bates and Autherine Lucy[3] were at the forefront of the struggle for integration, the most publicized image of the African American woman on the movie screen was that of a whore played by Dorothy Dandridge in *Carmen Jones*.[4]

Dorothy Dandridge, an entertainer on the vaudeville circuit from age 5, began her film career with performances in *A Day at the Races* (1937) and *Going Places* (1939) and continued through several 1940s musicals up through the 1950s when she appeared in *Tarzan's Peril* (1951) as an abducted African princess. Her performance as Carmen made her a celebrity. *Carmen Jones* (1954) was 'the 1950's most lavish, most publicized, and most successful all-Black spectacle' (Bogle 1988: 169). The film's release coincided with the revival of the musical *Porgy and Boss* (1953) featuring Leontyne Price in a highly acclaimed production on international theatre tour. Dandridge went on to play Price's filmic counterpart. *Carmen Jones* is a loose interpretation of Bizet's nineteenth-century opera, which was based on a work by French novelist Prosper Merimée about a Spanish Gypsy peasant girl (Carmen) who works in a tobacco factory in Seville, Spain. In the opera, Carmen is a promiscuous woman who accords toreador Escamillo her sexual favours after having professed her love for the sergeant, Don José. The screenplay *Carmen Jones*, written by Harry Kleiner, produced and directed by Otto Preminger, with incredibly stereotyped lyrics conceived and perceived to be 'Black dialect' (replete with 'dese', 'dat's' and 'dis's') by Oscar Hammerstein II, is transplanted to a parachute factory in the American South during 1943. After 'hair-pulling fights between black females, the inevitable barroom brawl, the exaggerated dialect, the animalistic passions and furies of the leads' (Bogle 1988: 169), Carmen Jones meets her demise, provoked by her whorish nature, at the hands of Joe, a student air force pilot whom she has rejected for Husky Miller, a prize fighter. Dandridge's character Carmen Jones embodies two stereotypes of African American women – those of whore and bitch.[5] She is sexually promiscuous, emasculating and foul-mouthed, and she carries a razor that she uses on one of her co-workers. Pauline Kael's description of Dandridge as 'fiery and petulant, with whiplash hips' (Kael 1982: 93) and Donald Bogle's as 'animalistic and elemental' (Bogle 1988: 169) are indicative of what critics said of Dandridge's portrayal of Carmen Jones.

The role garnered Dandridge an Academy Award nomination for Best Actress – the first time a Black woman was so honoured.[6] Dandridge received a three-year contract with Twentieth Century Fox Studios under Darryl F. Zanuck which stipulated that she would star in one movie a year with a starting salary of $75,000 per picture (Robinson 1966: 74). Several achieved notoriety for their controversial implications of inter-racial love rather than for her acting ability. In *Island in the Sun* (1957), Dandridge became the first African American actress to be cast opposite a White actor (John Justin) as a serious romantic interest. The cast included James Mason, Joan Fontaine, Joan Collins and Michael Rennie, and co-starred Harry Belafonte. This was the first of at least three films in which she was so cast. Dandridge was the first African American woman contracted as a leading lady in an American film; as such, according to the formula, she would have to kiss or indicate romantic intimacy with her leading man. The producer vacillated because, according to her manager Earl Mills, he 'could not decide how to handle the Caucasian–Negro relationship' (quoted in Robinson 1966: 75). The producers were unwilling to break the stereotypical mould even for the acclaimed actress and legendary beauty. In *Tamango* (1959), for example, she was cast as a scantily clad African slave opposite Curt Jurgens as a sea captain who falls in love with her. The kissing scenes remained in the French release but were removed for the English release. Nevertheless, distribution was hampered in the United States because of a section in the Motion Picture Production Code that prohibited mis-cengenation on screen. Dandridge completed her three films cast opposite a White actor in each of them, but did not receive further acclaim for her acting until she again played a whore (Bess) in *Porgy and Bess* (1959), for which she received the Golden Globe Award as Best Actress in a Musical. By today's standards Carmen and Bess seem to exemplify characteristics of the liberated woman, but according to the moral expectations of the African American community these women were sexually promiscuous.[7]

In 1965, the first African American actress to grace the cover of *Life* magazine (1954) was found dead from an overdose of antidepressant pills. Dandridge was dedicated to achieving recognition as a dramatic actress. After talking with director Reuben Mamoulian she believed that she would play Cleopatra, but the role went to Elizabeth Taylor. After the many years she had struggled in her career, and after achieving acclaim, there is no doubt that Dandridge was disappointed and perhaps depressed regarding her career. When the Hollywood offers subsided she exclaimed, 'I could play the part of an Egyptian or an Indian or a Mexican, and I'm certainly not the only one … there are other Negro actors and actresses who can do the same thing' (quoted in Robinson 1966: 80). Dandridge had confidence in herself as an actress – of the roles proffered by Hollywood's movie moguls she said, 'more often than not – and more often than I would like – the role calls for a creature of abandon whose desires are stronger than their sense of morality' (quoted in Robinson 1966: 80).

Latinas in commercial films were treated no more equitably than their Black sisters. Hollywood film-makers projected the same images of the Latinas as those that Pettit (1980) maintains are manifested in the conquest fiction of Anglos. He asserts:

> Authors of conquest fiction tend to divide all Spanish Mexican women into two categories. A majority of dark-skinned half-breed harlots and a minority of Castilian dark ladies who are actually no darker than the American heroines, and may or may not be virtuous. ... The one similarity between these two types of women is that both are 'naturally' sexual. However, their sexuality takes different forms, each based on color. The sexual behavior of the Castilian dark ladies is carefully programmed and controlled. The sexual behavior of the half-breed women is spontaneous, constant, and entirely lacking in control, if not design. (Pettit 1980: 20)

Hollywood applies this natural sexual image to all Latin women – the only distinction is through a false verisimilitude that implies that all Latinas in urban settings are Puertorriqueña, and all Latinas in rural settings are Mexicana. White actresses playing Latinas are also limited to the same stereotypes as in the case with Jane Russell as Rio in *The Outlaw* (1943), where the release was delayed until 1947 because of publicized censorship feuds; and Linda Darnell as Chihuahua in *My Darling Clementine* (1946); Jennifer Jones as Pearl Chayez, a half-breed whorish wretch in *Duel in the Sun* (1946); and even with Lena Horne's character Claire Quintana in *Death of a Gunfighter* (1969); they were women of easy virtue, prostitutes, madams or concubines. Latina actresses should have had little trouble securing roles that would permit them to play a greater latitude of minority roles as well as White or generic women's roles, because they could 'pass' for women of other nationalities. As George Hadley-Garcia wrote in 1990, negative film images of Latinas continue to persist because of 'the sexism which overlaps the standard racism and xenophobia' (Hadley-Garcia 1990: 111). Moreover, when Latina actresses are cast in roles depicting other nationalities, although these roles imply diversity, frequently they are characterizations of members of another outcast minority group. Mexican actress Lupé Velez once said in reference to roles in which she had been cast, that 'she had portrayed Chinese, Eskimos, Japanese, squaws, Hindus ... Malays, and Javanese' (Woll 1980: 60).

The roles designated to Delores Del Río, one of Hollywood's first Latina stars, exemplifies this practice. Although she occasionally played the aristocratic Castilian, she was more frequently stereotyped. She, too, began as an actress during the silent screen era in the 1920s, playing 'exotic heroines'. Throughout the 1920s, 1930s and into the 1940s, Del Río portrayed a French peasant in *What Price Glory* (1926), a Russian peasant in *Resurrection* (1927), a half-Indian in *Ramona* (1928) and a Polynesian in *Bird of Paradise* (1932) (Gaiter 1983: 23D). She also played the role of Carmen in *Loves of Carmen* (1927), of which critic Mordaunt Hall (1927) wrote: 'The alluring Miss Del Río with her bright eyes, pretty lips and lithe figure, gives a decidedly unrestrained portrait of the faithless creature.' Between 1925 and 1943, Del Río was featured in at least 14 Hollywood films. During the 1930s and 1940s she appeared in *The Girl of the Rio* (1932) as a cantina dancer in this unsuccessful film that raised the ire of the Mexican government, which levelled a formal protest for its derogatory representation of Mexican law; and in *In Caliente* (1935), a sequel to *The Girl of the Rio* with the same cast and the same opposition from the Mexican government. *Flying Down to Rio* (1932) features Del Río as a Brazilian, once again generating controversy because she sports a two-piece bikini; and African American actress Etta Moten as a dark-skinned South American who sang 'The Carioca'. Del Río, who insisted upon being recognized as a Mexican in her publicity releases, tired of these stereotypical roles and returned to Mexico during the 1940s where she continued to perform on stage and screen and was instrumental in the founding of the Mexican film industry (Gaiter 1983: 23D). She starred in John Ford's *The Fugitive* (1947), filmed in Mexico, as a Chicana mother of an illegitimate child who sacrifices her life to save the Anglo priest (Henry Fonda); and resurfaced in Hollywood in two roles as a Native American – the first, as the mother of Elvis Presley in *Flaming Star* (1960), and in *Cheyenne Autumn* (1964), John Ford's 'apology to the Indians' in which Native Americans are decimated but in a more 'sympathetic' manner.

Rita Moreno, a Puertorriqueña and who, like Dandridge, also appeared on the cover of *Life* in 1954, began her career as a film actress in *So Young, So Brave* (1950) and continued to play stereotyped roles similar to those of Del Río. Her film credits include *Pagan Love Song* (1950), *Latin Lovers* (1953) and *Untamed* (1955); in 1956 she received critical recognition as a talented actress for her role as the Siamese Princess Tuptim in *The King and I*. During this period of her acting career, Moreno says that she portrayed 'the Indian lady with feathers in her head or the Latin lady who's always demeaned and never winds up with a man, especially if he's a white man' (Bermel 1965: 38). Moreno's comment reverberates with the Anglos' fear of 'genetic pollution' referenced above; the same fear they have of the African Americans intermingling with White women.[8] After a four-year hiatus, during which Moreno performed on the legitimate stage, she returned to Hollywood in 1961 in the role of Anita in *West Side Story*. As Anita, Moreno portrays a Puertorriqueña who is the razor-tongued, street-wise friend of Maria (a suntanned Natalie Wood!). The story focuses on Maria, a Puertorriqueña who has just arrived in Spanish Harlem from Puerto Rico. Anita warns Maria of the dangers of failing in love with a White boy, which Maria promptly does when she falls in love with Tony's close friend Riff, the leader of the Jets. Their relationship ignites the fermenting feud between rival street gangs, the Jets (White boys) and the Sharks (Puertorriqueño), advancing the conflict in the film.

There are both overt and subliminal messages of ubiquitous promiscuity regarding the character of the Puertorriqueña in the film. The constancy of derogatory lyrics with pretentious accents (as in *Carmen Jones* and *Porgy and Bess*; this time in conceived Puerto Rican lyrics by Stephen Sondheim), compounded with decidedly risqué costumes for the era in which the film was produced, heighten this promiscuity. The lyrics of 'America', a duet sung by Rosalia and Anita, contain both positive and negative descriptions of Puerto Rico but the negative descriptions prevail. The introduction to this song implies that the long Hispanic names are ridiculous and continues in the following pejorative manner: 'Always the population growin''/And the money owing/And the babies crying/Hundreds of people in each room!' The diffuse dialogue in negative reference to large Hispanic families subliminally reinforces the stereotyped beliefs held by mainstream America. The image of the promiscuous Latina is effectively buttressed by placing Anita on the side of her bed skimpily clad in undergarments as she suggestively sings: 'Anita's gonna get her kicks/Tonight/We'll have our private little mix/Tonight/He'll walk in hot and tired, poor dear/Don't matter if he's tired/As long as he's here/Tonight!'

Costuming women in red in both theatre and film productions is universally synonymous with 'loose women' (see note 5) and there is certainly a proliferation of red in the costumes of the Latinas in this film. Presumably red is reflecting the fire smouldering inside the character wearing it. Maria's virtuous white 'coming out' dress flaunts a red waist sash; the majority of the Puertorriqueña wear red; and the lavish crinoline slips underneath Anita's black 'mourning' skirt are red (which are revealed when some of the Jets attempt to rape her); and Maria wears a red dress in the final scene of the film. The colour red combined with low-cut, suggestive blouses and tight skirts exemplifies the attire of the whore, and its repeated use implies that this mode of dress is indigenous to Latinas. And finally, the conclusion pays homage to all of the earlier prototypes of film containing inter-racial relationships – the Latina cannot wed the Anglo – she or he in this case must die.

Costumes and lyrics are only two of the negative images presented in this film, but they are two of the strongest subliminal production elements that serve to lull an audience into a false sense of reality. In both film and theatre, music and colour are utilized to manipulate moods and attitudes. The majority of the Anglo critics hailed this film as a masterpiece, with one notable dissenter – Pauline Kael (1966). They did not comment on the negative stereotypes; perhaps because they believed – as critic Stanley Kaufman believed – that 'we are seeing street gangs for the first time as they really are' and by extension Latinas (quoted in Kael 1966: 131). A positive statement such as this can be made without any personal knowledge of Puerto Ricans or gang members because the stereotyped images are imprinted in the spectator's subconscious. The people whose images were negatively affected did complain, however. Although the Puerto Rican Action Coalition implored Paramount to remove the 'racist' film *West Side Story* from circulation, Paramount President Frank Yablans refused. The films continued to play throughout the USA, and Hollywood honoured it with ten Academy Awards, including one for Best Colour Costume Design. Rita Moreno received an Oscar for Best Supporting Actress for her role as Anita (Pickard 1977: 175–6). Moreno subsequently played a stripper in *Marlowe* (1969) and Alan Arkin's mistress in *Poppi* (1969), while simultaneously continuing her illustrious stage career. Morena is the only woman to have received an award in every media – the Academy Award, the Emmy and the Tony.

American cinema has presented a similarly distorted picture of the African American family structure,[9] bolstered by 'documentation' from sociological studies. This distortion has led to a corresponding distortion of the depiction of African American women. From the latter half of the 1960s through the 1970s, many Black Americans gradually shifted from an integrationist to a separatist ideology. The separatist ideology is sometimes referred to as the 'Black Power Movement', which meant rejection of the White man's images of fun, beauty, profit and virtue, replacing them with Black images ... was cultural, political, social, religious, and economic' (Berry and Blassingame 1982: 419). The contemporary feminist movement evolved almost simultaneously, and African American women were involved in both movements. These activities coincided with a spate of sociologically based studies that argue that the Black family is dominated by women and that this domination is responsible for the deterioration of the Black family in America. Although many Black men and women verbally denounced these assertions, many embraced them. Paula Giddings (1984: 319) explains:

> Some Black intellectuals of the time were not content merely to rele-gate Black women to the political – or biological – back seat of the movement. Sociologists, psychiatrists, and the male literati accused Black women of castrating not only their men but their sons; of having low self-esteem; of faring badly when compared to the virtues of White women. Black women were unfeminine, they said; how could they expect the unflagging loyalty and protection of Black men?

These seeds of derision sown among African American men and women blossomed on the silver screen during the late 1960s through the mid-1970s and have resurfaced to haunt us in the ongoing heated debates about the Steven Spielberg adaptation of Alice Walker's novel *The Color Purple* (1984).[10] The sociological theories provided both Black and White males with justification for their maltreatment of Black women. African American men such as Amiri Baraka, Eldridge Cleaver and Malcolm X espoused male domination of women (albeit the latter's attitude was tempered by his religious beliefs). These attitudes were reflected in film through the exploitation of African American women by both Black and White males. White males more often than not cast Black women primarily as con-cubines, prostitutes and superbitches, achieving monetary success from the films. Black men, portraying pimps and pushers, exploited, brutalized and destroyed their Black women on the silver screen for all to see, even though for many it was a one-film deal.

. . .

The Liberation of L.B. Jones (Columbia 1970) was the vehicle that laun-ched Lola Falana, a vocalist and dancer, into film. Falana starred as Emma Jones, wife of the wealthiest Black man in Somerset, Tennessee, Lord Byron Jones (Roscoe Lee Browne), who publicly humiliates her husband by becoming the concubine of Willie Joe Worth (Anthony Zerbe), a redneck cop. She discontentedly lounges around (like Cassy) in her own bourgeois home, half-clad in sexy lingerie, reading movie magazines. Canby refers to Falana as being 'like an all-black Jean Harlow . . . an admirable, not entirely conventional slut' (Canby 1970: 6C: 1).

Melinda (Vonetta McCee) in the film *Melinda* (Metro-Goldwyn-Mayer, 1972) is the concubine of a White Mafia boss (Paul Stevens). She is slashed to death early in the film, providing the motivation for narcissistic Frankie J. Parker (Calvin Lockhart) to avenge her murder by karate kicking and chopping his way through hoodlums for the remainder of the film.

Although Lonne Elder III (an accomplished playwright and screenwriter for the Oscar-nominated *Sounder*) wrote the screenplay and Hugh A. Robertson was the director, the two Black men alleged that the White movie moguls 'kept pushing for all sex and violence' (Mitchener 1975: 243). Veteran actress Rosalind Cash (Terry Davis) who played a respectable business executive contends that she vigorously fought to develop a character that was more than a 'black whore' (Ward 1977: 223). The Terry Davis character indicated that African American women are business women also. This film was popular among African Americans who had complained about the 'blaxploitation' fare. It grossed $1,560,000 in domestic film rentals (Parish and Hill 1989: 216).

In each of these early blaxploitation films it is apparent that the writers were in a quandary as to what to do with women. The shallow characters are more illustrative of Barbie Dolls (her first appearance was in 1959) – engaged in nothing more than maintaining their beauty, revealing flesh while changing their clothes, and developing variations of seductive poses – rather than complex, loving human beings. Manifestly, the film-makers of these films recognized the marketability of beautiful Black women on the screen and that their beauty had to be combined with sex. After several decades of mammies, maids, tragic mulattoes and matriarchs, however, they did not know quite what to do with this combination. The subsequent phase of blaxploitation temporarily resolved this confusion.

'Blaxploitation' refers to films that feature predominantly Black casts, are sometimes authored by Black writers and guided by Black directors, but always hastily produced on a shoestring budget by White-owned Hollywood studios that earn millions of dollars from their enterprise. Earlier films in this genre featured Black men in the leading roles functioning in a male *métier* (e.g. *Shaft* 1971; *Superfly* 1972; *Across 110th Street* 1972; and *The Mack* 1973). Women in these films were incidental; they created the 'ambience' of the ghetto as prostitutes, whores and drug addicts. With the arrival of *Coffy* (1973) starring Pam Grier, however, women became the focal point and the next phase of blaxploitation combined beauty and sex with violence which engendered sexploitation films and the arrival of the 'superbitch'.

The superbitch embodies characteristics similar to those ascribed to the matriarch (dominating woman) combined with the description of the bitch delineated above. Pam Grier achieved stardom as the superbitch supreme throughout the first half of the 1970s. She appeared on the covers of both *Ms.* – which celebrated her as a liberated woman – and *New York*, which exalted her as a sex goddess (Bogle 1989: 399). Grier, initially a switchboard operator for American International Pictures, eventually grossed millions for this company after becoming their contract star. She was featured in more than a dozen films, the majority of which were produced by AIP, brandishing such titles as *Coffy* (1973), *Black Mama, White Mama* (1973), *Foxy Brown* (1974), *Sheba, Baby* (1975), and *Friday Foster* (1975). Grier starred as a nurse, a prostitute, a private investigator, and a glamour magazine photographer who sports very sexy attire and literally castrates men on the screen. In *Foxy Brown* alone, Grier thrashes a call girl in a bar, slashes the throat of another woman, cremates two men to death, and castrates a third and delivers his genitals in a pickle jar to his woman friend as a warning. She strutted her sexiness through the decadent ghetto world of pimps, pushers and prostitutes, variously armed with profanity, a spear gun and a sawn-off shotgun, the tools of her trade that facilitated her cleansing the community of these seedy elements. It did not matter what Grier's slated role was, her character type remained the same – whorish superbitch who bedded with anyone including her professed enemies. When AIP's box-office dollars for Grier movies began to dwindle in 1975, her contract was not renewed (Parish and Hill 1989: 145).

The Pam Grier movies exploited sex and women during the era of the contemporary women's liberation movement. The creation of this machismo character provided soft pornography for men and a vicarious pleasure and satisfaction for some feminists who believed that these images were positive examples of equitable casting. These films represented the female counterparts to the popular male films such as *Shaft* (1971), *Superfly* (1972) and *The Attack* (1973); the audience is told in the latter that 'a pimp is only as good as his product – and his product is women'. This statement is visually reinforced as the audience is bombarded with the display of Black women as whores and prostitutes who are referred to and addressed as 'bitches'. Fortunately, the popularity of these films was ephemeral. Unfortunately, with the death of blaxploitation films, Black actresses became unemployed. They were no longer in demand because the industry was unwilling to cast them in any but the dehumanized sex-object roles.

Indeed, commercial films of the 1980s have neglected to provide alternatives to these images as evidenced in the film *Fort Apache, the Bronx* (1981), where men refer to women as 'bitches' and 'fuckin' sluts', and which features Pam Grier, who received critical praise for her role as Charlotte, a drugged-out prostitute who wanders through a decadent community populated with pushers, pimps, prostitutes and arsonists in the South Bronx, where she shoots two cops at close range during the film's opening, and randomly slits the jugulars of men with a razor blade concealed under her tongue for no apparent reason, until the middle of the film when she blunders and is killed by her would-be victim. Grier's absence is

inconsequential to the community as well as to the film's progression.
...

Latina actresses were more difficult to ascertain in the contemporary film industry because their numbers are scant and because some are cross-cast. Presumably there is a younger generation of Latina actresses who, like their predecessors, have changed their names, and there are many women who are not easily identifiable as Latinas. The women who attained celebrity status were white-skinned: Rita Hayworth (née Margarita Cansino) and Racquel Welch (née Raquel Tejada), whose anonymity permitted them a 'greater variety of screen roles and identities' (Cortés 1985: 99, 100; Hadley-Garcia 1990: 178).

Although Rachel Ticotin continues in roles that are non-generic regarding race, she continues as nothing more than a male appendage. She was Melina, a prostitute in *Total Recall* (1990); Kim Brandon, single mother and woman-friend of Rollie (Bryan Brown) in *The Deadly Art of Illusion* (1991); Grace, concubine to the dope-pusher, but actually an undercover detective in *One Good Cop* (1991). Incidentally, the popular 1986 science fiction film *Aliens* featured Private Vasquez, a fierce machine-gun-toting Latina (possibly a flirtation with gender-bending?) who was very impressive as being equal to the boys when it came to combat. The role, however, was played by a suntanned White actress (Jenette Goldstein). It is still not clear as to why this character had to be Latina, and since she was, considering the paucity of roles, why was a Latina not cast?

The 1990s do not envisage brighter horizons for Aframerican and Latina women. The options of roles that Aframerican and Latina actresses are offered continue to illustrate what James Baldwin (1975: 93) said of the intentional misrepresentations in *Carmen Jones* 40 years ago:

> *Carmen Jones* has Negro bodies before the camera and Negroes are associated in the public mind with sex. Since to lighter races, darker races always seem to have an aura of sexuality, this fact is not distressing in itself. What is distressing is the conjecture this movie leaves one with as what Americans take sex to be.

Commercially successful films continue to manifest this ignorance. Spike Lee's *Do the Right Thing* (Universal 1989), in which Latina Rosie Perez ('all you do is curse', Tina) is used only as a sex object (as women are continually used in his subsequent films); *A Rage in Harlem* (1991) features Robin Givens – replete with red dress – as Isabelle, a prostitute (whose rendition has been compared to Dorothy Dandridge in *Carmen Jones*) redeemed by Forrest Whitaker; *New Jack City* (1991), where

Aframericans in addition to fulfilling their sexual expectations are accorded parity with males through their ability to unblinkingly blow someone's head off at close range with an Uzi (reminiscent of Pam Grier's 1970s characters); to name a few.

The same year that Black and Hispanic people formed the Committee Against Fort Apache, the National Association for the Advancement of Colored People (NAACP) announced that, '1980 had been the worst year for black actors and actresses since 1970' (Sterritt 1983: 12), and withheld the Image Awards (Black version of the Oscar) for Best Actress after it was realized that Cicely Tyson was the only actress who played in a role large enough to qualify for nomination (*Bustin' Loose*, 1981). There were no Black actresses in a leading role in 1982, and in 1983, in an act of desperation, the Image Award was bestowed on Jennifer Beals – an actress whose African American heritage was publicly ambiguous – for her part in *Flashdance* (certainly not a Black film). Her nomination was accompanied by an explanation from Willis Edwards, then president of the NAACP's Hollywood Beverly Hills branch, who maintained 'that the Image Awards were created to honor individuals – black or white – who present a positive image for minorities' (London 1983: 1). The 1990 Image Award for the category of Best Actress was suspended because there were not enough leading performances to adjudicate (Givens 1991: 38). Although 29 per cent of the feature films cast women, only 10 per cent of principal roles in both film and television were awarded to African American women (Eivens 1991: 36).

There is a glimmer of hope in Matty Rich's *Straight Out of Brooklyn* (1991) and John Singleton's *Boyz N the Hood* (Columbia 1991), two films that, although focused on men, portray African American women realistically. The former sensitively addresses the complexities surrounding wife battering and child abuse; the latter presents diverse images of Aframericans. Among the characters represented in *Boyz N the Hood* are the responsible single mother who recognizes the necessity of a father–son relationship and delivers the adolescent to his father, completes her master's degree and opens her own business; the single mother who attempts to raise two sons but errs in lavishing affection on one to the neglect of the other; the 'crackhead' mother whose toddler is frequently wandering the street in traffic; and finally a refreshing young high school woman who verbalizes that she will not become sexually active because of her man-friend's demands but that she will determine when she is ready. The latter character is contrasted with a young woman of the same age who hangs with the 'Boyz' but nevertheless articulates her malcontent with the way in which they reference women when she asks 'why we always gotta be bitches, hoes and hootches?' Rae Dawn Chong and Jennifer Beals are at least two African American actresses frequently cross-cast. And although cross-casting on the one hand is positive, on the other, cross-casting solely light-skinned actresses hearkens back to earlier filmic practices that exclude the darker-skinned sisters. The same is true for Latina actresses. Del Río, Miranda and Velez were vocal about their Latin heritage; there were darker Latinas whose careers were truncated because of their colour; and finally there were those who could pass.

For the most part, attention to the plight of the image of Black women in film has been precipitated by Black women such as Ruby Dee and Alice Childress, who long ago published articles addressing the issue of the Black woman's image in literature and the visual arts, and Saundra Sharp, who maintained in 1982 that young Black actresses were still being offered 'four or five lines on a stupid comedy show, a bit part as a prostitute or a dope addict, or straight T and A' (Dempsey and Gupta 1982: 69). Her words continue to be echoed in 1991 by a new generation of actresses who lament the absence of diverse roles for women of colour: 'when you are an ethnic woman of color, you play the hooker or you don't work' (Givens 1991: 40).

Aframerican and Latina actresses continue to struggle alone – making achievements, winning awards, but alone – there is no support system, and 'Hollyweird' allows only one 'success' at a time. Like their foremothers Nina Mae McKinney, Freddie Washington, Lena Horne, Dorothy Dandridge, Cicely Tyson, Delores Del Río, Carmen Miranda, Lupé Velez and Maria Montez (to whom Pam Grier has been compared) whose beauty is renowned, a prerequisite for Hollywood films, and who have won numerous accolades against all odds, to maintain gainful employment in the motion picture industry. There is a paucity of roles for women in general, but there are even fewer for African American and Latina actresses. Whereas White women have taken the opportunity to portray African American and Latina women – among them Jeanne Crain, Janet Leigh, Linda Darnell, Jennifer Jones, Susan Kohner and recently Jenette Goldstein – 'women of colour' are not offered the option to play themselves and certainly not to play a White woman or even a role believed to be a White woman's. Finally, while White Hollywood simultaneously celebrates Meryl Streep, Demi Moore, Julia Roberts, Melanie Griffith, Jodie Foster and others, only one African American actress at a time is considered a 'box-office attraction'. 'Hollyweird' currently recognizes Whoopi Goldberg (who has had an uphill battle in 'tinsel town'), but remains ignorant of Sheryl Lee Ralph, Lynn Whitfield, Vanessa Bell Calloway and Kimberly Russell.

Today when Black women writers are acclaimed for literary works (Alice Walker, Toni Morrison and Terry McMillan – all three appeared on the

New York Times Best Seller's List simultaneously in 1992), and when women of colour own their own publishing houses (e.g. Kitchen Table: Women of Color Press), are publishing books internationally and multi-culturally (*Charting the Journey: Writings by Black and Third World Women; Women's Fiction From Latin America: Selections From Twelve Contemporary Authors*; and *Bridges of Power*, among many other titles), there is no indication from the Hollywood film industry that complex stories about Aframericans and Latinas are imminent.

Films have long ceased to be innocuous entertainment. In fact, when dealing with Aframericans and Latinas, Hollywood has never been apolitical.[11] Hollywood designs and distributes entertainment for the dominant culture. Art has been abused for the sake of maintaining the status quo. After all, the business of Hollywood is illusion. Lamentably there is no distinction made between mythology and actuality. Films that have been released irrespective of opposition from minorities impart a clear message that the White-controlled studios, distribution centres, and critics do not give a damn about the derogatory images of minorities if there is a profit to be made in those images. The film industry can no longer be permitted to be irresponsible; they must be held culpable for their decision making. The reason that stereotypes continue to abound is, as Gordon W. Allport (1981: 200) states, that they are socially supported, continually revived and hammered in, by our media of mass communication – by novels, short stories, newspapers, movies, stage, radio and television. Western society continually espouses the need for universality in art. But this has become an excuse to give the public a homogenized universality that appeals solely to White people – if it deviates from their cultural understanding, then it has no validity. This is a prime example of cultural genocide. American film has buttressed institutional teachings of mainstream America to invalidate all that is different, as well as to convince the 'different' that they and their culture are invalid.

Although White Hollywood exercises the luxury of remakes (often of bad films), the diverse stories of African American and Latin women have not been told even once. There are African American and Latina independent film-makers telling those stories. Women such as Julie Dash, Michelle Parkerson, Allile Sharon Larkin, Ayoka Chenzira, the late Kathleen Collins, Leslie Harris, Marta N. Bautis, Sylvia Morales, Pilar Rodriguez, Teresa 'Osa' and many others have been recording the African American women's experiences for more than a decade, without acknowledgement from Hollywood – and with nominal acknowledgement from critics.[12] And their stories will survive just as their cultures have survived in spite of the multifarious means employed by Anglos to nullify them.

Notes

1. Films featuring the half-breed Latina character include *The Outlaw* (1943) and *My Darling Clementine* (1946); films on the 'tragic mulatto' include *The Debt* (1912), *The Outlaw* (1913), *Imitation of Life* (1934 and 1959) and *Pinky* (1949).

2. For an indication of box-office returns on contemporary Black films see Parish and Hill (1989). It is important to note that, with the advent of videotapes, some of these films are still reaping profits. Pam Grier's films are excellent examples; released in 1988, the package was promoted as 'sex for the price of five'.

3. Rosa Parks refused to relinquish her bus seat to a White man, precipitating the Montgomery Bus Boycott and the beginning of the Civil Rights Movement; Etta Baker, an activist and Coordinator of Dr Martin Luther King, Jr's, Southern Christian Leadership Conference (SCLC), Daisy Bates, President of the Arkansas National Association for the Advancement of Colored People (NAACP) chapter and publisher of the Arkansas State Press, led the integration of Central High School during the 1957 school integration crisis in Little Rock, and Autherine Lucy, the first African American to desegregate the University of Alabama at Tuscaloosa.

4. Dorothy Dandridge had been in films since the early 1940s, but the role that gained her position as a movie star was that of *Carmen Jones* in the film of the same title.

5. Indeed, Donald Bogle describes how Dandridge outfitted herself and altered her behaviour in Otto Preminger's office to convince him that the role belonged to her, because Preminger believed that Dandridge was 'too sleek and sophisticated for the role of a whore' (Bogle 1988: 168).

6. Hattie McDaniel won an Academy Award for Best Supporting Actress of 1939, for her mammy performance in *Gone With the Wind*. Beah Richards was nominated in 1967 for Best Supporting Actress in *Guess Who's Coming to Dinner*. The second African American woman to receive an award in the history of the Academy is Whoopi Goldberg who won for Best Supporting Actress in 1991. Incidentally, Goldberg plays an intermediary to the White stars in the film *Ghost*.

7. Other films characterizing Black women in this manner were the remake of *Imitation of Life* (1959), in which a White actress portrays the irrepressibly sexual and fiery, tragic mulatto Sarah Lane whose Black blood lures her to degraded occupations and compels her to hide in her room, engaged in licentious gyrations to African American jazz. Juanita Moore, who plays Sarah Lane's mother, won an Oscar nomination for Best Supporting Actress for her subservient performance to Claudette Colbert in this 1959 remake of the 1934 classic based on the novel by Fannie Hurst, a White woman. Although the stereotypical names have been changed from Aunt Delilah to Annie and from Peola to Sarah Jane, the negative stereotypes remain unchanged. *Sapphire*

(1959), a British-made film scripted by Janet Green, a White woman, also features the tragic mulatto theme in which the murdered Sapphire is found dead at the film's beginning, dressed in a red petticoat that does not match the rest of her luxurious lingerie. During the ensuing investigation by White detectives to establish the murderer, it is determined that Sapphire was a Negro passing for White and engaged to be married to a White man; she clandestinely frequented Black hangouts and had secret friendships with Black men.

8. The rationale for the lynching of Black men that occurred in the USA during the nineteenth and up until the mid-twentieth century was predicated on this fear.

9. Independent Black film-makers have made some positive and realistic family films, most notably *The Learning Tree* (1969) by Gordon Parks (a Hollywood exception, based on Parks's childhood); *The Sky is Grey* (1972) by Stan Lathan; *The Killer of Sheep* (1977); *Bless Their Little Hearts* (1984) by Billy Wood-berry; *To Sleep With Anger* (1990) by Charles Burnett; *Daughters of the Dust* (1991) by Julie Dash; and *Nothing But A Man* (1963), a White independent film by Michael Roemer. Also see the special issue of *The Nation Scapegoating the Black Family, Black Women Speak* (1989 July 24/31) – a diverse group of Black women, including educators, legislators and other professional women, address issues concerning the Black family.

10. Although there were many, Tony Brown's articles and Minister Louis Farra-kahn's tapes were perhaps the most critically severe in their attacks (see Brown 1986). This syndicated column, in addition to thanking the Academy of Motion Picture Arts and Sciences 'for not rewarding Purple People for their lack of self-love', levels scurrilous personal attacks against Whoopi Goldberg, Oprah Winfrey and Margaret Avery. In addition, Minister Louis Farrakahn took time out of his busy schedule to produce a long-running commercial audiotape that derides *The Color Purple* and also levels personal attacks against the artists.

11. Nor, for that matter, films depicting any group of colour – including Indians, Asians and others. For an introduction to this issue see Miller (1980).

12. For a more comprehensive listing see Michelle Parkerson (1990).

References

Allport, G.W. (1981) *The Nature of Prejudice* (25th anniv. edn). Reading, MA: Addison-Wesley.

Anzaldúa, G. (1990) Bridge, drawbridge, sandbar or island: lesbians-of-color Hacienda Alianzas, in L. Albrecht and R.M. Brewer (eds) *Bridges of Power: Women's Multicultural Alliances*. Philadelphia: New Society Publishers.

Baldwin, J. (1975) Carmen Jones: the dark is light enough, in L. Patterson (ed.) *Black Films and Filmmakers: A Comprehensive Anthology from Stereotype to Superhero*. New York: Dodd, Mead.

Bates, K.G. (1991) They've gotta have us, *The New York Times* magazine, 14 July: 15.

Bermal, A. (1965) Getting out from under an image, *Harper's Magazine*, April: 38.

Berry, M.F. and Blassingame, J.W. (1982) *Long Memory: The Black Experience in America*. New York: Oxford University Press.

Blackwood, M. (1986) Stereotypes: beyond the 'mammie', in C. Brunsdon (ed.) *Films for Women*. London: British Film Institute.

Bogle, D. (1988) *Blacks in American Films and Television: An Illustrated Encyclopedia*. New York: Garland.

Bogle, D. (1989) *Toms, Coons, Mulattoes, Mammies, and Bucks: An Interpretive History of Blacks in American Films* (expanded edn). New York: Continuum.

Brinton, C., Christopher, J.B. and Wolff, R.L. (1964) *Civilization in the West*. Englewood Cliffs, NJ: Prentice Hall.

Brown, T. (1986) Whoopi for the Academy Awards, *The Indianapolis Recorder*, April 3:11.

Canby, V. (1970) The liberation of L.B. Jones, *The New York Times*, 19 March: 60.

Cortés, C.E. (1985) *Chicanas in Film: History of an Image in Chicano Cinema: Research, Reviews, and Resources*. Binghamton, NY: Bilingual Review Press.

Dempsey, M. and Gupta, U. (1982) Hollywood's color problem, *American Film*, April: 66–70.

Gaiter, D.J. (1983) Dolores Del Río, 77, is dead: film star in U.S. and Mexico, *The New York Times*, 13 April: 23D.

Giddings, P. (1984). *When and Where I Enter: The Impact of Black Women on Race and Sex in America*. New York: William Morrow.

Givens, R. (1991) Why are Black actresses having such a hard time in Hollywood?, *Ebony*, June: 36–40.

Hadley-Garcia, G. (1990) *Hispanic Hollywood: The Latin in Motion Pictures*. New York: Citadel.

Hall, M. (1927) *The New York Times*, 27 September.

Kael, P. (1966) 'West Side Story', in *I Lost it at the Movies*. New York: Bantam.

Kael, P. (1982) *5001 Nights at the Movies: A Guide from A to Z*. New York: Holt, Rinehart & Winston.

Kakutani, M. (1981) Lena Horne: aloofness hid the pain, until time cooled her anger, *The New York Times*, sec. 2, 3 May: DI.

Kelley, R. (1986) *The Shaping of the American Past*. Englewood Cliffs, NJ: Prentice Hall.

London, Michael (1983) Beals named as NAACP Image Awards nominee, *Los Angeles Times*, 9 November: C6:1.

Mercado, L. (1974) *A Puerto Rican American Speaks*, in E. Mapp (ed.) *Puerto Rican Perspectives*. Methuen, NJ: Scarecrow.

Miller, R.M. (1980) *Kaleidoscopic Lens: How Hollywood Views Ethnic Groups*. Englewood, NJ: Jerome S. Ozer.

Mitchener, C. (1975) Black movies, in L. Patterson (ed.) *Black Films and Film-*

making: A Comprehensive Anthology from Stereotypes to Superheros. New York: Dodd, Mead.

Parish, J.R. and Hill, G.H. (1989) *Black Action Films.* Jefferson, NE: McFarland.

Parkerson, M. (1990) Did you say the mirror talks?, in L. Albrecht and R.M. Brewer (eds) *Bridges of Power: Women's Multicultural Alliances.* Philadelphia: New Society.

Pettit, A.G. (1980) *Images of the Mexican American in Fiction and Film.* College Station:Texas A&M University Press.

Pickard, R. (1977) *The Oscar Movies from A–Z.* London: Frederick Muller.

Robinson, L. (1966) Hollywood's tragic enigma, *Ebony,* March: 70.

Sterritt, D. (1983) In film, progress is obvious but not enough and affects only certain groups, *Christian Science Monitor,* 9 May: 11–13.

Ward, F. (1977) Black male images in films, in E. Kaiser (ed.), *A Freedomways Reader: Afro-America in the Seventies.* New York: International Publishers.

Woll, A.L. (1980) Bandits and lovers: Hispanic images in American film, in R.M. Miller (ed.) *The Kaleidoscopic Lens: How Hollywood Views Ethnic Groups.* Engelwood, NJ: Jerome S. Ozer.

15

WOMEN AND SOAP OPERA: RESISTIVE READINGS

Mary Ellen Brown

Soap opera knowledge supports largely feminine friendship and gossip networks by allowing for a system where those who have such knowledge are supported and where such knowledge is legitimated. In addition, we can see the beginning of a tendency to break the rules – both narrative and social – and to question established boundaries through parody and laughter. In this chapter we shall look more carefully at how the text itself is brought into dialogues where it can be used to structure a resistive reading or where a potentially resistive reading can be rejected. In all cases, the resistance is measured in terms of the subordination of women in our culture, hence the facets of female power can be seen as a crucial factor in the creation of resistive meaning.

Female Power

A negotiation of female power evidences itself in both text and audiences. There is evidence in these interviews to suggest that female characters are judged in terms of power; that power is, in many cases, indicated by a female character's ability both to speak and to be seen. ... In the following conversation, we see this idea taken a step further:

> **Ellen:** *Coronation Street* is famous also because it has great bawling-out, stand-up fights between women.

MEB: The first time I saw that was on *Coronation Street*.
Ellen: Between Ena Sharples –
MEB: But she's so old.
Ellen: Between Ena Sharples and –
MEB: Annie would be too sophisticated.
Ellen: Well, no. Annie has got a good bag for that.
MEB: She's got a good mouth on her! (Laughter)

Here we see that women willing to literally fight it out can be viewed as powerful. The women being depicted on *Coronation Street* in the above conversation are older women (Ena Sharples was in her nineties at the time), hence the pleasure of seeing two women fight is not in seeing them as sexual objects but as fighting women, able to use their bodies in this way. On *Coronation Street*, older women are considered to have interesting lives and sometimes to be daring and courageous. In this case, there is a bit of resistance embedded in the text itself.

In another case, when a female character is not as strong as she could be, these *Days of Our Lives* fans take note of it.

Sue: How do you feel about the women?
Emma: Well, Marlena, she's the doctor, the psychiatrist. She was at the hospital. She had her office and had patients and then she suddenly gets involved with Roman and police work. She just slipped out of character. Now she is going back [Roman is dead at this point], of course.
Sue: Do you think she is a strong woman character?
Emma: Fairly.
Sue: That's what I feel, fairly. I'd like to see her really get stronger as a person.
Emma: She's very well liked. Seems to be very popular.
Sue: I think she's real popular, but I'd still like to see her be a little more independent or something. I don't know.
Karen: You know who is the best? Gwen. Wasn't she wonderful when she refused to lean on Larry? She has some good lines.

Marlena's popularity means that she may well continue to be a character on the show, but this group of fans would like to see her make use of the power she should have by virtue of her position as a psychiatrist. Gwen, on the other hand, is popular because of the strength of her character and also because she has been given 'some good lines'. Gwen's power is, at least partially, in what she is able to say. Within the discussion the shifting emphasis between producer, character, actor, and audience in terms of the source of power for these female characters is evidence of the dialogic nature of conversations about soap operas. The power of the female voice seems to be recognized and appreciated by these fans. Another example of this affirmation follows:

> *Ellen:* That's definitely a lot of the pleasure in watching it. It's the way things are said.
> *MEB:* Particularly the put-down, I take it.
> *Ellen:* The put-downs, the rudeness. It's kind of stylized rudeness.
> *MEB:* Well, the power of the women seems to have to do with their –
> *Ellen:* Their mouths.
> (Laughter)

But evidence of female power is not the only marker of resistive reading. We have already seen how groups of women constantly negotiate their position within traditional families and romantic relationships in the context of soap opera networks. Now let us look at two groups of teenage soap opera viewers – one, a group of young teenage girls who are fans of the Australian *Sons and Daughters*, and another, British fans of *Neighbours* and *Brookside*. The *Sons and Daughters* fans are mainly working-class, high school friends whose formal contact with the feminist movement is slight. They are close to the age where Australian teens, like British teenagers, will choose whether to continue their education beyond the age of 16. The second group of teenagers are college-age young people from a British university studying in the United States, some of whom are committed feminists. With each group it is possible to distinguish the way that a resistive reading hinges on the social, cultural, and political positions of audience members.

Strategies and Tactics

Patricia Palmer's study *Girls and Television* (1986) tells us a bit about the general television viewing practices of Australian teenage girls. The viewers in her study, from working-class schools are, she finds, devoted and enthusiastic and watch more television than boys. Girls' viewing, according to her findings, peaks between the ages of 13 and 14. Although two out of the five schools Palmer used in her study were coeducational, talk about television programs by girls was almost always with other girls. Girls, according to Palmer's finding, 'had a detailed knowledge of programs their friends watched and liked and the favorite show of their group at school' (p. 32). In fact, according to Palmer, girls often form their friendship groups based on which television programs are their favorites. Girls did not, as a rule, discuss their television involvement with parents, teachers, or other adults; however, as Palmer notes: 'It was certainly gratifying to girls if parents viewed their programs, as long as they did not interrupt by talking or asking for translations, in the case of parents who did not speak English' (pp. 43–4).

An attitude of ownership of certain programs was usual and the young women often referred to their favorites as 'my programs'. Parents in Palmer's study were quite flexible about allowing television viewing of programs of which they did not approve; however, they sometimes were critical of their daughters' viewing practices, criticizing them for watching soap operas in particular. The girls reported an overwhelmingly negative perspective on most television by their teachers, but when a teacher was a television fan, these girls felt supported. As one of Palmer's group members remarked:

> Cheryl: My science teacher likes it, she watches all the 'Prisoner' programs and things like that. It's good to come to school and have, you know, a good conversation with the teacher. You feel you are in the right, then, you know. (p. 51)

Although Palmer concludes that girls' use of television contributed to their narrowing their future choices by the educational decisions they made during early teenage years, she also acknowledges the pleasure that the girls she interviewed experienced in talking about television. 'While their talk is often intense, it is also punctuated by laughter. What girls learn from television can have serious, and negative, consequences but there is no doubt that the process of doing so affords them great enjoyment' (p. 67). In my view, the laughter and enjoyment of television may themselves be appropriations of television's strategies, and their gathering together to share this enjoyment means that they may be doing more than simply absorbing the ideology that these shows seem to represent. A close look at responses to a specific program can help to clarify how the process of reading takes place within a particular group of girls.

The teenagers whom we look at here are longtime fans of *Sons and Daughters*,[1] two of them having watched it since its inception in 1981. The act of watching this particular soap then put these teenagers in the position of choosing as their cultural capital a particularly trashy soap – an initial act of defiance usually of their parents and teachers in itself and a common one among teenagers. Although sharing many similarities with the American daytime soap operas, also noted for their excessive trashiness, *Sons and Daughters* also has significant differences. The plots on *Sons and Daughters* move exceptionally fast (thus counteracting the universal teenage complaint of boredom), and they emphasize different aspects of the narrative than do plots of American daytime soap operas. This can be seen by the way the show deals with weddings.

The major wedding on *Sons and Daughters* during the period when I interviewed the teenagers was that of Wayne and Susan. When Wayne, the villain, and Susan (a good, honest, and strong young woman) are married, Wayne has kidnapped Susan's younger brother to persuade her mother to influence Susan to marry him. In addition, he has framed Glen, Susan's real love, so that Susan will think Glen has betrayed her. The wedding itself is, of course, a gathering of all of the show's characters. It features a fistfight between Wayne and Glen and a last-minute appeal to Susan by Glen for a chance to prove his innocence. All of this is similar to what might happen at an American daytime soap opera wedding, but the remarkable thing about this wedding is that the program shows less than a minute of the actual ceremony. As one of the young women in the interview group put it, there was no necessity to show it because 'everyone knows what goes on at a wedding.' This is markedly different than the usual portrayal of weddings on American daytime soap operas. On *Days of Our Lives*, Roman and Marlena's first wedding lasted three days, giving the entire 'real time' text of the wedding ceremony. Wayne and Susan's wedding on *Sons and Daughters* provides us with an example of the way that the text itself contributes to teenage resistive readings of romantic sentiment, of which the wedding is the culminating symbolic act.

To look at specific examples of the ways that teenage girls talk about *Sons and Daughters* in light of commonly held beliefs that audiences do not question dominant ideological assumptions in relation to soap operas, let us turn to the recorded conversations.

The first aspect to be noted is that this group evidenced a decided preference for individualistic characters, particularly those who defied social norms.

> *Diana:* I like the people or the characters. They do things that people we know wouldn't do. Sort of, we've been told, no I could never do that to another person, but they go right out to hurt another person's feelings, or something like that. And we just like to see what happens when it does happen.

The conflicts of teenage girls mentioned by Taylor (1987) ... in relation to the expectation that they be proper young ladies rather than seek their independence as boys do, seem to be played out in the admiration of a character who is not a nice person. Contrary to notions of being good, their favorite characters tended to be villains.

> *MEB:* Which characters do you like?
> *Jan:* Wayne.
> *MEB:* What is it about Wayne?
> *Jan:* Because he is such a little devil and is like a split personality: like to his wife he is such an angel and then when she is out of the room he turns and his whole face changes. And the type of clothes he wears changes and he goes right out, you know, to hurt other people. Like he uses old family friends, like his next-door neighbor Charlie and all that, for their money. She doesn't have a clue what her money's invested in but he uses her anyway.
> *Diana:* I think he's good because he does it without anyone knowing what he's doing.

The pleasure here seems to be appreciation of Wayne's ability to get away with things, to use people without getting caught, but also to get along in the world. Thus Wayne is a kind of role model for resistance. Female villains are also admired for, among other things, being at the center of the action.

> *MEB:* Well, Jan said that Alison is a winner, but Caroline's not. Do you agree with that?
> *Diana:* She doesn't play as major a role and you know, she doesn't get involved in as many activities that Alison does, type of thing. Not as adventurous type of thing. Alison gets into more trouble.
> *Jan:* Yeah, I think it's because Alison's got more drive and more ambition to do things and she knows who to contact to get in touch with people and get about what she wants to do. Whereas Caroline just sort of fumbles her way toward it and whatever she does isn't really a big thing to the series at all ... so you know...
> *Diana:* She's just taking every day as it comes type of thing ... whereas Alison, she plans ahead.

Alison is admired as a role model in avoiding the passive expectations of women. Decisive action, then, is a high priority with these viewers, one that contrasts sharply with the statement by a 15-year-old girl in Hudson's (1984) study, 'Whatever we do, it's always wrong' (p. 31). The idea of simply taking every day as it comes, which is the fear of many educators about girls limiting their economic choices by early decisions on school options, is not the admired characteristic among these fans, whereas planning ahead and knowing what one wants are appreciated. This would seem to broaden young women's options rather than decrease them. Of course, there are also other influences in these young womens' lives, but if we consider television viewing and fanship a contributing factor, then these conversations must be looked at as seriously as the content of the program.

With the exception of the strong matriarch, the saintly characters are disliked by this group of fans. However, those characters who exhibit socially aberrant behavior, or who at least behave or act defiantly, are admired.

MEB: I expected you to like the teenage characters.
Diana: Like Andy and Craig and . . .
Jan: I like Andy. He's good.
Diana: I don't know, I suppose Craig – he's all right, but he's such a goody-goody – he's always doing good things for everyone, you know. I suppose in that teenager there would be a good adventurous side and that would be Andy, and there'd be the really nice side, and that would be Craig. They've sort of split the individual up into two characters. There's not just one – I suppose Ginny would be the character where she is really nice to people and adventurous. Ginny would be the . . .
MEB: I'm trying to remember which one Ginny is.
Jan: She is the one who wears the really odd clothes, she puts together with the long – sort of hair.
MEB: She's the one that's just had that thing fall on her.
Jan: Yeah.
MEB: So she's the one that you like?
Diana: She's all right. She doesn't like blend in with the rest of the *Sons and Daughters'* characters, but she uses her language differently. Her odd clothes make it more interesting to listen to her and everything, but that's about it.
Jan: Her character's really outstanding.
MEB: What do you mean, she uses language?
Jan: Like soft-spoken and everything, she doesn't care what she says, she's outgoing and . . .
Diana: Loud . . .

It is clear in the above example that the manner in which the characters are constructed is clear to these viewers. The idea expressed here that Craig and Andy are two sides of a single character construction is indicative of the group's awareness that the characters in soaps are constructs, that these girls were able to like characters seemingly without the process of identi-fication clearly demanded by narratives with a single hero or heroine whose ability to be identified with is coded for the audience by her or his well-roundedness. Although the latter type of character relationship with audiences is clearly rewarded in terms of dominant viewership, its invitation was not accepted by these teenage girls. Andy and Craig were clearly, to the speaker, only parts of a character construction.

Moreover, the power of speech is evident in the above excerpt from the interview. This quoted section is complex in the group members' understanding of how, for example, the codes of dress that Ginny is given affect how we code her speech ('She uses her language differently. Her odd clothes make it more interesting to listen to her and everything'). That visual codes and oral codes can be related seemed clear to these readers. In addition, the power of Ginny's speech (she uses language) was quite clear to this particular *Sons and Daughters* fan. That power is used by the character of Ginny to contradict what 'nice' girls might be allowed to say. ('She doesn't care what she says, she's outgoing and ...' – 'Loud'). These fans valued characters for their power over hegemonic discourse (niceness for girls) and for the freedom to use voice quality to assert a position of strength in nonconformity. Ginny makes herself heard, and this is a valued behavior.

The following example ... is an instance of how the conversation about *Sons and Daughters* slips between analysis of the construction of the soap's plot and storytelling or performance on the part of the speakers of the group, including the 'filling in' process that brings the others up to date on the current plot:

> *Jan:* Most of what happens is based on revenge for what someone's done to them or working around greed for money, I think, and someone else's wife.
> *Diana:* Or husband, as Alison.
> *Jan:* Love of money and revenge. I think it is going to be pretty, um, shall we say dramatic for a while seeing as Alison is in such a critical condition at the moment in hospital.
> *Diana:* Is she in hospital?
> *Jan:* She's in a coma.
> *Diana:* Well, I haven't seen it for three days.
> *Jan:* She got stuck in the freezer with David.
> *Diana:* Yes, I saw that bit.
> *Jan:* Yeah, well they had no air and she went into a coma.
> *Diana:* Oh no!
> *Jan:* Yes and, um – Craig's mother drew the people out into the open and arrested them and Craig got off the hook.
> *Diana:* Good one!

Although the conversation begins with an analysis of the plot possibilities, it slips into the process of storytelling ('seeing as Alison is in such a critical condition'), and when it is discovered that one member of the group has not watched for 3 days, the intensity of the conversations heightens while the drama of Alison's coma and the courage and cleverness of Craig's mother are disclosed. The act of storytelling, recounting complicated and unpredictable plot structures, catching one's friends up on missed episodes, obviously is a major source of pleasure for these soap opera fans. Within the boundaries of such storytelling groups, these young women are verbally powerful.

Teenage girls' gossip networks and friendship systems centering on soap operas and other television programs, as Palmer has pointed out, are often systems in which girls take the power to exclude both boys and adults. Even when boys and adults are tolerated, it is only on the girls' terms. As Palmer's interviews indicated, girls often are happy to have others watch with them as long as they don't 'interrupt.' This is a reversal of the usual gender and adult–child power relationships. As de Certeau (1986) and many others have pointed out, the power to speak, control of the speech act, regulation of who may speak and under what conditions, is one of the central strategies by which the dominant system maintains control.

The hegemonic necessity to win over subordinated groups to particular ideological stances that in turn support their own subordination seems to be at least partially tactically subverted by the rich oral culture that Australian girls enjoyed around *Sons and Daughters*. Some romantic notions, like the wedding ceremony as life goal, are challenged by the text itself and these teenage viewers consume the text in ways that begin to distinguish power relationships within the construction of the text. Their awareness of the narrative constructions of these relationships and their willingness to challenge dominant notions of feminine dependency may indicate that these young women are using soap operas in ways that may support a resistance to the ideology of dependence and romance discussed earlier.

The following is excerpted from a conversation with British fans in their early twenties who watch soap operas primarily with their friends. At the time of the interview, Jen, an outspoken feminist member of the group whom I have quoted extensively, was studying in the United States for 6 months but would shortly return to Britain to finish her education at a polytechnical institute near London. She is from a working-class family and grew up in Manchester. In the following conversation, she is clearly attuned to the politics of the character she describes. The politics, in the first example, concern labor unions rather than women's issues.

Jen: You know ... that when *Brookside* first started it was a lot more political than it is now, and it had a lot of following because of it. And they had one particular character in there who was married to Sheila,

Bobby Grant, who was a member of his union and also a member of Militant – do you know Militant? It's a faction of the Labour party, extreme left faction of the Labour party. And every week, without fail, there used to be an opportunity for him to make some kind of political speech. And then they kept moving him up in the series, his job kept getting better, and then he went into management, but he was still in the union. And the guy who plays Bobby Grant actually was a member of Militant and the reason he was in that program was because he saw it as an opportunity to get across his political message.

Steve: Phil Redman, who came up with the idea for that program, started it specifically because he wanted a forum for these ideas in a way that could reach everybody.

MEB: So it was really political?

Jen: There is a lot of political sermon in it, and then they tried to really dilute his character. And when he became an executive of something, they tried to portray him as somebody who'd sold out the shop floor members of the union to make a deal with the bosses. And the guy who plays Bobby Grant quit the series because he wouldn't portray a union boss in that light, because it was when the union was getting really bad press, and everything, and he didn't want to add anything to that. And also, he just didn't want to be a party to that. So they just killed off his character, because he refused to play that part.

Jen, in the passage above, is comfortable with the political position expressed in the early episodes of *Brookside*. A preferred reading is one in which the audience member agrees with the ideological stance presented and thus has no trouble accepting the point of view portrayed in the piece. If we look at Stuart Hall's (1980) classification of viewers' possible responses to television as preferred, negotiated, or oppositional readings, we can see that some soap operas present a preferred reading in some aspects for some people. Thus these viewers are not reading against the grain when they view and interpret soap operas, but with the grain.

An antiunion audience member, on the other hand, might reject the positive reading entirely and thus read against the grain. His or her reading would be termed *oppositional* using Hall's criteria because the ideological message is so offensive that the reading is interpreted completely negatively. A negotiated reading would fall somewhere in between. An audience member could also approve of unions in general but find Militant too extreme. Or another viewer might interpret Bobby Grant's actions not as selling out but as a reasonable compromise. Any number of possibilities can be incorporated in a negotiated reading.

Sometimes reading with the grain can produce a preferred and resistive reading because the soap opera itself appears to take such a stand. This is the case earlier when young teenagers read the wedding as pretty routine and of little interest in and of itself. It is apparent that the soap opera itself can support a nondominant reading, which in the case of the union story in *Brookside* would be antimanagement and in the case of *Sons and Daughters* would be antimarriage. However, we can see clearly in the union story the retraction or 'clawing back' of the story. When it goes so far as to threaten hegemonic stability, the character is made to compromise the union's position in the story. When the ideological point of view in the story changes, the audience doesn't automatically change with it. Instead, the viewer may change her reading strategy to a negotiated or oppositional one.

The younger group of viewers of *Sons and Daughters*, in the following conversation, fail to read the text in an oppositional manner and give a preferred reading instead. In general, their readings of the text are not as overtly political as are Jen's, and in this case their reading is consistent with the dominant one.

Sara: I think that's because they don't relate them to, like we are, they just relate them as characters, they have made these characters up and put them on tele, that's why they didn't sort of ... like we don't really know what sort of work Gordon and that's in, except that they invest their money and they've got a business, we don't know exactly what sort of business they've got ... so we can't really say oh, he couldn't have that much money with that sort of job, you know, or maybe he should go into that sort of job, we don't sort of...
Diana: ... you know wondering what he works at, to get so much money and everything; how Caroline gets so much money.
Jan: Yeah, because it's not important to the program, it's not important how they get their money, just they have the money and they are what they are and what happens to them being what they are.
MEB: How come?
Sara: Because most people don't work sort of 24 hours a day once they finish their job they stop and that's it. That's the end of their job and then, you know, you're not really fussed about it. You don't want to switch on the tele and watch someone else work, it probably would be boring.
Diana: Because the only important thing is the characters and what they do. Like the money only comes into it if Wayne is blackmailing someone for money or trying to get more money invested or something like that and then the money is brought into the program, you know

what they do, but otherwise it's not mentioned because the program's based on the relationship between people rather than what people do.

Such lack of interest in money is often a part of dominant female conditioning, so much so that women sometimes fail to take the responsibility for their own finances or make poor judgments in relation to money. In this case, the audience member's preferred reading supports dominant notions that soap operas reinforce women's subordination relating to money issues – at least some of the time.

It is the ideology in question that constitutes the opening for a resistive reading. Such ideology can be contained within the narrative itself or it can be contained in the way viewers use the narrative in the context of their own social positioning. It is therefore impossible to say that all soap operas provoke a resistive reading just as it is also not always possible to predict how a resistive reading will take place. Ideologies change their inflection as do soap operas and as do the people who participate in soap operas networks. Many inflections of various ideologies exist within a given audience structured as it is by their social, cultural, or racial position, for example.

Just as it is rare to have a mainstream film address women's issues as directly as *Thelma & Louise* does, it is also rare that a soap opera addresses social issues as precisely as did *Brookside* in its early programs. Consequently, let us turn to situations that present less specific resistance within the soap opera itself.

In the following two examples, a soap opera's treatment of female characters is brought into question. The first is about *Neighbours* in its British run.

> *Jen:* You know what's really interesting about Jane, I think, because she was always portrayed as Jane, Jane, she's the brain. She was really, really intelligent when she's at school, but very awful in a conventional sense. When she left, she became very beautiful overnight. She got that job as a secretary. And yet she's supposed to be super, super brains, and the best she could get was [a job] as a secretary. She did not mind, though, did she?

This viewer is offering a critique both of the soap opera and also of society in general, where intelligent women are able to secure only conventionally female jobs. A similarly smart and educated man might be employed in a job with greater status and pay. And if a man were underemployed for his talents, he would surely mind, she implies. Thus the capping statement, 'She did not mind, though, did she?' conveys sadness on the part of the speaker and an acute personal awareness of the pain of such a position. Also in this statement is an implied criticism of the school system when Jen says that Jane is intelligent 'in the conventional sense,' presumably in the sense that the knowledge that schools convey is knowledge that doesn't question established rules. The fact that Jane has become beautiful overnight indicates to the speaker that, for women in the world of work, the real value is beauty – not intelligence, and that Jane is now doing socially acceptable women's work and can be rewarded for this by being seen as beautiful. Thus we can see that this conversation is a critique of the portrayal of women on the program and of a system where conventions oppress women in a number of ways. Still, Jen seems to negotiate this meaning in relation to her own identity.

In the next quotation about the British soap opera *EastEnders*, the character of Angie, once married to Den, has adopted his daughter, who, it turns out, had also been adopted earlier by Den. The conversation is about Angie.

> *Jen:* She adopted his daughter. She was adopted when she was very young, and she didn't find out she was adopted until she was quite old. She tried to get in touch with her biological parents, and that was so real. They came around in the end. It was so outrageous the way they did it because her birth mother, when she finally found her, had exactly the same hair, same dress. What are they trying to say here? I mean that was really powerful, I thought, that they were trying to say family ties, the way you turn out to be, is not a socialized thing, it's the naturalized thing ... I was actually considering writing to them about not looking for Angie, now, because it was really out of order.

This passage questions a number of assumptions that are evident in the visualization of the program as well as the plot. Jen questions the biological basis for socialization but also the value that the program (and society) place on the birth mother over the adoptive mother. This skepticism brings up the question of maternity rather than the often expressed problem of paternity frequently at issue in the American daytime soap operas ... Concern with whom one's mother is could be seen to imply an interest in matriarchal descent. This time Jen does not accept with resignation the situation as she did in looking at Jane's work situation, but is obviously angry that the program has overstepped the boundaries that she considers appropriate in dealing with women's issues even for a popular media form. Here she gives the program an oppositional reading.

Commenting about the lack of politics in *Neighbours*, the same British fan sees it as only political enough to add a bit of interest.

Jen: They just live out their roles. Scott's the boy next door and Kylie is the girl next door with a bit of rebellion put in for good measure, you know, but not too much, just enough to make mommy and daddy slightly angry. Enough to make people think. There's a little edge, but not enough to tarnish the image.

She has obviously not bought into the untarnished image of the girl next door. Thus there are clear distinctions made by the audience about what constitutes resistance to dominant ideology on the soaps and what doesn't. Jen obviously watches but finds it necessary to negotiate quite frequently.

Sometimes, oppositional readings become funny. In discussing *Neighbours* again, the same person says:

I cried when Marge married 'The Bish.' I did, I cried. I was so embarrassed, I cried. She married the Bishop Harold. I don't know why. I've always cried at weddings. I don't think it's for the reasons most people cry – another one bites the dust.

Here the traditional feminine response at a wedding, crying, gets turned around as an ironic expression of sorrow that another woman has succumbed; the tears show disappointment at defeat rather than joy. Thus we see that this resistive reading ... involves the appropriation of certain behaviour for an ironic reading of a dominant institution, in this case marriage.

Jen is looking, of course, at these examples of British and Australian soap operas as a feminist. And needless to say, some fans of soap operas are feminists (see also Ang 1985). However, most of the women and girls we look at in this study would not call themselves feminists; but when confronted with specific situations, either on a soap opera or in actual life, they often speak from a perspective that acknowledges their partial rejection of domestic role expectations, gender-defined double standards, in favor of feminine empowerment ...

Resistance

For such a resistive reading to reach outside the boundaries of the soap opera network and thereby transgress into areas of overt politics, thus becoming adopted as a political stance of the viewer in life situations, several variables need to come into play. These are

a. the political economy of the patriarchal family, which may be more or less exploitative in different contexts;
b. a genre that caters to women and the emotional tone of their lives;

c. the alternative interaction networks that soap operas facilitate;

d. the development of solidarity bases that give women support outside of the patriarchal family;

e. the development of a fund of strategic knowledge, not just about the genre itself but around the language of the genre and the life context of women;

f. the carnivalesque atmosphere of the genre, that is, the release from the dogmatism of the social norms surrounding the patriarchal family and broader social institutions; and

g. finally, the emergence of resistive readings, the conscious questioning of the existing structure of domestic roles and a rethinking of how these roles may be structured.

In the case of soap opera fanship, it is where all of these variables are present in the spoken text that a reading is likely to be resistant.

There are many critics who negate the possibility of a resistive reading of any type of television. Their position is that society reproduces itself in the repetitive stories of television – in the systems of reward and punishment shown, in the patterns of heroism and villainy, in the absence of non-hegemonic political positions. In other words, television can only be seen to legitimate the existing social order (Newcomb and Alley 1983, p. 21). Similarly, it is often assumed that women must leave their feminine plea-sures behind in order to become liberated; but, in fact, these feminine pleasures may give them space to evaluate their lives in light of existing dominant notions of femininity as well as some nondominant strategies with which to challenge the system on another level.

There are four areas that are important in the generation of resistive readings: talk, boundaries, strategic knowledge, and the lowering of nor-mative controls. There is *first* the necessity for the talk to take place. Not only are soap operas constructed in such a way that they elicit talk, but it is also obvious that a large amount of the pleasure that women derive from soap operas is in talking about them. It is in this *spoken text* that most of the meaning generation concerning everyday life and the construction of identity for audiences takes place.

The second important area is the developing of boundaries within which it is safe to talk freely – that is, to speak in feminine discourse. Many soap opera gossip networks are loose knit but others are more formalized neighborhood-based 'video clubs.' Often relatives, particularly mothers and daughters, or close friends are a part of one's gossip network. Australian teenage networks frequently have large informal groups of fans. But no matter how the groups are organized, the important thing seems to be that these fan groups set boundaries and within these boundaries one is free to speak as one pleases.

The third area is strategic knowledge. Regular soap opera viewers not only know the codes and conventions of soap operas, which gives them a way of talking that outsiders don't understand, but they can also access strategic knowledge, that is, knowledge of women's oppression.

The fourth area is the lowering of normative controls and this is expressed in carnivalesque laughter, or laughter that involves the inversion of the normal order of things – particularly in the way that soap operas are defiantly considered by many women as valuable cultural capital when dominant culture finds them trash or rubbish, that is, not acceptable in official designations of high art or what might be taught in school, for example.

At this point, let us list evidence that supports the notion that the young teenagers negotiate their reading actively rather than passively when they consume *Sons and Daughters*, at least part of the time. First, the television program that these teenagers chose to watch was itself defiant of hegemonic notions of the 'proper' text. It earned its trashy reputation because of its simple plots, its low production costs, its melodramatic morality, and its narrative structure. Second, these young women discussed the narrative structure in some detail, acknowledging the constructedness of the narrative itself. Third, they preferred characters who defy social norms, and they liked this characteristic in women as well as in men. In addition, they liked characters who took control of their voices, who 'use language differently,' that is, who use dominant structures on their own behalf. Although there were times when the group did not resist the expectations of feminine behavior as it is constructed in dominant terms, there were also times when they did. These conversations seem to indicate that these young women understand at some level the constraints of subordination. All of these points are supported by both the pleasure they experience and the freedom they feel to speak seriously and in fun about these soap opera narratives within their friendship networks, networks in which they themselves are in control (Brown 1991). In the group of college-age British viewers, we have seen that the nature of resistive reading practices, when the readers are ideologically feminists, is still to some degree controlled by what goes on in the text. We can only think differently when our social and cultural positions are compared with those in a given text, when rather than being sucked in by the text we are challenged to think for ourselves to the extent that there is room within dominant discourse to do this. This space to think for ourselves is in a constant state of flux, governed by our own emotional closeness or distance from its politics and our fluctuating capacity to think rationally outside of our conditioning, controlled as it is by the discourses to which we are each subjected.

Feminism and the Soap Opera Text

The work of Foucault (1975) on archaeology ... delineates the power of discourse to shape what is considered truth in a given discursive tradition. He defines discourse by its parameters of containment, by which he refers to those discursive practices that surround a social practice and ultimately construct a dominant 'reality' for the practice under consideration. Foucault (1982) relates the power to make one's own meaning within dominant discourse to a will to power combined with a will to knowledge. He sees all power relationships as containing within their structure the possibility of resistance: 'Every power relationship implies, at least in potential, a strategy of struggle, in which the two forces are not superimposed, do not lose their specific nature, do not finally become confused. Each constitutes for the other a kind of permanent limit, a point of possible reversal' (p. 225).

Thus when I refer to an element of popular culture as a site of struggle, I mean that, although popular culture is embedded in ideology, the possibility of struggle is always there for subordinated groups. Soap operas contain their own ideological contradictions because they are a product of hegemonic culture that embodies the very contradictions it seeks to disguise. Fiske (1988) has called the site of potential resistance 'a personified cultural process held in a moment of temporary stability when shifting social allegiances come together at the moment of semiosis' (p. 246). If we picture the moment of the reading of a particular text as the point where specific aspects of our lives come together with the issues and ideological notions inherent in a text, then certain possible stances of resistance can manifest themselves in our individual readings. Then when we bring the meanings garnered from those readings to bear in conversations, the spoken text can become a way of expressing resistance. If one is then in a position to have his or her resistances acknowledged and validated by a group of people, it may be possible for one to begin to work politically at the level of everyday life.

Not all women's talk is resistive, but that which recognizes, rather than denies, oppression is very likely to be able to question prevalent ideological assumptions and therefore women's own construction in discourse, thereby making it potentially resistive. In soap opera texts, there is usually no clear feminist message although the issues brought up are of interest to women, whether they are feminists or not. Other political issues such as those having to do with class can also come up, particularly in British soap operas like *EastEnders* or *Brookside*. Thus audience members can either appreciate the politics of the soap opera or not, or they can struggle with the ideas presented in order to negotiate an ideological position for themselves.

Let us return briefly to the movie *Thelma & Louise*. The following statement was made by a fan after viewing the text: 'My women friends and I have gone over that cliff together so many times.' There are three aspects of this resistive reading that are particularly important and that, in fact, make this particular moment a moment of resistive pleasure. The first is 'my women friends and I'; the second is going 'over that cliff'; and the third is 'so many times.' The first emphasizes solidarity among women. The 'going over the cliff' accomplishes a symbolic transgression of boundaries necessary to rock the stability of the status quo. It is an impossible and deadly act, at the same time courageous and open ended. And the repetition of this feeling 'so many times' confirms the existence and duration of the problem.

For me, the third party in the transaction, to hear it from a friend who overheard it provided a particularly resistive reading because many of us are now involved. Thus resistive pleasure comes not only with an understanding of the political implications of the mere existence of such a film, of its availability in mainstream movie houses and on videotape, and of its political messages for many women, particularly feminists, but also with our acknowledging its existence by talking about it. In other words, part of the pleasure here is the allowing into the discourse of mainstream film a position and space known only to the subordinated. Additionally, the recognition of the conversation with others as a powerful force in relation to subordination is of great value.

Although women have historically been subordinate, the meaning of women's friendship groups has changed in the eyes of dominant culture. In the nineteenth century, women's supposed asexuality meant that they could have close and loving relationships with their female friends without such friendships being considered threatening (Faderman 1981; Smith-Rosenberg 1975). It has been suggested that such relationships were problematized after the 1920s with the popularization of theories of Freudian and neo-Freudian psychoanalysis because these saw female relationships as sexual, bringing up possible sanctions against lesbianism because these theories considered it normal behavior to be heterosexually active. This led to the popular image of the older single woman as not normal (Walby 1990). Some writers see this as an attack on first-wave feminism because it involved strong bonding among women (Jefferys 1985; Millett 1977). Thus the political, cultural, and social atmosphere in which we live determines how we construct our gendered identity. Seen in a society that stresses individuality as a mark of mature functioning, the politics of connectedness can be discursively turned into a resistive and powerful position.

Soap opera provides images and plots that are of special interest to women, that are sufficiently open and sufficiently related to a woman's life context to be worked on by women together to generate symbols of resistance and ways of rethinking the role definitions of women, and consequently those of men also. The fact that groups of women do this together gives them a space where they can be enabled to fully work out issues and then to work them into their consciousness. It then provides the social support to carry these decisions out in practice. In addition, a soap opera group does not bring down on itself the anathema that the suffragists or the women's groups in the 1970s women's movement did because its purpose is overtly nonpolitical in the traditional sense of the word. However, as we have seen, politics can be reconceptualized on the level of culture where soap opera gossip networks can be thought of as not only political but perhaps even subversive.

Note

1. *Sons and Daughters* is an Australian teenage soap opera. The first U.S. teen soap opera, *Swans Crossing*, began in June 1992 on the Fox network. These soap operas are aimed at children aged 11–13 and a little older, often called the 'tween' market. In the United States, I have seen young girls' peer networks centered on soap opera viewing start as young as 7, and of course children watch at much younger ages.

References

Ang, I. (1985) *Watching 'Dallas': Soap Opera and the Melodramatic Imagination.* London: Methuen.

Brown, M.E. (1991) Strategies and tactics: Teenage girls and Australian soaps. *Women and Language, 16,* 22–8.

de Certeau, M. (1986) *The Practice of Everyday Life,* trans. S.F. Randall. Berkley: University of California Press.

Faderman, L. (1981) *Surpassing the Love of Men: Romantic Friendship and Love Between Women from the Renaissance to the Present.* London: Junction.

Fiske, J. (1988) Critical response: Meaningful moments. *Critical Studies in Mass Communication, 5,* 246–51.

Foucault, M. (1975) *The Birth of the Clinic: An Archeology of Medical Perception* (A.M. Sheridan Smith, Trans.). New York: Vintage.

Foucault, M. (1982) Afterword: The subject and power, in H.L. Dreyfus and P. Rabinow (eds), *Michel Foucault: Beyond Structuralism and Hermeneutics*, pp. 208–26. Brighton: Harvester.

Hall, S. (1980) Encoding/decoding, in S. Hall, D. Hobson, A. Lowe, and P. Willis (eds), *Culture, Media, Language*, pp. 128–38. London: Hutchinson.

Hudson, B. (1984) Femininity and adolescence, in A. McRobbie and M. Nava (eds), *Gender and Generation*, pp. 31–53. London: Macmillan.

Jeffrys, S. (1985) *The Spinster and her Enemies: Feminism and Sexuality 1800–1930*. London: Pandora.

Millet, K. (1977) *Sexual Politics*. London: Virago.

Newcomb, H. and Alley, R. (1983) *The Producer's Medium*. New York: Oxford University Press.

Palmer, P. (1986) *Girls and Television*. Sydney: New South Wales Ministry of Education.

Smith-Rosenberg, C. (1975) The female world of love and ritual. *Signs*, *1*, 1–29.

Taylor, S. (1987) *The Tender Trap: Teenage Girls, Romantic Ideology and Schooling*. Unpublished paper, Educational Studies Department, Brisbane College Advanced Education, Kelvin Grove Campus.

Walby, S. (1990) *Theorizing Patriarchy*. Oxford: Blackwell.

FREUD VS. WOMEN

16

THE POPULARIZATION OF THERAPY ON DAYTIME TALK SHOWS

Jane Shattuc

I am often amazed at the confessions, emotions and community of daytime talk shows. Women discuss and debate 'the problems of self-esteem in little girls' on *Oprah* on 19 April 1994, with a missionary zeal rarely found on network TV. Of all TV programming, the four major daytime talk shows are the most directly linked to the therapeutic discourse. Not only do they invoke Freud's concept of the 'talking cure' with their emphasis on the free flow of talk, but two-thirds of their programmes deal with psychological or socio-psychological issues. Typical are: a *Donahue* programme devoted to a test designed to enable couples to understand their strengths and weaknesses (31 January 1994); a *Geraldo* programme on 'women who have taken back their lying, cheating dog of a husband' (23 March 1994); and a *Sally* programme on couples who do not want to have children (31 March 1994).

Daytime talk shows rely overwhelmingly on experts out of the mental health industry: psychologists, social workers, therapists and self-help book authors. They use the language of psychology, whether it be Freudian (*repression, drives, the unconscious*) or American 12-step revisions (*dysfunctionality, healing, addiction, codependency*). Much like Freud's freeing of the unconscious, talk shows depend on the belief that 'real' emotion, conflicts and psychological truths will surface; between the spontaneity of the free-for-all discussion and the scrutiny of the expert, audience and host repression will give way.

According to Mimi White, daytime talk shows are not the only example of how American TV thrives on the therapeutic for emotional power. Shows as diverse as *Alf, 700 Club* and *Love Connection* depend on 'the confessional and therapeutic discourses' as both 'the subject of programming and its mode of narrativization'.[1] White's thesis broadens the definition of therapy beyond the common understanding of therapy as the healing of emotional problems, offering a more complex and sinister view: the media and their use of confessional formats to exert a form of social control. TV as an agent of the dominant culture exercises its power over unwitting viewers by naturalizing therapeutic psychology as a neutral method to free the self, when it is in fact the very opposite: a form of social control. Talk-show viewers learn to police themselves in the name of 'mental health'.

White's point of view extends Michel Foucault's belief in the 'productive power' of modern times, which 'works to manage and manipulate people by instilling in them a specific sort of interpretation of who they are and what they want'.[2] In *The History of Sexuality* he argues that the confession – a principal feature of talk shows – serves as a central means to elicit truth in our culture. It establishes a power hierarchy of interlocutor and confessor. The analyst or therapist becomes 'the authority who requires the confession, prescribes and appreciates it and intervenes in order to judge, punish, forgive, console, and reconcile; a ritual in which the truth is corroborated by the obstacles it has surmounted in order to be formulated'.[3] It is important, then, to question the degree to which daytime talk shows take part in a larger power hierarchy which uses the therapeutic concepts of 'self-knowledge', 'self-actualization', and 'emotional freedom' to regiment and control viewers. But the shows' rhetoric is not that simple. Their conventions, values and ultimate power spring from the feminist movement as a challenge to patriarchy. As a result, the relationship of the shows to the dominant power is not easily located. Although Foucault offers a cautionary model against a rush to characterize the shows as feminist, his critical stance does not allow for the possibility of emancipatory movements such as feminism.[4] This chapter traces how the contradictory tensions between the dominant culture and insurgent cultures are played out in a popular medium.

To begin, daytime talk shows throw into question the top-down therapeutic logic of the therapist/interlocutor and patient/confessor. If we look at the direct influences of the American revisions of Freudian psychoanalysis – humanist therapy, the self-help movement and feminist therapy – which have directly affected the logic of the shows, we see in the talk show a set of power relations much more complex and vertiginous than Foucault's. Who is the therapist? The expert? The host? The studio audience? Who are the patients? Those on stage with the reductive name tags such as 'female gang member', 'incest survivor' and 'husband locked her to bed'?

Or 'we' the viewers? Or Oprah, who routinely confesses her abusive childhood and displeasure with her body? And to what degree are the confessions, emotions and interactions understood as 'truth'?

Psychology is changing in the late twentieth century as therapy moves from the confessional to the public arena. Indeed, TV therapy is closer to testimonials of faith than to the guilt-ridden whispers of the confessional. No longer is the therapeutic a matter of secrets pried from the unconscious. Rather, therapy is an ideology based on the power to affirm the survival of emotional weakness, repression and subordination – all sensibilities derived from feminist therapy. Obviously, the daytime talk shows are not as theoretically inclined or as systematic as traditional clinical therapies, yet one needs to make manifest the implicit role of American psychology. If therapy is an agency designed to bring about emotional adjustment and/or social control, we should look more closely at the specifics of its talk-show incarnation – after all, 19 million people tune into *Oprah* daily. With an audience of 80 per cent women, the shows are not only the leading form of daytime entertainment but a powerful element in the creation of femininity.

The Humanist Challenge to Freud

The daytime talk show gets its wider therapeutic 'can-do' logic from the American revisions of Freud's psychoanalysis. In many ways it is misleading to liken its seemingly obsessive talk to Freud's talking cure, which called for free association, the individual's saying whatever comes to mind. Such unconsidered speech breaks down social constraints on communication and rationality, allowing the patient to reveal subconscious desires through certain compulsive repetitions.[5] When Anna O. (Bertha von Pappenheim) dubbed Freud's method 'the talking cure', she could not have foreseen the highly orchestrated world of televised talk as a Freudian venue. Under the industrial formula of a seven-segment structure, commercial breaks and the studio taping process, TV's talking cure emanates more from the preconstructed clash of 'I's, or knowing egos, than from the dark, uncontrolled id of Freud's theory of the unconscious.

The daytime talk shows have reinvented talking as a curative as a consequence of ego psychology and the American cultural psychology. Many twentieth-century clinical psychologists have sought to limit the authority of the Freudian therapist and Freud's highly prescriptive theory of the unconscious, to which only the therapist has access. Ego psychology argues that the ego develops a measure of independence from the unconscious and the id. Psychologists such as Erik Erikson, Heinz Hartmann and T.C.

Kroeber argued that the ego is not as dependent on the id as Freud postulated. They viewed it as a rational agency responsible for the individual's intellectual and social actions.[6] Hartmann said that such a position offered a more balanced consideration of the biological and social cultural aspects of human behaviour.[7]

Evolving out of the anti-authoritarian post-Second World War climate, individual-oriented therapy extended ego theory to grant the patient active agency and control. The most successful rethinking of therapist authority occurred in the 1960s with the growing activist American orientation and the psychological community's parallel theory of self-actualization. The patient became a self-determining figure in regard to mental health. As early as 1927 Alfred Adler broke with Freud and argued that personality was determined by conscious elements – social and interpersonal factors – rather than by a controlling unconscious to which only the therapist had access. Psychoanalyst Karen Horney in the late 1930s argued for the critical role that active 'self-esteem' played in human development. In the 1960s Erich Fromm, a member of the Frankfurt School, 'explicitly rejected Freudian notions of innate, undesirable human traits (for example, death instinct or aggressive instinct) and emphasized the positive nature of human nature'.[8] By 1969 psychologist George Miller was arguing in the *American Psychologist* 'to give psychology away to the people'.[9]

The American revisions of Freud put the patient in charge of her or his mental health. Rachel Hare-Mustin points out Freud's authoritarianism. In his famed case of Anna O., he revealed his misogyny when he blamed Anna's neuroses and departure from his therapy on her mother without questioning her disturbing relationship with her father. Moreover, Freud refused to question how the incident might reveal the limits or problems of his practice.[10] It is the Freudian analyst who serves as the model for Foucault's powerful secular interlocutor whose silence provokes the supine patient into a submissive confessional mode. At issue then is whether, with the rise of self-determination in American therapy, the unequal power relations dissolve? Or are they reinvented in a more complex and insidious form wherein the patient polices himself or herself in the name of 'self-actualization'? In its self-help ethos, the daytime talk show offers an explicit case of the potential value and problems of the self-determination model of American psychology.

Through its fragmented structure, the talk show undercuts the rigours of therapeutic practices and reduces the power of the therapist or expert; it should not be confused with the precision and authority of Freudian psychoanalysis or even clinical psychology. However, talk shows are predicated on a belief in the individual's active cognition of his or her problems. For example, a *Geraldo* programme on 'strange obsessions' (9 March 1994) opens with each guest describing her or his compulsion (agoraphobia, obsessive hair-pulling, self-hate). 'Shani' tells of her fear 'that God was after me and that he would zap me'. 'Sandy' describes her obsession with numbers: 'I would have to rinse the cup either three or seven or a hundred times.' 'Heather' declares, 'I was totally obsessed by the mirror ... Part of the hair obsession was I get concerned with it being even and symmetrical ... I couldn't stop it at the time.' Even though the programme plays into a tabloid sensationalism that depicts these women as bizarre curiosities, each is asked to evaluate her problem as a dispassionate observer. Rivera addresses them as rational thinkers able to distinguish between healthy and unhealthy behaviours, as he pronounces them 'courageous' copers.

...

By the 1960s and 1970s American humanist therapy represented a new psychology, or the 'third force' (the first and second forces: psychoanalysis and behaviourism). It was based on a belief in an inherent tendency toward self-actualization, growth and enhancement, rather than in Freud's more negative theory concerning such instincts and drives as masculine sadism, feminine masochism and a death wish. It called for renewed attention to the specifics or individualism of clients' problems as opposed to the prescriptions of Freudian theory and the authority of the therapist.[11]

Rational emotive therapy (RET) is the most influential of these self-actualization revisions and a source for the recent self-help movement. Rejecting the role of the unconscious and early childhood experience, it opposes any logic of indirect or inactive methods of change. The therapy is highly confrontational: the therapist/practitioner points out 'unscientific' or irrational assumptions, ideas and beliefs that seem to be at the core of a problem. With a rational emotive modality, many people get blocked in attempting to achieve happiness and self-actualization. They become neurotic because they turn their strong preferences for success, approval and comfort into absolutes: shoulds, musts, demands.

Born of this post-Freudian therapy, talking or self-disclosure has become the most common mechanism for the individual to make manifest his or her neurotic behaviours. No longer is self-disclosure the result of involuntary slips such as Freud's talking cure; it is the result of an active decision to overcome shame, guilt and inhibition. During a daytime talk show a guest is expected to break through the guilt-ridden, chaotic world of internalized emotion to the rational and open world of personal narrative, human interaction and community. Yet this unburdening process has tested limits of the liberal bourgeois openness: the established press continually condemns the shows as excessive. For example, Janet Maslin of the *New York Times* calls them 'muck marathons'.[12] And Anna Quinlan, a *Times* columnist, describes them as 'the dark night of split levels'.[13] There is no self-consciousness that privacy might be a luxury of middle-class life; people can distance themselves from other people and other classes in particular. The anger on the shows reveals the limits of what the middle class defines as 'proper' public display of private emotions and activities.

Self-actualization and Daytime Talk Shows

The active or cognitive approach of American therapy on daytime talk shows is twofold. There is the self-help approach based on basic 'no non-sense' prescriptions that the patient, TV guest or audience member can administer, such as the couples test on *Donahue* (31 January 1995), as mentioned earlier. The test enables couples to evaluate their capacity to endure. The guests (selected audience members) are asked to react to a series of statements on a yes/no basis, such as 'I am very satisfied with the amount of affection that I receive from my partner', 'We have clearly decided how we will share household responsibilities', and 'At times I feel pressure to participate in activities my partner enjoys.' Although the announced purpose of the test is to help couples decide if they should marry, the deeper sense is to get them to start 'talking' about their relationships.

. . .

The usual daytime talk show is structured in this fashion: its first quarter identifies the problem; in the second quarter the audience begins to confront guests' inconsistencies as the host plays moderator; in the third and fourth quarters the therapist becomes engaged, but often audience members point out the lack of logic in or the irrationality of a belief system and begin to offer their solutions even before the therapist (if present) enters the talk arena. The solutions combine a generalized knowledge of therapy and popular wisdom derived from everyday pragmatism. The emotive and cognitive methods of RET practice read like a litany of daytime talk show practices: shame-attacking exercises; role playing; unconditional acceptance of guests by host and expert; use of forceful statements; and behavioural techniques as reinforcement; penalizing; assertiveness; activity homework assignments; bibliotherapy; and skill training. *Geraldo* has obsessive compulsives enact examples of their obsessions, in part as a therapeutic test and in part as a demonstration of the problems. *Oprah* invites back guests who have been assigned home activities to remedy compulsive spending. A therapist on *Sally* tells a beleaguered wife to speak up and direct her anger at her unfaithful husband. Even though the audience is already familiar with these basic methods, most appearances of an expert or therapist are predicated on his or her book as a continuation of a programme's limited therapy.

Additionally, programmes about personal relational issues, such as 'Married Women Who Have Affairs with Married Men' on *Sally* (23 February 1994), depend on the confrontational logic of rational emotive practice. For the first 20 minutes *Sally* teases out the stories of two women in disguise, Ann and Laura, who are having affairs. After establishing the issue, the host lets her audience confront the women.

> FIRST AUDIENCE MEMBER: Where are your morals? When you get married, you take vows. They are down in hell, baby! ... I was married 35 years and some woman came took off with my husband.
> ANN: I do not want to take off with him. I just want the sex.
> FIRST AUDIENCE MEMBER: Well, there are people who do fall in love.
> ANN: This is true. When you let emotions get in the way of sex...
> FIRST AUDIENCE MEMBER: What about my emotions? 35 years!
> SECOND AUDIENCE MEMBER: You know, I've been married since I'm 19 to the same man. I will be married 40 years. OK? You're a very selfish person. You're a liar and cheat. If you're not satisfied, then you satisfy yourself. You don't go out [applause], you go out of the marriage. You, the blonde, you want excitement? You're sleeping with a married man. You're also a cheat. Take up bungee jumping or sky diving.

Obviously, the *Sally* staff have slanted the debate by populating the audience with women who have lost a husband to another woman. And because the audience is usually a stand-in for the at-home viewer or the average American, the 'normal' psyche of the viewer is set in opposition to the 'promiscuous psychosis' of the guests. Although usually not so morally unified, the audience of the show functions in this confrontational role more than the expert/therapist, who plays a much smaller and more deferential role under the host's control. Here, one could argue that the audience has so internalized the policing practices of modern psychology that the therapist has become an inconsequential element. Yet, the therapist remains a central agent who synthesizes the audience's disparate advice.

In this *Sally* programme, the relationships expert Dr Gilda Carle appears halfway through the discussion. Her first act is to hug a crying woman whose husband has just confessed to cheating on her. Carle asks, 'Can you tell me how you feel?' Hunched over in grief, the woman responds, 'I feel sick.' Raphael pipes up from the audience, 'I don't blame her.' Carle reacts, 'I don't blame her either. This is exactly what happens when people do cheat.' Carle's role is more classically therapeutic than the audience's; she exudes the feminine virtues of understanding, nurturing and bourgeois etiquette. She coaches the docile woman to assert herself by speaking up to her domineering husband.

. . .

Daytime talk shows' techniques are a loose reworking of a rational emotive therapy's disputational method for overcoming unrealistic and irrational feelings and actions. It involves detecting irrational beliefs, debating them, showing why they are irrational, and reformulating them. RET works on specific problems and hence is easily adapted to the fragmented format of the talk show. Talk-show therapy is at best 'band-aid' therapy, not the fundamental psychic reorientation that Foucault's model implies. Its logic downplays environmental factors or an awareness of what might be described as social subjectivity. It depends on a problem/solution format which, according to the founder of rational emotive therapy, Albert Ellis, 'places man squarely in the center of his universe and of his emotional fate and gives him almost full responsibility for choosing to make or not make himself seriously disturbed'.[14] The therapeutic logic of talk shows offers the potential for a high degree of self-absorption. Audience members often jump to the microphone to tell their own stories, seemingly competing for the most egregious example of personal pain. As a result, talk shows are frequently indicted for their excessive emphasis on egomaniacal 'I', or what Christopher Lasch sees as the cultural narcissism of the post-1960s period. The individual is so caught up in self-examination and self-determination that she or he denies any larger social causation.[15] Depression has its social roots, yet it is denied here. Philip Rieff proclaims that this individualism in American therapy leads to a severely limited sense of ethics wherein the self determines experience and Western culture 'stands for nothing'.[16] This selfish ideology leads Wendy Kaminer to label talk shows as part of a new pathological individualism.[17] Yet in all these cases it is simplistic to blame recent postmodern culture because American ideology has always had its roots in individualism. From Tocqueville's treatise on American culture to the entrepreneurial capitalism of the nineteenth century to the populist movement, the American discourse of individualism transcends the late twentieth century and the psychology of the world of the marketplace.

. . .

Talk Shows and Feminism

In the end daytime talk shows are not caught up purely in pragmatic individualism; they also solicit a collective consciousness – the female audience. Like all cultural practices, the shows exert contradictory demands for power. But their claim to personal fulfilment through commercial consumption is counterbalanced by their veiled feminism and a con- sciousness of the inequalities of power. Their principal social aim has been to build up women's self-esteem, confidence and identity. Unlike most self- help books about which Simmonds writes, the shows take place in an arena of collective feminine experience. The form of their practice results from the women's movement and feminist therapy – specifically, the consciousness- raising group as a democratic forum – a place where women create com- munity in the absence of authority by drawing on their social experiences and morality. Here advice does not come top-down but from within the group and its shared oppression.

Through their rewriting of feminism, daytime talk shows retain their moral power. This role cannot be reduced to the complex therapeutic power of a consumerist culture but involves the nascent claims to power for women as a subordinated group. Ultimately, *Oprah* and the other shows offer a utopian vision of female equality, a vision that keeps them from falling into problems associated with the pragmatic individualism of modern mass culture: selfishness, isolation and alienation, as well as the stultifying nihilism of Foucauldian scepticism. If the individual polices herself or himself for society through talk shows, the process is always complicated by the dissident values of American feminism. The shows are venues where women of different races and classes attempt to claim power.

Historically, feminist psychology represents a further elaboration of the American rewriting of Freud than does ego psychology. By the mid-1970s feminist psychologists had firmly critiqued Freudian theories for depen- dence on a male developmental model, for attributing biological inferiority to women because of anatomical differences between sexes. This resulted in a tendency to see women as passive, dependent, and of lesser moral stature. Feminist theorists have attacked three major constructs of Freud's person- ality theory of women: penis envy, the Oedipus complex and the focus of female sexuality as the vagina and not the clitoris. Whereas psychoanalytic feminists in media studies have been attracted to Freud's comprehensive theory of masculine domination through the Oedipal scenario, practicing psychologists for two decades have critiqued psychoanalysis as oppressive to women.

In 1975 Julia Sherman detailed ways that psychoanalysis has been destructive to women patients:

> (1) the authoritative relationship that analysts have with patients, which promotes dependency and mystification; (2) the analytic practice of locating the problem and the blame within women – 'victimizing the victim'; (3) providing a negative view of women; (4) providing a view of women as to engender iatrogenic disease; and (5) handy rationales for the oppression of women.[18]

That year the American Psychological Association created a task force on sex bias and sex role stereotyping in psychotherapeutic practice. The panel argued that psychoanalytic practice often insisted on Freudian interpretation, ignoring reality factors (for example, how the patient felt about the therapist or a given incident). Many Freudian therapists maintained that vaginal orgasm was a prerequisite to emotional maturity. They also problematically labelled female assertiveness and ambition as unhealthy, a form of penis envy.[19]

A major goal of feminist therapy has been egalitarianism, whether in personal relationships or in therapeutic practice. Feminist reform shares the self-actualization orientation of the third movement of American humanist psychology. Feminists developed several humanist techniques which are loosely replicated by daytime talk shows: sharing, group discussion and assertiveness training. What differentiated feminist therapy was and is the implicit assumption of unequal power relations between men and women. Using the humanist model, feminist therapists reconfigured the image of women as active, complex and ever-changing individuals who have capacity to choose, to assign meaning to their lives, and to be autonomous.[20]

Feminist therapy (unlike other humanist therapies) returns to the environment (not childhood *per se*) as a determining element of female psychology. Where many humanist psychologists saw feminine and masculine as given categories, feminist therapy involves analysis of the social construction of sex roles and power; therefore there is always a sense of shared, not isolated victimization. Nevertheless, the logic of the therapy has been resolutely active. Feminist therapy turns the humanist concept of self-actualization around and places it within a critique of social constraint. Feminism named the process 'empowerment', which has become a central discourse of talk shows. In fact, an audience member jumped up during a discussion of bad husbands and announced to Oprah: 'It's about power and empowerment.'

The Feminist Psychologist, the Women Experts of Talk Shows

As stated earlier, daytime talk shows overwhelmingly populate their programmes with female experts. In my three-month study, four out of every five therapists (PhDs, MDs, MSWs or 'psychotherapists') were women. Male experts are typically medical doctors, investigators or agency heads empowered by their official knowledge. Although knowledge is also a factor, women experts are called more often to carry out their practices on stage – to nurture, interact and solve dilemmas by offering short-term solutions. Although all four hosts have stated a vague allegiance to feminism, it falls to the experts who are not officially tied to the shows to represent feminist ideology. Both their on-camera advice and their self-help books often approximate toned-down and broadly applied feminist therapy manuals. The experts are the central popularizers of feminist theory on TV.

The feminisms of the therapists diverge widely. According to Ann Kaplan, in the 1970s and 1980s there were loosely four broad types of 'feminism':

- bourgeois feminism (women's concern to obtain equal rights and freedom, within a capitalist system);
- Marxist feminism (the linking of specific female oppressions to the larger structure of capitalism and to oppressions of other groups: gays, minorities, the working classes and so on);
- radical feminism (the designation of women as different from men and the desire to establish separate female communities to forward women's specific needs and desires);
- poststructural feminism (the idea that we need to analyse the language order through which we learn what our culture calls 'women' – distinct from a group called men – as we attempt to bring about change beneficial to women).[21]

Generally, the women therapists of daytime talk shows come out of bourgeois feminism. They believe that equal rights are attainable once women become aware of the social and sexual repressions to which they are victim. Like Gilda Carle's quick answers, their therapy tends to be blind to the differences caused by race, sexual preference and class. Because their advice is constrained by TV's segmented form, it is often reduced to exercises, simple cause-and-effect models and self-help formulas to which 'anyone' can have access. For all of bourgeois feminism's critique of women's oppression, these experts espouse a democratic notion of equal sharing of power between men and women as opposed to a negative social critique of male domination.

For example, *Donahue* aired the programme 'Daughters Who Are Unusually Close to Their Fathers' (9 March 1994), on which the therapist Dr Victoria Secunda argues that the problem stems from the father's need to be idealized by his daughter. The daughter is attracted to him because of his absence from the difficulties attendent upon her rearing; the mother is devalued as the disciplinarian. Secunda's solution: the parents must equally share the responsibilities of child rearing. But Donahue continually tempers her critique by stating that he approves of father/daughter closeness. He declares, for instance, 'If you ask me (and nobody has) we want to first celebrate the wonderful love and mutual affection and admiration.'

Another example is the *Oprah* programme devoted to how to get married (14 March 1994). Oprah introduces Dr Pat Allen and her book, *Getting to 'I Do'*[22] and states that Allen promises the audience that 'if you follow her advice, you will snag a man within a year!' The programme starts with the patriarchal belief in a male-centred model of femininity where women scheme to marry. But it turns out that Allen's argument is predicated on the assumption (as Oprah puts it) that all men and women have 'masculine and feminine energy'. In fact, Allen's first words are 'Everyone is both masculine and feminine.' She continues, 'There is no such thing as a woman that is too masculine.' A few minutes later, she proclaims, 'The problem is we don't need to marry any more. Men can go to a gourmet cooking class and we can go to a sperm bank.' The audience laughs wildly and applauds at her declaration of female independence. But Oprah keeps on course: 'What is really great about this marriage thing . . .' 'So if you want to get married . . .' But Allen later argues that 'we still have as much a man's liberation movement ahead as we have a woman's'. Her position becomes that men have the right to be feminine – an issue of universal victimization.

Here, we also get the mixed message from the therapist that although women and men are blends of masculinity and femininity, the terms *masculine* and *feminine* are essentialized as active and passive, respectively. And what women need to do to get married is return to their feminine selves. Such a contradictory message – which combines a male-centred model and feminism – is endemic to the shows, which tend to cater to both sides on the gender issue. But this is an unusual programme in that both sides are evoked by one therapist. Even when critic Naomi Wolf attempts to point out the problems of essentializing feminine behaviour as passive, the continual interrupting by Allen, commercial breaks, Oprah's interjections and audience questions keep a clearly articulated counterstatement from being made.

Ultimately, good talk show therapists must be good performers, neither beacons of rationality nor politically astute feminists. They are in an odd way comparable to the itinerant performers of the nineteenth century. There are the 'star' or repeat therapists, who are discovered and nurtured and appear regularly on a particular show. Carle is a *Sally* regular, as is Randy Rolfe on *Geraldo*. Many therapists travel what is known in the business as the 'talk-show circuit'. For example, Secunda appeared on three different talk shows between 9 March and 30 June 1994. Although the therapists are not paid, they get to publicize their services and books (Carle's *Interchange Communications Training*, or Secunda's most recent volume, *Women and Their Fathers*).

As much as the therapist represents psychology and feminism, she is rated on her performative skills. The 'original' model is Dr Joyce Brothers, the first 'star' therapist of daytime TV. The therapist is inserted *deus ex machina*, usually, into the third or fourth segment of a show. According to an interview (21 June 1994) with executive producer Rose Mary Henri of *Sally*, therapists are chosen for their ability to relate emotionally to the guests and audience. Feminine, colourful clothing is prescribed. Their style is somewhere between that of the old medicine show 'doctor' hawking his quick remedy and that of the hero who comes to the rescue in an old-time melodrama.

Carle has replaced Brothers as the prototypical therapist on talk shows in the 1990s. Acknowledging her debt to Brothers, Carle has done more than 100 talk shows in the past five years. Unlike Brothers, she has a degree not in psychology but in organizational studies. Her consulting firm specializes in communication, and she has advised IBM and the New York City government. Having written no books, she self-promoted herself onto talk shows by means of a video infomercial she sent to the producers. Once she appeared on *Geraldo*, her career took off. Recompense is exposure for her and her firm; she maintains that she does the work because she 'cares'. Given format time constraints (a therapist averages two minutes per guest), Carle argues that she does not do 'therapy' on the shows but gives 'therapeutic tips'.[23]

According to Henri, Carle is considered 'an excellent TV therapist' in the industry because 'she can emotionally identify with the guests and speak a simple jargon-free therapy'. Secunda, who is more measured in performance and language, is described less enthusiastically as 'formal'. One can perhaps conclude that part of Naomi Wolf's problem in her appearance as an expert on *Oprah*'s getting-to-the-altar programme was that Pat Allen outperformed her with quick upbeat statements, use of the inclusive 'we', direct address to the audience, and expansive gestures. But all the therapists can neatly offer tentative solutions within their allotted minutes.

A typical performance entails the therapist's interacting with the guests while turning to the audience to put a therapeutic point across. For example, after hugging and stroking the crying wife in the previously mentioned programme on affairs, Carle with intense emotion asks the audience: 'What about the other party? What about the spouse? What if the other party finds out? All we have been hearing about is: me, me, me.' Applause erupts. We see close-ups of the approving women in the audience who have been cheated on. Pleased by their reaction to her performance, Carle continues: 'One of things we have to do is to take that "m" in me and turn it around to "w" in we.' More enthusiastic applause. The dual performative style undercuts the authenticity of the therapist's interaction with her 'patients'. Her gestures are ultimately an 'act' in that her object is to reach the larger viewing audience. Carle represents a crass caricature of the productive power involved in any authoritative claim as to what is *correct* femininity or the *truth* in regard to mental happiness on talk shows. She, as so many like her, evokes the 'we' of feminism, effacing social difference and the implicit power involved in defining an all-inclusive category.

Although the established media would attack Carle's astute use of 'sound bites' as pandering to the lowest emotions, I argue that her method is an example of classic show-womanship. It is naive to believe that there can be authenticity on national TV, a discourse on which the daytime talk shows trade. ... Viewers do not automatically look upon the therapist as genuine. We may cringe at the callous use of a woman guest's private pain for public promotion, but talk shows are not traditional therapy. They are shows.

The therapist is not the only performer. Unlike medicine shows and vaudeville, everyone performs on talk shows. They are closer to public performances of personal narratives of emotional pain, frustration and recovery. The guests and audience members do not come as naive to the TV arena. Audience members primp in the rest-room upon arrival to look 'good' if the camera catches them. Before the taping they play musical chairs as they shift seats, in order to get as close as they can to the host and the microphone. They vie to ask questions. They have watched the programmes and have absorbed many of the conventions. They call the hosts by first names. Generally, they know what are permissible questions and behaviour (many are savvy enough to ask their questions straight to the camera). They have thought out their narratives beforehand. They speak the language of talk shows and therapy. For example, many elderly women in the *Donahue* audiences seem prepared for the host's game of flirting and attempt to top him by embarrassing him with their forwardness.

A *Sally* programme on 23 February 1994 was stopped when a husband confessed his affairs to his wife, but it was the wife's decision to resume taping. Asked by Sally why she wants it to continue, the woman says, 'I must stop and realize that my husband must love me to come on the show and tell everybody that [applause] he is sorry and that he wants to try and make our relationship and our marriage work.' It was an occasion when actions and beliefs could affirm the importance of their lives before a 'jury' numbered in millions. With daytime talk shows, we are caught between anger at the exploitation of people's emotions for profit and awe at this venue for testimonials where average women elect to perform and are validated and empowered by their performances.

Talk's Psychic Structure: The Feminist Consciousness-raising Group

It is not the courtroom but the consciousness-raising group that is the logic of the daytime talk shows. Patricia Mellencamp argues: 'It's not too far-fetched to imagine daytime talk as the electronic syndicated version of consciousness-raising groups of the women's movement.' For her, they represent a shift away from the arcane worlds of medicine, psychiatry and law, 'away from the experts and toward self-help, away from individuality and toward a group or collective mentality'.[24]

Gloria-Jean Masciarotte points out that a 1966–67 outline of the rules of consciousness-raising 'could form the production notes for Phil Donahue or Oprah Winfrey's shows':

The 'bitch session' cell group

- A. Ongoing consciousness expansion
    1. Personal recognition and testimony
    2. Personal testimony methods
        - a. Going around the room with key questions on key topics
        - b. Speaking out experience at random
        - c. Cross-examination
    3. Relating and generalizing individual testimony
- B. 'Starting to stop' – overcoming repressions and delusions ... daring to share one's experience with the group.[25]

Consciousness-raising groups have always been a hybrid: part therapy and part political activism. When *Donahue*, the prototype feminine-issues daytime talk show, began in 1967, consciousness-raising groups were evolving from a political organizing tool to an arena where women shared personal information and discovered commonalities.[26] The groups and even their talk-show incarnation have been held together by empowering women through collectively constructing self-esteem.

'Self-esteem' has been attacked by academic feminists as an empty concept that daytime talk shows use to avoid more complex problems, such as social repression.[27] Yet self-esteem remains central for the feminist therapy movement. Jana Sawicki in her claim for Foucauldian feminism argues that such criticism reveals a lack of awareness of the class and gender bias involved in political awareness: 'A principal aim of feminism has been to build women's self-esteem – the sense of confidence and identity necessary for developing an appositional movement.'[28]

Daytime talk shows have taken this mission of feminism one step further in the 1980s and 1990s. What neither Mellencamp nor Masciarotte takes note of is the degree to which talk shows avoid critical analysis of the context of male power. Central to the consciousness-raising group of feminism is a form of political education. According to feminist psychologist Diane Kravetz, 'Understanding the nature of female oppression in a sexist society has been essential for assessing needs, establishing goals, and providing alternative programs and services.' Consciousness-raising groups are where 'institutional structures and social norms, as well as individual attitudes and behaviors, provide the framework for analysis'.[29] They have moved from political groups to emotional 'support' groups in the language of the 1980s and 1990s. The shows mirror this depoliticization in focusing on the individual and the proactive nature of humanist therapy in understanding cultural malaise. Their analysis takes place in a historical and institutional vacuum, preferring the narratives of virtue and transcendence over the negativism and complexity of social analysis. This sensibility underlines Donahue's epiphany about being a homemaker in his biography: 'I don't know how the hell they [women] do it. My fantasies about "my four sons" have been lowered, and my consciousness raised.'[30] The shows' sense of consciousness-raising has to do with women's day-to-day experiences and how individual women can immediately effect changes rather than with a more detached view of the political origins of the experiences.

Much like the consciousness-raising groups, the shows range from cognitive-oriented discussions, as in rational emotive therapy, to a more personal, emotional sharing. Although the consciousness-raising process involves discovering the social or external roots of those experiences related to living in a sexist environment, the shows avoid clear social categories, such as economic power or even the patriarchy. They phobically avoid male bashing, doing at most one or two openly feminist topics a season. As a result, their critique of masculine power is always implied and rarely stated. It is primarily through programming – woman as a social category, the value of lived experiences, and the nonhierarchical structure – that programme makers convey the shows' feminism.

Because the shows are public arenas they do not evoke the intimacy and thoroughness of therapy or even consciousness-raising groups. But because of their ties to a social ideology such as feminism, their discursive structure involves testimonials rather than confessions. Here, feminism becomes more a secular religion than a political practice. The testimonial or witnessing has a long history in American fundamentalism and media evangelism.[31] And it has been reinvigorated in the 12-step movement, a secular model of witnessing. The original religious sense of the practice means the public testimony given by Christian witnesses to Christ and his saving power. Within evangelicalism the act of standing up and speaking one's religious experience is a social obligation – done without regard for personal safety and comfort.[32] The feminism that underlies the daytime talk shows has changed the logic of therapy: women are no longer passive sufferers but, rather, witnesses to the power of overcoming oppression. This extends the role that witnessing has played in women's history, beginning with abolition and then extending to suffrage and temperance.[33]

Masciarotte argues that 'the talk show's subject is not an ego-centered version of the talking cure in which the free flow of the subject's voice echoes back strong individual boundaries. But rather talk shows construct a serial spectacle of "I"s.'[34] The transgression or problem is no longer a sign of individual shame; instead, it is part of a larger problem and the individual's experience becomes one of many examples.

Like Christians overcoming evil through faith, the women in the daytime talk show audience attest the power of the individual and the feminine community by speaking their individual experience of the evils of social subordination and testify to their strength or survival to their community. The pre-taping audiences in which I have participated have the feel of a congregation. The women interact as friends exchanging views, compliments and intimacies as if they are part of a larger ethos.

Consider a programme devoted to HIV-positive men and women (*Oprah*, 17 February 1994). The project becomes the reconciliation of an HIV-positive daughter and her estranged mother. Not only does the programme present a formerly homophobic mother who supported her dying son, but also audience members who are HIV-positive get up one by one and testify to the understanding or lack of support of their families. In fact, the programme is a follow-up of a programme a week earlier in which a closeted HIV-positive guest, Brian, 'came out' on national TV (and to his family afterward). Asked why he did it by Oprah during the second programme, Brian responds that he had to 'unburden' himself and that he did it for others. And as the camera pans across a row of the audience, Oprah says: 'Brian is not alone. These are faces of the people who have tested HIV-positive. Some of them have been spat upon, yelled at, kicked out of classrooms, thrown out on the street and outright disowned by everybody that they loved. But they are here today to tell their stories of life – in this age of AIDS.' The issue is not gendered. The concept of healing through narratives and community remains the springboard for faith.

Feminism, like all ideologies, shares with religion a spirituality of community and a myth of utopian transcendence – a world of gender equality. Hence, daytime talk-show programmes on makeovers, superstar women in second careers and returning reformed guests from earlier programmes emphasize the ability to grow, change and transcend. It should come as no surprise that many of the non-therapy topics of the programmes have a quasi-religious sensibility: 'Random Acts of Kindness' (*Oprah*, 15 February 1994); 'People on Schindler's List' (*Donahue*, 28 February 1994); 'Visionaries' (*Sally*, 3 March 1994); 'Holocaust Heroes' (*Oprah*, 18 March 1994); 'Angels Who Have Altered People's Lives' (*Donahue*, 31 March 1994); 'Faith Healing' (*Geraldo*, 1 April 1994). For all talk shows are indicted as part of the 'new' culture of victimization, they are as caught up in affirming the ideals of familial love, the transcendence of emotional pain, and equality.

In *Life Stories* Charlotte Linde defines the individual narrative as an oral unit that is told over many occasions. Conventionally, it includes certain landmark events, such as choice of profession, marriage, divorce and religious or ideological conversion, if any. Both in its content (the items that it includes and excludes) and in its form (the structures that are used to make it coherent), it is the product of a member of a particular culture. ... Indeed, the notion of a 'life story' itself is not universal, but is the product of a particular culture.[35]

Each programme, then, becomes a variation on the feminine community as each guest brings her life story to the televized theatre. Robyn Warhol and Helena Michie suggest that such life stories are central to the 12-step programmes and the concept of recovery – a process on which talk shows draw for their therapeutic logic. Whereas Alcoholics Anonymous looks to the frame provided by Bill W. and his story of alcoholism and recovery as the frame for alcoholics' own stories, daytime talk-show guests and audi-

ence look to the long tradition of melodrama and the long narrative tradition of mythic female virtue, victimization and transcendence.[36]
...

Conclusion

Essentially, daytime talk shows are not feminist; they do not espouse a
clearly laid-out political position for the empowerment of women. They
often champion women who deny themselves for the good of the family.
The shows do represent popular TV at its most feminist, nonetheless; they
articulate the frustrations of women's subordination in a 'man's world'.
They are not authoritarian in the way that TV traditionally displays the
therapeutic. They give a voice to normally voiceless women: working-class
women, housewives, lesbians, sexually active older women, among others.
What is important is that they speak for themselves and are valued for their
experience, even if their stories are highly prescribed. Moreover, the shows
represent a practical application of a central debate in cultural studies
through their employment of the therapeutic: the tension between theories
of power and control as described by Freud and Foucault and an active/
activist individual who has the capacity to think and disagree.

For daytime talk shows, we need to rewrite Foucault's theory of the
confession: the only credible interlocutor is a 'recovering' interlocutor, for
he or she too must testify to her or his weakness to belong to the community. For all their technological distance, the shows are about
belongingness – community in late capitalism. It is no wonder that Winfrey,
as a self-confessed victim of child abuse, drugs and self-hate, is the most
highly paid woman interlocutor. The private has become public. The personal is political. And the ability to confess publicly has become a sign of
power and control. Such public therapy is an ideology that combines the
negative hermeneutics of Freudian subjectivity with the affirmation of the
active individual within a shared community. And that tension is ultimately
the therapeutic power of talk on TV.

Notes

1. Mimi White (1992) *Tele-vising: Therapeutic Discourse in American Television*,
   p. 8. Chapel Hill: University of North Carolina Press.
2. Charles Guigon, paper presented as part of the Humanities Seminars at the
   University of Vermont, Burlington, VT, 27 October 1994, 3.

3. Michel Foucault (1977) *The History of Sexuality, Volume 1: An Introduction*, trans. Robert Hurley, pp. 61–2. New York: Pantheon.

4. For examples see Jana Sawicki (1991) *Disciplining Foucault: Feminism, Power and the Body*. New York: Routledge; and Isaac D. Balbus (1988) Disciplining women: Michel Foucault and the power of feminist discourse, in Jonathan Arac (ed.) *After Foucault: Humanistic Knowledge, Postmodern Challenges*, pp. 138–60. New Brunswick, NJ: Rutgers University Press.

5. Barnaby B. Barratt (1993) *Psychoanalysis and the Postmodern Impulse: Knowing and Being Since Freud's Psychology*, p. 190. Baltimore: Johns Hopkins University.

6. E.H. Erickson (1946) Ego development and historical change, *The Psychoanalytic Study of the Child*, vol. 2. New York: International Universities Press; and T.C. Kroeber (1964) The coping functions of the ego-mechanisms, in R.W. White (ed.) *The Study of Lives*. New York: Atherton Press.

7. Heinz Hartmann (1964) *Essays on Ego Psychology*, pp. 158–9. New York: International Universities.

8. Steven Starker (1989) *Oracle at the Supermarket: The American Preoccupation with Self-Help Books*, p. 112. New Brunswick: Transaction.

9. George C. Miller (1969) Psychology as a means of protecting human welfare, *American Psychologist*, 24: 1074.

10. Rachel T. Hare-Mustin (1983) An appraisal of the relationship between women and psychotherapy *American Psychologist*, 38: 593.

11. Starker, op cit., p. 113.

12. Janet Maslin (1993) In Dirty Laundryland, *New York Times*, 10 October, p. 9.1.

13. Anna Quinlan (1991) The human condition, *New York Times*, 2 May, p. A25.

14. Albert Ellis (1973) *Humanistic Psychotherapy: The Rational-Emotive Approach*, p. 3. New York: Julian Press.

15. Christopher Lasch (1978) *The Culture of Narcissism*, p. 10. New York: Norton.

16. Phillip Rieff (1987) *The Triumph of the Therapeutic: Uses of Faith After Freud*, p. 65. Chicago: University of Chicago Press.

17. Wendy Kaminer (1993) *I'm Dysfunctional, You're Dysfunctional: The Recovery Movement and Other Self-Help Fashions*, p. 38. New York: Vintage.

18. Susan Sturdivant (1980) *Therapy with Women: A Feminist Philosophy of Treatment*, p. 52. New York: Springer.

19. *American Psychologist* (1975).

20. Sturdivant op cit., 87.

21. Ann Kaplan (1992) Feminist criticism and television, in Robert Allen (ed) *Channels of Discourse, Reassembled*, p. 251. Chapel Hill: University of North Carolina.

22. Patricia Allen and Sandra Harmon (1994) *Getting to 'I Do'*. New York: William Morrow.

23. Warren Berger (1995) Childhood trauma healed while-u-wait, *New York Times*, 8 January, p. 33.

24. Patricia Mellencamp (1990) *High Anxiety: Catastrophe, Scandal, Age, and Comedy*, p. 218. Bloomington, IN: Indiana University Press.

25. Gloria-Jean Masciarotte (1991) C'mon girl: Oprah Winfrey and the discourse of feminine talk, *Genders*, 11: 91.

26. Judith Worell and Pam Remer (1992) *Feminist Perspectives in Therapy: An Empowerment Model for Women*, p. 101. Chichester: John Wiley.

27. Two examples are Janice Peck's attack on Winfrey's repeated use of her programme in her article 'Talk about racism: framing a popular discourse of race on Oprah Winfrey', in *Cultural Critique* (Spring 1994), p. 89. Also Vicki Abt, a sociology professor at Pennsylvania State University, has been quoted in the *New York Times* as saying: 'If you watch the talk show doctors, their advice is always a cliché, something about self-esteem.' See Warren Berger, op cit., 33.

28. Sawicki, op cit., 106.

29. Diane Kravetz (1980) Consciousness-raising and self help, in A.M. Brodsky and R.T. Hare-Mustin (eds) *Women and Psychotherapy: An Assessment of Research and Practice*, p. 268. New York: Guilford.

30. Phil Donahue and Co. (1979) *My Own Story: Donahue*, p. 109. New York: Simon & Schuster.

31. See Janice Peck (1993) Selling goods and selling God: advertising, televangelism and the commodity form, *Communication Inquiry*, 17(1): 5–24.

32. Walter Elwell (ed.) (1984) *Evangelical Dictionary of Theology*, p. 1175. Grand Rapids, MI: Baker Book House.

33. Nancy Hardesty (1984) *Women Called to Witness: Evangelical Feminism in the 19th Century*. Nashville, TN: Abington Press; and Barbara Epstein (1981) *The Politics of Domesticity: Women, Evangelism, and Temperance in Nineteenth Century America*. Middletown, CN: Wesleyan University Press.

34. Masciarotte, op cit., 86.

35. Charlotte Linde (1993) *Life Stories: The Creation of Coherence*, p. 11. New York: Oxford University Press.

36. Robyn Warhol and Helena Michie (1995) Twelve-step teleology: narratives of recovery/recovery as narrative, in S. Smith and J. Watson (eds) *Getting a Life: Everyday Uses of Autobiography in Postmodern America*. Minneapolis: University of Minnesota Press.

WHAT GIRLS WANT
THE INTERSECTIONS OF LEISURE AND POWER IN FEMALE COMPUTER GAME PLAY

17

Heather Gilmour

Once subordinate to other cultural forms, computer software, both pleasurable and practical, is moving from the margins to the centre of culture and industry. Yet all too often, women and girls have been left on the sidelines of the high-tech playing field. Software industry developers and researchers have become increasingly aware of this disproportion, and a wave of software targeting the girl market is now being produced amid widespread discussions about what it is that girls really want in computer games. Developed by companies committed to girls, a few of these products, such as Mattel's *Fashion Barbie* and Girl Games's *Let's Talk about ME!* and *Let's Talk about ME! Too*, recently attained considerable success in the marketplace, proving what many have long suspected: that girls represent a target audience with great potential. Still, instead of challenging those entrenched divisions between boys and girls as players of electronic games, the discourse around these products has unfortunately tended to strengthen the traditional divisions between genders. Like some of their less successful predecessors (such as Her Interactive's *McKenzie & Co.*), these products feature girl-coded topics such as dating, fashion, hairstyles and social protocols, leading both developers and consumers to conclude that 'good' software must be specifically gendered.

Thus, girls continue to be essentialized as emotional, highly social, neo-Victorian subjects while males are defined as competitive and technologically inclined – an old binary that has come to inform discussions about new technology. Here is how one journalist 'distilled' such information from various panels presented at the 1994 Computer Games Developers Conference:[1]

Men seem to like:	*Women seem to like*:
Repeating actions to get to the next level	Solving problems among characters
Action (shooting, running, jumping)	Storytelling and characters
Solving puzzles to overcome specific obstacles	Picking up clues and learning from characters in the game
Measuring their skills	Getting credit for trying
Turning off the sound	Using music to add to the fun
The challenge of negative comments from the game	Encouragement and support from the game
Lots of definite and rigid rules	Fewer, simpler, variable rules
Winning through competition and individual prowess	Winning through cooperation
Playing until someone wins	Quitting when they get bored

Such lists are commonplace not only in popular articles and from the proliferating educational panels at conferences and trade shows, but also in the research around electronic games. For example, Maria Klawa, a researcher of interactive games, concludes, 'Boys and girls use software and video games differently. Girls like characters and relationships between them, while boys like fast action.' Electronic Arts Kids spokesperson Catherine Wambach describes an interactive program that 'had an area where you could construct a character and playhouse. The boys could have cared less. The girls wanted to bring that character out, and bring it into physical reality. They'd spend hours on the pictures, houses and clay forms of those characters.'[2] Even when the evidence suggests the contrary, researchers provide explanations that seem designed to keep traditional binaries in place. For instance, the popularity of Nintendo's *Tetris* with female players would seem to counter the belief that women prefer character interaction, since this is a game of spatial relations with no characters. Yet, Dr. Gini Graham Scott, a sociologist commissioned by Nintendo to study this phenomenon, claims that *Tetris* causes women to experience an endorphin rush because it satisfies the feminine craving for order: 'It's the woman who handles the decor; it's usually the guy who messes things up.' Asserting that *Tetris* appeals to women's holistic ways of seeing things, Scott even ties the game's popularity to prehistoric gender behaviour. 'Men were the hunters – they focused on killing for survival; women were the gatherers – they see the whole picture.'[3] It is disturbing that essentializing explanations such as these originate with experts and then gain acceptance in the popular imagination.

Michel Foucault observed that juridical systems of power produce the subjects they subsequently come to represent. Indeed, software production and much current research have produced a girl consumer whose definition is only in opposition to a putative standard 'boy'. Such definitions can be as distorting for boys as they are for girls. It is difficult to reconcile boys' alleged disinterest in character development with the popularity of fantasy games like *Dungeons and Dragons* which, according to Patricia Marks Greenfield, 'involve complex characters with a medieval flavor who go on adventures together and meet a wide variety of circumstances. ... One distinguishing mark of this type of game is that there are so many more possible happenings and characters than in a traditional game.'[4] Additional counter-evidence can be provided by Multi-User Dungeons (MUDS) where players (mostly boys) develop elaborate character relationships and create environments – two activities stereotyped as female. In short, the gendered binary of assumed preferences in software says more about the ideologies and assumptions of researchers and developers who speculate on the topic than about any essential differences between the sexes, yet these specula-tions are recirculated back to consumers through advertising and popular journalism, encouraging kids to choose those products that are supposedly appropriate to their gender. It is not surprising, then, that such differences also appear even in the innovative studies of Yasmin Kafai, who analyses gender differences in games designed (rather than merely consumed) by girls and boys.[5]

This essay explores issues of socialization and gender around computers and computer games, and seeks to clarify how girls relate to interactive media. While not denying that differences between boys and girls do occur in their use of computers and games, I will argue that these differences are attributable to the cultural gendering of leisure and play, rather than to inherent biological differences. Historical discourses around leisure reveal that current 'discoveries' by researchers about girls' interests and play preferences are clearly linked to much older discussions about what con-stitutes appropriate feminine leisure activity. These considerations led me to test how gender differences around software are being actualized by chil-dren in three Los Angeles schools. My object was to do my own analysis of girls' behaviour with computers and then weigh my findings against pop-ular theories of what girls want in software. At the same time, I contextualize both current theories about girls and my own research within historical discourses around feminine leisure.

Continuities in the Discourse around Leisure

Any inquiry into computers and culture must observe the intersection of computers as they are used at school for educational purposes and at home as a leisure activity. This relationship is crucial because while boys and girls may sometimes use the computer in the classroom in similar ways, their leisure use is markedly different, and this discrepancy, in turn, influences classroom behaviour. Children's use of computers, then, has to be considered in both of these contexts.

Instead of viewing computer use in terms of the effects that a new technology has on society, I regard computer use as a social act, influenced by long-standing cultural beliefs about education, leisure and gender. In this sense, computers are not a force that drives the course of society or human behaviour, but objects that become embedded in elaborate cultural codes and social patterns. A review of the history of women, girls and leisure indicates that present-day patterns of computer game play are inflected by much older beliefs about feminine leisure.

Karla Henderson has theorized women's place in the history of leisure via a periodizing scheme that includes six eras from 1907 to the present. For Henderson, women's relationship to leisure was conceived differently in each period, and can be related to the dominant social ideologies of the time.[6] While I agree with Henderson's notion that discourses about gender and leisure must be located within broader ones about gender and culture, I see the relationships between leisure, gender and culture less as a series of separate eras than as a continuity of ideas about the contested nature of the feminine.

Henderson observes the historical invisibility of women in the literature about leisure, which she attributes to the assumption that men have traditionally been dominant in the public sphere, whereas women's roles have been confined to the private sphere. According to Henderson, discussions of girls and leisure have reinforced the notion that leisure ought to enhance girls' education as feminine subjects.[7] In other words, not only has the actual participation of females in leisure activities been governed by traditional conceptions of femininity, but these notions have also governed the production of discourse around the topic. There is some continuity between the literature on girls and computing today and historical discourses about girls and leisure. Although a great deal has been written about the implications of gender in the educational use of computers, much less has been written on girls' use of computers and software as leisure – and much of that tends to assume that girls' leisure preferences are skewed toward educational software. Much work remains to be done on girls' pleasures in leisure itself. Contemporary perceptions about gender and leisure, then, must be viewed as part of an ongoing discussion about how girls and boys ought to behave, and how it is proper for them to spend their time.

As has been abundantly remarked in research on gender and leisure, women have less free time than men, largely due to the conflation of public and private spheres for women, who often come home to a 'second shift' of work, whereas men in general associate time at home with leisure. Because girls are acculturated, in part, by observing their mothers' roles, some girls experience this time pressure at surprisingly early ages. Citing a 1910 study, Henderson claims that girls made fewer demands than boys for recreation, and thus were seen as less interested in it. She notes here, 'Further examination of this perception indicated that many girls as "little mothers" were so tired from their household tasks when they came to the playground that they had little energy to play.'[8] This perception still has relevance today, as Susan Shaw's studies of adolescents have shown: there is 'a statistically significant difference in obligatory and nonobligatory time between males and females, with females spending more time than males in obligatory activities. Females tend to spend more time than males at school, doing schoolwork at home, and doing chores.'[9]

The reigning discourse about girls' preferences in interactive entertainment submits that girls prefer cooperative games to competitive ones. This assertion is part of a much longer discussion. The late 1900s and early 1920s were periods when the importance of athletics was stressed for all children, including girls. As Henderson explains, however, girls' games and sports were considered to be properly group activities; team play and competition were downplayed. Girls and women of this period were encouraged to join clubs because they provided opportunities for members to work together, and group participation and cooperation were stressed.[10] Clearly, the notion that girls ought to be, or rather are, primarily social beings has become naturalized. Popular and academic discussions of what girls want in interactive media invariably highlight group play, cooperation and social interaction. Foucault has argued that discourses proliferate within certain power relationships. By enforcing an essentialist view of the female as social and group oriented (read: not intellectual and not independent), dominant discourses about interactive media continue to appeal to the same structures of power that have historically guided discussions of gender.

Method

The incorporation of ethnographic methods into cultural studies suggests a refusal to theorize female readers of culture monolithically, as well as a willingness to observe difference and lived experience. Several contemporary studies of female audiences have called on empirical or ethnographic methods: Marsha Kinder's *Playing with Power in Movies, Television, and Video Games*, Angela McRobbie's 'Dance and Social Fantasy', Janice Radway's *Reading the Romance* and Jackie Stacey's *Star-Gazing: Hollywood Cinema and Female Spectatorship*.[11] Informed by these approaches, my research method followed three paths: ethnographic observation in schools, a broad survey of students and follow-up interviews with teachers and students.

By first observing kids at school (a setting that is part of their daily lives, rather than an artificial environment like a laboratory or focus group), I was able to formulate questions that would guide my survey and interviews. I noted the behaviour of kids in computer classes, seeking to discover who asks questions, who is more aggressive or tentative with computers, who works with others and who works alone, and how students and teachers interact.

For the survey, I compiled a 22-item questionnaire ... and distributed it to 180 students (45 girls and 45 boys each at two different schools) to obtain an overview of their opinions, preferences and habits. While some of the conclusions I reached have been widely discussed in previous literature, others were surprising. The surveys were valuable insofar as they added a broader perspective and, I suspect, allowed greater candour. As a research tool, however, the survey is rooted in a social science methodology that looks for generalities, while I was primarily interested in the heterogeneous and local aspects of girls' experiences with computers.

Hence, in addition to these surveys, I interviewed a number of girls in greater depth to gain a fuller understanding of their opinions. Assuming that there would be some variations or contradictions between the spoken and written responses, I saw the interviews as one way of moving beyond the anonymity of the survey to locate individual responses within personal experience and social context.

Originally, I intended to work in three Los Angeles private schools with different demographics: Pilgrim School, the most ethnically diverse private school in the nation; the Sinai Akiba Academy, a Jewish private school that uses more interactive software than most; and Marlborough School, one of the oldest girls schools in Los Angeles. Although all three schools are private, there are striking differences in class between Marlborough and the others. Located in the wealthy Hancock Park neighborhood, Marlborough has a tuition of about $13,000 per year, more than double those of Pilgrim (which is situated in a multiracial neighbourhood near downtown Los Angeles) and Sinai Akiba (which is in a predominantly Jewish neighbourhood in Westwood). Whereas Marlborough is reputed to be the city's most prestigious school for girls, one that protects them from competition with boys who are presumably favoured by teachers, Sinai Akiba attempts to integrate the premises of Judaism with first-rate education for a homogeneous community, and Pilgrim strives for academic excellence while preparing an ethnically diverse population for college.

I chose to work in private schools for several reasons. First, while a number of studies of children and computer use have already been done in public schools, private schools have been for the most part neglected. Second, the demographics of private schools are more easily differentiated. Moreover, I found that private schools offered greater ease of access to kids, and far superior computer labs and software resources than were available in the LA Unified School District's schools, particularly since, according to a 1995–96 study by Quality Education Data, California ranked last nationally for number of students per computer.

At Pilgrim and Sinai Akiba, the teachers were forthcoming, and I was able to watch and speak with students as much as I liked. Despite their initial enthusiasm, the school administrators at Marlborough finally decided that my research came at a bad time of year for their students. Nonetheless, I was able to interview a Marlborough student and her mother at length.

My research in the schools allowed me to study kids from a variety of ethnic and class backgrounds. Further work remains to be done by observing kids in their homes since, as mentioned earlier, computers and software are used in both educational and recreational ways, and each of these patterns of use informs and has impact on the other.

Research Findings

Observation

At the Sinai Akiba Academy (K–8), Marilyn, the computer teacher, makes an effort to integrate computer classes with other subjects. There are no programming classes. Kids use educational games, in addition to typing, math, art and word-processing programs.

Rick, the computer teacher at the Pilgrim School (K–12), places more emphasis on applications such as drawing and word-processing programs because he finds it hard to integrate existing interactive software into other teachers' syllabi. The Pilgrim School also offers optional programming classes.

My first impression from observation at both schools was that kids act much more traditionally than I would have thought. It seemed that girls were more hesitant to work their way through interactive software and programming exercises, and stopped frequently to ask questions, whereas boys seemed more independent. The more I watched, however, the less convinced I became of this finding. Some girls, particularly if they are familiar with a program, are quite aggressive, and some boys ask many questions. I noted that traditionally gendered behaviour is related to what computers and software are used for, and in what settings, rather than being a function of computers or software as such. In other words, it is more instructive to look at how a technology is used within a social context than to draw conclusions about technology without concern for its actual use.

At the Pilgrim School, writing and drawing applications are often used for class exercises, as in one first-grade project that involved drawing sea creatures and writing sentences about them. Both boys and girls had many questions about typing, spelling, and opening and closing their documents. The students' writing, however, strongly reflected traditional notions of gender. Many boys wrote sentences that implied action or violence, such as: 'I draw a hammershark. He eats fish in the ocean', 'The whales are surrounding a pile of fish and trying to eat them', and 'The sharks are surrounding a whale. The whales are jumping in and out of the water.' Most of the girls' sentences described their affective relationship to the creatures they had drawn, such as, 'My whale is nice. I love whales, do you?', 'I love whales' and 'I like whales, they are pretty.' This class, then, expressed more traditional gender behaviour in terms of the content of their projects than in their approach to the computer. I noticed a similar dynamic in Marilyn's third-grade class at Sinai Akiba. For one project, students made stationery that included their names and clip art. Although boys and girls seemed equally comfortable with the software used here, most girls selected images of unicorns, fairies or ballerinas, while most boys chose sports images.

Much popular and academic literature argues that girls prefer to use computers in pairs or groups, and boys to work alone, yet I found that both boys and girls pair up and work alone with about equal frequency. Most pairs were same-sex. Sometimes, pairs were composed of one leader, who understood the program, and one follower, who needed help, and this pattern was true for boys and girls.

Gender differences are much more apparent in the Pilgrim School's programming classes. Invariably, many more boys than girls are enrolled – usually in a ratio of about four to one. The girls I observed were relatively silent, while boys tended to engage Rick in discussion about their assignments and computing in general. For example, in Rick's grades 9 through 12 Pascal class, several boys involved Rick in a discussion about how they might hack their way into Rick's locked files. These results are not especially surprising, since gender differences become more pronounced toward adolescence (kids in the programming classes are much older than the first and third graders I described earlier) and programming is perceived, like math and science, as a male-coded activity.

In short, my observations suggested a number of questions. To what extent is the popular perception by researchers that girls are less comfortable or aggressive with computers a product of researchers' biases? How would 'aggressiveness' be quantified? Is 'aggressiveness' the same as computer competence, as is usually assumed? As one of my survey respondents explained, 'Girls are much better at computers because girls understand technology more. They don't just rush in putting things together.' Girls' responses to computers and software seem to be more strongly determined by how computers are used than by attitudes about properties inherent in the technology itself.

Marlborough School

Although my interaction with Sharon (pseud.) and her mother was methodologically unlike the rest of my research, I [use it . . .] to point up the way that class inflects the relationship between gender and technology. I contend that Sharon's and her mother's attitudes about the relative lack of importance of computer education at school have their roots in a class privilege that regards knowing the nuts and bolts of computing as non-essential to the type of professions into which it is assumed these girls will eventually enter.

A great uproar has been caused by the experiences of Marlborough students on the Internet. Girls have been caught using school computers to download pornographic images and engage in racy conversations with men in chat rooms. This concern with the invasion of the protected space of the private school by a questionable public influence has a long history in the development of communications technologies. At Marlborough, the stakes in controlling what goes on within the school gates are all the higher because of the upper-class ethos of the school. A recent issue of *Ultra Violet,* the school paper, contains a two-page special report on the Internet, titled 'Sex, Lies, and the Internet'. Some contributors were repelled by the men they encountered on the Internet and shared their experiences as cautionary tales. 'Have you ever been on-line and received an instant message that says, "Wanna talk dirty?" from some guy named "HotPimp" or "JoBlo?" Well, I have, and it makes me sick.'[12] Another writer challenged Marlborough's new list of rules for Internet use, some of which are: 'Attention to grammar, spelling, and arid content in an E-mail message is important, as you want individuals who receive your message to see your best work and respond intelligently', 'Answer E-mail in a timely manner', 'NEVER impersonate someone else on-line. Further, allowing others to believe you are an adult when you are not is wrong and potentially dangerous,' and 'Marlborough School does not sanction the use of the Internet to explore resources that are pornographic, violent, or abusive. Use of the system for these purposes, at school or at home, will result in revocation of ALL privileges and possible disciplinary action.' Like Sharon in our interview, the author of the *Ultra Violet* article found these rules condescending and inappropriate, 'as if Marlborough girls were a group of immature children who were computer illiterate'.[13] The issue of what a 'Marlborough girl' is or is not lies at the root of both arguments. The administrators' rules express their anxiety that the prized internal order of the school might be disturbed, especially when exposed to the public realm of the Internet. The students' responses imply that because the girls are part of this internal order, administrators need not restrict them; they know better than to behave in a manner that would discredit the school. Clearly, the concern for upper-class status evidenced by the discourses around computers at Marlborough is quite different from the more pragmatic approach taken at Pilgrim and Sinai Akiba.

While it was irrelevant to consider gender differences in the recreation use of computers at a girls school like Marlborough, this issue did arise at the other two institutions. For example, the computer teacher at Sinai Akiba expressed concern that her attention was unfairly distributed, since boys ask for help during free time while playing games or exploring the Internet, whereas girls do not make as many similar demands. She felt that this situation represents a closed loop in which boys who ask for her time learn more, grow more interested and ask for still more attention. This description brings Henderson's observations to mind; although referring to the 1910 study, the following statement speaks directly to Marilyn's fear: 'A "chicken-and-egg" situation seemed to create these acknowledged constraints on females' play behavior. Because females made fewer demands, they received less assistance. A lack of supervision and instruction resulted in a lack of involvement and thus, fewer demands.'[14]

Indeed, most of the boys who responded to my survey said that they play computer games daily or every other day from a half-hour to an hour on average; most girls play much less – about once a week for 15 minutes. This behaviour is, of course, overdetermined by such factors as gender coding, lack of appealing software for girls and lack of marketing channels. Yet, beyond these issues, many of the girls I surveyed responded in ways such as 'I have too many things to do' or 'I'm too busy' when asked how often they play games. One 12-year-old girl suggested that I improve my survey by choosing the word 'use' instead of 'play'. She said that, as the oldest child in her household, she is expected to help supervise her three younger sisters and assist with housework. This leaves her little time to play, she said, although she does use the computer for homework. Part of the reason for these responses may be that girls and boys also have different perceptions of how much free time they have and how they are supposed to spend it. Clearly, answers about how many hours per week they play games are as heavily influenced by what kids believe is an acceptable answer as by what the empirical number actually is.

Computers in the Domestic Sphere

The home can be seen as a place where the use of computers for leisure and education intersect. In my survey, most boys and girls used their home computer for both entertainment and homework. Lily Shashaani reports that in her study of 1,700 secondary school children, 68 per cent of boys and 56 per cent of girls have access to a computer at home. The percentage of male students as primary users of the computer, however, was twice that of female students, and a higher percentage of boys said that they had first learned about computers at home.[15] In my research, the percentage of home-computer owners is much higher – all but one of the kids at the Sinai Akiba Academy had a computer at home, as did the majority of Pilgrim School children. These are private schools, which are typically attended by children of a higher economic bracket, whereas Shashaani's study was of public schools. Nevertheless, in my study, when a home computer was available, boys were the more frequent users, particularly for leisure and Internet activities...

According to Shashaani, substantial stereotyping of computers as the purview of boys and men occurs at home.

Studies have shown that parents, especially fathers, encourage their sons more than their daughters to learn about computers. Parents most often purchase computers and computer games for their sons, and not for their daughters. ... [A] lack of female-user role models at home may influence girls' self-confidence that learning and working with computers are difficult tasks, and that computers are in 'the masculine domain'.[16]

Likewise, Ann Colley cites a recent meta-analysis of 172 studies of the different socialization of boys and girls by parents which 'found that the only area which showed a significant effect for both mothers and fathers was encouragement of sex-typed activities and perceptions of sex-stereo-typed characteristics, where parents emphasize gender stereotypes in play and in household tasks'.[17] Indeed, none of the girls I surveyed said that they had been bought a computer or cartridge entertainment system, while for many of the boys, this was the case. Moreover, many of my respondents said that their father or brother was their entrée into computer and software use. Fathers and brothers were also mentioned as an important way in which kids keep up with new software developments. Only two of my respondents listed women as their initial link to computing or software. As David Morley has observed, the use of media within the home must be considered with respect to established patterns of gender behaviour within the family.[18] These patterns could have implications for girls' relationships to computers and software outside the home as well.

Computers in the classroom

Computers, then, represent a significant element of boys' leisure, while for girls they are a less important part of any free time. Extracurricular rela-tionships to computers and software extend into the classroom. Computers in educational uses perform, broadly, in two fashions. At times, they are used to run educational software that is integrated into wider class syllabi. Other computer classes, such as those in programming, are exercises in learning computer logic and critical thinking. The different uses to which computers may be put in schools complicate attempts to generalize or even theorize about gender in educational computing. According to Colley:

Computing is often associated with math or science, academic areas which are male-dominated. Indeed, children's attitudes to computing have been found to be similar to their attitudes to science and to be associated with attitudes to math. Although more enrollments in computer courses have been recorded for males, it has been pointed out that further scrutiny of the statistics shows that males outnumber females in programming courses, and that males spend more time programming than females, while similar numbers of males and females or even a majority of females is found when enrollments for other computing applications, especially word processing, are considered. Word processing can be regarded either as a computer application, or as an extension of typing, which is a female-dominated vocational skill and which has been stereotyped for females in studies of perceptions of school subjects.[19]

Colley's finding was partially upheld in my research. The association of computers with math and science was noted frequently. At the Pilgrim School, there were many more boys than girls in programming classes. One girl with whom I spoke said that boys are better at using computers because 'Men can relate better to machinery. They find machinery more interesting starting from bulldozers at age three up to hedge clippers at age thirty-five.' One boy surveyed wrote that boys were better at computers 'because boys are more nerds than girls'. On the other hand, many boys and girls responded that there is no correlation between gender and computer ability, and several thought it was sexist of me even to pose the question.

While teachers and students sometimes argue that there is no difference between boys' and girls' use of computers at school, it seems that some differences do exist. Educational software can exacerbate existing differences. Some educational software still employs the metaphors of traditional shoot-'em-up video games. In *Math Blaster*, one of the reward games is a classic arcade-style activity in which the player shoots space trash. In *Pilgrim Quest*, there are leisure areas where users can hunt or fish – after the fashion of traditional computer dexterity games. Research has shown that this type of activity is generally more appealing to boys than girls, presumably because of its similarity to games in which boys have previous expertise.[20] Also, in the popular educational games *Pilgrim Quest* and *Oregon Trail*, the few characters represented on-screen are male. As is often the case with entertainment software, even seemingly 'genderless' characters in educational software are conventionally male – for example, in *Word Attack III*, Mostly Chrome, a shiny sphere, is male. This bias, however subtle, only exacerbates an already existing inequity of experience and comfort with computers and computer software between girls and boys.

Social pressure forms another possible influence on girls' use of computers at school. As Colley notes, 'according to social learning theory, it is assumed that one major concern of females who participate in male-stereotyped areas of interest or achievement, in addition to beliefs concerning their lack of competence, is that they may be negatively rewarded because they are behaving in an unfeminine way'.[21] Indeed, the one real 'tomboy' I encountered in my research seemed rather an outsider from the girls' circle. This particular girl is extraordinarily competent with computers, uses several on-line services, e-mails, faxes, and plays a variety of flight simulation games. Her younger sister, however, was quick to define herself as 'exactly the opposite of my sister. I am not a tomboy.' This response may have as much to do with sibling rivalry as it does with perceptions of gender constraints, but it did point out that among many girls (and boys), it is often preferable to associate oneself with others who follow fairly traditional patterns of gender.

Given the stringent strictures of gender, particularly during youth, it is not surprising that many boys felt they were better at computers and computer games than girls – in a sense, they have to be. Considering the stakes in upholding masculinity, being a 'tomboy' is one matter, being a 'sissy' is a much more serious transgression. On the other hand, a number of boys surveyed answered that boys and girls are equal in terms of their ability – many of them wrote: 'We are all equal' or 'Boys and girls do equally well on the computer.' What was more surprising was that some girls believed that they were not only equal to but better than boys at using computers and games. While kids' attitudes toward computers frequently reflect traditional notions of gender, they sometimes challenge convention. These various responses must be located within larger cultural tensions. For numerous reasons, most boys have a relationship with computers and computing that most girls do not. At the same time, the responses from teachers and students indicate that there is an impulse toward gender equality. The traditional and the progressive, then, are simultaneously at play in behaviours and attitudes around computers.

Approaching Gender and Computing

My study revealed that the interplay between gender and the use of computers involves a negotiation between established orders and liberatory beliefs and behaviours that challenge convention. Before spending much time with kids, I had more utopian ideas about the ease with which gender might be transgressed. Yet despite cultural restraints, girls still express their belief in gender equality and have a wide range of preferences in software. Thus, what is definitive is that there is much more variety among girls than is typically assumed.

Precisely because of its institutional supports, Judith Butler challenges the category *woman* as grounds for theoretical pronouncements.

If one 'is' a woman, surely that is not all one is; the term fails to be exhaustive, not because a pregendered 'person' transcends the specific paraphernalia of its gender, but because gender is not always constituted coherently or consistently in different historical contexts, and because gender intersects with racial, class, ethnic, sexual, and regional modalities of discursively constituted entities. As a result, it becomes impossible to separate out 'gender' from the political and cultural intersections in which it is invariably produced and maintained.[22]

The same argument applies to 'girls'. My study shows that girls at Pilgrim School (which privileges fairly conventional approaches to computing) have a different experience with computers than girls at Marlborough School (where computer use intersects with upper-class ideologies and class anxieties). The experience of girls at Sinai Akiba (where computer use is often meshed with Judaism, as when students use software to make greeting cards for Jewish holidays) is an example of yet another social context that inflects computer use. Girls' use of computers must therefore be situated within heterogeneous cultural factors.

Given the social strictures placed on gender, particularly in relationship to computing, it is simplistic to say that girls can just transcend gender. In this sense, the question becomes not one of dispensing with the notion of gender entirely, but rather of how to mutate its directives. Shaw claims that involvement in non-traditional activities especially benefits girls.

For adolescent girls, the need for activities which encourage independence and autonomy may be particularly great. ... Since girls live in a male-dominated world, it may be important for them to challenge traditional 'feminine' roles through participation in nontraditional activities. Indeed, this would seem to be consistent with the notion of identity development being enhanced through challenging activities and through the exploration of alternative ideas and alternative identities.[23]

According to Henderson, leisure activities provide the space for such resistance: 'If leisure experiences represent situations of choice and self-determination, they also provide opportunities for individuals to exercise personal power, and such power can be used as a form of resistance to imposed gender constraints or restrictions.'[24] Yet the problem remains: given the available software, girls have little choice but to learn to negotiate texts that are constructed along highly traditional lines of gender. Even the newest software designed by women for girls hails them as future subjects within this essentialist system.

Girls may be inscribed within powerful circles of the social, but within those circles they maintain their heterogeneity. The only way to approach gender and computing, practically or theoretically, then, is to resist that which works to restrict feminine behaviour, pleasure and self-definition, and to encourage that which presses beyond conventional notions of the feminine as a monolithic category. Donna Haraway formulates a utopian cyborg world in which science and technology can provide fresh sources of power as old dichotomies are called into question.[25] Only when it dispenses with traditional relations of power can computer software begin to fulfil Haraway's vision. Producing products that girls would enjoy becomes, from this standpoint, a pleasure, not a problem.

. . .

Notes

1. Russel DeMaria (1994) Battle of the sexes, *Electronic Entertainment*, September: 34.
2. Maria Klawa and Catherine Wambach, quoted in Dana Blankenhorn (1994) Research on kids' software use complete, *Clarinet Electronic News Service*, 5 May.
3. Gini Graham Scott, quoted in Janice Crony (1994) Boys' club, *PlayRight*, 1(2): 20–4.
4. Patricia Marks Greenfield (1984) *Mind and Media: The Effects of Television, Video Games, and Computers*, p. 105. Cambridge, MA: Harvard University Press.
5. Yasmin B. Kafai (1996) Gender differences in children's constructions of video games, in Patricia M. Greenfield and Rodney R. Cocking (eds) *Advances in Applied Developmental Psychology*, vol. II. Norwood, NJ: Ablex Publishing.
6. Karla A. Henderson (1993) A feminist analysis of selected professional recreation literature about girls/women from 1907–1990, *Journal of Leisure Research*, 25(2): 165–81.
7. Ibid., p. 166.
8. Ibid., p. 170.
9. Susan Shaw (1995) Leisure and identity formation in male and female adolescents: a preliminary examination, *Journal of Leisure Research*, 27(3): 245.
10. Henderson, op cit., p. 171.
11. Marsha Kinder (1991) *Playing with Power in Movies, Television, and Video Games: From Muppet Babies to Teenage Mutant Ninja Turtles*. Berkeley: University of California Press; Angela McRobbie (1984) Dance and social fantasy, in Mica Nava and Angela McRobbie (eds) *Gender and Generation*. New York: Macmillan; Janice Radway (1984) *Reading the Romance: Women, Patriarchy, and Popular Literature*. Chapel Hill: University of North Carolina

Press; Jackie Stacey (1994) *Star-Gazing: Hollywood Cinema and Female Spectatorship*. London: Routledge.

12. Christina Gregory (1995) Talkin' dirty on-line, *Ultra Violet*, 26(3): 8.
13. Moye Ishimoto (1995) Disagreeing with the computer agreement, *Ultra Violet*, 26(3): 8.
14. Henderson, op cit., p. 171.
15. Lily Shashaani (1994) Gender differences in computer experience and its influence on computer attitudes, *Journal of Educational Computing Research*, 11(4): 349.
16. Ibid., p. 362.
17. Ann Colley (1995) Gender effects in the stereotyping of those with different kinds of computing experience, *Journal of Educational Computing Research*, 12(1): 20.
18. David Morley (1986) Family Television: *Cultural Power and Domestic Leisure*. London: Routledge.
19. Colley, op cit., 20.
20. See Rosemary E. Sutton (1991) Equity and computers in the schools: a decade of research, *Review of Educational Research*, 61(4): 475.
21. Colley, op cit., 20.
22. Judith Butler (1990) *Gender Trouble: Feminism and the Subversion of Identity*, p. 3. London: Routledge.
23. Shaw, op cit., 247.
24. Karla A. Henderson (1994) Perspectives on analyzing gender, women, and leisure, *Journal of Leisure Research*, 26(2): 15.
25. Donna Haraway (1991) *Simians, Cyborgs, and Women: The Reinvention of Nature*, p. 61. New York: Routledge.

GLOSSARY

alternative media Various partisan radio stations, magazines, newspapers and other media systems produced by and about and usually for subcultures, social movements or political interests outside the mainstream that, typically, reject established values or doctrines. Usually the goal is communicating about the community's goals and philosophy, so they produce little or no profit. Niche media, in contrast, are aimed at narrowly defined but potential profitable segments of a market. Some scholars emphasize how alternative media enable groups to express and maintain their resistance to dominant messages. Others warn of recuperation, when dominant powers or authorities, rather than merely taking over or incorporating alternative voices, make limited concessions to oppositional voices and thereby coopt them.

audiences People – individuals or, more properly, differentiated groups – who receive mass communications. The term focuses on their social and interpretative work, as distinguished from markets or consumers, the role emphasized by advertisers or media producers. Indeed, while some early work on audiences understood them to be relatively passive, current scholarship often focuses on how audiences make meaning, and thus conceive of audiences as necessarily active.

censorship Process for blocking, withholding, regulating or deleting part or all of some message, because it is deemed offensive or illegal. Often refers to state actions to prevent dissemination of a message or to group actions to block access.

class Formation comprising people with similar relationship to the means of production in that society and therefore with similar material, social and cultural position. In consequence, societies are stratified – property ownership, power, status and material rewards are unequally distributed across classes. In the nineteenth century, the German philosopher Karl Marx argued that different forms of social consciousness correspond to class position.

closure or **ideological closure** The term refers to a strategy or feature of a text that encourages audience members to make sense of it (fictional or factual narratives) in a particular way.

commercialization The process by which the design, production and marketing of products, including cultural products, is made popular in order to increase profits. Although some early notions stressed how gearing cultural products to the 'least common denominator' would maximize profit, more recent scholars emphasize that media producers may be more interested in certain niche markets.

cultivation analysis Assumes that repeated, long-term exposure to consistent messages will shape heavy viewers' attitudes and expectations about the world. Exposure to 'deviant' definitions of reality shown on television will lead to perceptions that such views are 'normal'. Cultural Indicators research undertaken by George Gerbner and associates at the University of Pennsylvania in the USA found a 'mainstreaming' or 'homogenizing' trend, such that the kinds of differences that one would expect to find based on other identity factors are overridden by media content.

cultural capital Making a distinction between economic, social, symbolic and cultural capital, the French sociologist Pierre Bourdieu defined the latter as the rewards and status that accrue from having knowledge of 'high' cultural products or access to the dominant cultural institutions.

cyberspace Coined by science fiction novelist William Gibson, this now refers to virtual social spheres created and sustained through electronic technologies. In cyberspace or virtual reality, people's activities and relationships are conducted through computer-mediated communication. So-called cyberfeminists critique the differences in power between men and women in cyberspace.

decoding The process of interpreting, or making meaning of, messages. Building on Frank Parkin's theory of meaning systems, various media scholars have pointed out that audiences may decode messages or texts (could be published articles, advertising, broadcast programming, films, music videos) at least three different ways: first, in the way that the texts' producers intended, resulting in the 'preferred' reading; second, they may engage in oppositional decoding, when they understand producers' intentions but produce a very different reading; third, a negotiated decoding results when the reader acknowledges the legitimacy of the dominant codes, but adapts the meaning to her or his own specific situation or social condition.

determinism The term refers to any theory positing a single cause for a large set of outcomes or transformations. Technological determinism largely attributes large-scale social, cultural and economic changes to technology or technological change; economic determinism posits that economic status explains how and why people act and think.

dichotomous thinking 'Either/or' ways of thinking that divides up phenomena (people as 'black' or 'white', as 'good' or 'bad', 'right' or 'wrong') into two opposite or 'bipolar' sets. Some linguists had posited that meaning is necessarily generated in opposition, but feminists criticize binary logic for suppressing ambiguities and overlaps, and for distorting multiplicity. None the less, bifurcated thinking exists. Although the terms vary in historically and culturally specific contexts, 'masculinity' (as the traits, characteristics, values and/or a particular way of looking that are said to be right or normative for men, necessary to be manly) continues to be contrasted with 'femininity' (as the traits, characteristics, values and/or a particular way of looking that is said to be right or normative for women, necessary to be womanly).

discourse   Originally, this was a linguistic concept referring to a set of written or oral utterances. As used in cultural studies, discourse refers to a set of statements that offer a way of representing knowledge of a particular topic. The French cultural historian Michel Foucault's point was that discourse produces the objects of knowledge; nothing has significant meaning outside discourse.

effects theory   (or **media effects tradition**) Idea (usually discredited) that certain media texts, more or less uniformly, directly produce consistent reactions. In its most exaggerated mechanistic form, when strong effects are said to very directly and immediately result among passive audiences, may be known as the 'magic bullet' or 'hypodermic needle' theory. British cultural studies scholar Stuart Hall proposes 'media effectivity' to refer to a broader conception of media's role in long-term social and cultural reproduction.

feminization   The process by which an occupation, institution or discourse becomes marked and thereby changed by the increasing presence of women. Examples of 'feminized' media occupations include the fields of magazine publishing, advertising and public relations, which some have referred to as 'pink' or 'velvet' ghettos. Women often form the majority of workers in these fields, thus allegedly causing status and salaries to decrease. This, in turn, results in men leaving the occupation, creating a further decrease in occupational status and pay. Feminization is also used to refer to efforts made by market-driven newspaper publishers to attract larger numbers of female readers by 'softening' or 'feminizing' news discourses so that they are more appealing to this audience (for example, more human interest-based stories, news about family, fashion, health and education).

feminism   A political philosophy and social–political movement. In some sense it is marked by an emancipatory concern to explain and overcome subordination and oppression of all kinds; it takes gender as a fundamental mechanism by which the world is structured. Among other feminisms, liberal feminists argue for equality across the sexes: equal rights, equal pay and equal access to education. Radical feminists generally celebrate women's distinctive culture, morality and psyche and argue that the gender is *the* central form of subordination throughout the world. Socialist feminists insist that patriarchy and capitalism are either single or dual systems of oppression that (re)produce women's subordination. Postmodern feminists reject the 'grand narrative' of 'feminism' (patriarchy as the root cause of inequality), arguing that gendered meanings and identities are plural, fluid and therefore contestable. Distinctions and continuities are sometimes offered between 'first wave' feminism, referring to the suffrage movements (in both the USA and UK) in the 1870–1920 period and 'second wave' feminism, referring to the women's movements of the 1960s and 1970s. Today, a new generation of 'third wave' feminists is now embracing a feminism marked by a commitment to a multiracial, multicultural and multisexual form of political activism.

frames US sociologist Erving Goffman has argued that people use certain 'principles of organization' to mark off and explain events, in order to understand and respond to social situations. Media frames, then, are routines or principles of selection used by media professionals to organize and package output, such as news stories. Some sociologists have emphasized how, over time, the hierarchical framing rules of inclusion and exclusion that are typically, tacitly and perhaps even unavoidably part of journalists' work acquire a natural, commonsense status.

gender Social construct referring to the cultural differentiation of male and female and, according to contemporary thought, the term for meaningful (as opposed to minor physiological) ways to discuss women and men, and differences between women and men.

genre Standard type of output of a particular medium, such as radio talk shows or science fiction movies that, by virtue of their content, conventions or aesthetics, audiences recognize as such. Many media organizations produce and market their content in terms of genres. Specific types of content are typical of particular media genres. An audience's prior knowledge of the structures and rules of different media genres conditions their expectations. Some genres are associated with a single gender (i.e. soap operas are for women; football games are for men).

hegemony The process by which groups in power secure (including by use of media) the consent or submission of less powerful groups in society. Italian political theorist Antonio Gramsci, trying to explain the rise of fascism in 1930s, argued that gaining this consent rests on presenting the class interests and definitions of 'reality' of the powerful as if they are 'natural' and 'universal'. When successful, the interests of these groups are rendered commonsensical. However, hegemony is never total and is always contested. To remain powerful, élites must make compromises and negotiate their position with less powerful groups in order to maintain their consent. As a result, it is always possible for alternative interests and definitions of reality to be mobilized counter-hegemonically or oppositionally.

homophobia Hatred of homosexuality or of lesbians and gay men. Homophobia is typically linked to a cultural fear of homosexuality – that it threatens or undermines the 'legitimacy' and cultural dominance of heterosexuality, patriarchy and the nuclear family.

identity A term referring to the ways in which we make sense of ourselves as belonging to a particular gender, 'race', nationality, sexuality, etc. Each of us has a number of identities based on a sense of being connected to others that share our experiences and history. Many feminists reject 'essentialist' notions of identity – for example, the notion that 'woman' means the same thing to all women across time, space, class, 'race', sexuality and ethnicity – instead, arguing for more fluid conceptions of identity.

identity politics Political or activist alignment based on strong commitment of the group to a particular identity (i.e. as members of a particular 'race', ethnicity, gender or sexuality) that points to the importance of that identity to explain the unequal distribution of power in society.

ideology A term associated with Marxist theory positing that the world-view of dominant economic groups in society conditions the meanings through which all economic groups comprehend the world. German philosopher Karl Marx argued that the ruling economic classes maintained their power through self-interested forms of knowledge. For feminists, the notion of patriarchy or patriarchal ideology refers to a social system in which men dominate women.

male gaze A psychoanalytic notion popularized in the 1970s by US film scholar Laura Mulvey who argued that mainstream films are constructed to allow men to identify with the male protagonist, and to see through his eyes. Female audiences also view films through this male gaze, thus eroticizing and objectifying female characters in a similar fashion to male audiences.

media production The panoply of complex industrial, institutional and group processes by which, in the context of capitalism, content – whether a television drama or a news story – is conceived, produced, revised, monitored and transmitted by a particular media organization.

naturalizing Ideological strategy for fixing and securing an otherwise slippery or historically specific idea in order to make it seem necessary, ageless, unchangeable and permanent. This process is especially apparent in the process of dichotomizing socially constructed masculinity and femininity and then representing them as 'natural' human divisions based on maleness and femaleness. What this fails to take into account is how cultural definitions of masculinity and femininity shift over time and vary across culture, usually to suit the interests of the dominant group.

objectification Feminists use this term to refer to the depiction of women as objects rather than as people. Many critics of pornography and of advertising that features women's body parts, for example, say that in treating women as commodities to be sold, these cultural forms contribute to the perpetuation of women's dehumanization and subordination.

patriarchy In its narrowest sense, a social system marked by rule or authority of the father. Patriarchy is sometimes used as a short-cut term referring to any political, social or cultural system in which men have privileged status that encourages or allows men to dominate women.

political economy In media studies, political economy refers to a conceptual approach that focuses on the ways in which the economic structures of society in general, and media corporations in particular, influence media content. Political economists analyse, for instance, how advertising, the growing concentration of media ownership and the power of certain influential sources shape media content in ways that perpetuate the socio-economic positions of powerful élite groups in society.

polysemy   Quality of texts meaning that they can be interpreted in multiple ways, although some may be more open and encouraging of multiple interpretations than others. Italian linguist Umberto Eco speaks of 'closed texts' as those that are constructed so as to attempt to limit readers' negotiations, while 'open texts' invite readers to adopt a more creative interpretative stance.

popular culture   A term that originally referred to cultural materials appealing to and/or emanating from 'the masses' or 'the people', as opposed to the 'high culture' of cultural élites. Popular culture now usually refers to particular expressive forms that require relatively little formal literacy to access and that are widely disseminated, for instance, Hollywood films or television situation comedies, as well as to non-mediated forms such as clothing, fads and sports. Studies of popular culture focus on the meanings that people construct from these cultural forms.

pornography   The etymological root 'porno' means 'prostitution' and the word 'graphos' means 'writing about'. Erotica, on the other hand, comes from the root 'eros' or passionate love. Radical feminists see pornography as the ultimate expression of men's hatred of women. US feminist Gloria Steinem sees pornography as being about the domination and violent objectification of women, whereas erotica suggests a desire for closeness and yearning for a particular person. Soft-core pornography (sexually suggestive representations) is now a typical feature in most media products (films, television, magazine features and advertising, etc.). Hard-core pornography (sexually explicit representations, showing an erect penis and accompanying acts of penetration), on the other hand, is still primarily found in licensed 'sex shops' and websites that restrict admittance to those over 18 years of age (the latter being achieved through requiring credit card payment to download images).

postcolonial theory   Critical interventionist practice and theorizing that studies past and present effects of colonialism, imperialism and the growing global power of Western states. Often, this theory is also concerned with Orientalism, that is, discourse that represents and cultivates the notion that 'Eastern' people are very different from 'Western' people, and are 'alien' and 'exotic'. Literary critic Edward Said says such discourse wrongly assumes a fixed, unchanging, reductive image of Eastern culture.

postmodernism   Anti-foundationalist theorizing positing that no single theory explains everything, that there can be no single 'big picture' (or 'grand narrative') or even a unified subject position (e.g. 'woman'). Postmodernists reject the meta-narrative of progress that is central to the modernist project. French theorist Jean Baudrillard argues that contemporary life in Western societies is characterized by dispersal, fragmentation and replacement of the 'real' with the 'image' (or simulacrum).

psychoanalysis   The term 'psychoanalysis' is used to refer to a body of theories about mental conditions and human behaviour as well as a method of investigating the underlying origins of the human unconscious. It also designates a set of therapeutic techniques for treating mental 'disorders'. The 'father' of psychoanalysis is the Austrian doctor Sigmund Freud, whose theories focused on the influence of unconscious mental forces such as repression. Among other ideas, Freud proposed that the analysis of dreams would allow us to understand the unconscious. Some feminist scholars find psychoanalytic theory to be unhelpful since it has sometimes been used to reify and justify women's subordinate status in society. Others have regarded certain psychoanalytic theories, such as those developed by the French psychoanalyst Jacques Lacan, as potentially productive since they provide possible clues about boys' and girls' differential entry into language as children (the 'Symbolic Order') and how these processes repress and subordinate 'the feminine'.

racism   This term refers to the institutionalized or informal policy of prejudice or bigotry against a particular 'race' of people. Refers to highly discredited notion that there are biologically distinct 'races' and that some are superior to others. Some feminists argue that in capitalist societies, there is an inter-structuring of discriminatory power differences based on gender, class and 'race' (or ethnicity, a broader social–cultural concept).

sexualization   A process by which cultural material that would not seem to be overtly about sex nevertheless includes sexual imagery and represents women in sexual terms. Visual representations in the news of women in sexy clothing, or even topless, for example, are geared to heterosexual male (or heterosexist) ideas about women as sexual objects.

socialization   Refers to complicated, life-long process through which we become social beings or how we learn the values, rules, ideologies and role relationships of our culture. Occupational (or professional) socialization refers to learning the values and rules of specific workplaces and jobs.

standpoint theory   Epistemology (or way of thinking) that thinking processes always reflect one's position, including one's experience over time, so thinking is never neutral or 'objective'. Some feminists have argued for the development of a feminist critique of science, arguing that contemporary scientific theories and modes of inquiry force women to accept the scientific standpoints of men as being 'neutral' and 'objective' truths, while the reverse is not true.

stereotypes   Representations of phenomena or people in terms of a few simple, exaggerated characterizations that are deemed to be 'natural' and their meanings to be 'fixed'. Stereotyping reduces everything about a person or a group to those few 'essential' traits. Although at any given point in time the normative notion of masculinity may reference toughness, invulnerability and violence, depictions of all men as only violent and tough reference a stereotype. Whether or not the concept stereotype is used, how groups, issues or social movements come to be portrayed in particular, narrow ways is tied to social struggles around the distribution of political and economic power.

symbolic annihilation   In the 1970s, feminist and gender-sensitive media scholars coined this term to refer to processes through which patriarchal institutions and ideologies, operating through the media, contribute to the maintenance of women's subordinate position in society by keeping them literally or essentially invisible, or by denigrating, marginalizing or ridiculing them.

MEDIA AND GENDER VIDEO RESOURCES

American Porn (Frontline/PBS Home Video, 60 mins). Porn as a $10 billion industry.

Barbie Nation (New Day Films, 54 mins). The culture and cult of Barbie.

Beyond Killing Us Softly (Cambridge Documentary Films, 33 mins). Resisting media sexism.

Bionic Beauty Salon (New Day Films, 22 mins). Teens' views of beauty culture.

Color Adjustment (California Newsreel, 88 mins). Television images of African American women and men on television.

The Date Rape Backlash: Media & the Denial of Rape (Media Education Foundation, 57 mins). Journalists' undermining of rape as an issue.

Dirty Business: Who's Profiting from Pornography. (Films for the Humanities & Sciences, 22 mins). Economics of pornography.

Dreamworlds 2 (Media Education Foundation, 56 mins). Interrogation of the images of women in music videos.

The Famine Within (Direct Cinema, 55 mins). Media's influence on women's ideas about weight.

Game Over (Media Education Foundation, 41 mins). Gender, 'race' and violence in video games.

Killing Us Softly 3 (Media Education Foundation, 34 mins). Advertising's portrayal of women.

Man Oh Man (New Day Films, 22 mins). Masculinity, inter-gender communication.

Mickey Mouse Monopoly (Media Education Foundation, 52 mins). Lessons about 'race' and gender embedded in Disney films.

Miss America (PBS Home Video, 120 mins). Investigates the pageant's sexual politics and commercialism.

Off the Straight and Narrow (Media Education Foundation, 63 mins). TV's changing portrayal of gays and lesbians.

Playing Unfair: The Media Image of the Female Athlete (Media Education Foundation, 30 mins). Sports journalism's fixation on femininity.

Pornography: First Amendment Right or State-Sanctioned Violence Against Women (CBS News Productions, 45 mins). Current debates about pornography.

Representation & the Media (Media Education Foundation, 55 mins). Stuart Hall's theory of cultural representations.

Reviving Ophelia (Media Education Foundation, 35 mins). How media shape girls' identities.

Selling Addictions (Media Education Foundation, 45 mins). How advertising takes advantage of women's vulnerabilities.

Slim Hopes (Media Education Foundation, 30 mins). Impact of advertising on women's body images.

Stale Roles, Tight Buns (OASIS, 29 mins). Images of men in advertising.

Telenovelas: Love, TV, and Power (Films for the Humanities & Sciences, 59 mins). Impact of telenovelas.

Tough Guise (Media Education Foundation, 82 mins, 57 mins abridged version). The media construction of violent masculinity.

Warning: The Media May be Hazardous to Your Health (Media Watch, 38 mins). Sexism and the fashion industry.

Western Eyes (National Film Board of Canada, 40 mins). Beauty concerns of teens of Asian descent.

INDEX

VIOLENCE AND THE MEDIA

Cynthia Carter and C. Kay Weaver

- Why is there so much violence portrayed in the media?
- What meanings are attached to representations of violence in the media?
- Can media violence encourage violent behaviour and desensitize audiences to real violence?
- Does the 'everydayness' of media violence lead to the 'normalization' of violence in society?

Violence and the Media is a lively and indispensable introduction to current thinking about media violence and its potential influence on audiences. Adopting a fresh perspective on the 'media effects' debate, Carter and Weaver engage with a host of pressing issues around violence in different media contexts – including news, film, television, pornography, advertising and cyberspace. The book offers a compelling argument that the daily repetition of media violence helps to normalize and legitimize the acts being portrayed. Most crucially, the influence of media violence needs to be understood in relation to the structural inequalities of everyday life. Using a wide range of examples of media violence primarily drawn from the American and British media to illustrate these points, *Violence and the Media* is a distinctive and revealing exploration of one of the most important and controversial subjects in cultural and media studies today.

Contents
Series editor's foreword – Acknowledgements – Introduction: violence and the media – Grim news – Fears of film – Television's crimes and misdemeanours – Pornofury – Advertising body parts – The dark side of cyberspace – Conclusion: the future of media violence – Glossary – References – Index.

192pp   0 335 20505 4 (paperback)   0 335 20506 2   (hardback)

MORAL PANICS AND THE MEDIA

Chas Critcher

- How are social problems defined and responded to in contemporary society?
- How useful is the concept of moral panic in understanding these processes?
- What does an examination of recent examples reveal about the role of the media in creating, endorsing and sustaining moral panics?

The term 'moral panic' is frequently applied to sudden eruptions of concern about social problems. This book critically evaluates the usefulness of moral panic models for understanding how politicians, the public and pressure groups come to recognize apparently new threats to the social order. The role of the media, especially the popular press, comes under scrutiny. Two models of moral panics are initially identified and explained, then applied to a range of case studies: AIDS, rave/ecstasy, video nasties, child abuse and paedophilia. Experience is compared across a range of countries, revealing many basic similarities but also significant variations between different national contexts. Common to all is an increasing focus on threats to children, evoking images of childhood innocence. The conclusion is that moral panic remains a useful tool for analysis but needs more systematic connection to wider theoretical concerns, especially those of the risk society and discourse analysis.

Contents

224pp   0 335 20908 4 (paperback)   0 335 20909 2 (hardback)